the
cricinfo
guide to

international
cricket
2007

edited by
**steven
lynch**

THE CRICINFO GUIDE TO INTERNATIONAL CRICKET 2007

Edited by Steven Lynch

Published by John Wisden & Co Ltd
© John Wisden & Co Ltd, 2006

"Cricinfo" is the registered trademark of Wisden Cricinfo Ltd
www.cricinfo.com

John Wisden & Co Ltd
13 Old Aylesfield, Golden Pot, Alton, Hampshire GU34 4BY

ISBN–10: 1-905625-01-4
ISBN–13: 978-1-905625-01-7

10 9 8 7 6 5 4 3 2 1

Typeset in Mendoza Roman and Frutiger by Typematter, Basingstoke
Printed and bound in Great Britain by Clays Ltd, St Ives plc

Distributed by Macmillan Distribution Ltd

CONTENTS

ABOUT CRICINFO

Cricinfo was founded in 1993, in the early days of the internet boom, by some expatriates who were working in the United States and wanted to find out the latest cricket scores. A network was quickly established, and soon **www.cricinfo.com** had mushroomed into one of the biggest single-sport websites in the world – which it remains – and by the turn of the millennium had sponsored a women's World Cup and the English County Championship.

Financial reality set in after the dotcom bubble burst early in the 21st century, and in 2003 Cricinfo merged with its main rival, Wisden.com, to produce an unrivalled site which married Cricinfo's scoring and statistical expertise to *Wisden*'s long-standing reputation for editorial excellence and its unmatched historical archive. Cricinfo continues to offer live scores, updated ball-by-ball for almost every international match, across a wide variety of formats, allied to informed bulletins and comment from a dedicated and talented editorial team around the world.

There are also regular columns, features and interviews, in addition to a worldwide news service and the searchable statistical database, **Statsguru**, which is explained in more detail overleaf. Cricinfo also offers video highlights and audio commentary for selected matches, as well as running cricket-management games and specialist areas for betting and cricket tours, and even an online shop. The entire *Wisden* archive is also online, dating back to the first Almanack in 1864: all *Wisden*'s essays and articles, such as the famous Five Cricketers of the Year, and its international match reports, are available to registered users.

Cricinfo's busiest month to date was March 2006, a hectic time for international cricket as England were touring India, Australia were in South Africa, New Zealand were entertaining West Indies, and Pakistan were playing in Sri Lanka. In that month alone Cricinfo had 9,097,074 separate visitors or "unique users": the daily record was established shortly before that, when 1.25 million people accessed the site on February 13, primarily for news of the one-day international between Pakistan and India and one of the VB Series finals in Australia. Around five million people followed Cricinfo's coverage of the first Test between Pakistan and India early in 2006.

Around 25% of Cricinfo's global audience comes from India, with approximately 20% from North America and 15% from both the United Kingdom and Australia. The most-read news story was the match report of the record-breaking one-day international at Johannesburg in March 2006, when South Africa somehow managed to overhaul Australia's record total of 434 for 4: around 685,000 people logged on to that bulletin. Of the player pages from which most of the profiles in this book are adapted, the most-viewed is Sachin Tendulkar's, while Kevin Pietersen recently overtook Andrew Flintoff as the most-viewed England player.

Cricinfo, which has offices in England, India, Australia, South Africa, Sri Lanka and Pakistan, is part of The Wisden Group, which also includes *Wisden Cricketers' Almanack*, the *Wisden Cricketer* and *Cricinfo* magazines, and Hawk-Eye Innovations, the leading ball-tracking technology.

INTRODUCTION

Welcome to the first edition of the **Cricinfo Guide to International Cricket**, which brings you details – in words and photographs, facts and figures – of 200 players, taken from the well-stacked database of Cricinfo, cricket's leading website. The idea for the book grew out of a conversation with Matthew Engel, the editor of *Wisden Cricketers' Almanack*, who wondered how many of the 30,000 people who make up a full house at Lord's could recognise everyone on the field. This book will help the 29,000 or so who probably couldn't: it includes a photograph of each player, gives a concise summary of his career, then mixes some unusual facts – mostly taken from Cricinfo's searchable database, Statsguru – with statistics for Tests, one-day internationals and first-class matches. There is also a selection of records, both country-by-country and overall.

We have tried to include every player likely to appear in international cricket in 2007, with a particular eye on the World Cup. Like all selectors, we will undoubtedly have left out someone who should have been included – but details of anyone who managed to escape our selectorial net can be found on Cricinfo.

Most of the profiles are edited and updated versions from Cricinfo's player pages, for which I must thank the site's current editorial staff, especially Sambit Bal (my successor as the site's global editor), Martin Williamson and Andrew Miller, and several former colleagues and contributors to the Cricinfo and Wisden websites, notably Kamran Abbasi, Tanya Aldred, Vaneisa Baksh, Lawrence Booth, Simon Briggs, Don Cameron, Tim de Lisle, Rabeed Imam, Lynn McConnell, Neil Manthorp, S. Rajesh, Christian Ryan, Rob Smyth, Telford Vice and John Ward. Thanks are also due to my wife Karina for her support, and to Christopher Lane, Matthew Engel, Hugh Chevallier, Nigel Davies and Harriet Monkhouse of Wisden, the typesetter Ray Rich, and Travis Basevi, the man who built StatsGuru. The majority of the photographs are from Getty Images, apart from a few reproduced by kind permission of the Pakistan Cricket Board and some specially shot for Cricinfo.

The statistics have been updated to **September 11, 2006**, the end of the international season in England. The figures have been taken from Cricinfo and include, for the first time in published form, the number of boundaries hit by each batsman in international cricket. The abbreviation "S/R" (strike rate) in the batting tables denotes runs per 100 balls; in the bowling it shows the balls required to take each wicket. A dash (–) in the records usually indicates that full statistics are not available (such as details of fours and sixes, or balls faced, in all domestic matches). Individual figures for players who have appeared for more than one side in official internationals include the additional matches, details of which are given in the player's "Facts" box. These matches are excluded in the national records sections, which explains any differences in the figures for the players concerned.

Steven Lynch
September 2006

ANY QUESTIONS? ASK STATSGURU

by S. Rajesh, Cricinfo's statistics editor

Which bowler has dismissed Ricky Ponting most often? What is Muttiah Muralitharan's average in innings when he has conceded more than 100 runs? Where has Rahul Dravid done best, and which ground has brought out the worst in him? If you want the answers to questions like these, your options are limited: if you don't happen to have a full set of *Wisden* handy, you could write to a statistician and wait ... or you can log on to Cricinfo, and click on "Statsguru". Many of the weird and wonderful facts in the player pages in this book came from Statsguru's mine of information.

Cricket is such a number-friendly game that it lends itself perfectly to statistical analysis, and Statsguru fulfils the need for an online tool which can weed out data and answer queries which would otherwise take you hours of examining *Wisden's* finer print. Want to analyse a batsman, a bowler, a fielder, a team, or a ground? Go to http://stats.cricinfo.com/guru, or click on "Statsguru" in the grey menu on the left of the Cricinfo home-page.

Let's go back to the questions mentioned above. The table below, adapted from Statsguru, shows which bowlers have done the best against the batsman who is arguably the best in the world. Darren Gough has dismissed Australia's captain Ricky Ponting eight times in Tests, but the other interesting bit is Ponting's average in the five innings in which he has been dismissed by Harbhajan Singh – it's a paltry 3.40, which suggests that it would be a good idea for India to bring on Harbhajan as early as possible when Ponting comes in. Check out the corresponding page for Herschelle Gibbs, and the answer is equally startling: Gibbs has fallen to Chaminda Vaas 12 times in international matches – three times in Tests, all for ducks, and nine times in ODIs: in those nine innings, he averages 3.11. And when you're talking about bowlers dominating top batsmen, it's hard to leave out Glenn McGrath: go to his Test-match page on Statsguru, and check out the filter which says "batsmen/fielder summary". No prizes for guessing which two batsmen are top of his bunnies list: it's poor old Mike Atherton (dismissed 19 times) and Brian Lara (15).

Bowlers who have dismissed Ricky Ponting most often in Tests

Bowler	Dismissals	Ponting's average in those innings
Darren Gough England	8	32.12
Anil Kumble India	7	88.57
Chaminda Vaas Sri Lanka	6	41.83
Harbhajan Singh India	5	3.40

Quite often with this sort of online searchable tool, the process of filtering through to get at the answers you want can be daunting. But this isn't the case with Statsguru, which has a two-layered filtering process. For elementary queries – things like runs or wickets per innings, series averages and career summaries – there's a basic page which is easier to navigate and quicker to come up with the answer. The queries are limited, but the output is still pretty exhaustive – the career summary, for example, reveals everything from averages against each side, and in each country, to performances in wins and defeats or at home and away, as well as more detailed figures like performances in each innings of a match, and at each batting position.

If your query is more intricate, though, then there's an advanced version as well. Want to know what Don Bradman's average was in innings when he passed 50? All you need to do is go to The Don's advanced-query page on Statsguru, put in "50" in the box which asks you for "Runs: from ...", and select the output format. If the average comes up as a mind-boggling 185.20, you've done it right. Follow a similar process for Muralitharan's bowling, and you'll discover that as at October 2006 he had gone for 100 or more runs in a Test innings 49 times, and taken 175 wickets at 37.21 in them.

Statsguru also scores with its ability to customise its output display according to the format you want. Steve Waugh's scores over his 18-year Test career can be viewed innings by innings, or series by series – or, most interestingly, as a cumulative career stat, which reveals just how spectacularly his batting average rose after a fairly sluggish start. After 26 Tests, he only averaged 30.52, but then came the 1989 Ashes series, and Waugh transformed himself from a pretty good batsman to a hugely prolific one.

Steve Waugh's cumulative batting chart

After Test no.	Runs	Average	100s/50s
10	271	20.84	0/2
25	1079	31.73	0/10
50	2387	36.16	4/14
75	4240	45.59	7/27
100	6288	49.51	14/37
130	8440	50.23	22/42
168	10927	51.06	32/50

And now to the last of those questions from the start: what is Rahul Dravid's *bête noire*, when it comes to venues? Strangely, it's his own home ground, the Chinnaswamy Stadium in Bangalore – in nine Test innings there, he has passed 50 just once, and averages a paltry 18.33, against his impressive overall 58.75. The table below shows how he's done at grounds where he has played more than three Tests (if you want to see the entire list, go to Statsguru and select the "ground averages" option on Dravid's page).

Rahul Dravid's average on each ground (more than three Tests)

Venue	Tests	Runs	Average	100s/50s
Kolkata	7	785	65.41	3/2
Delhi	5	456	65.14	1/2
Nagpur	5	453	64.71	1/3
Ahmedabad	4	431	61.57	1/1
Mohali	6	470	58.75	1/3
Mumbai	6	504	56.00	1/3
Chennai	6	331	36.77	0/4
Bangalore	5	165	18.33	0/1

If all this statistical talk has got you going, then here are a few questions which will have you clicking for Statsguru: who dismissed Graham Gooch lbw most often (hint: it wasn't Terry Alderman)? And what if the question is restricted only to the matches in which Gooch was the captain? Off which bowler did Mark Taylor take most catches, and how many? And who was Malcolm Marshall's 300th Test victim?

Happy hunting!

PLAYER INDEX

PLAYER INDEX

ABDUL RAZZAQ

Full name	**Abdul Razzaq**
Born	**December 2, 1979, Lahore, Punjab**
Teams	**Lahore**
Style	**Right-hand bat, right-arm fast-medium bowler**
Test debut	**Pakistan v Australia at Brisbane 1999-2000**
ODI debut	**Pakistan v Zimbabwe at Lahore 1996-97**

THE PROFILE   Abdul Razzaq was once rapid enough to open the bowling, and remains composed enough to bat anywhere, although he is discovering that the lower order suits him nicely. His bowling, which first got him noticed, is characterised by a galloping approach, accuracy, and reverse-swing. But it is his batting that is more likely to win matches. He has all the shots, and is particularly strong driving through cover and mid-off off front or back foot. He has two gears: block or blast. Cut off the big shots and he can get bogged down, although he is very patient, as demonstrated by a match-saving 71 in almost six hours against India at Mohali in March 2005. Just before that he had batted bewilderingly slowly at Melbourne, scoring 4 in 110 minutes. But when the occasion demands he can still slog with the best of them: England were pillaged for 51 in 22 balls in December 2005. Razzaq was originally touted as Pakistan's best allrounder since Imran Khan, but his career hasn't been plain sailing. He suffered a slump, particularly in bowling, between 2002 and 2004, but has recently rediscovered some of his old guile, if not his nip. And if the pitch is helpful to seam – as Karachi's was for his only Test five-for in 2004, and also against India there in January 2006 – he can still be a considerable danger. Razzaq's allround performance in that win over India was easily his most emphatic: he made 45 and 90 to add to seven wickets.

THE FACTS   Abdul Razzaq took a hat-trick against Sri Lanka at Galle in June 2000 ... He is one of only four players to have scored a hundred and taken a hat-trick in Tests: the others were England's Johnny Briggs, Wasim Akram of Pakistan and the New Zealander James Franklin ... Razzaq took 7 for 51 – still his best figures – on his first-class debut, for Lahore City v Karachi Whites in the Quaid-e-Azam Trophy final at Thatta in November 1996 ... His highest score is 203 not out, for Middlesex v Glamorgan at Cardiff in 2003, when he shared a stand of 320 with Ed Joyce ... His record includes four ODIs for the Asia XI ...

THE FIGURES
Batting and fielding

	M	Inns	NO	Runs	HS	Avge	S/R	100	50	4s	6s	Ct	St
Tests *to 11.9.06*	43	72	8	1828	134	28.56	41.00	3	6	216	22	12	0
ODIs *to 11.9.06*	217	187	47	4297	112*	30.69	80.49	2	22	322	100	29	0
First-class *to 11.9.06*	101	157	24	4487	203*	33.73	–		8	21	–	–	23	0

Bowling

	M	Balls	Runs	Wkts	BB	Avge	RpO	S/R	5i	10m
Tests *to 11.9.06*	43	6650	3521	95	5–35	37.06	3.17	70.00	1	0
ODIs *to 11.9.06*	217	9339	7209	236	6–35	30.54	4.63	39.57	3	0
First-class *to 11.9.06*	101	16277	9613	295	7–51	32.58	3.54	55.17	10	2

ABDUR RAZZAK

Full name **Khan Abdur Razzak**
Born **June 15, 1982, Khulna**
Teams **Khulna**
Style **Left-hand bat, slow left-arm orthodox spinner**
Test debut **Bangladesh v Australia at Chittagong 2005-06**
ODI debut **Bangladesh v Hong Kong at Colombo 2004**

THE PROFILE The latest in Bangladesh's seemingly never-ending supply of left-arm spinners, Abdur Razzaq (no relation to the similarly named Pakistan allrounder) made his mark when he helped unheralded Khulna to their first-ever National Cricket League title in 2001-02. Tall, with a high action, he was also instrumental in Victoria Sporting Club's surprise triumph in the 2002-03 Dhaka Premier Division. He was given his A-team debut during the five-match one-day series against Zimbabwe early in 2004, and took the opportunity well with 15 wickets, including a matchwinning 7 for 17 in the third encounter on the batting paradise of Dhaka's Bangabandhu National Stadium. He has an uncanny ability to pin batsmen down, although the position of his bowling arm during delivery is a worry, and his action has been reported in the past. Bangladesh's coaching staff are using video technology to help iron out anything suspicious. He took 3 for 17 on his one-day debut against Hong Kong in the Asia Cup in Colombo in 2004, but was reported for a suspect action after the next match, against Pakistan. Left out of the Champions Trophy in England later that year, "Raj" played just one ODI – against Zimbabwe in January 2005 – before he was recalled for the home series against Sri Lanka in February 2006. He made his Test debut two months later, called up for the second Test against Australia on a turning track at Chittagong (even the Aussies played three spinners), but failed to take a wicket.

THE FACTS Abdur Razzaq's best bowling in ODIs remains his 3 for 17 on debut against Hong Kong, but he also took 3 for 36 against Australia (dismissing Adam Gilchrist, Ricky Ponting and Andrew Symonds, all lbw) at Chittagong in April 2006 ... His best first-class figures of 7 for 11 (10 for 62 in the match) came for Khulna against Sylhet at Sylhet in 2003-04 ... Razzaq's economy rate of 3.82 runs per over is the best by anyone for Bangladesh in ODIs, and is surpassed among current bowlers only by Shaun Pollock (3.76) and Prosper Utseya (3.79) ...

THE FIGURES
Batting and fielding

	M	Inns	NO	Runs	HS	Avge	S/R	100	50	4s	6s	Ct	St
Tests to 11.9.06	1	2	0	15	15	7.50	57.69	0	0	2	0	0	0
ODIs to 11.9.06	22	15	9	90	21	15.00	75.63	0	0	3	2	6	0
First-class to 11.9.06	35	55	7	943	83	19.64	56.23	0	5	–	–	13	0

Bowling

	M	Balls	Runs	Wkts	BB	Avge	RpO	S/R	5i	10m
Tests to 11.9.06	1	180	99	0	–	–	3.29	–	0	0
ODIs to 11.9.06	22	1149	733	30	3–17	24.43	3.82	38.30	0	0
First-class to 11.9.06	35	7916	3412	117	7–11	29.16	2.58	67.65	4	1

ANDRE ADAMS

Full name	**Andre Ryan Adams**
Born	**July 17, 1975, Auckland**
Teams	**Auckland, Essex**
Style	**Right-hand bat, right-arm fast-medium bowler**
Test debut	**New Zealand v England at Auckland 2001-02**
ODI debut	**New Zealand v Sri Lanka at Sharjah 2000-01**

THE PROFILE A bowling allrounder, Andre Adams adds a touch of dash to New Zealand's batting armoury with his hard-hitting skills – he has scored his one-day runs at better than a run a ball. He started as a fast bowler before throttling back to a brisk medium with the occasional faster one. He did well against England in 2001-02, starting with 2 for 25 in the first one-dayer (and making 28 not out), then lifting the match award for 3 for 13 and 25 not out in the second game. But a stress fracture to the lower back hindered him, allowing Jacob Oram to move ahead in the pecking order, and some eyebrows were raised about his attitude. Adams returned for the 2003 World Cup, but made little impact beyond another award-winning performance, against West Indies, when he followed 35 from 24 balls with 4 for 44. He lost his place again, and seemed destined to remain on the outer until called up towards the end of the 2004 NatWest Series in England. He didn't actually play, but did sign up with Essex for the rest of the season: he returned there the following two years as well. Although he took six wickets on debut against England at Auckland early in 2002 – in a match New Zealand won to square the series – Adams looks unlikely to add to his solitary Test cap. But he is very much in the one-day frame, and earned a central contract from New Zealand Cricket for 2006-07.

THE FACTS Adams has made two centuries in first-class cricket – both of them for Essex ... He made a footnote in history in the last ODI against South Africa at Centurion in November 2005, when he was super-subbed out of the game before it had even started ... In ODIs against India Adams has taken 17 wickets at 13.82, more than twice as many as against any other country (eight v England) ...

THE FIGURES
Batting and fielding

	M	Inns	NO	Runs	HS	Avge	S/R	100	50	4s	6s	Ct	St
Tests *to 11.9.06*	1	2	0	11	37	9.00	90.00	0	0	3	0	1	0
ODIs *to 11.9.06*	39	31	10	409	45	19.47	104.87	0	0	31	18	7	0
First-class *to 11.9.06*	68	88	6	1958	124	23.87	–	2	9	–	–	43	0

Bowling

	M	Balls	Runs	Wkts	BB	Avge	RpO	S/R	5i	10m
Tests *to 11.9.06*	1	190	105	6	3–44	17.50	3.31	31.66	0	0
ODIs *to 11.9.06*	39	1729	1494	52	5–22	28.73	5.18	33.25	1	0
First-class *to 11.9.06*	68	13051	6418	246	6–25	26.08	2.95	53.05	9	1

AFTAB AHMED

Full name	**Aftab Ahmed Chowdhury**
Born	**November 10, 1985, Chittagong**
Teams	**Chittagong**
Style	**Right-hand bat, right-arm medium-pacer**
Test debut	**Bangladesh v New Zealand at Chittagong 2004-05**
ODI debut	**Bangladesh v South Africa at Birmingham 2004**

THE PROFILE Aftab Ahmed first came to the attention of the Bangladeshi selectors after scoring 79 against South Africa in the Under-19 World Cup in 2002, and the following year he was pitched into the Test squad to face England, despite having failed to impress in two earlier warm-up matches. His selection was initially viewed with suspicion by the local media, who regarded Aftab as something of a one-day cowboy, and indeed his desire to belt the cover off the ball has resulted in some all-too-brief performances. His potential, however, is plain to see, and his selection for the seminal tour of England early in 2005 was evidence of the selectors' faith, which he repaid at Chester-le-Street with a defiant, carefree 82 not out, the highest score for Bangladesh in the Test series. He also finished off the historic one-day win over Australia at Cardiff, smashing Jason Gillespie for four and six to seal victory. His medium-pacers have potential as well, as he showed with an astonishing one-day haul of 5 for 31 against New Zealand at Dhaka in November 2004. He led Bangladesh to a 3-2 series victory with an unbeaten 81 in the final match against Zimbabwe in January 2005. Since then, barring that run-a-ball 82 at the Riverside, he's hit a lean patch: he hasn't reached 30 in a Test, while in one-dayers he hit a couple of fifties against the Kenyans early in 2006, but failed to impress against Australia.

THE FACTS Exactly half Aftab Ahmed's ODI wickets came in one spell, his 5 for 31 against New Zealand at Dhaka in November 2004 ... His best bowling analysis in first-class cricket is 7 for 39, for the Bangladesh Cricket Board XI against Central Zone in India's Duleep Trophy in 2004-05 ... Aftab's solitary first-class century was 129 for Chittagong against Dhaka in Dhaka in 2002-03 ... He also made 91 for Bangladesh Under-19s in a youth Test against England, captained by Alastair Cook, at Taunton in August 2004 ...

THE FIGURES

Batting and fielding

	M	Inns	NO	Runs	HS	Avge	S/R	100	50	4s	6s	Ct	St
Tests to 11.9.06	10	20	1	395	82*	20.78	58.08	0	1	60	3	4	0
ODIs to 11.9.06	39	39	4	863	81*	24.65	81.10	0	6	95	19	6	0
First-class to 11.9.06	25	47	3	1189	129*	27.02	63.95	1	5	–	–	17	0

Bowling

	M	Balls	Runs	Wkts	BB	Avge	RpO	S/R	5i	10m
Tests to 11.9.06	10	210	176	3	1–28	58.66	5.02	70.00	0	0
ODIs to 11.9.06	39	605	504	10	5–31	50.40	4.99	60.50	1	0
First-class to 11.9.06	25	1110	539	20	7–39	26.94	2.91	55.50	1	0

AJIT AGARKAR

Full name	**Ajit Bhalchandra Agarkar**
Born	**December 4, 1977, Bombay**
Teams	**Mumbai**
Style	**Right-hand bat, right-arm fast-medium bowler**
Test debut	**India v Zimbabwe at Harare 1998-99**
ODI debut	**India v Australia at Kochi 1997-98**

THE PROFILE Slight, fiery and gifted, Ajit Agarkar has never quite come to terms with being touted as Kapil Dev's replacement as India's matchwinner with bat and ball. The ingredients are there, and in the right proportions. But they have never quite formed the right long-lasting mix. Agarkar is a brisk, energetic fast-medium bowler from Mumbai, and his entry into international cricket in 1998 – with an avalanche of wickets that made him the fastest to 50 wickets in ODIs – was matched for speed only by an astonishing batting slump a couple of years later that saw him collect seven consecutive Test ducks against Australia. But all India knows he can bat, because tailenders simply do not score half-centuries in 21 balls, as Agarkar did in a one-dayer against Zimbabwe late in 2000, or score Test centuries at Lord's, as he did in some style in 2002, making a nonsense of a Test average of about 17. His aggression is an asset, but his body doesn't seem to be able to support it. India's succession of left-arm quicks have relegated Agarkar to Test afterthought now – he played four matches in 2005-06 and managed only five wickets – but he's still a feature in the one-day side, grabbing nine wickets in five games in the West Indies in June 2006, and he was close to playing in the Tests there. If he can find his confidence, and develop some more strength, Agarkar could even now be very special for India.

THE FACTS Agarkar took his 50th wicket in his 23rd ODI, a record for India ... He made seven successive ducks in Tests against Australia in 1999-2000 and 2000-01, and averages only 7.42 against them, compared with 42 against England and 30.66 against Sri Lanka ... Agarkar has taken 46 ODI wickets against Sri Lanka, and 45 against Zimbabwe ... Among Test century-makers, only Pakistan's Saqlain Mushtaq (14.48) has a lower batting average than Agarkar's 16.79 ...

THE FIGURES

Batting and fielding

	M	Inns	NO	Runs	HS	Avge	S/R	100	50	4s	6s	Ct	St
Tests *to 11.9.06*	26	39	5	571	109*	16.79	52.82	1	0	83	3	6	0
ODIs *to 11.9.06*	165	99	26	1166	95	15.97	84.24	0	3	94	22	47	0
First-class *to 11.9.06*	69	90	15	1900	109*	25.33	–	2	8	–	–	24	0

Bowling

	M	Balls	Runs	Wkts	BB	Avge	RpO	S/R	5i	10m
Tests *to 11.9.06*	26	4857	2745	58	6–41	47.32	3.39	83.74	1	0
ODIs *to 11.9.06*	165	8146	6842	252	6–42	27.15	5.03	32.32	2	0
First-class *to 11.9.06*	69	11860	6032	207	6–41	29.14	3.05	57.29	9	0

ALOK KAPALI

Full name **Alok Kapali**
Born **January 1, 1984, Sylhet**
Teams **Sylhet**
Style **Right-hand bat, legspinner**
Test debut **Bangladesh v Sri Lanka at Colombo 2002**
ODI debut **Bangladesh v Sri Lanka at Colombo 2002**

THE PROFILE A talented but erratic legspinner and a batsman of undoubted potential, Alok Kapali has a burgeoning reputation as an allrounder, particularly in the one-day game. He made a promising Test debut against Sri Lanka in 2002, and impressed with his technique and temperament in an otherwise disappointing match. Batting as high as No. 6, in spite of a first-class average in the mid-teens, he made starts on both occasions without being able to go on, and has since demonstrated a bold attitude towards quick bowling. His bowling has improved, since disappearing for more than five an over on debut, and against Pakistan at Peshawar in August 2003, when still only 19, he became the first Bangladesh bowler to take a hat-trick in Test cricket, a performance that secured his side their maiden first-innings lead, at the 23rd attempt. Following a string of poor performances he was dropped from the one-day squad before the Champions Trophy in England in September 2004, and was later omitted from the 20-man training squad for the 2005 tour of England. He was recalled to the national squad early in 2006, but did little of note beyond an innings of 55 in one of the one-dayers against Kenya, and failed in his only Test outing, against Sri Lanka, which followed a career-best 156 for Sylhet against Chittagong. Time is still on his side, but he needs to inject more consistency into his allround game.

THE FACTS Half of Alok Kapali's Test wickets came during his hat-trick (Bangladesh's first in Tests) against Pakistan at Peshawar in August 2003: he ended the innings with the wickets of Shabbir Ahmed, Danish Kaneria and Umar Gul ... His highest Test score is 85, against West Indies at Chittagong in 2002-03: it came less than a fortnight after his highest ODI score of 89 not out, also against West Indies, at Dhaka ... He took 7 for 33 for Sylhet against Barisal at Sylhet in 2001-02 ...

THE FIGURES

Batting and fielding

	M	Inns	NO	Runs	HS	Avge	S/R	100	50	4s	6s	Ct	St
Tests *to 11.9.06*	17	34	1	584	85	17.69	48.62	0	2	80	3	5	0
ODIs *to 11.9.06*	55	52	3	964	89*	19.67	65.66	0	5	76	4	21	0
First-class *to 11.9.06*	56	99	4	2278	156*	23.97	–	3	10	–	–	29	0

Bowling

	M	Balls	Runs	Wkts	BB	Avge	RpO	S/R	5i	10m
Tests *to 11.9.06*	17	1103	709	6	3–3	118.16	3.85	183.83	0	0
ODIs *to 11.9.06*	55	1124	939	15	2–29	62.60	5.01	74.93	0	0
First-class *to 11.9.06*	56	4924	2282	82	7–33	27.82	2.78	60.04	4	1

HASHIM AMLA

Full name	**Hashim Mahomed Amla**
Born	**March 31, 1983, Durban, Natal**
Teams	**Dolphins**
Style	**Right-hand bat, occasional right-arm medium-pacer**
Test debut	**South Africa v India at Kolkata 2004-05**
ODI debut	**No ODIs yet**

THE PROFILE An elegant, stroke-filled right-hander blessed with the temperament to make the most of his talent, Hashim Amla was the first South African of Indian descent to reach the national squad. His elevation was hardly a surprise after he reeled off four centuries in his first eight innings in 2004-05, after being appointed captain of the Dolphins (formerly Natal) at the tender age of 21. Ahmed, his older brother by four years, also plays for them, but there is little doubt that the younger Amla is the better player. He is also a devout Muslim, whose requests to have logos promoting alcohol removed from his playing gear have been successful so far. Amla toured New Zealand with the Under-19s in 2000-01, he captained South Africa at the 2002 Under-19 World Cup, and, after starring for the A team in 2004-05 – he made two hundreds against New Zealand A – made his Test debut against India. He was not an instant success, with serious questions emerging about his technique as he mustered only 36 runs in four innings against England later that season, struggling with an ungainly crouched stance and a bat coming down from somewhere in the region of gully. But when he was handed a second chance in April 2006 he made it count, with 149 against New Zealand at Cape Town, helping to ensure a draw. Amla remains a candidate to become South Africa's captain eventually, and possesses easily the most impressive beard in the game.

THE FACTS Amla's highest score is 249, made in nearly 11 hours, for the Dolphins against the Eagles at Bloemfontein in March 2005 ... He made his first-class debut for KwaZulu-Natal at 16, against Nasser Hussain's 1999-2000 England tourists (and scored 1) ... In his next match, in February 2002, Amla made his maiden first-class hundred – 103 against Easterns at Durban ...

THE FIGURES
Batting and fielding

	M	Inns	NO	Runs	HS	Avge	S/R	100	50	4s	6s	Ct	St
Tests to 11.9.06	7	13	0	364	149	28.00	46.84	1	1	48	0	6	0
ODIs to 11.9.06	0	–	–	–	–	–	–	–	–	–	–	–	–
First-class to 11.9.06	61	101	11	4250	249	47.22	–	12	22	–	–	43	0

Bowling

	M	Balls	Runs	Wkts	BB	Avge	RpO	S/R	5i	10m
Tests to 11.9.06	7	6	4	0	–	–	4.00	–	0	0
ODIs to 11.9.06	0	–	–	–	–	–	–	–	–	–
First-class to 11.9.06	61	150	101	1	1–10	101.00	4.04	150.00	0	0

JAMES ANDERSON

Full name	**James Michael Anderson**
Born	**July 30, 1982, Burnley, Lancashire**
Teams	**Lancashire**
Style	**Left-hand bat, right-arm fast-medium bowler**
Test debut	**England v Zimbabwe at Lord's 2003**
ODI debut	**England v Australia at Melbourne 2002-03**

THE PROFILE A strapping, genuinely quick fast bowler, James Anderson had played only three one-day games for Lancashire in 2002 – he'd played more for his club, Burnley – before being hurried into England's one-day squad in Australia that winter as cover for Andy Caddick, following an impressive stint at the Academy there. He didn't have a number – or even a name – on his shirt, but a remarkable ten-over stint, costing just 12 runs, in century heat at Adelaide earned him a World Cup spot. There, he produced a matchwinning spell against Pakistan before a sobering last-over disaster against Australia. Nonetheless his star was very much in the ascendant, and he took five wickets in the first innings of his debut Test, against Zimbabwe at home in 2003, almost to order. A one-day hat-trick followed against Pakistan ... but from then on, his fortunes began to wane. South Africa's batsmen made his new go-faster hairstyle look a bit foolish, and although he toured Bangladesh and Sri Lanka in 2003-04 and South Africa the following winter, he was a peripheral net bowler – and a shadow of his former self when he did get on the field. Previously silent critics noted that his head pointed downwards at delivery, supposedly leading to a lack of control. Anderson sat on the sidelines until injuries led to a recall at Mumbai in 2005-06, and took six wickets in England's series-levelling triumph. But back home he collected a lower-back stress fracture, which kept him out for most of the 2006 season.

THE FACTS Anderson was the first man to take an ODI hat-trick for England, against Pakistan at The Oval in 2003: Steve Harmison followed suit in 2004 ... Anderson was the cover star on the first edition of the new *Wisden Cricketer* magazine in 2003 ... His best figures of 6 for 23 came for Lancashire against Hampshire at Southampton in 2002, his first season ... Anderson was the Cricket Writers' Club's Young Cricketer of the Year in 2003 – the first unanimous choice since the award began in 1950, as all 175 members who voted went for him ...

THE FIGURES

Batting and fielding

	M	Inns	NO	Runs	HS	Avge	S/R	100	50	4s	6s	Ct	St
Tests *to 11.9.06*	13	18	12	89	21*	14.83	36.92	0	0	4	0	11	0
ODIs *to 11.9.06*	50	19	9	69	12*	6.90	36.50	0	0	2	4	7	0
First-class *to 11.9.06*	52	61	30	311	37*	10.03	–	0	0	–	–	19	0

Bowling

	M	Balls	Runs	Wkts	BB	Avge	RpO	S/R	5i	10m
Tests *to 11.9.06*	13	2221	1353	41	5–73	33.00	3.65	54.17	2	0
ODIs *to 11.9.06*	50	2452	1972	75	4–25	26.29	4.82	32.69	0	0
First-class *to 11.9.06*	52	8830	5151	190	6–23	27.11	3.50	46.47	8	1

RUSSEL ARNOLD

Full name	**Russel Premakumaran Arnold**
Born	**October 25, 1973, Colombo**
Teams	**Nondescripts**
Style	**Left-hand bat, offspinner**
Test debut	**Sri Lanka v Pakistan at Colombo 1996-97**
ODI debut	**Sri Lanka v South Africa at Lahore 1997-98**

THE PROFILE A tall, angular left-hander and a patient accumulator, Russel Arnold began his Test career in 1997 as an opener, but despite solid scores then, and on his recall for the Asian Test Championship two years later, he lost out to Marvan Atapattu as Sanath Jayasuriya's long-term partner. Short of runs by late 2000, he dropped into the middle order. When a loss of form and confidence by Jayasuriya gave Arnold another chance at the top in 2002, he did not disappoint, scoring 62 and 109 in a valiant rearguard at Old Trafford – but failure in the series that followed left him on the sidelines again after the 2003 World Cup. He has played only one Test since then – in Australia in 2004 – but was a regular member of the one-day side, at least until a new selection committee wanted new blood late in 2004. Arnold's future looked bleak for a while, but he worked furiously on his game in the nets, and scored heavily in domestic cricket. Finally, with various replacements failing to impress, he won a recall for the one-dayers in New Zealand in December 2004. His ability to adapt his game to the situation makes him an ideal No. 6 in limited-overs cricket, and an unselfish approach explains the high esteem in which he is held by team-mates. A cool head under pressure helps when chasing, and he adds great value in the field with a safe pair of hands. His offbreaks occasionally come in useful too.

THE FACTS Arnold has a share in Sri Lanka's record ODI partnerships for the fifth wicket (166 with Sanath Jayasuriya) and the sixth (133 with Marvan Atapattu) ... He has scored three first-class double-centuries, the highest 217 not out for Nondescripts against Moors in Colombo in March 1996: he also scored 209 against Somerset in 1998 ... Arnold made 851 runs in ODIs in 2001 ... He took 7 for 84 for Nondescripts at Kurunegala in February 1997 ...

THE FIGURES

Batting and fielding

	M	Inns	NO	Runs	HS	Avge	S/R	100	50	4s	6s	Ct	St
Tests *to 11.9.06*	44	69	4	1821	123	28.01	44.58	3	10	222	3	51	0
ODIs *to 11.9.06*	165	143	37	3738	103*	3526	72.37	1	26	269	20	46	0
First-class *to 11.9.06*	163	247	22	9257	217*	41.14	–		25	41	–	–	147	0

Bowling

	M	Balls	Runs	Wkts	BB	Avge	RpO	S/R	5i	10m
Tests *to 11.9.06*	44	1334	598	11	3–76	54.36	2.68	121.27	0	0
ODIs *to 11.9.06*	165	2084	1683	37	3–47	45.48	4.48	56.32	0	0
First-class *to 11.9.06*	163	9774	4555	156	7–84	29.19	2.79	62.65	4	0

NATHAN ASTLE

Full name	**Nathan John Astle**
Born	**September 15, 1971, Christchurch, Canterbury**
Teams	**Canterbury, Lancashire**
Style	**Right-hand bat, right-arm medium-pacer**
Test debut	**New Zealand v Zimbabwe at Hamilton 1995-96**
ODI debut	**New Zealand v West Indies at Auckland 1994-95**

THE PROFILE One of cricket's free spirits, Nathan Astle became a lively international allrounder without losing his breezy confidence. He began at Canterbury as an unregarded batsman and the most parsimonious of medium-pace bowlers, but his batting developed quickly. First he became a free-scoring one-day player, and then Glenn Turner, the national coach at the time, helped turn him into a first-rate Test batsman, who made his mark with consecutive hundreds in the West Indies in 1995-96. Astle ripped up the record-books with his 222 against England at Christchurch in March 2002, the fastest Test double-century, reached from only 153 balls. A knee injury which needed an operation forced him out towards the end of 2003, but he still toured England the following year. Astle is also an expert slip catcher, and is now an occasional medium-paced partnership-breaker. He seemed to be on the way out in 2005-06, after the new coach John Bracewell apparently decided to go for younger blood, but Astle still ended the season with the award as New Zealand's one-day batsman of the year. He was left out of the one-day side, then got back in after injuries to others and scored a matchwinning 90 not out against Sri Lanka at Christchurch, only to be dropped again for the next game, to widespread amazement. But Astle bounced back, made another 90 against Sri Lanka and 118 – his 16th one-day hundred – against West Indies, and is set fair for a fourth World Cup in 2007.

THE FACTS Astle has scored 16 ODI centuries, ten more than any other New Zealander ... He averages 56.63 in ODIs against England, but only 22.44 against South Africa: in Tests he averages 55 against West Indies, but 3.14 against Pakistan ... Astle and Australia's Glenn McGrath are the only two players who have been involved in two hundred partnerships for the tenth wicket in Tests ... Astle played for Lancashire in 2006, his fourth English county ...

THE FIGURES
Batting and fielding

	M	Inns	NO	Runs	HS	Avge	S/R	100	50	4s	6s	Ct	St
Tests to 11.9.06	79	133	10	4650	222	37.80	49.62	11	24	606	39	69	0
ODIs to 11.9.06	212	207	14	6890	145*	35.69	72.74	16	40	695	83	80	0
First-class to 11.9.06	165	262	23	9051	223	37.87	–	19	48	–	–	127	0

Bowling

	M	Balls	Runs	Wkts	BB	Avge	RpO	S/R	5i	10m
Tests to 11.9.06	79	5634	2119	51	3–27	41.54	2.25	101.47	0	0
ODIs to 11.9.06	212	4768	3741	99	4–43	37.78	4.70	48.16	0	0
First-class to 11.9.06	165	13172	4775	148	6–22	32.26	2.17	89.00	2	0

MARVAN ATAPATTU

Full name	**Marvan Samson Atapattu**
Born	**November 22, 1970, Kalutara**
Teams	**Sinhalese Sports Club**
Style	**Right-hand bat, occasional offspinner**
Test debut	**Sri Lanka v India at Chandigarh 1990-91**
ODI debut	**Sri Lanka v India at Nagpur 1990-91**

THE PROFILE Marvan Atapattu can be a vulnerable starter, but he is hard to dislodge once set, his signature shot the high-elbow cover-drive. On lifeless pitches he is an elegant master of the percentages, the ideal foil for Sanath Jayasuriya, his opening partner almost throughout his Test career. All Atapattu's big Test innings – he has scored six double-centuries – have been slow affairs, but the most tortuous part of his international career was its start: it took him nearly seven years to establish himself, but his average has been climbing steadily since then. He was appointed one-day captain in April 2003: he had been expected to take over the Test team too, but the selectors appointed Hashan Tillakaratne instead. After some indifferent results Atapattu did finally take charge in May 2004 – and immediately made 170 and 249 against Zimbabwe. Quickly he halted the slide and established himself as a strong leader. On the surface he is quiet and reserved, and his captaincy pedigree was not entirely obvious – but within the dressing-room he is straight-talking and positive, firm and fair in his dealings with players and aggressive in his approach to the game. By mid-2004 the team's fortunes had changed: Sri Lanka won the Asia Cup, and whitewashed South Africa. A back problem that required surgery forced him to miss the 2006 tour of England, where Mahela Jayawardene deputised impressively, and with Atapattu's relationship with the national selectors remaining a prickly one after past clashes there is some doubt whether he will return as captain.

THE FACTS Atapattu has made six Test double-centuries (three against Zimbabwe), behind only Don Bradman (12), Brian Lara (eight) and Wally Hammond (seven) ... He made a nightmare start to his Test career, scoring only one run in his first six innings: 0 and 0 v India at Chandigarh in 1990-91, 0 and 1 v Australia in Colombo in 1992-93, and 0 and 0 v India at Ahmedabad in 1993-94: his next Test was not until March 1997 ... Atapattu's highest score is 253 not out for Sinhalese Sports Club v Galle in Colombo in February 1996 ...

THE FIGURES

Batting and fielding

	M	Inns	NO	Runs	HS	Avge	S/R	100	50	4s	6s	Ct	St
Tests *to 11.9.06*	88	152	15	5330	249	38.90	–	16	15	667	3	57	0
ODIs *to 11.9.06*	253	246	28	8233	132*	37.76	67.72	11	59	702	15	70	0
First-class *to 11.9.06*	224	340	49	14246	253*	48.95	–	47	50	–	–	148	0

Bowling

	M	Balls	Runs	Wkts	BB	Avge	RpO	S/R	5i	10m
Tests *to 11.9.06*	88	48	24	1	1–9	24.00	3.00	48.00	0	0
ODIs *to 11.9.06*	253	51	41	0	–	–	4.82	–	0	0
First-class *to 11.9.06*	224	1302	692	19	3–19	36.42	3.18	68.52	0	0

MALINGA BANDARA

Full name	**Charitha Malinga Bandara**
Born	**December 31, 1979, Kalutara**
Teams	**Ragama**
Style	**Right-hand bat, legspinner**
Test debut	**Sri Lanka v New Zealand at Colombo 1997-98**
ODI debut	**Sri Lanka v New Zealand at Wellington 2005-06**

THE PROFILE Malinga Bandara was earmarked from an early age as a legspinner of great potential. He doesn't turn it a long way, but varies his pace intelligently. His school performances won him selection for an Under-19 tour of India in 1997, the Youth World Cup in South Africa, and the Sri Lanka A tour of England in 1999. In between, he made his Test debut against New Zealand in May 1998, but looked all at sea and was not considered again for some time. But he bowled consistently in domestic cricket, taking 45 wickets in 2000-01, and a match haul of 11 for 126 against England A in March 2005 confirmed his growing confidence. It also interested Gloucestershire, as they looked for a mid-season replacement for Upul Chandana: Bandara outbowled his more senior team-mate in county cricket in 2005, taking 45 wickets at 24.15 to Chandana's 16 at 42.25, although admittedly the pitches were drier and more suited to legspin when Bandara arrived. His performances helped him win a Test return against India at the end of 2005, and he finally took his first wicket (MS Dhoni) more than six years after his debut. He chipped in with useful wickets and handy runs, and toured England in 2006 ahead of Chandana: he didn't play in the Tests, but deputised for Muralitharan in the one-day series, which his side swept 5-0. Earlier his two four-wicket hauls had helped Sri Lanka reach the finals of the VB Series in Australia in February 2006.

THE FACTS Bandara took 8 for 49 (and 3 for 77) as Sri Lanka A beat England A in Colombo in March 2005 ... His highest score came the following month, also for Sri Lanka A, against Pakistan A at Dambulla: he made 79, and put on 171 for the ninth wicket with Prasanna Jayawardene ... Bandara averages 12.11 with the ball in ODIs against South Africa – and 51.50 against Bangladesh ...

THE FIGURES

Batting and fielding

	M	Inns	NO	Runs	HS	Avge	S/R	100	50	4s	6s	Ct	St
Tests to 11.9.06	8	11	3	124	43	15.50	51.66	0	0	14	2	4	0
ODIs to 11.9.06	19	9	2	85	28*	12.14	77.98	0	0	5	3	4	0
First-class to 11.9.06	100	135	29	1966	79	18.54	–	0	8	–	–	62	0

Bowling

	M	Balls	Runs	Wkts	BB	Avge	RpO	S/R	5i	10m
Tests to 11.9.06	8	1152	633	16	3–84	39.56	3.29	72.00	0	0
ODIs to 11.9.06	19	878	703	23	4–31	30.56	4.80	38.17	0	0
First-class to 11.9.06	100	12836	6647	255	8–49	26.06	3.10	50.33	9	2

CARLTON BAUGH

Full name	**Carlton Seymour Baugh junior**
Born	**June 23, 1982, Kingston, Jamaica**
Teams	**Jamaica**
Style	**Right-hand bat, wicketkeeper**
Test debut	**West Indies v Australia at Port-of-Spain 2002-03**
ODI debut	**West Indies v Australia at Kingston 2002-03**

THE PROFILE Carlton Baugh seemed to be West Indies' original choice to replace the long-serving Ridley Jacobs behind the stumps, even though he did not start out as a keeper for Jamaica. Baugh was tidy enough when he deputised for the injured Jacobs in two Tests at home against Australia early in 2003, and won a place as a batsman alone for one match in South Africa later that year. Baugh first caught the eye for West Indies B, smacking a rapid undefeated 100 against Barbados at Bridgetown in March 2003, then climbed in against the touring Australians at Georgetown, carting Stuart MacGill for 16 in one over on his way to an unbeaten 115 for a Carib Beer XI, which sealed that Test call-up. He played twice more in England in 2004, making 68 in the third Test at Manchester. Baugh's flowing strokeplay seemed ideal for one-dayers, but a highest score of 29 in his first six matches wasn't enough, and Denesh Ramdin grabbed the gloves for the tours of Sri Lanka and Australia in 2005. Baugh earned something of a surprise recall when Zimbabwe toured early in 2006, and although he again failed to set the world alight he kept his place until the final match of the Indian series that followed. Ramdin might be the man in possession, but Baugh is a more explosive batsman and could edge back in time for the World Cup, when West Indies' pool games will be played in his home town of Kingston, Jamaica.

THE FACTS Although he plays for Jamaica Baugh has never played a first-class match at Sabina Park in Kingston ... He has extended three of his seven first-class centuries into scores of 150 or more – the highest is 158 not out for the West Indians against Free State at Bloemfontein in December 2003 ... Baugh's father, also Carlton, played four times for Jamaica in the early 1980s ...

THE FIGURES
Batting and fielding

	M	Inns	NO	Runs	HS	Avge	S/R	100	50	4s	6s	Ct	St
Tests to 11.9.06	5	10	0	196	68	19.60	56.48	0	1	26	1	4	1
ODIs to 11.9.06	12	11	5	146	29*	24.33	81.56	0	0	11	6	6	0
First-class to 11.9.06	49	84	11	2764	158*	37.86	–	7	12	–	–	87	14

Bowling

	M	Balls	Runs	Wkts	BB	Avge	RpO	S/R	5i	10m
Tests to 11.9.06	5	0	–	–	–	–	–	–	–	–
ODIs to 11.9.06	0	0	–	–	–	–	–	–	–	–
First-class to 11.9.06	0	0	–	–	–	–	–	–	–	–

IAN BELL

Full name **Ian Ronald Bell**
Born **April 11, 1982, Walsgrave, Coventry**
Teams **Warwickshire**
Style **Right-hand bat, right-arm medium-pace bowler**
Test debut **England v West Indies at The Oval 2004**
ODI debut **England v Zimbabwe at Harare 2004-05**

THE PROFILE Ian Bell was earmarked for greatness long before he was drafted into the England squad in New Zealand in 2001-02, aged 19, as cover for the injured Mark Butcher. Tenacious and technically sound, Bell is in the mould of Michael Atherton, who was burdened with similar expectations on his England debut a generation earlier. Like Atherton, it is Bell's mental attitude to the game that has set him apart. When in form, he is particularly adept at leaving the ball outside off, and he has received glowing reviews from all his coaches, including Rod Marsh, a man not given to hyperbole. Bell had played only 13 first-class matches when called into that England squad, although he did score 836 runs at 64 for Warwickshire in 2001. Under the spotlight, his form slumped, but by 2004 he was on the up again. He finally made his Test debut against West Indies in August 2004, stroking 70 at The Oval, before returning the following summer to lift his average to an obscene 297 against Bangladesh, including a maiden Test century at Chester-le-Street. Such rich pickings soon ceased: found out by McGrath and Warne, like so many before him, Bell mustered just 171 runs in the 2005 Ashes series. But, like a true class act, he bounced back better for the experience, stroking 313 runs in three Tests in Pakistan, including a classy century at Faisalabad. And when Pakistan toured in 2006, Bell repeated the dose, with elegant hundreds in each of the first three Tests.

THE FACTS After three Tests, and innings of 70, 65 not out and 162 not out, Bell's average was 297.00: he raised that to 303.00 before Australia started getting him out – only Lawrence Rowe (336), David Lloyd (308) and "Tip" Foster (306) have ever had better batting averages in Test history ... He made 262 not out for Warwickshire against Sussex at Horsham in May 2004, sharing a county-record seventh-wicket stand of 289 with Tony Frost: he also scored 231 against Middlesex at Birmingham in 2005 ...

THE FIGURES

Batting and fielding

	M	Inns	NO	Runs	HS	Avge	S/R	100	50	4s	6s	Ct	St
Tests to 11.9.06	18	32	5	1287	162*	47.66	53.24	5	7	142	4	18	0
ODIs to 11.9.06	23	21	3	783	88	43.50	71.44	0	6	71	2	2	0
First-class to 11.9.06	100	172	17	6756	262*	43.58	–		17	35	–	–	61	0

Bowling

	M	Balls	Runs	Wkts	BB	Avge	RpO	S/R	5i	10m
Tests to 11.9.06	18	102	64	1	1–33	64.00	3.76	102.00	0	0
ODIs to 11.9.06	23	88	88	6	3–9	14.66	6.00	14.66	0	0
First-class to 11.9.06	100	2713	1478	47	4–4	31.44	3.26	57.72	0	0

TINO BEST

Full name	**Tino la Bertram Best**
Born	**August 26, 1981, Richmond Gap, St Michael, Barbados**
Teams	**Barbados**
Style	**Right-hand bat, right-arm fast bowler**
Test debut	**West Indies v Australia at Bridgetown 2002-03**
ODI debut	**West Indies v Bangladesh at Kingstown 2003-04**

THE PROFILE   Tino Best brings qualities to the West Indian bowling attack that were missing for too long. He is aggressive, confident and energetic, and carries the fight to the very end. He topped the domestic averages with 39 wickets in 2003, and was selected for the third Test against Australia at home that May, although he didn't take a wicket. He impressed against England in 2004, at least with his enthusiasm – his figures, as West Indies slumped to seven defeats out of eight, weren't great, and he was memorably psyched out by Andrew Flintoff while batting at Lord's: after being advised to "mind the windows", Best obliged by trying to blast the ball into the pavilion, and was immediately stumped. He then injured his back and missed the rest of the tour. With the ball, he has been likened to his fellow Barbadian, the great Wes Hall, especially in exuberance and speed, although he isn't as tall. Best can nudge the speedo over 90mph, but still needs to tighten up – he lost his place in the West Indies side in May 2006 after ten wayward overs in an ODI against the callow Zimbabweans cost 70 runs. He has also had the odd run-in with umpires, chiefly over letting slip the odd high full-toss – he was banned from bowling in Sri Lanka because of this in July 2005, and hasn't played a Test since. But Best will be back, huffing and puffing, as long as his body can stand the strain.

THE FACTS   Best was banned from bowling after sending down a beamer to Sri Lanka's Rangana Herath at Kandy in July 2005, only the third time this has happened in a Test: he was also been taken off by the umpires after a similar incident in a domestic match in 2003 ... Best's best ODI figures of 4 for 35 came on his debut, against Bangladesh at Kingstown in May 2004 ... He took 7 for 33 (11 for 66 in the match) for Barbados against Windward Islands at Crab Hill in January 2004 ...

THE FIGURES
Batting and fielding

	M	Inns	NO	Runs	HS	Avge	S/R	100	50	4s	6s	Ct	St
Tests to 11.9.06	12	19	2	174	27	10.23	49.15	0	0	20	1	1	0
ODIs to 11.9.06	11	7	3	44	24	11.00	81.48	0	0	4	0	3	0
First-class to 11.9.06	48	61	13	582	42*	12.12	–	0	0	–	–	13	0

Bowling

	M	Balls	Runs	Wkts	BB	Avge	RpO	S/R	5i	10m
Tests to 11.9.06	12	1851	1171	26	4–46	45.03	3.79	71.19	0	0
ODIs to 11.9.06	11	506	427	13	4–35	32.84	5.06	38.92	0	0
First-class to 11.9.06	48	6794	4104	153	7–33	26.82	3.62	44.40	6	1

ANDY BLIGNAUT

Full name	**Arnoldus Mauritius Blignaut**
Born	**August 1, 1978, Salisbury (now Harare)**
Teams	**Mashonaland, Lions**
Style	**Left-hand bat, right-arm fast-medium bowler**
Test debut	**Zimbabwe v Bangladesh at Bulawayo 2000-01**
ODI debut	**Zimbabwe v West Indies at Singapore 1999-2000**

THE PROFILE Laid-back Andy Blignaut hails from an Afrikaner farming family. His strongest suit is his pace bowling, and he returned Zimbabwe's best figures on Test debut – 5 for 73 against Bangladesh in April 2001. He also managed a first-ball duck, although as a stroke-playing left-hander, he has a terrific eye for the ball, and a couple of Test nineties to his name. He's a fine fielder as well. After growing disenchanted with cricket he sat out 2001-02, amid whispers of disputes with administrators and fellow players. Blignaut tried several jobs including, briefly, male modelling. But in August 2002 he returned, and in his first game back took 5 for 79 against Pakistan. He cemented his place with some steady performances during the World Cup and in England later in 2003. Early the following year he claimed Zimbabwe's first Test hat-trick. But he was one of the 15 "rebel" players involved in a bitter stand-off with the board, and was eventually sacked. In June 2004 he joined the growing exodus from Zimbabwe by signing for Tasmania. But they released him early – his time there was dogged by injury – and in February 2005 he returned "unconditionally" to Zimbabwe. He was nonetheless part of the strike against the board later that year, and spent 2005-06 playing in South Africa for the Lions. He was touted as a possible successor to Tatenda Taibu as captain, but refused to play again until the board paid the substantial amounts Blignaut said they owed him.

THE FACTS Blignaut took Zimbabwe's first (and so far only) Test hat-trick, against Bangladesh at Harare in 2003-04 ... He averages 31.60 with the ball in Tests at home, but 67.75 overseas ... Blignaut has scored two first-class centuries, including 194 for Mashonaland against Manicaland at Mutare in September 2003 ... He has twice reached the nineties in Tests, both times during national-record stands with Heath Streak ... Blignaut has also played for Tasmania and Durham ...

THE FIGURES

Batting and fielding

	M	Inns	NO	Runs	HS	Avge	S/R	100	50	4s	6s	Ct	St
Tests to 11.9.06	19	36	3	886	92	26.84	68.57	0	6	102	23	13	0
ODIs to 11.9.06	51	40	8	625	63*	19.53	106.65	0	5	62	13	11	0
First-class to 11.9.06	56	89	5	2303	194*	27.41	–	2	14	–	–	38	0

Bowling

	M	Balls	Runs	Wkts	BB	Avge	RpO	S/R	5i	10m
Tests to 11.9.06	19	3173	1964	53	5–73	37.05	3.71	59.86	3	0
ODIs to 11.9.06	51	2270	2021	49	4–43	41.24	5.34	46.32	0	0
First-class to 11.9.06	56	8052	4819	133	5–73	36.23	3.59	60.54	3	0

NICKY BOJE

SOUTH AFRICA

Full name	**Nico Boje**
Born	**March 20, 1973, Bloemfontein, Orange Free State**
Teams	**Eagles**
Style	**Left-hand bat, left-arm orthodox spinner**
Test debut	**South Africa v India at Mumbai 1999-2000**
ODI debut	**South Africa v Zimbabwe at Harare 1995-96**

THE PROFILE   Such is the sporting gene-pool in the Boje family that mother, father and all three children played at least one sport at provincial or international level. Nicky Boje captained South African Schools, and was selected for three successive years as a middle-order batsman. He opened the bowling for his own school – Grey College in Bloemfontein, which also produced Hansie Cronje – and then switched to left-arm spin on the coach's command, because nobody else could turn the ball. Boje spent four long years after his initial national-squad selection quietly desperate to be regarded as a middle-order batsman who bowled usefully, but a spinner he remained. He worked furiously on his bowling as a result, and matchwinning analyses in both India and Sri Lanka finally established him as the Test No. 1 in 2000-01, a position he briefly surrendered to Claude Henderson in Australia in 2001-02, and then to Robin Peterson and Paul Adams in 2003. However, he had a big role to play in the final Test of the 2003-04 New Zealand tour, when his eight-wicket haul helped South Africa to a series-levelling win. Without often threatening to run through sides, he is now close to 100 wickets in both Tests and one-dayers. His batting ability remains untarnished, as a pair of one-day hundreds and a Test-match 85 testify. Boje is of the bright, inquisitive breed of internationals who prefers a cameraman's long lens to a boring dressing-room, and a craft market or temple to a hotel room.

THE FACTS   Boje's two one-day hundreds came in the space of three innings (the middle one was 64) against New Zealand in 2000-01, when he was being tried at No. 3 ... He has been reluctant to tour India since his name cropped up in connection with the Hansie Cronje match-fixing scandal: despite his protestations of innocence the police denied him immunity from prosecution if he returned ... Boje averages 24.57 with the ball in Tests against India, but 71.66 against England ... His record includes two ODIs for the Africa XI ...

THE FIGURES
Batting and fielding

	M	Inns	NO	Runs	HS	Avge	S/R	100	50	4s	6s	Ct	St
Tests *to 11.9.06*	43	62	10	1312	85	25.23	48.32	0	4	184	6	18	0
ODIs *to 11.9.06*	115	71	18	1414	129	26.67	88.70	2	4	135	13	33	0
First-class *to 11.9.06*	162	240	45	6329	116	32.45	–		5	36	–	–	95	0

Bowling

	M	Balls	Runs	Wkts	BB	Avge	RpO	S/R	5i	10m
Tests *to 11.9.06*	43	8620	4265	100	5–62	42.65	2.96	86.20	3	0
ODIs *to 11.9.06*	115	4541	3415	96	5–21	35.57	4.51	47.30	1	0
First-class *to 11.9.06*	162	33757	14604	447	8–93	32.67	2.59	75.51	20	2

SHANE BOND

Full name	**Shane Edward Bond**
Born	**June 7, 1975, Christchurch, Canterbury**
Teams	**Canterbury**
Style	**Right-hand bat, right-arm fast bowler**
Test debut	**New Zealand v Australia at Hobart 2001-02**
ODI debut	**New Zealand v Australia at Melbourne 2001-02**

THE PROFILE   Shane Bond, for a while world cricket's most famous ex-policeman, is one of the fastest and most dangerous fast bowlers around ... when he's fit. Unfortunately for New Zealand, that hasn't been too often since his impressive introduction to international cricket in 2001-02, when his 21 wickets in the VB Series helped keep the Aussies out of the finals for once. Bond has suffered stress fractures in his back (something of an occupational hazard for fast bowlers) and also in his feet (rather less so). He zipped to 50 one-day wickets in only 27 matches, which included 6 for 23 as he unsettled the Aussies again in the 2003 World Cup. But those injuries have cost him numerous caps, and planned county stints with Warwickshire in 2003 and Gloucestershire in 2006. He has played only 14 Tests, in he which he has taken 64 wickets at an enviable average. His speciality is the fast, inswinging yorker, which he used to great effect against the callow Zimbabweans in 2005, when most of his ten wickets in the Bulawayo Test were lbw or caught in the cordon. He reached 50 wickets in that match, only his 12th Test, and shook up the West Indians with 5 for 86 as they narrowly failed to chase 291 at Auckland in March 2006. But a knee injury sidelined him on the South African tour that followed: fingers, and much else, are crossed in New Zealand that he can regain full fitness.

THE FACTS   Bond was the first super-sub to win a Man of the Match award in an ODI, after coming off the bench to take 6 for 19 against India at Bulawayo in 2005-06 ... Those are New Zealand's best figures in ODIs, beating Bond's own 6 for 23 against Australia in the 2003 World Cup ... In ODIs he has taken 22 wickets against Australia at 10.45 – but in Tests against them he has only three wickets at 96.33 ... Bond has made little impact with the bat in international cricket, but scored 100 for Canterbury v Northern Districts in Christchurch in 2004-05 ...

THE FIGURES

Batting and fielding

	M	Inns	NO	Runs	HS	Avge	S/R	100	50	4s	6s	Ct	St
Tests to 11.9.06	14	14	7	123	41	17.57	42.12	0	0	15	3	5	0
ODIs to 11.9.06	45	19	10	152	31*	16.88	78.75	0	0	11	7	9	0
First-class to 11.9.06	48	53	20	671	100	20.33	–	1	2	–	–	21	0

Bowling

	M	Balls	Runs	Wkts	BB	Avge	RpO	S/R	5i	10m
Tests to 11.9.06	14	2478	1378	64	6–51	21.53	3.33	38.71	4	1
ODIs to 11.9.06	45	2306	1621	87	6–19	18.63	4.21	26.50	3	0
First-class to 11.9.06	48	7985	4154	164	6–51	25.32	3.12	46.68	8	1

MARK BOUCHER

SOUTH AFRICA

Full name	**Mark Verdon Boucher**
Born	**December 3, 1976, East London, Cape Province**
Teams	**Warriors**
Style	**Right-hand bat, wicketkeeper**
Test debut	**South Africa v Pakistan at Sheikhupura 1997-98**
ODI debut	**South Africa v New Zealand at Perth 1997-98**

THE PROFILE It is a measure of the rapidity of Mark Boucher's rise that no-one is quite sure exactly how many records he holds. Fastest man to 100 dismissals, highest score by a nightwatchman, most innings without a bye ... they have tumbled out so quickly that it has been difficult to keep up. Probably his most significant achievement, however, came in only his second Test, against Pakistan at Johannesburg in February 1998, when he and Pat Symcox added 195, a new Test record for the ninth wicket, from a desperate 166 for 8. Boucher had made his debut a few months previously when still not 21, rushing to Sheikhupura to replace the injured Dave Richardson, who retired after the Australian tour that followed. Boucher was not everyone's first choice to succeed him – Nic Pothas had also been waiting patiently – but once Boucher got his hands into the gloves, he refused to let them go. He found conditions in England difficult, in the 1998 Tests and the 1999 World Cup, but demonstrated courage and determination in what became a run of 75 consecutive Tests. Those qualities brought him three hundreds in his first 25 matches, and he was also named vice-captain when Shaun Pollock took over from Hansie Cronje, recognition of his willingness to get down and scrap when his team needed it. And Boucher scrapped successfully to regain his spot when a form dip eventually did cost him his place – to Thami Tsolekile, and then AB de Villiers – late in 2004.

THE FACTS Only Ian Healy (395) has made more dismissals than Boucher in Tests, and only Adam Gilchrist (393) heads him in ODIs ... His 125 against South Africa at Harare in 1999-2000 was a Test record for a nightwatchman until Jason Gillespie surpassed it in 2006 ... Boucher's run of 75 consecutive Tests between 1997-98 and 2004-05 is a South African record ... His figures include one Test for the World XI and two ODIs for the Africa XI ...

THE FIGURES
Batting and fielding

	M	Inns	NO	Runs	HS	Avge	S/R	100	50	4s	6s	Ct	St
Tests *to 11.9.06*	96	136	17	3582	125	30.10	50.48	4	23	457	11	350	14
ODIs *to 11.9.06*	217	158	39	3175	76	26.68	80.29	0	19	242	42	303	17
First-class *to 11.9.06*	153	226	33	6574	134	34.06	–		8	40	–	–	517	27

Bowling

	M	Balls	Runs	Wkts	BB	Avge	RpO	S/R	5i	10m
Tests *to 11.9.06*	96	8	6	1	1-6	6.00	4.50	8.00	0	0
ODIs *to 11.9.06*	217	0	–	–	–	–	–	–	–	–
First-class *to 11.9.06*	153	26	26	1	1-6	26.00	6.00	26.00	0	0

NATHAN BRACKEN

Full name   **Nathan Wade Bracken**
Born   **September 12, 1977, Penrith, New South Wales**
Teams   **New South Wales**
Style   **Right-hand bat, left-arm fast-medium bowler**
Test debut   **Australia v India at Brisbane 2003-04**
ODI debut   **Australia v West Indies at Melbourne 2000-01**

THE PROFILE The search for a Test-class left-armer, a universal pursuit, first led Australia to Nathan Bracken. Tall and slim like Bruce Reid, Bracken bowls a full length, moves the ball both ways in the air and off the seam, and fitted easily into Australia's rampant one-day squad in 2000-01. He has also been instrumental in resuscitating New South Wales's fortunes, including 6 for 27 in their 2004-05 final win over Queensland and an amazing 7 for 4 earlier that season when South Australia fell for just 29 at the SCG. A shoulder injury cut short his maiden Ashes tour in 2001 after only two matches, but after a spell on the sidelines he returned to the side during the 2003 World Cup, when Jason Gillespie dropped out with a heel injury. Bracken's Test debut finally came in 2003-04, but in three outings against the powerful Indian batting line-up he failed to make real inroads. In the spring of 2004 he was omitted from Cricket Australia's list of centrally contracted players, but returned to the ODI scene for the Super Series late the following year and became a regular in green and gold, prompting him to withdraw from a planned county stint with Worcestershire. However, he played only two Tests in 2005-06, and faces a head-to-head battle with Mitchell Johnson for the position as Australia's No. 1 left-armer.

THE FACTS Bracken's figures of 7-5-4-7 for New South Wales against South Australia at Sydney in December 2004 were described as "more like a PIN number than a bowling analysis" in the *Sydney Morning Herald*, which also called his yorker-heavy bowling to the South Africans "foot theory" ... He is 6ft 5ins (195cm) tall ... Seven of his 12 Test wickets have come at Brisbane ... Bracken took 3 for 21 in his only ODI against England, and has never played against Pakistan ... He averages 16.07 in ODIs against India – but 94 against Zimbabwe ...

THE FIGURES

Batting and fielding

	M	Inns	NO	Runs	HS	Avge	S/R	100	50	4s	6s	Ct	St
Tests to 11.9.06	5	6	2	70	37	17.50	62.50	0	0	7	0	2	0
ODIs to 11.9.06	38	10	6	84	21*	21.00	85.71	0	0	2	4	7	0
First-class to 11.9.06	55	73	26	820	38*	17.44	–	0	0	–	–	15	0

Bowling

	M	Balls	Runs	Wkts	BB	Avge	RpO	S/R	5i	10m
Tests to 11.9.06	5	1110	505	12	4-48	42.08	2.72	92.50	0	0
ODIs to 11.9.06	38	1906	1377	65	5-67	21.18	4.33	29.32	1	0
First-class to 11.9.06	55	10890	4607	177	7-4	26.02	2.53	61.52	8	0

IAN BRADSHAW

Full name	Ian David Russell Bradshaw
Born	July 9, 1974, Hopewell, Christ Church, Barbados
Teams	Barbados
Style	Left-hand bat, left-arm fast-medium bowler
Test debut	West Indies v New Zealand at Auckland 2005-06
ODI debut	West Indies v England at Gros Islet 2003-04

THE PROFILE Ian Bradshaw has the demeanour and posture of a man well beyond his years, although he is no longer exactly a youngster. It's not surprising when one considers the responsibility he carried, often as captain of the regionally dominant Barbados team – and he was West Indies' Under-19 skipper before that, leading a side in England in 1993 that included Shivnarine Chanderpaul. He projects a calm and composed façade, reflecting his disciplined approach to the game, has a refreshingly diligent work ethic, and a highly developed cricket brain. He's from the Jimmy Adams mould, seeing consistency as the cornerstone of good performance, and his nippy left-arm bowling provides the kind of ballast needed to anchor the West Indian team. Indeed, after a rich haul of wickets in his initial games, Bradshaw went mostly wicketless in English conditions apparently suited to his style of bowling in 2004, but still played a vital role by stifling runs, which gave the other bowlers a chance to express themselves. Cricinfo called him "the West Indian Energizer Bunny" after an unbroken spell of 25 overs in stifling heat against India in Antigua in June 2006. He is more than handy with the bat, with a first-class century under his belt, and he memorably helped Courtney Browne – another Barbados captain – win the Champions Trophy final against England in the dark at The Oval in September 2004.

THE FACTS Bradshaw took six wickets on his Test debut, in March 2006 when he was nearly 32, but has taken only three more wickets in four Tests since ... He scored 34 not out, and put on 71 with Courtney Browne in near-darkness to steer West Indies to victory over England in the final of the Champions Trophy at The Oval in September 2004 ... Bradshaw scored 109 not out for Barbados v England A at Bridgetown in January 2001 ...

THE FIGURES

Batting and fielding

	M	Inns	NO	Runs	HS	Avge	S/R	100	50	4s	6s	Ct	St
Tests to 11.9.06	5	8	1	96	33	13.71	26.96	0	0	11	0	3	0
ODIs to 11.9.06	43	24	8	235	37	14.68	65.45	0	0	14	4	6	0
First-class to 11.9.06	45	67	11	1213	109*	21.66	–	1	5	–	–	25	0

Bowling

	M	Balls	Runs	Wkts	BB	Avge	RpO	S/R	5i	10m
Tests to 11.9.06	5	1021	540	9	3–73	60.00	3.17	113.44	0	0
ODIs to 11.9.06	43	2148	1548	58	3–15	26.68	4.32	37.03	0	0
First-class to 11.9.06	45	8272	4014	157	6–34	25.56	2.91	52.68	2	0

DWAYNE BRAVO

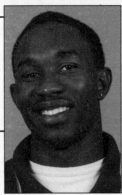

Full name	**Dwayne John Bravo**
Born	**October 7, 1983, Santa Cruz, Trinidad**
Teams	**Trinidad & Tobago, Kent**
Style	**Right-hand bat, right-arm fast-medium bowler**
Test debut	**West Indies v England at Lord's 2004**
ODI debut	**West Indies v England at Georgetown 2003-04**

THE PROFILE   Dwayne Bravo is that creature long needed by West Indies, an allrounder. He made his Test debut at Lord's in July 2004, and took three wickets in the first innings with his medium-paced swingers. He also showed a cool enough temperament to forge a confident start at the crease, displaying a straight bat even though his team was facing a big England total of 568. His follow-ups were even better. By the end of the series, West Indies were down and out, but at least they knew they had unearthed a special talent in Bravo. He scored plenty of runs and claimed a bunch of wickets in the four Tests, but nowhere was his ability more evident than at Manchester, where he top-scored and then restricted England with a six-wicket haul. He hit 107 against South Africa in Antigua in April 2005 as his maiden century, and played an even better innings the following November, a magnificent 113 at Hobart which forced the rampant Australians to wait till the fifth day to complete victory. He was restricted by a side injury early in 2006, but pronounced himself fit to face the Indians in June, going on to enjoy a memorable one-day series against them. Born in Santa Cruz, like Brian Lara, Bravo made his one-day debut in April 2004, on the tenth anniversary of Lara's 375. He has represented Trinidad & Tobago at every level since the Under-15s, and given his maturity and agility in the field, and his assurance with the bat, he is very much one to watch.

THE FACTS   Bravo's second Test century – 113 at Hobart late in 2005 – came during a stand of 182 with his fellow-Trinidadian Denesh Ramdin, and came the day after Trinidad & Tobago qualified for the soccer World Cup for the first time ... He was West Indies' leading wicket-taker (with 16) in his first Test series, in England in 2004 – and also scored 220 runs ... Bravo was one of only eight players offered central contracts by the cash-strapped West Indian board in June 2006, although a later sponsorship dispute put that in doubt ...

THE FIGURES
Batting and fielding

	M	Inns	NO	Runs	HS	Avge	S/R	100	50	4s	6s	Ct	St
Tests *to 11.9.06*	16	30	1	956	113	32.96	45.74	2	5	120	1	13	0
ODIs *to 11.9.06*	43	33	10	513	62*	22.30	76.56	0	2	33	3	15	0
First-class *to 11.9.06*	66	122	6	3490	197	30.08	–		7	17	–	–	47	0

Bowling

	M	Balls	Runs	Wkts	BB	Avge	RpO	S/R	5i	10m
Tests *to 11.9.06*	16	2403	1295	36	6–55	35.97	3.23	66.75	2	0
ODIs *to 11.9.06*	43	1634	1415	45	3–24	31.44	5.19	36.31	0	0
First-class *to 11.9.06*	66	6044	3319	110	6–11	30.17	3.29	54.94	6	0

STUART BROAD

Full name	**Stuart Christopher John Broad**
Born	**June 24, 1986, Nottingham**
Teams	**Leicestershire**
Style	**Left-hand bat, right-arm fast-medium bowler**
Test debut	**No Tests yet**
ODI debut	**England v Pakistan at Cardiff 2006**

THE PROFILE Stuart Broad was shaping up to be an opening bat just like his dad, Chris, until he suddenly shot up. Already well over six feet, he grew three inches over the winter of 2005-06. He had already transformed himself into a fast-medium bowler good enough to play for England Under-19s. And by the end of the 2006 season he was called into the full England one-day side, and also muscled his way into the list of probables for the Champions Trophy in India. Talk about a meteoric rise: "I thought I may as well try bowling because I can't just stand around in the field all day," he explains away the change that, in 2005, brought him nine cheap wickets in three U-19 ODIs against Sri Lanka, and 30 first-class wickets at 27.69 for Leicestershire too. And it got even better in 2006, as he collected four five-fors before that increasingly inevitable one-day summons. But his game could yet change again: Broad junior has aspirations to be an allrounder. Progress so far has been good. At just 19 he replaced James Anderson in the West Indies with England A, then made an impressive start to his full international career, keeping a cool head in the mayhem of a Twenty20 international, then claiming the early wicket of Shoaib Malik on his ODI debut, at Cardiff at the end of August 2006. He's got a smooth action, and as long as his physique stands up to all that bowling – and all that growing – he has a glittering future.

THE FACTS Broad took nine wickets for 72 in three Under-19 ODIs against Sri Lanka in England in 2005 … He scored 54 not out in an unbroken last-wicket stand of 127 with Chris Read (150*) for England A against the Pakistanis at Canterbury in July 2006: he later improved his highest score to 65 not out for Leicestershire against Derbyshire at Grace Road … Broad's father, Chris, scored 1661 runs in 25 Tests for England in the 1980s, scoring six centuries – including three in Australia in 1986-87, when he was the International Player of the Season …

THE FIGURES
Batting and fielding

	M	Inns	NO	Runs	HS	Avge	S/R	100	50	4s	6s	Ct	St
Tests to 11.9.06	0	–	–	–	–	–	–	–	–	–	–	–	–
ODIs to 11.9.06	5	3	3	9	8*	–	60.00	0	0	0	0	1	0
First-class to 11.9.06	25	31	8	387	65*	16.82	41.30	0	2	–	–	8	0

Bowling

	M	Balls	Runs	Wkts	BB	Avge	RpO	S/R	5i	10m
Tests to 11.9.06	0	–	–	–	–	–	–	–	–	–
ODIs to 11.9.06	5	214	185	5	3–57	37.00	5.18	42.80	0	0
First-class to 11.9.06	25	3840	2402	80	5–83	30.02	3.75	48.00	4	0

SHIVNARINE CHANDERPAUL

Full name	**Shivnarine Chanderpaul**
Born	**August 16, 1974, Unity Village, Demerara, Guyana**
Teams	**Guyana**
Style	**Left-hand bat, occasional legspinner**
Test debut	**West Indies v England at Georgetown 1993-94**
ODI debut	**West Indies v India at Faridabad 1994-95**

THE PROFILE Crouched and crabby at the crease, Shivnarine Chanderpaul proves there is life beyond the coaching handbook. He never seems to play in the V, or off the front foot, but uses soft hands, canny deflections and a whiplash pull to maintain an average in the mid-forties as he approaches a century of Tests. Early on he had a problem converting fifties into hundreds, and also missed a lot of matches, to the point that some thought him a hypochondriac. That was rectified when a large piece of floating bone was removed from his foot late in 2000, and, suitably liberated, he set about rectifying his hundreds problem too, collecting three in four Tests against India early in 2002, and two more against Australia the following year, including 104 in the successful chase for a world-record 418 in Antigua. A good run in South Africa in 2003-04 preceded a tough one at home against England – only his second lean trot in a decade – but he rediscovered his form in England, narrowly missing twin tons in the 2004 Lord's Test, and was a major contributor as West Indies surprisingly won the Champions Trophy that September. The following year he was appointed captain during an acrimonious contracts dispute, and celebrated with 203 at home in Guyana, although he was too passive in the field to prevent South Africa taking the series. In April 2006 he stood down, after a tour of Australia where he struggled at the crease and in front of the microphone.

THE FACTS Chanderpaul averages 71.86 in Tests against India, but only 28.77 against Zimbabwe ... He scored 303 not out for Guyana against Jamaica at Kingston in January 1996 ... At Georgetown in April 2003 Chanderpaul reached his century against Australia in only 69 balls – the third-fastest in Test history by balls faced ... Eleven of his Test hundreds have come in the Caribbean, and only three overseas ... Chanderpaul once managed to shoot a policeman in the hand in his native Guyana, mistaking him for a mugger ...

THE FIGURES
Batting and fielding

	M	Inns	NO	Runs	HS	Avge	S/R	100	50	4s	6s	Ct	St
Tests to 11.9.06	98	168	22	6531	203*	44.73	42.75	14	38	759	16	41	0
ODIs to 11.9.06	191	179	22	5715	150	36.40	70.30	3	38	486	47	58	0
First-class to 11.9.06	198	323	53	13882	303*	51.41	–		39	66	–	–	120	0

Bowling

	M	Balls	Runs	Wkts	BB	Avge	RpO	S/R	5i	10m
Tests to 11.9.06	98	1590	786	8	1–2	98.25	2.96	198.75	0	0
ODIs to 11.9.06	191	716	617	14	3–18	44.07	5.17	51.14	0	0
First-class to 11.9.06	198	4472	2352	56	4–48	42.00	3.15	79.85	0	0

CHAMU CHIBHABHA

Full name	**Chamunorwa Justice Chibhabha**
Born	**September 6, 1986, Masvingo**
Teams	**Mashonaland**
Style	**Right-hand bat, right-arm medium-pace bowler**
Test debut	**No Tests yet**
ODI debut	**Zimbabwe v New Zealand at Harare 2005-06**

THE PROFILE Chamu Chibhabha is a promising allrounder who bats up the order and bowls more-than-useful seamers. He was fast-tracked into the national side in 2005 after the loss of several senior players, and after an inauspicious start – he made a duck in a one-dayer against India and struggled in the under-19 Afro-Asia Cup – he came good with back-to-back fifties in the opening matches of the tour of the West Indies early in 2006, showing a penchant for the upright off-drive. Chibhabha comes from the townships, and was well coached under Zimbabwe Cricket's development programme. He has a sound technique, with the discipline to play straight. In the Caribbean he suffered from a back problem that affected his nagging medium-pace bowling, so he was forced to concentrate on his batting, and showed character and promise in the crucial No. 3 position. He was particularly impressive against the West Indian quick bowlers, but now needs to gain experience and work on building big innings. He is a superb fielder, usually in the covers.

THE FACTS Chibhabha scored 55 in his second ODI, against West Indies at St John's in April 2006, and added 67 and 40 in his next two matches before being sidelined by injury … His highest first-class score (66 for Mashonaland) is one lower than his best in ODIs, although he also made 83 not out in a one-dayer against Bangladesh A at Bulawayo … Chibhabha's sister Julia is one of Zimbabwe's leading cricket scorers …

THE FIGURES

Batting and fielding

	M	Inns	NO	Runs	HS	Avge	S/R	100	50	4s	6s	Ct	St
Tests to 11.9.06	0	–	–	–	–	–		–	–	–	–	–	–
ODIs to 11.9.06	9	9	0	265	67	29.44	56.50	0	2	26	1	6	0
First-class to 11.9.06	17	31	0	594	66	19.16	–	0	3	–	–	8	0

Bowling

	M	Balls	Runs	Wkts	BB	Avge	RpO	S/R	5i	10m
Tests to 11.9.06	0	–	–	–	–	–	–	–	–	–
ODIs to 11.9.06	9	126	134	3	2–39	44.66	6.38	42.00	0	0
First-class to 11.9.06	17	1837	1104	42	5–96	26.28	3.60	43.73	1	0

ELTON CHIGUMBURA

Full name	**Elton Chigumbura**
Born	**March 14, 1986, Kwekwe**
Teams	**Manicaland**
Style	**Right-hand bat, right-arm medium-pace bowler**
Test debut	**Zimbabwe v Sri Lanka at Harare 2003-04**
ODI debut	**Zimbabwe v Sri Lanka at Bulawayo 2003-04**

THE PROFILE Elton Chigumbura, who was fast-tracked into the Zimbabwe national side not long after his 18th birthday after several leading players fell out with the board early in 2004, made his first-class debut for Mashonaland in the Logan Cup when only 15. In Zimbabwean domestic cricket he is a genuine allrounder, an aggressive batsman at No. 4 or 5 and a seamer who comes on as first or second change. He took to the game at Chipembere Primary School in the Highfield township of Harare. A protégé of coach Stephen Mangongo, he won a Zimbabwe Cricket Union scholarship to Churchill High School, and plays for the Takashinga club. He played in two Under-19 World Cups, and took four wickets as Zimbabwe sensationally toppled Australia in the second one, in Bangladesh in February 2004. He looked out of his depth when given a Test cap a month later, but appeared much improved by the time of the Champions Trophy in England the following September. He was forced to sit out much of 2005 after sustaining a stress fracture of the back. When fit, Chigumbura is Zimbabwe's fastest bowler, clocking in above 140kph (87mph). In the West Indies early in 2006 he played only as a batsman, and his only success was an innings of 60 off 59 balls in the fourth one-dayer, but coach Kevin Curran noted his increasing maturity and greater self-discipline. He particularly enjoys the lofted drive, and is a good, athletic outfielder.

THE FACTS Chigumbura took 4 for 17 (and Tinashe Panyangara 6 for 31) when Zimbabwe bundled Australia out for 73 in the Under-19 World Cup at Bogra in 2004 ... His highest score in first-class cricket is 130 not out, for Zimbabwe A against Bangladesh A, also at Bogra early in 2004 ... Chigumbura's strike rate in ODIs is a healthy 83.47 runs per 100 balls ... Against West Indies at Port-of-Spain in May 2006 he took four catches, all near the long-on boundary ...

THE FIGURES
Batting and fielding

	M	Inns	NO	Runs	HS	Avge	S/R	100	50	4s	6s	Ct	St
Tests to 11.9.06	6	12	0	187	71	15.58	40.12	0	1	28	3	2	0
ODIs to 11.9.06	38	34	3	677	77	21.83	83.47	0	5	63	17	14	0
First-class to 11.9.06	31	55	3	1568	130*	30.15	–	1	13	–	–	12	0

Bowling

	M	Balls	Runs	Wkts	BB	Avge	RpO	S/R	5i	10m
Tests to 11.9.06	6	829	498	9	5–54	55.33	3.60	92.11	1	0
ODIs to 11.9.06	38	459	551	10	3–37	55.10	7.20	45.90	0	0
First-class to 11.9.06	31	3065	1887	45	5–54	41.93	3.69	68.11	1	0

STUART CLARK

AUSTRALIA

Full name	**Stuart Rupert Clark**
Born	**September 28, 1975, Sutherland, Sydney, NSW**
Teams	**New South Wales**
Style	**Right-hand bat, right-arm fast-medium bowler**
Test debut	**Australia v South Africa at Cape Town 2005-06**
ODI debut	**Australia v World XI at Melbourne 2005-06**

THE PROFILE Stuart Clark is a tall and lanky opening bowler often described as "in the Glenn McGrath mould". Appropriately, in his opening Test series in South Africa early in 2006, 30-year-old Clark replaced McGrath, who was caring for his sick wife, and experienced a dream entry: 20 wickets at 15.75 made him Player of the Series. A borderline selection for the first Test, he earned victory with 5 for 55 and 4 for 34, the third-best match figures by an Australian debutant after Bob Massie and Clarrie Grimmett. A former real-estate agent in Sydney who crams in study for a commerce and law degree, Clark was a late cricket developer, finally emerging at 27 after a battle with body as much as talent. Not to be confused with NSW team-mate Michael Clarke, or Michael Clark, the Western Australian left-armer, this Clark earned a central contract with 45 wickets in 2001-02, but lost it the following summer after ankle and rib injuries. Hernia surgery was next, quickly followed by a leg problem, but he took 40 wickets in NSW's 2004-05 Pura Cup triumph. Clark, who troubles batsmen with his height (197cm) and seam movement, made his one-day debut in 2005-06, and was a sound limited-overs performer in his first summer. The child of Indian-born parents who met in England, he wants to be the chief executive of New South Wales Cricket when he grows up. After his dramatic entry into Test cricket's playground, that may not be for some time.

THE FACTS During the memorable 2005 Ashes tour, Clark was twice called into the Australian squad from county cricket with Middlesex as cover for injured bowlers, but did not play in a Test ... His nickname is "Sarfraz", after a vague resemblance – in appearance and run-up – to the former Pakistan fast bowler Sarfraz Nawaz ... Clark's international debut was against the World XI in Melbourne in October 2005, and his first wicket was Kevin Pietersen ...

THE FIGURES

Batting and fielding

	M	Inns	NO	Runs	HS	Avge	S/R	100	50	4s	6s	Ct	St
Tests *to 11.9.06*	4	5	2	31	13*	10.33	46.20	0	0	4	0	2	0
ODIs *to 11.9.06*	15	3	2	33	16*	33.00	100.00	0	0	3	1	4	0
First-class *to 11.9.06*	65	86	26	774	35	12.90	–	0	0	–	–	19	0

Bowling

	M	Balls	Runs	Wkts	BB	Avge	RpO	S/R	5i	10m
Tests *to 11.9.06*	4	882	394	21	5–55	18.76	2.68	42.00	1	0
ODIs *to 11.9.06*	15	804	688	23	4–55	29.91	5.13	34.95	0	0
First-class *to 11.9.06*	65	13389	6577	223	6–84	29.49	2.49	60.04	9	0

MICHAEL CLARKE

Full name **Michael John Clarke**
Born **April 2, 1981, Liverpool, New South Wales**
Teams **New South Wales**
Style **Right-hand bat, slow left-arm orthodox spinner**
Test debut **Australia v India at Bangalore 2003-04**
ODI debut **Australia v England at Adelaide 2002-03**

THE PROFILE Michael Clarke was being touted as Australia's next captain before he'd even played a Test. And when he marked his eventual debut with 151 against India in October 2004, his future looked even brighter than the yellow motorbike he received as Man of the Match. Another thrilling century followed on his home debut, and his first Test season ended with the Allan Border Medal. Then came the fall. Barely a year later came the fateful phone-call: dropped after 15 century-less Tests. He was told to tighten his technique, especially early on against swing. Clarke remained a one-day fixture, but had to wait until the low-key Bangladesh series early in 2006 to reclaim that Test place. Until his sacking he was a ravishing shot-maker who did not so much take guard as take off: he radiated a pointy-elbowed elegance reminiscent of the young Greg Chappell or Mark Waugh – who both also waited uncomplainingly for a Test opening then started with a ton. Unlike them, Clarke cut his teeth in Australia's one-day side. His impact in pyjamas was startling: 208 runs before being dismissed. His bouncy fielding and searing run-outs, usually from square on, add to his value, while his left-arm tweakers can surprise (they shocked six Indians in a Test at Mumbai). A cricket nut since he was in nappies, "Pup" honed his technique against the bowling machine at his dad's indoor centre. A future star transformed into a genuine one ... but one now working on regaining that golden-boy status.

THE FACTS Clarke scored a century on his Test debut, 151 against India at Bangalore in 2004-05, and the following month added another in his first home Test, 141 against New Zealand at Brisbane: only two other batsmen have done this for Australia – Harry Graham and Kepler Wessels ... Clarke played county cricket for Hampshire, under the captaincy of Shane Warne ... He averages 57.14 in Tests in India, almost double his average at home (29.90) ... A skin-cancer scare late in 2005 persuaded Clarke to swap a traditional cap for a wide-brimmed sunhat ...

THE FIGURES
Batting and fielding

	M	Inns	NO	Runs	HS	Avge	S/R	100	50	4s	6s	Ct	St
Tests to 11.9.06	22	34	2	1123	151	36.22	54.51	2	4	141	11	18	0
ODIs to 11.9.06	82	73	19	2393	105*	44.31	84.34	2	17	215	14	33	0
First-class to 11.9.06	75	128	10	4722	201*	40.01	–	15	17	–	–	72	0

Bowling

	M	Balls	Runs	Wkts	BB	Avge	RpO	S/R	5i	10m
Tests to 11.9.06	22	158	75	8	6–9	9.37	2.84	19.75	1	0
ODIs to 11.9.06	82	1022	910	25	5–35	36.39	5.34	40.88	1	0
First-class to 11.9.06	75	1107	631	15	6–9	42.06	3.42	73.79	1	0

RIKKI CLARKE

ENGLAND

Full name	**Rikki Clarke**
Born	**September 29, 1981, Orsett, Essex**
Teams	**Surrey**
Style	**Right-hand bat, right-arm fast-medium bowler**
Test debut	**England v Bangladesh at Dhaka 2003-04**
ODI debut	**England v Bangladesh at Chittagong 2003-04**

THE PROFILE Tall and well-balanced, Rikki Clarke is strong off the front foot, with a classy straight-drive. With the ball, it's like watching a video of Martin Bicknell, even down to the floppy hair. But the jury is still out about his international credentials, after a rapid rise came screeching to a halt in 2004. After winning a 2nd XI Championship medal with Surrey in 2001, he picked up a Division One winners' gong the following year, and within 12 months had been fast-tracked into the Test team, when Andrew Flintoff withdrew from the Bangladesh tour with a groin injury. Born in Essex but brought up in commuter-belt Surrey, Clarke cracked a century on debut against Cambridge, and shortly afterwards added a majestic unbeaten 153 against Somerset. He won the Cricket Writers' Club's prestigious Young Cricketer of the Year award in 2002, and was called up for the Champions Trophy in Sri Lanka. However, after disappointing tours of Bangladesh, Sri Lanka and the West Indies, he failed to impress in the one-day internationals in England in 2004, and was unceremoniously dumped, amid whispers that he had had too much too soon. That was it until 2006, when he exhibited increased maturity after being named as Surrey's vice-captain. He improved his career-highest score twice, secondly with a fine 214 against Somerset, and steamed past 1,000 runs for the first time. And, as the nation fretted about Flintoff's fitness, Clarke began to be mentioned again as a plausible stand-in.

THE FACTS Clarke was the 14th player to take a wicket (Imran Nazir of Pakistan) with his first ball in an ODI, at Manchester in 2003: the only other England bowler to do it was Geoff Arnold, also of Surrey, in 1972 ... Clarke made 107 not out on his first-class debut, for Surrey against Cambridge UCCE at Fenner's in 2002: he added 153 not out in his fifth match, against Somerset at Taunton ... He went 12 ODIs without making more than 11, before top-scoring with 39 against Pakistan at Lord's in September 2006: in his last Test to date he made 55, against Bangladesh at Chittagong in October 2003 ...

THE FIGURES

Batting and fielding

	M	Inns	NO	Runs	HS	Avge	S/R	100	50	4s	6s	Ct	St
Tests to 11.9.06	2	3	0	96	55	32.00	37.94	0	1	8	1	1	0
ODIs to 11.9.06	20	13	0	144	39	11.07	62.06	0	0	12	1	11	0
First-class to 11.9.06	66	108	12	3900	214	40.62	–	10	15	–	–	77	0

Bowling

	M	Balls	Runs	Wkts	BB	Avge	RpO	S/R	5i	10m
Tests to 11.9.06	2	174	60	4	2–7	15.00	2.06	43.50	0	0
ODIs to 11.9.06	20	469	415	11	2–28	37.72	5.30	42.63	0	0
First-class to 11.9.06	66	5687	3952	95	4–21	41.60	4.16	59.86	0	0

PAUL COLLINGWOOD

Full name **Paul David Collingwood**
Born **May 26, 1976, Shotley Bridge, Co. Durham**
Teams **Durham**
Style **Right-hand bat, right-arm medium-pace bowler**
Test debut **England v Sri Lanka at Galle 2003-04**
ODI debut **England v Pakistan at Birmingham 2001**

THE PROFILE While Paul Collingwood was flitting around the fringes of the England team, it seemed that he was perhaps the first specialist fielder to earn regular selection in a Test squad. He made the one-day side in 2001, but four years and numerous tours later had won only three Test caps. The third of those, however, was the single biggest match of his generation: the decider against Australia at The Oval in 2005, where his responsible batting helped secure the draw and the Ashes. He still seemed destined to be the uncomplaining stand-in – but that winter he struck 96 and 80 at Lahore, and added a brilliant century against India, as England struggled with injuries. Then at home in 2006 he cracked a coruscating 186 against Pakistan at Lord's, to make a middle-order place his own at last. He had already become probably the finest fielder around, capable of breathtaking moments at backward point or in the slips. With the bat he stands still, plays straight, and has all the shots. In Australia in 2002-03 he started the one-dayers as 12th man, but was soon spanking a memorable maiden century against Sri Lanka at Perth – a round 100 that cemented his spot for the 2003 World Cup. His bowling, which verges towards the dibbly-dobbly, is negligible in Tests, but given the right conditions he can be irresistible in one-dayers – as at Trent Bridge in 2005, when he followed a rapid century against Bangladesh with 6 for 31, England's best one-day figures.

THE FACTS Collingwood's century and six wickets in the same match – against Bangladesh at Nottingham in 2005 – is unmatched in ODI history: his 6 for 31 that day are also England's best one-day bowling figures ... He has made his highest score of 190 twice – for Durham against the Sri Lankans at Chester-le-Street in 2002, and against Derbyshire at Derby in 2005 ... In a bid to improve his game Collingwood played club cricket in Melbourne in 2000-01, and won the award as the leading grade cricketer of the season ... In September 2006 he became the 11th man to play 100 ODIs for England ...

THE FIGURES

Batting and fielding

	M	Inns	NO	Runs	HS	Avge	S/R	100	50	4s	6s	Ct	St
Tests to 11.9.06	15	28	3	1027	186	41.08	41.24	2	3	112	9	20	0
ODIs to 11.9.06	100	89	20	2251	112*	32.62	74.09	2	12	168	24	54	0
First-class to 11.9.06	132	231	17	7446	190	34.79	–	16	35	–	–	138	0

Bowling

	M	Balls	Runs	Wkts	BB	Avge	RpO	S/R	5i	10m
Tests to 11.9.06	15	432	245	1	1–33	245.00	3.40	432.00	0	0
ODIs to 11.9.06	100	2271	1900	50	6–31	38.00	5.01	45.42	1	0
First-class to 11.9.06	132	7976	4021	100	5–52	40.21	3.02	79.76	1	0

WEST INDIES

PEDRO COLLINS

Full name	**Pedro Tyrone Collins**
Born	**August 12, 1976, Boscobelle, St Peter, Barbados**
Teams	**Barbados**
Style	**Right-hand bat, left-arm fast-medium bowler**
Test debut	**West Indies v Australia at Port-of-Spain 1998-99**
ODI debut	**West Indies v Pakistan at Sharjah 1999-2000**

THE PROFILE   A fast-medium left-armer, Pedro Collins has bowled alongside genuine pacemen like Curtly Ambrose, Courtney Walsh and Ian Bishop, but initially failed to display the kind of stamina required to sustain long spells. Collins was a keen footballer before he fell into cricket, and his bowling follows the lineage of Bernard Julien and Garry Sobers: like them he finds enough swing into the right-hander to cause the best of them difficulty. In November 1998 he took three wickets in 11 balls for West Indies A against India, which led to his Test debut against Australia the following March. For a long time after that, he was best remembered for an injury of the cruellest kind, when a Jason Gillespie delivery trapped a testicle outside his box. After getting his breath back he worked on his fitness, and returned to the side in 2001-02, with a higher arm action and an extra yard of pace. He took just nine wickets in West Indies' series victory over India, but that included Sachin Tendulkar three times. He struggled on India's flat pitches, though, before terrorising Bangladesh in 2002-03. Then, after struggling against the Aussies, Collins didn't play for close to a year. But he returned to take on England in March 2004 and immediately removed Michael Vaughan, before taking three more wickets to herald a successful comeback to the side. He is now a regular cog in a young West Indian pace attack which includes Fidel Edwards, his half-brother.

THE FACTS   Uniquely, Collins has three times taken a wicket with the first ball of a Test – and the victim each time was Bangladesh's Hannan Sarkar ... He averages 21.00 with the ball in Tests v New Zealand, but 102.33 v Pakistan ... Collins opened the bowling against England at Bridgetown in April 2004 (and several times subsequently) with his half-brother, Fidel Edwards ... In two home Tests against Australia in 2003 Collins took 1 for 263 – he recovered with 25 in five matches against England and Bangladesh the following year ...

THE FIGURES
Batting and fielding

	M	Inns	NO	Runs	HS	Avge	S/R	100	50	4s	6s	Ct	St
Tests to 11.9.06	32	47	7	235	24	5.87	33.52	0	0	30	0	7	0
ODIs to 11.9.06	30	12	5	30	10*	4.28	60.00	0	0	1	0	8	0
First-class to 11.9.06	93	116	28	557	25	6.32	–	0	0	–	–	25	0

Bowling

	M	Balls	Runs	Wkts	BB	Avge	RpO	S/R	5i	10m
Tests to 11.9.06	32	6964	3671	106	6-53	34.63	3.63	65.69	3	0
ODIs to 11.9.06	30	1577	1212	39	5-43	31.07	4.61	40.43	1	0
First-class to 11.9.06	93	16399	8332	307	6-53	27.14	3.04	53.41	6	0

COREY COLLYMORE

Full name	**Corey Dalanelo Collymore**
Born	**December 21, 1977, Boscobelle, St Peter, Barbados**
Teams	**Barbados**
Style	**Right-hand bat, right-arm fast-medium bowler**
Test debut	**West Indies v Australia at St John's 1998-99**
ODI debut	**West Indies v India at Toronto 1999-2000**

THE PROFILE Corey Collymore isn't genuinely fast, but he is accurate and aggressive at a shade above fast-medium. His sprint to the crease is reminiscent of Malcolm Marshall's, but there the similarities largely end: Collymore's open-chested delivery seems to limit his ability to move the ball away from right-handers. He has suffered from the bane of modern fast bowlers – stress fractures. But he is a determined man, who recovered from injuries when critics had written him off at the end of the 2000 England tour, and fulfilled his promise to get back into the game. He took four wickets on his return to the one-day side in Zimbabwe in 2001, as West Indies beat India in the final of the Coca-Cola Cup, and after a moderately successful 2003 World Cup he was recalled to the Test team for the home series against Sri Lanka. He responded with five wickets in the drawn first Test, and 7 for 57 in the second as West Indies sealed a seven-wicket victory. Despite that, Collymore remained a fringe member of the side, frequently left out then included mid-series to add experience. In England in 2004 he often opened the bowling, but although he put the ball in the right place his inability to put the wind up batsmen meant he was largely ineffective. But still he hung in there, taking another seven-wicket haul against Pakistan at Sabina Park in June 2005, and 15 wickets in the four matches against India the following year.

THE FACTS Collymore's 11 for 134 against Pakistan in June 2005 are the best match figures in any Test at Kingston, Jamaica – and his 7 for 57 against Sri Lanka at Sabina Park two years previously are West Indies' best figures in an innings there ... Collymore averages 11.35 with the ball in Tests against Sri Lanka – and 63.44 against England ... He has taken 48 wickets at 22.79 in home Tests, and 27 at 41.66 away ...

THE FIGURES

Batting and fielding

	M	Inns	NO	Runs	HS	Avge	S/R	100	50	4s	6s	Ct	St
Tests to 11.9.06	23	40	21	149	16*	7.84	30.97	0	0	15	0	5	0
ODIs to 11.9.06	69	26	12	73	13*	5.21	34.27	0	0	4	0	12	0
First-class to 11.9.06	72	105	49	428	20	7.64	–	0	0	–	–	24	0

Bowling

	M	Balls	Runs	Wkts	BB	Avge	RpO	S/R	5i	10m
Tests to 11.9.06	23	4735	2219	75	7-57	29.58	2.81	63.13	4	1
ODIs to 11.9.06	69	3310	2410	69	5-51	34.92	4.36	47.97	1	0
First-class to 11.9.06	72	12440	5886	230	7-57	25.59	2.83	54.08	9	1

ALASTAIR COOK

ENGLAND

Full name	**Alastair Nathan Cook**
Born	**December 25, 1984, Gloucester**
Teams	**Essex**
Style	**Left-hand bat, occasional offspinner**
Test debut	**England v India at Nagpur 2005-06**
ODI debut	**England v Sri Lanka at Manchester 2006**

THE PROFILE   Those in the know were saying that the tall, dark and handsome Alastair Cook was destined for great things very early on. A stylish left-hander with a simple approach to batting, Cook was thrown straight in at the deep end by Essex only a year after he left Bedford School, where he broke all sorts of records. He had captained England in the Under-19 World Cup in Bangladesh early in 2004, making two centuries in leading them to the semi-finals. He scored his maiden first-class hundred against Leicestershire in 2004, impressing his seasoned Essex team-mates Andy Flower and Darren Gough. Following a fine season in 2005, in which he scored a double-century for Essex against the touring Australians, he was called up by England after injuries struck the following spring. He had been touring the Caribbean with England A when the SOS came but, unfazed, he racked up 60 in his first Test innings, against India at Nagpur, then added a magnificent 104 to become the 16th England batsman to make a century on debut. He succumbed to illness himself before that tour was done, but bounced back with 89 against Sri Lanka at Lord's in May 2006, then made sure his name was on MCC's honours board by adding 105 against Pakistan two months later. He made another upright century in the next Test, at Manchester, causing ripples so wide that, in Australia, Glenn McGrath was moved to nominate a veteran of seven Tests as one of his prime targets for the 2006-07 Ashes series.

THE FACTS   Cook was the 16th England batsman to make a century on his Test debut: the previous two (Andrew Strauss and Graham Thorpe) were also left-handers ... Like his England team-mates Marcus Trescothick and Simon Jones, Cook was born on Christmas Day: his stand of 127 with Trescothick against Sri Lanka at Lord's in 2005 was the second-highest in Tests by unrelated players who share a birthday, behind the 163 of Vic Stollmeyer and Kenneth Weekes (both born January 24) for West Indies at The Oval in 1939 ... Cook won the Cricket Writers' Club's Young Cricketer of the Year award in 2005, and was the runner-up in 2006 too ...

THE FIGURES
Batting and fielding

	M	Inns	NO	Runs	HS	Avge	S/R	100	50	4s	6s	Ct	St
Tests to 11.9.06	9	16	2	761	127	54.35	44.73	3	3	91	0	7	0
ODIs to 11.9.06	2	2	0	80	41	40.00	86.95	0	0	12	0	0	0
First-class to 11.9.06	51	90	10	3717	195	46.46	54.72	10	21	–	–	55	0

Bowling

	M	Balls	Runs	Wkts	BB	Avge	RpO	S/R	5i	10m
Tests to 11.9.06	9	0	–	–	–	–	–	–	–	–
ODIs to 11.9.06	2	0	–	–	–	–	–	–	–	–
First-class to 11.9.06	51	138	107	3	3–13	35.66	4.65	46.00	0	0

AUSTRALIA

MARK COSGROVE

Full name	**Mark James Cosgrove**
Born	**June 14, 1984, Elizabeth, Adelaide, South Australia**
Teams	**South Australia, Glamorgan**
Style	**Left-hand bat, occasional right-arm medium-pacer**
Test debut	**No Tests yet**
ODI debut	**Australia v Bangladesh at Fatullah 2005-06**

THE PROFILE Mark Cosgrove is a big man with an even larger reputation. Darren Lehmann wants his left-handed protégé to play in the 2007 World Cup, and Cosgrove made a smooth transition to the international side after a bumpy rise that centred as much around his weight as his heavy hitting. He may be out of place in modern-day gym culture, but has shown that cricket can still cater for all shapes. Cosgrove even upstaged Lehmann during a brilliant 2005-06 season which started with a month-long suspension for returning unfit from club cricket in England. The ultimatum from South Australia was: lose five kilos or your state contract. Even those who tut whenever Cosgrove's red cheeks puff hard or he falls to ill-disciplined shots were stunned by the response: a one-day 109 against Queensland, then 184 against Victoria and 89 off Western Australia. Barely stopping for breath, he hammered 736 Pura Cup runs at 66.90, and 591 at 73.87 in one-dayers. He made an impressive ODI debut against Bangladesh in April 2006, moving his feet to the spinners and driving strongly. He's better known for his punishment of anything outside off stump from the fast men, particularly off the front foot. Not that his back-foot play is shabby – he once lofted Andy Bichel into the stands at Adelaide with an unbelievable square drive. For a while the only threat appeared to be the scales. After his superb displays since his suspension, Cosgrove's headline-attracting waistline can now be ignored ... maybe even celebrated.

THE FACTS Cosgrove scored 74 in his first one-day international, against Bangladesh at Fatullah in April 2006: only Phil Jaques (94) and Kepler Wessels (79) have made higher scores on ODI debut for Australia ... He played for Australia Under-19, and the Academy ... Cosgrove's nickname is "Baby Boof", after another chunky South Australian left-hander, Darren "Boof" Lehmann ... He played for Glamorgan in 2006, and made 233 for them against Derbyshire at Derby ...

THE FIGURES
Batting and fielding

	M	Inns	NO	Runs	HS	Avge	S/R	100	50	4s	6s	Ct	St
Tests to 11.9.06	0	–	–	–	–	–	–	–	–	–	–	–	–
ODIs to 11.9.06	1	1	0	74	74	74.00	107.24	0	1	7	2	0	0
First-class to 11.9.06	36	66	4	2624	233	42.32	65.55	6	17	–	–	29	0

Bowling

	M	Balls	Runs	Wkts	BB	Avge	RpO	S/R	5i	10m
Tests to 11.9.06	0	–	–	–	–	–	–	–	–	–
ODIs to 11.9.06	1	24	12	0	–	–	3.00	–	0	0
First-class to 11.9.06	36	972	579	13	1-0	44.53	3.57	74.76	0	0

DAN CULLEN

AUSTRALIA

Full name	**Daniel James Cullen**
Born	**April 10, 1984, Woodville, Adelaide, South Australia**
Teams	**South Australia, Somerset**
Style	**Right-hand bat, offspinner**
Test debut	**Australia v Bangladesh at Chittagong 2005-06**
ODI debut	**Australia v Bangladesh at Chittagong 2005-06**

THE PROFILE South Australia's impressive list of slow bowlers has a new addition: after Clarrie Grimmett, Ashley Mallett, Terry Jenner and Tim May, meet offspinner Dan Cullen. An exciting dyed-blond deceiver, Cullen is tipped eventually to replace Shane Warne as Australia's top spinner, and has developed similar characteristics to the hero he chased for an autograph as a ten-year-old. A crafty heavy-turner who can send down the occasional mysterious doosra, Cullen has shown that he is unafraid to upset batsmen with flight, dip, spin ... or verbal banter. At 20 in 2004-05, he burst into the Pura Cup with 43 wickets at 30.37, and while his second summer was harder – there was a broken finger to go with 27 victims at 47.88 – he was named the Bradman Young Cricketer of the Year. "He has all the toys, he is young and he has got a bit of fire about him," said Warne. "He will definitely play for Australia." That prediction was fulfilled in Bangladesh early in 2006, when – after being given the baggy green by his hero Warne – Cullen formed part of a three-pronged spin attack for the second Test, taking one wicket in his 14 overs. He stayed on for the one-day series, and was economical, securing a central contract ahead of the Victoria legspinner Cameron White. A student of Jenner, who has Warne as his most famous client, Cullen had more chances to run into his hero in England in 2006, where he was playing for Somerset.

THE FACTS When Cullen made his Test debut at Chittagong in April 2006 alongside Shane Warne and Stuart MacGill, it was the first time since January 1999 that Australia had fielded three specialist spinners in the same side (Warne, MacGill and Colin Miller against England at Sydney) ... Cullen has played one Test and three one-day internationals, and still hasn't batted ...

THE FIGURES

Batting and fielding

	M	Inns	NO	Runs	HS	Avge	S/R	100	50	4s	6s	Ct	St
Tests to 11.9.06	1	0	–	–	–	–	–	–	–	–	–	0	0
ODIs to 11.9.06	3	0	–	–	–	–	–	–	–	–	–	2	0
First-class to 11.9.06	26	34	14	334	42	16.70	–	0	0	–	–	7	0

Bowling

	M	Balls	Runs	Wkts	BB	Avge	RpO	S/R	5i	10m
Tests to 11.9.06	1	84	54	1	1–25	54.00	3.85	84.00	0	0
ODIs to 11.9.06	33	165	98	2	2–25	49.00	3.56	82.50	0	0
First-class to 11.9.06	26	6284	3347	83	5–38	40.32	3.19	75.71	4	0

KEITH DABENGWA

Full name **Keith Mbusi Dabengwa**
Born **August 17, 1980, Bulawayo**
Teams **Matabeleland**
Style **Left-hand bat, slow left-arm orthodox spinner**
Test debut **Zimbabwe v New Zealand at Bulawayo 2005-06**
ODI debut **Zimbabwe v India at Harare 2005-06**

THE PROFILE An allrounder from Matabeleland, Keith Dabengwa is a left-hand batsman who also bowls orthodox left-arm spin. Small and slight in build, he is also an athletic fielder. He learned his cricket at Baines Junior and Milton High School in Bulawayo, and good league performances earned him a place at the CFX Academy in 2001. He's cheerful and unassuming, but nevertheless works very hard at his game, as was shown by his award as the Student of the Year during his time at the Academy. Since then he has represented Matabeleland regularly, without creating headlines until he clattered a remarkable 161 against Midlands at Kwekwe in a Logan Cup match in April 2005 – he came in with his side drowning at 83 for 6, and hit 21 fours as they recovered to post 360. His developing allround talents earned him a place in the national squad in 2005-06, but although he made his Test debut against New Zealand he struggled to make an impression in a floundering side. He was originally a bowler who could bat, but his flighted spinners have rarely earned him much success. As a batsman he is steady, but can indulge in some powerful leg-side hitting when in the mood. It's possible that a lack of confidence is responsible for his failure to fulfil his undoubted allround potential so far.

THE FACTS Dabengwa's first two ODI appearances came as a supersub: in the second one he took 2 for 17, a catch and a run-out against Kenya ... His best first-class score of 161 is well over double his next-highest, 72 against Manicaland in April 2005... At 25, Dabengwa was the oldest member of Zimbabwe's team for the one-day series in the West Indies early in 2006 ... He played club cricket in England for Hampshire club Lymington in 2006 ...

THE FIGURES
Batting and fielding

	M	Inns	NO	Runs	HS	Avge	S/R	100	50	4s	6s	Ct	St
Tests to 11.9.06	3	6	0	90	35	15.00	64.28	0	0	14	2	1	0
ODIs to 11.9.06	6	4	1	33	21*	11.00	49.25	0	0	2	0	3	0
First-class to 11.9.06	31	55	4	1017	161	19.94	–	1	4	–	–	32	0

Bowling

	M	Balls	Runs	Wkts	BB	Avge	RpO	S/R	5i	10m
Tests to 11.9.06	3	432	249	5	3–127	49.80	3.41	87.60	0	0
ODIs to 11.9.06	6	203	171	3	2–17	57.00	5.05	67.66	0	0
First-class to 11.9.06	31	3726	2323	41	5–76	56.65	3.74	90.87	2	0

JAMIE DALRYMPLE

Full name	**James William Murray Dalrymple**
Born	**January 21, 1981, Nairobi, Kenya**
Teams	**Middlesex**
Style	**Right-hand bat, offspinner**
Test debut	**No Tests yet**
ODI debut	**England v Ireland at Belfast 2006**

THE PROFILE   Kenyan-born Jamie Dalrymple is a genuine allrounder – an offspinner in the mould of his Middlesex predecessor (and now county coach) John Emburey, although he varies his pace a little more, and a capable batsman who knows his limitations and sticks to them. He made an impression at Oxford, with a double-century in the 2003 Varsity Match – he took five first-innings wickets for good measure – and followed that with 105 not out (out of 161 for 1) in the one-day game between the two sides a week later. His Middlesex opportunities were limited at first, but in May 2004 he cracked 244 against Surrey, followed eight days later by a matchwinning hundred in the C&G Trophy against Glamorgan at Lord's. In 2006, as England cast around in the absence of several established stars, he was called up for the mid-season one-day internationals. He made his debut against Ireland, alongside his Middlesex team-mate Ed Joyce, and after that gentle start was one of England's few successes in the 5–0 thrashing by Sri Lanka, never failing to reach 30 in his five innings, with 67 at Lord's his best effort. Duncan Fletcher, always a fan of multi-faceted players, ensured that he was drafted into the squad for the second Test against Pakistan in July 2006, and it was a close-run choice between him and Monty Panesar – but Panesar edged the final vote, and took eight wickets to confine Dalrymple to the one-day arena (and Middlesex) for the time being.

THE FACTS   Dalrymple was only the sixth batsman to make a double-century in the Varsity Match, with 236 not out for Oxford against Cambridge in 2003: only the Nawab of Pataudi senior (238*) had made a higher score in the match at that time ... He reached double figures in his first nine ODI innings, before a duck against Pakistan at Edgbaston in September 2006 ... Dalrymple's 244 at The Oval in May 2004 is the highest score for Middlesex against Surrey, beating Denis Compton's 235 in 1946 ... His Oxford University team-mates in 2002 included his brother, Simon ...

THE FIGURES

Batting and fielding

	M	Inns	NO	Runs	HS	Avge	S/R	100	50	4s	6s	Ct	St
Tests to 11.9.06	0	–	–	–	–	–	–	–	–	–	–	–	–
ODIs to 11.9.06	11	10	0	321	67	32.10	79.85	0	2	23	2	5	0
First-class to 11.9.06	63	105	10	3422	244	36.02	–	5	18	–	–	35	0

Bowling

	M	Balls	Runs	Wkts	BB	Avge	RpO	S/R	5i	10m
Tests to 11.9.06	0	–	–	–	–	–	–	–	–	–
ODIs to 11.9.06	11	474	351	9	2–13	39.00	4.44	52.66	0	0
First-class to 11.9.06	63	8457	4681	108	5–49	43.34	3.32	78.30	1	0

DANISH KANERIA

Full name	**Danish Parabha Shanker Kaneria**
Born	**December 16, 1980, Karachi, Sind**
Teams	**Karachi, Habib Bank, Essex**
Style	**Right-hand bat, legspinner**
Test debut	**Pakistan v England at Faisalabad 2000-01**
ODI debut	**Pakistan v Zimbabwe at Sharjah 2001-02**

THE PROFILE A tall, wiry legspinner, and only the second Hindu to play Test cricket for Pakistan, Danish Kaneria mastered the dark arts of wrist-spin at an early age. His stock ball drifts in to the right-hander, and he has a googly as cloaked as any in recent history. His whirling approach is reminiscent of Abdul Qadir's, and he has now picked up the baton from Mushtaq Ahmed as Pakistan's premier legspinner. Kaneria was hyped as a secret weapon when England toured Pakistan in 2000-01, and although his impact in that Test series was minimal, he has since made his mark. Initially he did so against the lesser lights of Bangladesh, but then turned it on against South Africa too, at Lahore in October 2003, when his five-for decided the match. Since then, Kaneria has confirmed himself as a matchwinner, inspiring Pakistan to victories over Sri Lanka at Karachi in 2004 and against West Indies in Jamaica in 2005. In between, two tours – to Australia and the graveyard of legspin, India – were arduous but satisfying stepping stones to the big league. In each series he outscalped the opposition's leading legspinner – first Shane Warne, then Anil Kumble – and although Pakistan still lost to Australia, Kaneria's 19 wickets were crucial in securing a morale-boosting draw in India. He ended 2005 with two more matchwinning last-day turns against England at home, but proved expensive when the teams reconvened the following summer in England, where he had previously had a lot of success with Essex.

THE FACTS Danish Kaneria was only the second Hindu to play Test cricket for Pakistan – the first, 1980s wicketkeeper Anil Dalpat, is his cousin ... He took 12 for 92 in his third Test, against Bangladesh at Multan in August 2001 ... Kaneria averages 16.41 against Bangladesh – and 42.31 against Australia ... He has conceded more than 100 runs in an innings 26 times in 40 Tests ... He had figures of 0 for 208 from 70 overs in one innings for Essex v Lancashire at Manchester in 2005, equalling the most expensive wicketless spell in the County Championship, set by Peter Smith, another Essex legspinner, in 1934 ...

THE FIGURES

Batting and fielding

	M	Inns	NO	Runs	HS	Avge	S/R	100	50	4s	6s	Ct	St
Tests *to 11.9.06*	40	54	27	175	29	6.48	43.53	0	0	23	1	11	0
ODIs *to 11.9.06*	16	8	6	6	3*	3.00	33.33	0	0	0	0	2	0
First-class *to 11.9.06*	99	120	61	511	47	8.68	–	0	0	–	–	32	0

Bowling

	M	Balls	Runs	Wkts	BB	Avge	RpO	S/R	5i	10m
Tests *to 11.9.06*	40	11035	5565	1698	7–77	32.92	3.02	65.29	11	2
ODIs *to 11.9.06*	16	776	590	12	3–31	49.16	4.56	64.66	0	0
First-class *to 11.9.06*	99	26377	12586	468	7–39	26.89	2.86	56.36	33	5

SOUTH AFRICA

AB de VILLIERS

Full name	**Abraham Benjamin de Villiers**
Born	**February 17, 1984, Pretoria**
Teams	**Titans**
Style	**Right-hand bat, occ. medium-pacer, wicketkeeper**
Test debut	**South Africa v England at Port Elizabeth 2004-05**
ODI debut	**South Africa v England at Bloemfontein 2004-05**

THE PROFILE Few Test newcomers can have been asked to play so many roles so quickly as AB de Villiers, and fewer still can have risen to the challenge with such alacrity that, at just 21, he was already being regarded as the future of South African cricket. de Villiers is a natural sportsman: tennis, golf, cricket or rugby could have been his calling. Cricket won out, however, and after starring in the national Under-19 team he made his debut for Titans in 2003-04, racking up five half-centuries in his 438 runs. He won his first Test cap the following season against England, and after a composed debut as an opener, he was handed the wicketkeeping gloves for the second Test at Durban, which he helped save with a maiden half-century down at No. 7. By the end of the series, however, he was going in first again, and after falling eight short of a deserved century in the first innings at Centurion, he made instant amends second time around. His development continued apace in the Caribbean, where he helped seal the series with a wonderful 178 at Bridgetown. Then came the almost inevitable dip in fortunes. In Australia in 2005-06 de Villiers managed just 152 runs at 25.33 – despite playing Shane Warne well – and missed the one-day VB Series. And in the re-match in South Africa, de Villiers managed only one good Test, hitting 50 and 46 at Durban, but added 97 at Centurion when New Zealand toured later in 2006.

THE FACTS AB de Villiers averages 74.40 in three Tests at Centurion – but only 7.50 from three at Johannesburg ... He scored 151, his maiden first-class century, for Titans v Western Province Boland at Benoni in October 2004, sharing a stand of 317 with Martin van Jaarsveld (236) ... de Villiers has never bowled in first-class cricket outside Tests: his two wickets (Daren Powell and Tino Best) came as West Indies piled up 747 in Antigua in 2005 ... His record includes two ODIs for the Africa XI ...

THE FIGURES

Batting and fielding

	M	Inns	NO	Runs	HS	Avge	S/R	100	50	4s	6s	Ct	St
Tests *to 11.9.06*	22	40	1	1607	178	41.20	53.94	3	10	218	4	29	1
ODIs *to 11.9.06*	19	19	0	402	68	21.15	74.30	0	1	50	8	7	0
First-class *to 11.9.06*	41	76	4	3115	178	43.26	59.22	5	22	–	–	71	2

Bowling

	M	Balls	Runs	Wkts	BB	Avge	RpO	S/R	5i	10m
Tests *to 11.9.06*	22	198	99	2	2–49	49.50	3.00	99.00	0	0
ODIs *to 11.9.06*	19	0	–	–	–	–	–	–	–	–
First-class *to 11.9.06*	41	198	99	2	2–49	49.50	3.00	99.00	0	0

MAHENDRA SINGH DHONI

Full name **Mahendra Singh Dhoni**
Born **July 7, 1981, Ranchi, Bihar**
Teams **Jharkhand**
Style **Right-hand bat, wicketkeeper**
Test debut **India v Sri Lanka at Chennai 2005-06**
ODI debut **India v Bangladesh at Chittagong 2004-05**

THE PROFILE   The spectacular arrival of Virender Sehwag was bound to inspire others to bat with the same approach. But the odds of a clone emerging from the backwaters of Jharkhand (formerly Bihar), whose state side has consistently floundered, were highly remote. That was until Mahendra Singh Dhoni arrived. He can be swashbuckling with the bat, and secure with the wicketkeeping gloves. His long hair adds to his dash. He started in first-class cricket in 1999-2000, making 40 and 68 not out on debut, but it wasn't until 2004 that he became a serious contender for national selection, after some stirring performances when the occasion demanded – a rapid hundred as East Zone clinched the Deodhar Trophy, and an audacious 60 in the Duleep Trophy final. But it was his two centuries against Pakistan A, in a triangular tournament in Kenya, that established him as a clinical destroyer of bowling attacks. In just his fifth one-day international – against Pakistan at Visakhapatnam in April 2005 – Dhoni cracked a dazzling 148, putting even Sehwag in the shade, and followed that with a colossal 183 not out against Sri Lanka in November, when he broke Adam Gilchrist's record for the highest score by a wicketkeeper in ODIs. He made an instant impact at Test level, too, pounding 148 at Faisalabad in only his fifth match, when India were struggling to avoid the follow-on. His keeping has improved – he was impressive in the Caribbean in 2006 – and he has quickly established himself as a key member of a revitalised side.

THE FACTS   Dhoni's unbeaten 183 against Sri Lanka at Jaipur in November 2005 is the highest score in ODIs by a wicketkeeper, and included 120 in boundaries – 10 sixes and 15 fours – a record at the time but later beaten by Herschelle Gibbs ... Dhoni's strike rate of 100.96 runs per 100 balls in ODIs is bettered only by Shahid Afridi (108.16) among players who have scored more than 1000 runs ... The only other Indian to score a century in an ODI in which he kept wicket is Rahul Dravid ...

THE FIGURES

Batting and fielding

	M	Inns	NO	Runs	HS	Avge	S/R	100	50	4s	6s	Ct	St
Tests to 11.9.06	13	20	1	602	148	31.68	72.88	1	3	76	14	38	9
ODIs to 11.9.06	48	43	13	1467	183*	48.90	100.96	2	8	131	45	44	9
First-class to 11.9.06	47	76	4	2550	148	35.41	–		4	15	–	–	137	23

Bowling

	M	Balls	Runs	Wkts	BB	Avge	RpO	S/R	5i	10m
Tests to 11.9.06	13	6	13	0	–	–	13.00	–	0	0
ODIs to 11.9.06	48	0	–	–	–	–	–	–	–	–
First-class to 11.9.06	47	18	20	0	–	–	6.66	–	0	0

TILLAKARATNE DILSHAN

Full name	**Tillakaratne Mudiyanselage Dilshan**
Born	**October 14, 1976, Kalutara**
Teams	**Bloomfield**
Style	**Right-hand bat, offspinner**
Test debut	**Sri Lanka v Zimbabwe at Bulawayo 1999-2000**
ODI debut	**Sri Lanka v Zimbabwe at Bulawayo 1999-2000**

THE PROFILE Tillakaratne Mudiyanselage Dilshan, who started life as Tuwan Mohamad Dilshan before converting to Buddhism, is a light-footed right-hander who burst onto the international scene with an unbeaten 163 against a strong Zimbabwe side in only his second Test in November 1999. Technically sound, comfortable against fast bowling, possessed of quick feet, strong wrists and natural timing, Dilshan has talent in abundance. But the bright start to his career was followed by a frustrating 15 months when he was shovelled up and down the order, and in and out of the side. After a lean series against England in 2001 – 51 runs in four innings – he didn't play another Test until England came calling again at the end of 2003. He came back mentally stronger, and determined to play his own natural aggressive game. This approach was immediately successful, with a string of good scores against England and Australia, and then – rather more surprisingly for someone who started as a wicketkeeper – came some matchwinning bowling performances with his offspin, in the one-day series against South Africa in August 2004. He has continued to be a steady influence in the middle order, although his Test average is still below 40. However, he brings an added dimension to the team, especially in one-day cricket, with his brilliant fielding – he effected four run-outs in the first final of the VB Series at Adelaide in February 2006, which came close to earning him the Man of the Match award.

THE FACTS Dilshan's 20 first-class centuries include a score of 200 not out while captaining North Central Province against Central in Colombo in February 2005 ... His highest Test score of 168 came against Bangladesh in Colombo in September 2005: he put on 280 with Thilan Samaraweera, a Sri Lankan fifth-wicket record in Tests ... Dilshan made his first ODI century against the Netherlands at Amstelveen in July 2006 ... He started as a wicketkeeper and has 23 first-class stumpings to his name ...

THE FIGURES
Batting and fielding

	M	Inns	NO	Runs	HS	Avge	S/R	100	50	4s	6s	Ct	St
Tests *to 11.9.06*	39	63	7	2056	168	36.71	56.11	4	9	266	4	44	0
ODIs *to 11.9.06*	96	82	18	1869	117*	29.20	78.52	1	7	154	8	48	1
First-class *to 11.9.06*	160	259	18	8957	200*	37.16	–	20	39	–	–	292	23

Bowling

	M	Balls	Runs	Wkts	BB	Avge	RpO	S/R	5i	10m
Tests *to 11.9.06*	39	528	271	6	2–4	45.16	3.07	88.00	0	0
ODIs *to 11.9.06*	96	1762	1406	35	4–29	40.17	4.78	50.34	0	0
First-class *to 11.9.06*	160	2520	1204	40	5–49	30.10	2.86	63.00	1	0

BOETA DIPPENAAR

Full name	**Hendrik Human Dippenaar**
Born	**June 14, 1977, Kimberley, Cape Province**
Teams	**Eagles**
Style	**Right-hand bat, occasional offspinner**
Test debut	**South Africa v Zimbabwe at Bloemfontein 1999-2000**
ODI debut	**South Africa v India at Nairobi 1999-2000**

THE PROFILE A year after making his Test debut in 1999, Boeta Dippenaar scored his maiden century against New Zealand at Johannesburg, before unluckily losing his place at the top of the order to the recalled Herschelle Gibbs. He grabbed his chance of returning to the Test team, after South Africa's disastrous 2003 World Cup, with an unbeaten 178 against lowly Bangladesh. But he remains on the fringe of the Test side, playing only one of the six matches against Australia in 2005-06. Prolific first-class run-scorers occasionally have their weaknesses exposed by top-class opposition, and so it was with Dippenaar, who quickly found that his tendency to play across and around his back-foot defensive strokes was costly against better bowlers. He worked hard to rectify the problem. He is not a tall man, yet he bats like one, seemingly able to reach the pitch of every ball bowled on or outside off stump and drive it through the covers. Reach and sweetness of timing are the foundations of his game; his ability as a cover fielder is a bonus. He has had great success opening the batting in one-dayers, and cemented his place after a fantastic series against West Indies in May 2005, when he averaged more than 100 and stroked a superb 123 at Bridgetown. Dippenaar revels in the outdoor pursuits which kept him busy as a boy growing up in Free State, and touring is almost as much an opportunity to fish new waters as it is to play cricket.

THE FACTS Dippenaar's highest Test score is 177 not out, against Bangladesh at Chittagong in April 2003: he and Jacques Rudolph put on 429 for the third wicket, a South African Test record ... He averages 66 in Tests against West Indies, but only 18.50 against Australia ... Dippenaar made 133 in an Under-19 Test at Leeds in 1995, against an England side captained by Marcus Trescothick and a new-ball attack of Andrew Flintoff and Alex Tudor ... His record includes three ODIs for the Africa XI ...

THE FIGURES

Batting and fielding

	M	Inns	NO	Runs	HS	Avge	S/R	100	50	4s	6s	Ct	St
Tests to 11.9.06	37	60	5	1715	177*	31.18	41.77	3	7	237	5	27	0
ODIs to 11.9.06	99	87	13	3234	125*	43.70	67.91	4	24	314	16	33	0
First-class to 11.9.06	111	187	17	7048	200*	41.45	–	21	30	–	–	83	0

Bowling

	M	Balls	Runs	Wkts	BB	Avge	RpO	S/R	5i	10m
Tests to 11.9.06	37	12	1	0	–	–	0.50	–	0	0
ODIs to 11.9.06	99	0	–	–	–	–	–	–	–	–
First-class to 11.9.06	111	19	13	0	–	–	4.10	–	0	0

RAHUL DRAVID

Full name	**Rahul Sharad Dravid**
Born	**January 11, 1973, Indore, Madhya Pradesh**
Teams	**Karnataka**
Style	**Right-hand bat, occasional wicketkeeper**
Test debut	**India v England at Lord's 1996**
ODI debut	**India v Sri Lanka at Singapore 1995-96**

THE PROFILE Rahul Dravid, who seamlessly blends old-world classicism with new-age professionalism, is the best No. 3 batsman to play for India. He already averages around 60 from there, more than any other No. 3 bar Bradman. But impressive as his stats are, they don't show his importance, or the beauty of his batting. When he started, he was pigeonholed as a stonewaller: his early nickname was "The Wall". But as the years passed, Dravid – who brings humility and intelligence to his study of the game – grew in stature, finally reaching maturity under Sourav Ganguly's captaincy. As a New India emerged, so did a new Dravid: first, he transformed himself into an astute middle-order one-day finisher, then strung together a series of awe-inspiring performances in Tests. His golden phase really began with a supporting act, at Kolkata early in 2001, when his 180 helped VVS Laxman create history against Australia. But from then on, Dravid became India's most valuable player, saving Tests at Port Elizabeth, Georgetown and Nottingham, and winning them at Leeds, Adelaide, Kandy and Rawalpindi. At one point he hit four double-centuries in 15 Tests. As India finished off their 2004 Pakistan tour with a win, thanks to Dravid's epic 270, his average crept past Tendulkar's – and he has stayed ahead. In October 2005 he was appointed captain of the one-day side, began with a 6-1 hammering of Sri Lanka at home and, after establishing a good rapport with coach Greg Chappell, soon succeeded Ganguly as the Test skipper too.

THE FACTS Dravid hit centuries in four successive Test innings in 2002, three in England and one against West Indies ... He kept wicket in 73 ODIs ... Unusually, Dravid averages more in away Tests (65.05) than at home in India (51.52) ... He averages more than 50 in Tests against all opponents except Australia (48.48) and South Africa (39.47) ... Dravid played county cricket for Kent, and has also played for Scotland ... His record includes one Test and three ODIs for the World XI, and one ODI for the Asia XI ...

THE FIGURES

Batting and fielding

	M	Inns	NO	Runs	HS	Avge	S/R	100	50	4s	6s	Ct	St
Tests *to 11.9.06*	104	176	22	9049	270	58.75	42.24	23	46	1120	13	146	0
ODIs *to 11.9.06*	293	272	35	9537	153	40.24	70.57	12	71	830	29	174	14
First-class *to 11.9.06*	217	354	50	17572	270	57.80	–		48	90	–	–	261	1

Bowling

	M	Balls	Runs	Wkts	BB	Avge	RpO	S/R	5i	10m
Tests *to 11.9.06*	104	120	39	1	1–18	39.00	1.95	120.00	0	0
ODIs *to 11.9.06*	293	186	170	4	2–43	42.50	5.48	46.50	0	0
First-class *to 11.9.06*	217	617	273	5	2–16	54.40	2.65	123.40	0	0

TERRY DUFFIN

Full name **Terrence Duffin**
Born **March 20, 1982, Kwekwe**
Teams **Matabeleland**
Style **Left-hand bat, occasional right-arm medium-pacer**
Test debut **Zimbabwe v India at Bulawayo 2005-06**
ODI debut **Zimbabwe v Kenya at Bulawayo 2005-06**

THE PROFILE A solid left-hand opener, Terry Duffin is a Mashonaland Districts player who made his name at Plumtree High School. He played for Zimbabwe Under-19s in 1998 and 2000 (he was injured in 1999), and progressed to the Academy in 2001, and captained them on his first-class debut. He was posted to the Midlands, and played there for three seasons. In 2004-05 he moved to Matabeleland, seeking greater stimulation, and at last began to realise his potential. He was selected for the team which toured Bangladesh that season, although he didn't play an international, and but for injury would probably have made his debut against New Zealand in August 2005. When the dust settled after the bitter player dispute in 2005-06, Duffin was one of the last left standing, and after signing a new contract he was appointed to succeed Tatenda Taibu as captain. Kevin Curran, the coach, nominated him after noting that he was one of the more mature players and commanded respect from the others, and he has done a sound job, unafraid to use innovative field placings, or a spinner during a powerplay when appropriate. In the West Indies early in 2006 Duffin's limitations as a batsman were exposed: he was able to survive, but showed no sign of being able to score at anywhere near the rate required in ODIs – his responsible style is better suited to Tests – and he was replaced as captain by Prosper Utseya when Bangladesh toured later in 2006. Stocky in build, he has had to watch his weight.

THE FACTS Duffin captained Zimbabwe on his ODI debut, against Kenya in February 2006 aged 23, and scored 53: he skippered in his first 13 ODI appearances before being relieved of the job ... Duffin also made 56 on his Test debut, against India ... He also captained the CFX Academy on his first-class debut, against Mashonaland in 2000-01, and was out for 0 ... Duffin's one first-class century was an innings of 117 for Matabeleland against Manicaland at Mutare in April 2005 ...

THE FIGURES

Batting and fielding

	M	Inns	NO	Runs	HS	Avge	S/R	100	50	4s	6s	Ct	St
Tests *to 11.9.06*	2	4	0	80	56	20.00	44.69	0	1	12	0	1	0
ODIs *to 11.9.06*	16	16	0	360	60	22.50	55.13	0	2	40	0	4	0
First-class *to 11.9.06*	35	66	4	1792	117	28.90	–		1	13	–	–	28	0

Bowling

	M	Balls	Runs	Wkts	BB	Avge	RpO	S/R	5i	10m
Tests *to 11.9.06*	2	0	–	–	–	–	–	–	–	–
ODIs *to 11.9.06*	16	0	–	–	–	–	–	–	–	–
First-class *to 11.9.06*	35	36	19	0	–	–	3.16	–	0	0

FIDEL EDWARDS

Full name **Fidel Henderson Edwards**
Born **February 6, 1982, Gays, St Peter, Barbados**
Teams **Barbados**
Style **Right-hand bat, right-arm fast bowler**
Test debut **West Indies v Sri Lanka at Kingston 2002-03**
ODI debut **West Indies v Zimbabwe at Harare 2003-04**

THE PROFILE Fidel Edwards had an extraordinary start in international cricket, the kind that can either haunt or add lustre to a career. He was spotted in the nets by Brian Lara ("I just bowled about four balls at him," said Edwards, "but he was talking to me before that") and called up for his Test debut after just one match for Barbados: he promptly took five Test wickets against Sri Lanka at Kingston in June 2003. He added five in his first overseas Test, and six in his first one-day international. Edwards has a slingy round-arm action not unlike Jeff Thomson's – or Lasith Malinga's – which leaves him vulnerable to back strains. It doesn't often seem to result in him straying down leg, though, which seems likely when you first see him, and his unusual action has caught out several distinguished batsmen. He is more of a protégé of his neighbour Corey Collymore than of his half-brother Pedro Collins, a left-armer – who replaced him when another injury (a hamstring this time) forced him out of the last three Tests against India in mid-2006. Edwards bowls fast, can swing the ball and reverse it too, but insists that he doesn't go for out-and-out pace – which is just as well, because he is learning that pace without control leads straight to the boundary at international level. He showed his increased maturity with a testing spell in Antigua in June 2006 that had India's Virender Sehwag in all kinds of trouble before that hamstring twanged.

THE FACTS Edwards had played only one first-class match – taking one wicket – before his Test debut against Sri Lanka at Kingston in June 2003, when he took 5 for 36 ... He also took 6 for 22 on his ODI debut, against Zimbabwe at Harare in November 2003 ... Edwards opened the bowling against England at Bridgetown in April 2004 (and several times subsequently) with his half-brother, Pedro Collins ... Edwards averages 29.96 with the ball in home Tests, but 54.00 overseas ... Unoriginally, his nickname is "Castro" ...

THE FIGURES
Batting and fielding

	M	Inns	NO	Runs	HS	Avge	S/R	100	50	4s	6s	Ct	St
Tests to 11.9.06	24	39	11	119	20	4.25	22.41	0	0	14	1	4	0
ODIs to 11.9.06	19	6	4	12	4*	6.00	31.57	0	0	0	0	2	0
First-class to 11.9.06	38	58	20	166	20	4.36	–	0	0	–	–	7	0

Bowling

	M	Balls	Runs	Wkts	BB	Avge	RpO	S/R	5i	10m
Tests to 11.9.06	24	4045	2675	62	5–36	43.14	3.96	65.24	4	0
ODIs to 11.9.06	19	939	684	24	6–22	28.50	4.37	39.12	1	0
First-class to 11.9.06	38	5830	3934	109	5–22	36.09	4.04	53.48	6	1

ENAMUL HAQUE

Full name	**Enamul Haque**
Born	**December 5, 1986, Sylhet**
Teams	**Sylhet**
Style	**Right-hand bat, slow left-arm orthodox spinner**
Test debut	**Bangladesh v England at Dhaka 2003-04**
ODI debut	**Bangladesh v Zimbabwe at Chittagong 2004-05**

THE PROFILE When Dav Whatmore took over as Bangladesh's coach in 2003, one of his first tasks was to locate a spinner to partner the effective but ageing Mohammad Rafique. And he seems to have found one in Enamul Haque junior. He was born in the hill country of Sylhet, on the eastern border, and there was some confusion about his age when he was selected for the Board President's XI in the opening match of England's 2003-04 tour: he was supposedly 16, although most people had him pegged as two years older than that. But that was nothing compared to the confusion he caused England's batsmen. In a giddy spell on the second afternoon, England lost four wickets for no runs, including three to Enamul. It propelled him straight into the first Test the following week, where, in tandem with Rafique, he bowled with skill and impressive composure to embarrass England's batsmen again. Enamul gives the ball a big rip from a high, economical action, and looks set to be a fixture in the squad for some time. He took 6 for 45 – and the historic final wicket – to send the country wild with an inaugural Test victory over Zimbabwe in January 2005, then added 7 for 95 (and 12 in the match) in the drawn second Test. He was kept out of the firing line in England later that year, but bounced back to play a part as Bangladesh nearly embarrassed Australia in the first Test of their 2006 tour.

THE FACTS Enamul's 7 for 95 – and 12 for 200 in the match – against Zimbabwe at Dhaka in 2004-05, are both Bangladesh Test records ... He also took 7 for 47 in an A-team Test against Zimbabwe at Bulawayo in February 2005 ... The "junior" is added to Enamul's name to distinguish him from an earlier Bangladesh left-arm spinner of the same name (born February 27, 1966, Enamul Haque senior played 10 Tests and 29 ODIs) ...

THE FIGURES

Batting and fielding

	M	Inns	NO	Runs	HS	Avge	S/R	100	50	4s	6s	Ct	St
Tests *to 11.9.06*	10	18	11	28	9	4.00	19.17	0	0	2	0	2	0
ODIs *to 11.9.06*	3	2	1	4	4*	4.00	133.33	0	0	0	0	5	0
First-class *to 11.9.06*	39	61	29	293	32	9.15	–	0	0	–	–	15	0

Bowling

	M	Balls	Runs	Wkts	BB	Avge	RpO	S/R	5i	10m
Tests *to 11.9.06*	10	2385	1198	32	7–95	37.43	3.01	74.53	3	1
ODIs *to 11.9.06*	3	180	129	4	2–37	32.25	4.29	45.00	0	0
First-class *to 11.9.06*	39	9441	4437	153	7–47	29.00	2.81	61.70	11	3

FAISAL IQBAL

Full name	**Faisal Iqbal**
Born	**December 30, 1981, Karachi, Sind**
Teams	**Karachi, Pakistan International Airlines**
Style	**Right-hand bat, occasional right-arm medium-pacer**
Test debut	**Pakistan v New Zealand at Auckland 2000-01**
ODI debut	**Pakistan v Sri Lanka at Lahore 1999-2000**

THE PROFILE A gutsy strokeplayer with a sound defence and attitude to boot, Faisal Iqbal is an exciting middle-order prospect. He was a prolific junior performer, but his elevation to Pakistan's Test squad was criticised as nepotism – he's the nephew of the great Javed Miandad, the coach when Iqbal made his debut in New Zealand in 2000-01. But he demonstrated that he was worth his place with three pleasing knocks then, and a counter-attacking 83 off 85 balls against Australia in Colombo in October 2002. He was particularly impressive against Shane Warne, using his feet superbly to seize the momentum for Pakistan, and did it all with a swagger reminiscent of his uncle. However, he couldn't repeat his performance in the rest of that series, or in two Tests in South Africa shortly afterwards. He lost his place, but continued to score heavily in domestic cricket, and that finally paid off three years later when he was recalled to replace the injured Inzamam-ul-Haq against India at home in Karachi in January 2006. Failure in the first innings meant the pressure was on in the second, but it didn't seem to affect Iqbal, who made an attractive 139, his first Test hundred, with some assured back-foot play and composed defence, helping Pakistan to a comfortable series-clinching win. A battling 60 followed against Murali in Colombo, then he got stuck in against England at Lord's in July to ensure a draw. He is probably the front runner to cement a spot when Inzamam retires.

THE FACTS Faisal Iqbal's maiden Test century, 139 at Karachi in January 2006, helped Pakistan defeat India by a record margin of 341 runs, even though they were 0 for 3 after the first over of the match, and later 39 for 6 ... His highest score is 200, for Karachi Blues v Sargodha in Karachi in January 2001 ... Iqbal's best in ODIs is 100 not out, against Zimbabwe at Harare in November 2002: in 16 other matches his highest score is 32 ... His uncle Javed Miandad is Pakistan's leading scorer in Tests, with 8832 runs from 124 matches ...

THE FIGURES
Batting and fielding

	M	Inns	NO	Runs	HS	Avge	S/R	100	50	4s	6s	Ct	St
Tests *to 11.9.06*	17	30	2	763	139	27.25	44.90	1	5	95	4	11	0
ODIs *to 11.9.06*	17	15	2	284	100*	21.84	60.29	1	0	21	4	2	0
First-class *to 11.9.06*	103	159	17	6080	200	42.81	–		13	33	–	–	80	0

Bowling

	M	Balls	Runs	Wkts	BB	Avge	RpO	S/R	5i	10m
Tests *to 11.9.06*	17	6	7	0	–	–	7.00	–	0	0
ODIs *to 11.9.06*	17	18	33	0	–	–	11.00	–	0	0
First-class *to 11.9.06*	103	138	98	1	1–6	98.00	4.26	138.00	0	0

DILHARA FERNANDO

Full name	**Congenige Randhi Dilhara Fernando**
Born	**July 19, 1979, Colombo**
Teams	**Sinhalese Sports Club**
Style	**Right-hand bat, right-arm fast-medium bowler**
Test debut	**Sri Lanka v Pakistan at Colombo 2000**
ODI debut	**Sri Lanka v South Africa at Paarl 2000-01**

THE PROFILE When Dilhara Fernando burst onto the international scene, young and raw, he soon inspired hope that he would be the long-term replacement for Chaminda Vaas as the cutting edge of Sri Lanka's attack. He has natural pace – six months after his debut he was timed at 91.9mph in Durban – hits the pitch hard, and moves the ball off the seam. He rattled India at Galle in 2001, taking five wickets and sending Javagal Srinath to hospital. At first he paid for an inconsistent line and length, but worked hard with the former Test opening bowler Rumesh Ratnayake and became more reliable. He also learnt the art of reverse swing, and developed a well-disguised slower one. But injuries intervened. Fernando was quick during the 2003 World Cup, but bowled a lot of no-balls – a problem he later blamed on a spinal stress fracture. He returned after six months, only for another one to be detected in January 2004. He was nursed back to fitness, and reclaimed his place in the national squad later that year. He has been thereabouts ever since, often going for a few in ODIs but always threatening wickets. Between injuries, he has been a Test regular too, although the no-ball problem resurfaced, and he was omitted after the first Test against Pakistan in March 2006 before returning later that year for the one-day series in England, which Sri Lanka swept 5-0, with Fernando grabbing three quick wickets in the first match, at Lord's.

THE FACTS Fernando averages 17.94 with the ball in Tests against Bangladesh – and 43.63 against India, even though his best figures of 5 for 42 came against them ... He averages 24.61 against England in ODIs, but 67.00 in 13 matches against South Africa ... Fernando's best bowling of 6 for 29 came as the Sinhalese Sports Club bowled Colts out for 68 in Colombo in November 1999 ... 34 (29%) of his ODI wickets have been left-handers ...

THE FIGURES
Batting and fielding

	M	Inns	NO	Runs	HS	Avge	S/R	100	50	4s	6s	Ct	St
Tests *to 11.9.06*	24	31	10	124	16	5.90	25.99	0	0	14	1	8	0
ODIs *to 11.9.06*	94	35	22	122	13*	9.38	58.65	0	0	9	1	16	0
First-class *to 11.9.06*	80	86	25	420	42	6.88	–	0	0	–	–	32	0

Bowling

	M	Balls	Runs	Wkts	BB	Avge	RpO	S/R	5i	10m
Tests *to 11.9.06*	24	3596	2201	69	5–42	31.89	3.67	52.11	3	0
ODIs *to 11.9.06*	94	4049	3596	116	4–48	31.00	5.32	34.90	0	0
First-class *to 11.9.06*	80	10707	6392	234	6–29	27.31	3.58	45.75	6	0

STEPHEN FLEMING

Full name	**Stephen Paul Fleming**
Born	**April 1, 1973, Christchurch, Canterbury**
Teams	**Wellington, Nottinghamshire**
Style	**Left-hand bat**
Test debut	**New Zealand v India at Hamilton 1993-94**
ODI debut	**New Zealand v India at Napier 1993-94**

THE PROFILE Maturity as a player and as a captain has finally brought reward for Stephen Fleming, New Zealand's longest-serving Test skipper. A season with Middlesex in 2001 laid the foundations of a successful re-evaluation of his batting methods: before, an inability to convert half-centuries into hundreds did little justice to his quality as a languid left-hander often reminiscent of another born on April Fools' Day – David Gower. But shortly after a breakout innings of 134 to steer New Zealand to a classy World Cup victory over South Africa, Fleming confirmed his greater batting consistency with an unbeaten 274 against Sri Lanka in Colombo in April 2003. And, following another county stint, with Yorkshire, he added an equally impressive 192 against Pakistan at Hamilton later that year. He's also a slip catcher up there with the very best. Fleming annexed three national records while playing Bangladesh at Chittagong in October 2004. His 87th Test meant he was the most-capped New Zealander, while his 150th innings was also a new high. And, when he moved to 81 of his eventual 202, he surpassed Martin Crowe's record aggregate of 5,444 Test runs. In 2005 he captained newly promoted Nottinghamshire to their first County Championship title since Richard Hadlee's last season there in 1987. Then, five months after having a benign tumour removed from his face, in April 2006 Fleming became the first New Zealander to win 100 Test caps, reaching the mark, appropriately enough, at Centurion Park: another double-century followed in the next match.

THE FACTS Fleming made 92 on his Test debut, against India at Hamilton in 1993-94 – and uniquely added 90 on his ODI debut, against India at Napier two days after that Test finished ... He averages 68.18 in Tests against Sri Lanka, but only 25.18 against Australia ... Fleming holds the New Zealand records for Test appearances, matches captained (and won), runs, and catches ... His record includes one ODI for the World XI ...

THE FIGURES
Batting and fielding

	M	Inns	NO	Runs	HS	Avge	S/R	100	50	4s	6s	Ct	St
Tests *to 11.9.06*	102	173	10	6545	274*	40.15	45.12	9	41	828	21	152	0
ODIs *to 11.9.06*	253	243	19	7184	134*	32.07	71.01	6	43	725	49	116	0
First-class *to 11.9.06*	222	364	31	14701	274*	44.14	–		31	86	–	–	297	0

Bowling

	M	Balls	Runs	Wkts	BB	Avge	RpO	S/R	5i	10m
Tests *to 11.9.06*	102	0	–	–	–	–	–	–	–	–
ODIs *to 11.9.06*	253	29	28	1	1–8	28.00	5.79	29.00	1	0
First-class *to 11.9.06*	222	102	129	0	–	–	7.58	–	0	0

ANDREW FLINTOFF

ENGLAND

Full name	**Andrew Flintoff**
Born	**December 6, 1977, Preston, Lancashire**
Teams	**Lancashire**
Style	**Right-hand bat, right-arm fast bowler**
Test debut	**England v South Africa at Nottingham 1998**
ODI debut	**England v Pakistan at Sharjah 1998-99**

THE PROFILE In 2005, "Freddie" Flintoff established himself as England's best allrounder since Ian Botham, reaping 402 runs and 24 wickets in an unforgettable Ashes series. It propelled him to the superstar status his admirers had long believed was within his grasp. Big, northern and proud of it, he hammers the ball, then uses his colossal frame to reach 90mph – which, with his accuracy and burgeoning mastery of reverse-swing, make him among the most intimidating bowlers around. Flintoff's precocious skills led to a Test debut at 20 in 1998, but two years later he was struggling with weight, motivation and back trouble. A spell at the Academy helped, and when England SOSed in 2001-02, he was a reformed character. India's spinners troubled him, but he tonked a maiden Test ton in New Zealand, and did well at home. But when England flew to Australia in October 2002, Flintoff could hardly walk after a hernia operation. He returned as the most economical bowler at the 2003 World Cup, then starred against South Africa in England, thumping a therapeutic 95 in the remarkable Oval comeback after a defiant Lord's century. In the Caribbean early in 2004 he finally learned to slip the handbrake and become a genuine attacking option with the ball. After an ankle operation, Flintoff inspired England to a nailbiting two-run victory over Australia at Birmingham in August 2005, followed by a century at Nottingham. Then he stepped into the breach as captain in India. But that left ankle flared up again, and England's talisman faced a worrying wait before the 2006-07 Ashes series.

THE FACTS Flintoff won 47 Test caps – and scored 2239 runs – before playing against Australia ... In 2005 Flintoff was only the fourth cricketer to be voted BBC Sports Personality of the Year, following Jim Laker (1956), David Steele (1975) and Ian Botham (1981) ... He took 68 Test wickets in 2005, beating Steve Harmison's 2004 record for an England bowler by one ... Flintoff averages 51.25 with the bat and 24.69 with the ball in Tests against West Indies ... His record includes one Test and three ODIs for the World XI ...

THE FIGURES

Batting and fielding

	M	Inns	NO	Runs	HS	Avge	S/R	100	50	4s	6s	Ct	St
Tests *to 11.9.06*	62	100	5	3127	167	32.91	64.95	5	22	426	74	44	0
ODIs *to 11.9.06*	102	90	12	2674	123	34.28	89.13	3	15	238	85	33	0
First-class *to 11.9.06*	154	242	17	7914	167	35.17	–	15	46	–	–	164	0

Bowling

	M	Balls	Runs	Wkts	BB	Avge	RpO	S/R	5i	10m
Tests *to 11.9.06*	62	11740	5827	186	5–58	31.32	2.97	63.11	2	0
ODIs *to 11.9.06*	102	3882	2840	110	4–14	25.81	4.38	35.29	0	0
First-class *to 11.9.06*	154	18043	8799	280	5–24	31.42	2.92	64.43	3	0

JAMES FRANKLIN

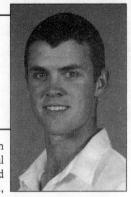

Full name	**James Edward Charles Franklin**
Born	**November 7, 1980, Wellington**
Teams	**Wellington, Glamorgan**
Style	**Left-hand bat, left-arm fast-medium bowler**
Test debut	**New Zealand v Pakistan at Auckland 2000-01**
ODI debut	**New Zealand v Zimbabwe at Taupo 2000-01**

THE PROFILE A left-arm medium-fast bowler who can swing the ball, James Franklin was introduced to international cricket when barely out of his teens after New Zealand suffered a run of injuries. Franklin made his one-day debut in 2000-01, and played two home Tests against Pakistan the same season, but struggled to make an impact and lost his place after the Sharjah Cup in April 2002. Back in domestic cricket he worked on his batting, which he had neglected, and filled out generally. He returned to the side in England in 2004. He was playing league cricket in Lancashire, but was called up when Shane Bond went home with a back injury. Franklin was included for the third Test at Trent Bridge, and although New Zealand lost he did his cause no harm with six wickets, five of them Test century-makers. He stayed on for the one-dayers that followed, and picked up the match award at Chester-le-Street for his 5 for 42 as England were skittled for 101. He was retained for the tour of Bangladesh, and took a hat-trick at Dhaka. Back home he took 6 for 119 against Australia in March 2005, and bowled superbly – getting the ball to reverse-swing – against Sri Lanka a month later, although his figures didn't reflect his excellence. More wickets followed against West Indies, then in April 2006 Franklin did his allrounder claims no harm with an unbeaten 122 – and a stand of 256 with Stephen Fleming – against South Africa at Cape Town.

THE FACTS Franklin is only the fourth man to have taken a hat-trick and scored a century in Tests – the others are Johnny Briggs of England and Pakistan's Abdul Razzaq and Wasim Akram ... The only other New Zealander to take a Test hat-trick was Peter Petherick in 1976-77 ... Franklin's highest first-class score is 208, for Wellington against Auckland in 2005-06: in the previous match, against Central Districts also at Wellington, he had taken his career-best figures of 7 for 30 ...

THE FIGURES

Batting and fielding

	M	Inns	NO	Runs	HS	Avge	S/R	100	50	4s	6s	Ct	St
Tests to 11.9.06	19	25	5	460	122*	23.00	40.31	1	1	46	3	7	0
ODIs to 11.9.06	41	25	6	221	29*	11.63	59.24	0	0	17	2	13	0
First-class to 11.9.06	84	124	19	2900	208	27.61	–	3	12	–	–	27	0

Bowling

	M	Balls	Runs	Wkts	BB	Avge	RpO	S/R	5i	10m
Tests to 11.9.06	19	3205	1970	70	6–119	28.14	3.68	45.78	3	0
ODIs to 11.9.06	41	1692	1468	37	5–42	39.67	5.20	45.72	1	0
First-class to 11.9.06	84	13764	7210	295	7–30	24.44	3.14	46.65	11	1

PETER FULTON

Full name	**Peter Gordon Fulton**
Born	**February 1, 1979, Christchurch, Canterbury**
Teams	**Canterbury**
Style	**Right-hand bat, occasional right-arm medium-pacer**
Test debut	**New Zealand v West Indies at Auckland 2005-06**
ODI debut	**New Zealand v Bangladesh at Chittagong 2004-05**

THE PROFILE Peter Fulton, a tall middle-order batsman nicknamed "Two-Metre Peter", initially made his mark on first-class cricket by extending his maiden century to 301 not out for Canterbury against Auckland in March 2003, in only his second full season. His 9½-hour innings, against an attack containing the Test bowlers Heath Davis and Brooke Walker, contained 45 fours and three sixes. Fulton, who has played a lot of club cricket in England, is a product of Canterbury Country, an area rich in cricket history but which had never previously produced an international player. His 301 also broke the monopoly of Otago, where the five previous New Zealand triple-centurions came from. The following season he scored consistently, making 728 runs at 42.82, including two more centuries, and – after a consistent tour of South Africa with New Zealand A – was called up to New Zealand's one-day squad for the tour of Bangladesh in November 2004. He played one match there, but it was another 12 months before he featured again. This time he made the most of his chance, with 70 not out, 32, 50 and 112 against Sri Lanka, which led to a Test baptism: he added 75 in his second match, as New Zealand took an unbeatable lead over West Indies. *Wisden* called him "one for the future, provided he could retain his simple, uncomplicated batting style": John Bracewell, New Zealand's coach, believes he has the tools to open, although he had problems there against South Africa early in 2006.

THE FACTS Fulton's 301 not out was the fifth-highest maiden century in all first-class cricket: the highest is 337 not out by Pervez Akhtar for Pakistan Railways in 1964-65 ... Fulton also scored 221 not out for Canterbury v Otago in Dunedin in 2004-05, when he shared an unbroken national sixth-wicket record stand of 293 with Neil Broom ... His uncle, Roddy Fulton, played for Canterbury and Northern Districts in the 1970s ...

THE FIGURES

Batting and fielding

	M	Inns	NO	Runs	HS	Avge	S/R	100	50	4s	6s	Ct	St
Tests to 11.9.06	5	7	0	185	75	26.42	46.25	0	1	27	3	3	0
ODIs to 11.9.06	10	10	2	382	112	47.75	77.64	1	2	29	5	5	0
First-class to 11.9.06	49	80	8	3389	301*	47.06	–	6	18	–	–	37	0

Bowling

	M	Balls	Runs	Wkts	BB	Avge	RpO	S/R	5i	10m
Tests to 11.9.06	5	0	–	–	–	–	–	–	–	–
ODIs to 11.9.06	10	0	–	–	–	–	–	–	–	–
First-class to 11.9.06	49	673	399	11	4-49	36.27	3.55	61.18	0	0

DAREN GANGA

WEST INDIES

Full name	**Daren Ganga**
Born	**January 14, 1979, Barrackpore, Trinidad**
Teams	**Trinidad & Tobago**
Style	**Right-hand bat, occasional offspinner**
Test debut	**West Indies v South Africa at Durban 1998-99**
ODI debut	**West Indies v South Africa at Cape Town 1998-99**

THE PROFILE Daren Ganga is a survivor at international level, bouncing back after seemingly flunking his last chance more than once. His 2000-01 tour of Australia was rather like Mark Ramprakash's debut Test series for England in 1991, featuring several characterful twenties and thirties – but, a studious opener whose limited supply of runs came mostly in the V, he could be becalmed all too easily. Like the unfortunate Ramprakash, he yo-yoed in and out of the Test side, and it wasn't until his fourth coming that he really made his mark, with back-to-back centuries against the mighty Australians in April 2003. Suddenly his phlegmatic approach seemed to be the ideal counterpoint for the rejuvenated Brian Lara, his fellow Trinidadian. But Ganga's form fell away again, and he was dropped after the first Test against South Africa in April 2005. Still it wasn't over: after missing ten Tests he was recalled for the tour of New Zealand early in 2006, and secured his place with 95 at Auckland, then led Trinidad & Tobago to the domestic title. He did well in the home series that followed against India, playing a calming role as a runner as West Indies hung on to save the first Test in Antigua, then making 135 and 66 not out in St Kitts' maiden Test. At 27 – nine years after what was probably a premature Test debut – Ganga was finally a senior member of the side and, with limited alternatives available, seemed set for an extended run.

THE FACTS Ganga made 265 for Trinidad & Tobago against Leeward Islands in Montserrat in March 2005, sharing a stand of 307 with Gregory Mahabir ... He has also passed 150 twice, both times against Windward Islands at Pointe-à-Pierre ... Ganga averages 49.14 in Tests against India, but only 10.66 against England ... His brother Sherwin also played for T&T ...

THE FIGURES
Batting and fielding

	M	Inns	NO	Runs	HS	Avge	S/R	100	50	4s	6s	Ct	St
Tests to 11.9.06	38	67	1	1765	135	26.74	40.21	3	7	237	2	25	0
ODIs to 11.9.06	33	32	1	802	71	25.87	61.03	0	9	67	7	11	0
First-class to 11.9.06	123	214	16	7149	265	36.10	–	17	33	–	–	80	0

Bowling

	M	Balls	Runs	Wkts	BB	Avge	RpO	S/R	5i	10m
Tests to 11.9.06	38	162	86	0	–	–	3.18	–	0	0
ODIs to 11.9.06	33	1	4	0	–	–	24.00	–	0	0
First-class to 11.9.06	123	572	302	3	1–7	100.66	3.16	190.66	0	0

SOURAV GANGULY

Full name **Sourav Chandidas Ganguly**
Born **July 8, 1972, Calcutta, Bengal**
Teams **Bengal, Northamptonshire**
Style **Left-hand bat, right-arm medium-pace bowler**
Test debut **India v England at Lord's 1996**
ODI debut **India v West Indies at Brisbane 1991-92**

THE PROFILE Some felt he couldn't play the bouncer, others swore he was divine on the off side; some laughed at his lack of athleticism, others admired his ability to galvanise a side. Sourav Ganguly's ability to polarise opinion has been an ongoing Indian soap opera. Nobody can dispute that he was India's most successful captain, forging a winning unit from a bunch of talented individuals, and nobody denies that he was among the best one-day batsmen, combining grace with surgical precision in his strokeplay. After he toured Australia at 19 his career stalled before a scintillating debut century at Lord's in 1996: soon he was forming a destructive opening partnership in one-dayers with Sachin Tendulkar. He took over the captaincy in 2000, and quickly proved to be tough and intuitive. India started winning overseas, and began a streak that took them all the way to the 2003 World Cup final. Later that year, Ganguly's unexpected, incandescent hundred at Brisbane set the tone for an epic series in which India fought the Aussies to a standstill. Victory in Pakistan turned him into a cult figure, but that turned out to be a watershed: things went pear-shaped when his loss of form coincided with India's insipid one-day performances. Breaking point came when his differences with new coach Greg Chappell were leaked. Two gritty innings at Karachi, as India succumbed to a humiliating defeat early in 2006, weren't enough to retain his place. A World Cup comeback is unlikely – but with Ganguly, nothing is impossible.

THE FACTS Ganguly made 131 on his Test debut, at Lord's in 1996, and scored 136 in his next innings, at Nottingham ... He is one of only four batsmen to score 10,000 runs in ODIs ... Ganguly averages 56.91 in ODIs against South Africa, but only 22.31 against Australia ... Only Sachin Tendulkar has scored more ODI hundreds than Ganguly's 22 ... Ganguly captained in 49 Tests, winning 21, both Indian records ... Ganguly's record includes one ODI for the Asia XI ...

THE FIGURES

Batting and fielding

	M	Inns	NO	Runs	HS	Avge	S/R	100	50	4s	6s	Ct	St
Tests to 11.9.06	88	140	12	5221	173	40.78	48.79	12	25	670	41	59	0
ODIs to 11.9.06	279	270	21	10123	183	40.65	73.79	22	60	991	168	96	0
First-class to 11.9.06	207	320	38	12277	200*	43.53	–		25	71	–	–	149	0

Bowling

	M	Balls	Runs	Wkts	BB	Avge	RpO	S/R	5i	10m
Tests to 11.9.06	88	2516	1419	26	3–28	54.57	3.38	96.76	0	0
ODIs to 11.9.06	279	4123	3470	93	5–16	37.31	5.04	44.33	2	0
First-class to 11.9.06	207	9695	5505	148	6–46	37.19	3.40	65.50	4	0

CHRIS GAYLE

Full name	**Christopher Henry Gayle**
Born	**September 21, 1979, Kingston, Jamaica**
Teams	**Jamaica**
Style	**Right-hand bat, offspinner**
Test debut	**West Indies v Zimbabwe at Port-of-Spain 1999-2000**
ODI debut	**West Indies v India at Toronto 1999-2000**

THE PROFILE A thrusting Jamaican left-hander, Chris Gayle earned himself a black mark on his first senior tour – to England in 2000 – when the new boys were felt to be insufficiently respectful of their elders. But a lack of respect, for opposition bowlers at least, has served Gayle well since then. Tall and imposing at the crease, he loves to carve through the covers off either foot, and has the ability to decimate the figures of even the thriftiest of opening bowlers. In a lean era for West Indian cricket in general – and fast bowling in particular – Gayle's pugnacious approach has become an attacking weapon in its own right, in Tests as well as one-dayers. His 79-ball century at Cape Town in January 2004, after South Africa had made 532, was typical of his no-holds-barred approach. Gayle's good run ended when England came calling early in 2004, and he averaged only 26 against their potent pace attack: Steve Harmison, in particular, fancied his chances, dismissing him four times in seven innings and exposing a lack of positive footwork. But men with little footwork often baffle experts, and after returning to form with an uncharacteristic century against Bangladesh, Gayle exacted his revenge on England's bowlers with a battering not seen since Lara's 400, before coming within a whisker of emulating Lara himself with 317 against South Africa in Antigua. Gayle also bowls brisk non-turning offspin, with which he has turned himself into a genuine one-day allrounder.

THE FACTS Gayle's 317 against New Zealand in Antigua in May 2005 has been exceeded for West Indies only by Brian Lara (twice) and Garry Sobers ... Only Lara (19) and Desmond Haynes (17) have scored more ODI centuries for West Indies than Gayle's 12 ... Gayle made 208 not out for Jamaica against West Indies B at Montego Bay in February 2001, sharing an unbroken opening stand of 425 with Leon Garrick ... His record includes three ODIs for the World XI ...

THE FIGURES

Batting and fielding

	M	Inns	NO	Runs	HS	Avge	S/R	100	50	4s	6s	Ct	St
Tests to 11.9.06	61	108	3	4079	317	38.84	55.38	7	25	648	30	65	0
ODIs to 11.9.06	138	135	7	4919	153*	38.42	78.31	12	26	591	67	63	0
First-class to 11.9.06	130	233	16	9589	317	44.18	–		22	50	–	–	121	0

Bowling

	M	Balls	Runs	Wkts	BB	Avge	RpO	S/R	5i	10m
Tests to 11.9.06	61	4274	1825	49	5–34	37.24	2.56	87.22	2	0
ODIs to 11.9.06	138	4716	3651	114	5–46	32.02	4.64	41.36	1	0
First-class to 11.9.06	130	9090	3661	97	5–34	37.74	2.41	93.71	2	0

HERSCHELLE GIBBS

Full name **Herschelle Herman Gibbs**
Born **February 23, 1974, Green Point, Cape Town**
Teams **Cape Cobras**
Style **Right-hand bat, occasional legspinner**
Test debut **South Africa v India at Calcutta 1996-97**
ODI debut **South Africa v Kenya at Nairobi 1996-97**

THE PROFILE Herschelle Gibbs was summoned from the classroom at 16 to make his first-class debut in 1990: his feet moved beautifully at the crease, but struggled to find the ground in real life. Admitting that a Test debut in front of 70,000 at Eden Gardens wasn't as nerve-wracking as sitting his final exams, as well as the fact that he reads little other than magazines and comics, contributed to a reputation for simplicity. In fact, Gibbs can be a warm and generous person. His passion for one-liners and verbal jousting continues to hamper his advancement, and his brush with career death in the match-fixing scandal added to the impression of one who had failed to grasp the magnitude of his impact on the nation's youth. At the crease, however, Gibbs can be invincible. No shot is beyond him, while Test-match opening has not tempered his desire for explosive entertainment. The speed of his hands is hypnotic, frequently allowing him to hook off the front foot and keep out surprise lifters. His trademark is the lofted extra-cover drive, hit inside-out with the certainty of a square cut. At backward point he is almost the equal of Jonty Rhodes. Gibbs has two double-centuries (and two more 190s) among his 14 Test tons, and 16 one-day hundreds too – the best of them in March 2006, when his 111-ball 175 powered South Africa to an amazing triumph at Johannesburg, overhauling Australia's massive 434 with a ball to spare in arguably the greatest one-day cracker of them all.

THE FACTS Gibbs and Graeme Smith are the only opening pair to share three stands of 300 or more in Tests: Gibbs shared another for the second wicket with Jacques Kallis ... He averages 67.42 in Tests against Pakistan, but only 23.30 against Sri Lanka ... Gibbs has been bowled in 33 (24%) of his Test innings ... Has been reluctant to tour India since he was implicated in the Hansie Cronje match-fixing scandal: the local police denied him immunity from prosecution if he returned ... Gibbs was banned for six months for his involvement with match-fixing, and was also briefly suspended in 2001 for smoking marijuana ...

THE FIGURES

Batting and fielding

	M	Inns	NO	Runs	HS	Avge	S/R	100	50	4s	6s	Ct	St
Tests *to 11.9.06*	79	135	6	5728	228	44.40	50.29	14	22	818	46	72	0
ODIs *to 11.9.06*	185	184	13	6117	175	35.77	82.09	16	25	712	87	77	0
First-class *to 11.9.06*	174	300	12	12637	228	43.87	–	31	54	–	–	142	0

Bowling

	M	Balls	Runs	Wkts	BB	Avge	RpO	S/R	5i	10m
Tests *to 11.9.06*	79	6	4	0	–	–	4.00	–	0	0
ODIs *to 11.9.06*	185	0	–	–	–	–	–	–	–	–
First-class *to 11.9.06*	174	138	78	3	2–14	26.00	3.39	46.00	0	0

ADAM GILCHRIST

Full name	**Adam Craig Gilchrist**
Born	**November 14, 1971, Bellingen, New South Wales**
Teams	**Western Australia**
Style	**Left-hand bat, wicketkeeper**
Test debut	**Australia v Pakistan at Brisbane 1999-2000**
ODI debut	**Australia v South Africa at Faridabad 1995-96**

THE PROFILE Going in first or seventh, wearing whites or coloureds, Adam Gilchrist has been the symbolic heart of Australia's steamrolling agenda and the most exhilarating cricketer of the modern age. It was arguably Gilchrist's belated Test arrival that turned the Australian XI from powerful to overpowering. He is a throwback to more innocent times, a flap-eared country boy who walked in a World Cup semi-final, and swatted his second ball for six while on a pair in a Test. "Just hit the ball," is how he described his batting philosophy. Employing a high-on-the-handle grip, he pokes good balls into gaps and throttles most others, invariably with head straight, wrists soft and balance sublime. Only at the death does he jettison the textbook, whirling his bat like a hammer-thrower. He bludgeoned 81 on debut, pouched five catches and a stumping, and has barely paused for breath since. Only recently has his appetite slowed: he was troubled by Andrew Flintoff's around-the-wicket barrage in 2005, and found the flaw difficult to overcome. But two of his Test innings rank among Australia's greatest: his unbeaten 149 against Pakistan at Hobart in November 1999 when all seemed lost, and a savage 204 at Johannesburg in February 2002. As a wicketkeeper he lacks Rod Marsh's acrobatics and Ian Healy's finesse, and he probably peaked at 30. But if he clutches few screamers he drops even fewer sitters. He is closing on Healy's record 396 Test dismissals, and already has the most centuries of any keeper-batsman.

THE FACTS Gilchrist was on the winning side in each of his first 15 Tests, the best start of any player ... He averages 68.44 in Tests against Pakistan, but only 29.95 against India ... Gilchrist averaged 171.50 in the series in New Zealand in 2004-05, with innings of 121, 162 and 60 not out: in all he averages 76.91 from 11 Tests against NZ ... As Ricky Ponting's stand-in he led Australia to their first series win in India for 35 years in 2004-05 ... Only Ian Healy (395) and Mark Boucher (364) have made more wicketkeeping dismissals in Tests, and Gilchrist leads the way in ODIs ... His record includes one ODI for the World XI ...

THE FIGURES
Batting and fielding

	M	Inns	NO	Runs	HS	Avge	S/R	100	50	4s	6s	Ct	St
Tests *to 11.9.06*	85	123	18	5124	204*	48.79	81.59	16	22	624	93	320	35
ODIs *to 11.9.06*	242	235	9	8233	172	36.42	96.76	14	45	996	123	348	45
First-class *to 11.9.06*	176	261	44	9759	204*	44.97	–	29	38	–	–	687	53

Bowling

	M	Balls	Runs	Wkts	BB	Avge	RpO	S/R	5i	10m
Tests *to 11.9.06*	85	0	–	–	–	–	–	–	–	–
ODIs *to 11.9.06*	242	0	–	–	–	–	–	–	–	–
First-class *to 11.9.06*	176	0	–	–	–	–	–	–	–	–

ASHLEY GILES

Full name **Ashley Fraser Giles**
Born **March 19, 1973, Chertsey, Surrey**
Teams **Warwickshire**
Style **Right-hand bat, slow left-arm orthodox spinner**
Test debut **England v South Africa at Manchester 1998**
ODI debut **England v Australia at The Oval 1997**

THE PROFILE The Ashley Giles story is an endearing tale of one man's triumph over the doubters. With a high-trotting approach climaxing in an energetic flurry of limbs, Giles doesn't have the most fluent action – possibly because he began life as a fast bowler – and was once derided as shuffling up like a wheelie-bin. But he is accurate, finds some turn and even more bounce, and established himself as England's No. 1 during the triumphant tour of Pakistan in 2000-01. He came close to retirement early in 2004 after a modest tour of the Caribbean, but instead claimed a matchwinning nine wickets at Lord's later that summer, including deceiving Brian Lara to bring up 100 in Tests: imbued with new confidence, he continued to chip in – with ball and, increasingly, bat – culminating in 59 at The Oval to help seal England's 2005 Ashes fairytale. Before that, Giles's most memorable moments had all come on the subcontinent: the rip-snorter that pitched outside leg and fizzed past Inzamam-ul-Haq's dangling bat into the stumps at Karachi in 2000-01; a Test-best 5 for 67 against India at Ahmedabad two years later, despite a niggling leg injury; and bouncing back after a dismal tour of Bangladesh in 2003-04 with 18 wickets in the series win in Sri Lanka. He has a strong arm and also fields well in the gully. Giles faced a new challenge in 2006: while he was sidelined with a persistent hip problem, Monty Panesar made his mark as England's slow left-armer.

THE FACTS Giles became the tenth Englishman to achieve the Test "double" of 1000 runs and 100 wickets, reaching the landmark at Cape Town in 2004-05, in the same match as Andrew Flintoff ... Unusually, his best bowling figures in Tests and ODIs are the same (5 for 57), a distinction he shares with India's Sandeep Patil (2 for 28 in both) ... Giles averages 26.91 with the ball in Tests against West Indies, but 55.63 against South Africa – and 112.00 against Bangladesh ... His best bowling figures are 8 for 90 (12 for 135 in the match) for Warwickshire at Northampton in June 2000 ...

THE FIGURES

Batting and fielding

	M	Inns	NO	Runs	HS	Avge	S/R	100	50	4s	6s	Ct	St
Tests to 11.9.06	52	77	12	1347	59	20.72	45.89	0	4	164	5	32	0
ODIs to 11.9.06	62	35	13	385	41	17.50	69.87	0	0	24	4	22	0
First-class to 11.9.06	176	245	45	5272	128*	26.36	–	3	22	–	–	79	0

Bowling

	M	Balls	Runs	Wkts	BB	Avge	RpO	S/R	5i	10m
Tests to 11.9.06	52	11688	5544	140	5–57	39.60	2.84	83.48	5	0
ODIs to 11.9.06	62	2856	2069	55	5–57	37.61	4.34	51.92	1	0
First-class to 11.9.06	176	36812	15696	536	8–90	29.28	2.55	68.67	26	3

JASON GILLESPIE

Full name **Jason Neil Gillespie**
Born **April 19, 1975, Darlinghurst, Sydney, New South Wales**
Teams **South Australia, Yorkshire**
Style **Right-hand bat, right-arm fast-medium bowler**
Test debut **Australia v West Indies at Sydney 1996-97**
ODI debut **Australia v Sri Lanka at Colombo 1996-97**

THE PROFILE   Jason Gillespie's bouncing mullet, hooked nose and Spofforth-like glare were a feature of Australia's pace attack in the first five years of the 2000s. Gillespie had played only 52 of a possible 92 Tests after his 1996-97 debut thanks to various ailments, including stress fractures in the back and a broken leg. Each time he recovered and, until dropped during the 2005 Ashes, had missed only two Tests since November 2002. He blossomed into half of Australia's statistically most-successful opening pair. But if Glenn McGrath's strength is his ability to make the ball do just enough, then Gillespie's flaw is his tendency for it to do too much. No other contemporary fast man elicits so many plays-and-misses. Operating from a shorter, reconfigured run-up, he is not so consistently quick, and in England he was treated like a medium-pacer. However, few Australian fast men can have owned such deep wells of tenacity. Gillespie bowls long spells in the hottest conditions – always uncomplainingly, always with seam upright and ball jagging both ways – and he had another long spell when he returned to the Test side against Bangladesh ... with the bat, as his maiden century turned into a magnificent 201. It was appropriate recognition for a hardy and valuable batting approach that also produced two unbeaten half-centuries – and a priceless 26 which sealed a hard-fought draw against India in 2004-05. The great-grandson of a Kamilaroi warrior, Gillespie occupies a significant niche in Australian history as the first acknowledged Aboriginal Test cricketer.

THE FACTS   Gillespie's 201 not out against Bangladesh at Chittagong in April 2006 was easily the highest score by a nightwatchman in a Test, beating Mark Boucher's 125 for South Africa v Zimbabwe at Harare in 1999-2000 ... Gillespie has never taken more than 20 wickets in a Test series, which he did in the 2002-03 Ashes series and in India in 2004-05 ... He has taken 50 wickets at 21.12 against West Indies, but only 10 at 37.50 against Pakistan ... He averages 2.80 with the bat against South Africa – and 247.00 against Bangladesh ...

THE FIGURES

Batting and fielding

	M	Inns	NO	Runs	HS	Avge	S/R	100	50	4s	6s	Ct	St
Tests to 11.9.06	71	93	28	1218	201*	18.73	31.96	1	2	146	8	27	0
ODIs to 11.9.06	97	39	16	289	44*	12.56	78.53	0	0	16	6	10	0
First-class to 11.9.06	141	188	48	2537	201*	18.12	–	1	6	–	–	56	0

Bowling

	M	Balls	Runs	Wkts	BB	Avge	RpO	S/R	5i	10m
Tests to 11.9.06	71	14234	6770	259	7–37	26.13	2.85	54.95	8	0
ODIs to 11.9.06	97	5144	3611	142	5–22	25.42	4.21	36.22	3	0
First-class to 11.9.06	141	27366	12796	503	8–50	25.43	2.80	54.40	19	1

HABIBUL BASHAR

Full name	**Qazi Habibul Bashar**
Born	**August 17, 1972, Nagakanda, Kushtia**
Teams	**Khulna**
Style	**Right-hand bat, occasional offspinner**
Test debut	**Bangladesh v India at Dhaka 2000-01**
ODI debut	**Bangladesh v Sri Lanka at Sharjah 1994-95**

THE PROFILE Impish and impulsive, Habibul Bashar has the style and strokes of a genuine Test player. Most of his runs come from cultured drives through midwicket, and most of his dismissals from a Hilditch-style addiction to the hook. Before Bangladesh's inaugural Test, "Sumon" promised he would kick the habit, but although he made 71 and 30 he was still out hooking ... twice. He has since carried Bangladesh's flimsy middle-order hopes, and inherited the captaincy from Khaled Mahmud in January 2004. After a shaky start in Zimbabwe, he came into his own with a century in St Lucia, as Bangladesh took a first-innings lead in their first Test in the Caribbean. He missed the Champions Trophy in England with an injured thumb – overall he has underperformed in ODIs for such an attacking player – but returned to captain in England in 2005 when, lo and behold, the hook habit cut him down twice at Lord's. But he restored pride with a hard-hitting 61 to conclude a disappointing series. Habibul's greatest moment as captain came a few weeks later at Cardiff, with a convincing five-wicket win over Australia in the NatWest Series. However, normal service resumed in September in Sri Lanka, where Bangladesh were blanked in both Tests and one-dayers. That he topped the Test averages was little consolation for Habibul, who called the tour his "worst ever". But things were looking up: he made 76 (and was run out for 7) as Bangladesh ran Australia awfully close at Fatullah in April 2006.

THE FACTS Habibul Bashar passed 2000 runs in Tests for Bangladesh before anyone else had reached 1000 ... He scored 94 and 55 in captaining Bangladesh to their first Test victory, against Zimbabwe at Chittagong in January 2005 ... Habibul has only missed two of Bangladesh's 44 Tests, at home against New Zealand in 2004-05 when he was recuperating from a broken thumb ... He averages 50.36 against Pakistan in Tests ... Habibul made his highest score of 224 for Biman Bangladesh v Khulna at Jessore in 2000-01 ....

THE FIGURES

Batting and fielding

	M	Inns	NO	Runs	HS	Avge	S/R	100	50	4s	6s	Ct	St
Tests *to 11.9.06*	42	83	1	2838	113	34.60	60.40	3	24	374	2	19	0
ODIs *to 11.9.06*	84	82	3	1708	74	21.62	60.09	0	12	–	8	16	0
First-class *to 11.9.06*	72	135	4	4616	224	35.23	–	6	34	–	–	30	0

Bowling

	M	Balls	Runs	Wkts	BB	Avge	RpO	S/R	5i	10m
Tests *to 11.9.06*	42	234	195	0	–	–	5.00	–	0	0
ODIs *to 11.9.06*	84	175	142	1	1–31	142.00	4.86	175.00	0	0
First-class *to 11.9.06*	72	754	491	8	2–28	61.37	3.90	94.25	0	0

BRAD HADDIN

AUSTRALIA

Full name	**Bradley James Haddin**
Born	**October 23, 1977, Cowra, New South Wales**
Teams	**New South Wales**
Style	**Right-hand bat, wicketkeeper**
Test debut	**No Tests yet**
ODI debut	**Australia v Zimbabwe at Hobart 2000-01**

THE PROFILE Brad Haddin holds the most nerve-fraying position in Australian cricket. He is the wicketkeeper-in-waiting, entrusted with warming the seat whenever Adam Gilchrist needs a rest. Slip up and be forgotten; perform well, as he has over the past couple of seasons, and suffer a speedy demotion when the incumbent returns. He's already seen off Darren Berry, Wade Seccombe and Ryan Campbell, but now has to look out for up-and-comers like Chris Hartley, Luke Ronchi and Adam Crosthwaite. At 29 Haddin has time – and talent – on his side for a lengthy international career, but the scheduling of Gilchrist's eventual departure will be crucial. The pressure of being No. 2 has not hindered Haddin's batting, and his keeping to a New South Wales attack swinging from Brett Lee to Stuart MacGill has remained sharp. In 2004-05 he scored 916 first-class runs at 57.25, leading the Blues to a one-wicket Pura Cup victory over Queensland, and he also posted an impressive limited-overs century for Australia A against Pakistan. Haddin followed that in 2005-06 with another 617 Pura Cup runs at 51.41, and capably filled in for Gilchrist in two VB Series games. He also shadowed Gilchrist on the 2005 Ashes tour. A former Australia Under-19 captain who grew up in Gundagai, Haddin began his senior domestic career in 1997-98 with the Australian Capital Territory in their debut Mercantile Mutual Cup season: two years later he was playing for NSW.

THE FACTS Haddin took up a novel batting position *behind* the stumps when facing a Shoaib Akhtar "free ball" (after a no-ball) in a Twenty20 game for Australia A against Pakistan early in 2005: he reasoned that he had more time to sight the ball, and if it hit the stumps it would confuse the fielders. It did hit the stumps, and he managed a bye ... Haddin was also the unwitting "villain" of the 2005 Ashes Test at Edgbaston: he was the man who threw a ball to Glenn McGrath, who badly sprained his ankle in catching it and missed the match, which England eventually won by just two runs ...

THE FIGURES

Batting and fielding

	M	Inns	NO	Runs	HS	Avge	S/R	100	50	4s	6s	Ct	St
Tests to 11.9.06	0	–	–	–	–	–	–	–	–	–	–	–	–
ODIs to 11.9.06	13	11	0	200	41	18.18	71.94	0	0	20	2	13	4
First-class to 11.9.06	74	123	13	4264	154	38.76	–	6	26	–	–	192	18

Bowling

	M	Balls	Runs	Wkts	BB	Avge	RpO	S/R	5i	10m
Tests to 11.9.06	0	–	–	–	–	–	–	–	–	–
ODIs to 11.9.06	13	0	–	–	–	–	–	–	–	–
First-class to 11.9.06	74	0	–	–	–	–	–	–	–	–

SOUTH AFRICA

ANDREW HALL

Full name **Andrew James Hall**
Born **July 31, 1975, Johannesburg, Transvaal**
Teams **Dolphins, Kent**
Style **Right-hand bat, right-arm fast-medium bowler**
Test debut **South Africa v Australia at Cape Town 2001-02**
ODI debut **South Africa v West Indies at Durban 1998-99**

THE PROFILE   Probably the only cricketer to have been shot at point-blank range and live to tell the tale, Andrew Hall has seized the opportunity to play international cricket with both hands. Which is remarkable really, considering that Hall fielded a bullet in his left hand when a mugger fired six shots at him at a cash machine late one night in 1998. Miraculously, the bullet caused no serious damage, and Hall recovered enough to win a place in South Africa's one-day side against West Indies in January 1999. He appeared to have slipped out of the selectors' minds until Australia arrived the following April for another one-day series. With Herschelle Gibbs struggling for form, Hall was tried as Gary Kirsten's opening partner. And he looked the part against Brett Lee, scoring a composed 46 – enough to win a place on the ensuing tour of Sri Lanka, where he made an equally impressive 81 against Murali at Galle. An allrounder who played indoor cricket for South Africa before breaking into the first-class game, Hall was initially seen as a bowler who batted down the order, then got pigeonholed as a one-day specialist. But as a late call-up in England in 2003 he took 16 wickets in the Tests, and ensured victory at Leeds with a buccaneering 99 not out. Then he defied the Indians for 588 minutes in the heat of Kanpur to make 163 as an emergency opener. Test opportunities have been few since, but he remains in the one-day frame.

THE FACTS   At Leeds in 2003 Hall was only the fifth man to be marooned on 99 not out in a Test, after Geoff Boycott, Steve Waugh, Alex Tudor and Shaun Pollock ... In the four innings either side of his 99 he made just one run, with three ducks ... Hall averages 23.66 with the ball in Tests against New Zealand – and 193.00 against West Indies ... He has played county cricket for Worcestershire and Kent ...

THE FIGURES
Batting and fielding

	M	Inns	NO	Runs	HS	Avge	S/R	100	50	4s	6s	Ct	St
Tests to 11.9.06	19	30	4	735	163	28.26	46.54	1	3	93	4	15	0
ODIs to 11.9.06	68	46	11	761	81	21.74	72.82	0	2	77	9	23	0
First-class to 11.9.06	115	169	23	4999	163	34.23	–	5	34	–	–	83	0

Bowling

	M	Balls	Runs	Wkts	BB	Avge	RpO	S/R	5i	10m
Tests to 11.9.06	19	2838	1511	39	3–1	38.74	3.19	72.76	0	0
ODIs to 11.9.06	68	2406	1848	65	4–23	28.43	4.60	37.01	0	0
First-class to 11.9.06	115	19802	9186	352	6–77	26.09	2.78	56.25	12	1

HARBHAJAN SINGH

Full name **Harbhajan Singh**
Born **July 3, 1980, Jullundur, Punjab**
Teams **Punjab**
Style **Right-hand bat, offspinner**
Test debut **India v Australia at Bangalore 1997-98**
ODI debut **India v New Zealand at Sharjah 1997-98**

THE PROFILE   Harbhajan Singh represents the spirit of the new Indian cricketer. His arrogance and cockiness – traits that earned him a rebuke from the establishment and suspension from India's National Cricket Academy – translate into self-belief and passion on the field, and Harbhajan has the talent to match. An offspinner with a windmilling, whiplash action, remodelled after he was reported for throwing, he exercises great command over the ball, has the ability to vary his length and pace, and can turn it the other way too. His main wicket-taking ball, however, is the one that climbs wickedly on the unsuspecting batsman from a good length, forcing him to alter his stroke at the last second. In March 2001, it proved too much for the all-conquering Australians, as Harbhajan collected 32 wickets in three Tests, while none of his team-mates managed more than three. Purists might mutter about a lack of loop and flight, but this was one of the greatest performances ever by a finger-spinner – at a time when orthodox offspin was supposed to be history. He has since been bothered by injury, while in Pakistan early in 2006 he finished with 0 for 355 in two Tests before bouncing back with five-fors against West Indies in St Kitts and Jamaica (5 for 13 in only 4.3 overs) in June. He had 50 Test caps and more than 200 wickets – and nearly 1000 runs with his occasionally explosive batting – before he turned 26, and remains very much part of India's master plan.

THE FACTS   Harbhajan's match figures of 15 for 217 against Australia at Chennai in 2000-01 have been bettered for India only by Narendra Hirwani (16 for 136 in 1987-88, also at Chennai) ... Harbhajan took 32 wickets at 17.03 in that three-match series: his haul at Kolkata included India's first-ever Test hat-trick, when he dismissed Ricky Ponting, Adam Gilchrist and Shane Warne ... He has taken 56 wickets at 24.17 in Tests against Australia, but only 15 at 57.33 against Pakistan ...

THE FIGURES

Batting and fielding

	M	Inns	NO	Runs	HS	Avge	S/R	100	50	4s	6s	Ct	St
Tests to 11.9.06	57	79	18	986	66	16.16	67.95	0	2	142	16	30	0
ODIs to 11.9.06	130	65	19	604	46	13.13	83.88	0	0	54	14	38	0
First-class to 11.9.06	112	147	33	2210	84	19.38	–	0	6	–	–	57	0

Bowling

	M	Balls	Runs	Wkts	BB	Avge	RpO	S/R	5i	10m
Tests to 11.9.06	57	15162	7108	238	8–84	29.86	2.81	63.70	19	4
ODIs to 11.9.06	130	7009	4804	154	5–31	31.19	4.11	45.51	2	0
First-class to 11.9.06	112	27039	12773	467	8–84	27.35	2.83	57.89	30	5

STEVE HARMISON

Full name	**Stephen James Harmison**
Born	**October 23, 1978, Ashington, Northumberland**
Teams	**Durham**
Style	**Right-hand bat, right-arm fast bowler**
Test debut	**England v India at Nottingham 2002**
ODI debut	**England v Sri Lanka at Brisbane 2002-03**

THE PROFILE   With his lofty, loose-limbed action and his painful knack of jamming fingers against bat-handles, Steve Harmison had long been likened, tongue-in-cheek, to the great Curtly Ambrose, when suddenly he loped in and produced a spell that Ambrose himself could hardly have bettered. West Indies were humbled for 47 at Kingston in March 2004, with Harmison taking a remarkable 7 for 12. It was a stunning riposte from a man who, only months earlier, had flown home crocked from Bangladesh with whispers about his attitude chasing him all the way. Harmison was held back before his 2002 Test debut by niggling injuries (including somehow dislocating his shoulder after catching his hand in his trouser pocket while bowling) and a tendency to homesickness on overseas tours, and he mixed magical spells with moments when the radar went on the blink. But in the Caribbean, the spiritual home of the fast bowler, he seemed finally to come of age. This was borne out with more wickets at home in 2004, as England won all seven Tests against West Indies and New Zealand. A dip followed in South Africa, but after a cathartic five-wicket haul against Bangladesh at home in Durham, he tore into Australia's top order at Lord's on the first morning of the 2005 Ashes series. He couldn't secure victory then, but popped up to seal the thrilling two-run win at Birmingham. He didn't hit such heights again until a year later, when his 6 for 19 routed Pakistan at Manchester, and set thoughts racing ahead to another Ashes encounter.

THE FACTS   Harmison's 7 for 12 at Kingston in March 2004, as West Indies were shot out for 47, are the best Test bowling figures at Sabina Park, beating Trevor Bailey's 7 for 34, also for England, in 1953-54 ... Harmison took 67 Test wickets in 2004, a record for an England bowler at the time (Andrew Flintoff beat it by one in 2005) ... His brother Ben also plays for Durham ... Harmison was born in Ashington, the same Northumberland village as football's Charlton brothers ... His record includes one Test for the World XI ...

THE FIGURES

Batting and fielding

	M	Inns	NO	Runs	HS	Avge	S/R	100	50	4s	6s	Ct	St
Tests to 11.9.06	45	60	16	505	42	11.47	61.21	0	0	69	9	6	0
ODIs to 11.9.06	44	20	12	64	13*	8.00	60.95	0	0	2	0	8	0
First-class to 11.9.06	130	179	49	1258	42	9.67	–	0	0	–	–	22	0

Bowling

	M	Balls	Runs	Wkts	BB	Avge	RpO	S/R	5i	10m
Tests to 11.9.06	45	9866	5157	179	7–12	28.81	3.13	55.11	8	1
ODIs to 11.9.06	44	2378	1978	64	5–33	30.90	4.99	37.15	1	0
First-class to 11.9.06	130	25443	13162	453	7–12	29.05	3.10	56.16	15	1

MATTHEW HAYDEN

Full name	**Matthew Lawrence Hayden**
Born	**October 29, 1971, Kingaroy, Queensland**
Teams	**Queensland**
Style	**Left-hand bat, occasional right-arm medium-pacer**
Test debut	**Australia v South Africa at Johannesburg 1993-94**
ODI debut	**Australia v England at Manchester 1993**

THE PROFILE Strength is Matthew Hayden's strength – both mental and physical. It enabled him to shrug off carping that he was too limited for Test cricket because of the way he plays around his front pad. Before his maiden first-class innings, he asked if anyone had made 200 on debut, then went out and smacked 149. The runs have rarely abated since. Tall and powerful, he batters the ball at and through the off side. He has also made himself a fine catcher in the cordon. Hayden's earliest Tests were all against South Africa and West Indies: he didn't impress, but patience and willpower won through, especially since 2000-01 when he slog-swept his way to 549 runs in India, an Australian record for a three-Test series. By the end of 2001 he had formed a prolific opening partnership with Justin Langer. Hayden belatedly came good in ODIs, and was ranked among the top three batsmen in both forms of the game by the 2003 World Cup. Later that year he hammered 380 against Zimbabwe, briefly borrowing the Test record from Brian Lara. He experienced a rare extended slump during 2004-05, and lost his one-day place. That lack of form and footwork continued in 2005, but a disastrous Ashes series was salvaged with 138 at The Oval. It was the awkward beginning of a resurgence that saved his career. Usually playing more patiently, he collected hundreds in the next three Tests, and passed 1000 runs in a calendar year for the fifth time.

THE FACTS Hayden held the record for the highest Test innings for six months, hitting 380 against Zimbabwe at Perth in October 2003: Brian Lara reclaimed the record with 400 not out, but Hayden's remains the highest score in a Test in Australia ... He has scored 17 of his 26 Test centuries in Australia, where his overall average is 63.76 ... His *worst* average against another country is 33.60 against Bangladesh ... Hayden now stands behind only Allan Border, Don Bradman, Ricky Ponting and Steve Waugh on Australia's list of century-makers ... His record includes one ODI for the World XI in January 2005 ...

THE FIGURES
Batting and fielding

	M	Inns	NO	Runs	HS	Avge	S/R	100	50	4s	6s	Ct	St
Tests *to 11.9.06*	84	150	12	7326	380	53.08	60.09	26	26	896	76	111	0
ODIs *to 11.9.06*	119	115	12	4131	146	40.10	75.90	5	26	419	50	46	0
First-class *to 11.9.06*	272	474	45	22935	380	53.46	–		74	96	–	–	274	0

Bowling

	M	Balls	Runs	Wkts	BB	Avge	RpO	S/R	5i	10m
Tests *to 11.9.06*	84	54	40	0	–	–	4.44	–	0	0
ODIs *to 11.9.06*	119	6	18	0	–	–	18.00	–	0	0
First-class *to 11.9.06*	272	1097	671	17	3–10	39.47	3.67	64.52	0	0

RYAN HIGGINS

Full name **Ryan Shaun Higgins**
Born **March 24, 1988, Harare**
Teams **Manicaland**
Style **Right-hand bat, legspinner**
Test debut **No Tests yet**
ODI debut **Zimbabwe v Kenya at Bulawayo 2005-06**

THE PROFILE Ryan Higgins is a capable middle-order batsman and a useful legspinner who produced some promising performances at the Under-19 World Cup in Sri Lanka early in 2006. He rescued Zimbabwe against Nepal with a battling 74 and two important wickets, while his bowling was also a key factor in the satisfying win over England, when he dismissed the opposing captain Moeen Ali and his predecessor Varun Chopra. Higgins was thrust into the full Zimbabwe squad for the one-day series against Kenya which followed immediately, with just one first-class match behind him. He bowled well despite his inexperience, even being used during the powerplays at times. He removed Steve Tikolo for 98 on his debut, then took 4 for 21 in his third match as Kenya were shot out for 122. He embarked on a steep learning curve in the West Indies, where he was unable to find much turn, but nonetheless showed a good attitude – and claimed the notable scalps of Ramnaresh Sarwan and Brian Lara in the sixth match at Port-of-Spain, before adding Shivnarine Chanderpaul and Dwayne Bravo in the next game. He is an attacking legspinner, although he does not give the ball a real rip, and he is developing a googly. Higgins also has the potential to contribute with the bat, where he has the virtue of playing straight. He was plucked out of school to begin his international career, and is still studying for his A-levels.

THE FACTS Higgins made his first-class debut – his only first-class match by September 2006 – a month after his 17th birthday, for Manicaland against Midlands at Kwekwe: he made a duck, but did take three wickets, including those of Doug Marillier and Prosper Utseya ... On his ODI debut he dismissed Kenya's Steve Tikolo for 98 ...

THE FIGURES

Batting and fielding

	M	Inns	NO	Runs	HS	Avge	S/R	100	50	4s	6s	Ct	St
Tests to 11.9.06	0	–	–	–	–	–	–	–	–	–	–	–	–
ODIs to 11.9.06	10	7	1	8	5	1.33	15.38	0	0	0	0	5	0
First-class to 11.9.06	1	1	0	0	0	0.00	0.00	0	0	0	0	1	0

Bowling

	M	Balls	Runs	Wkts	BB	Avge	RpO	S/R	5i	10m
Tests to 11.9.06	0	–	–	–	–	–	–	–	–	–
ODIs to 11.9.06	10	517	351	13	4–21	27.00	4.07	39.76	0	0
First-class to 11.9.06	1	276	166	3	2–99	55.33	3.60	92.00	0	0

WAVELL HINDS

Full name	**Wavell Wayne Hinds**
Born	**September 7, 1976, Kingston, Jamaica**
Teams	**Jamaica**
Style	**Left-hand bat, right-arm medium-pacer**
Test debut	**West Indies v Zimbabwe at Port-of-Spain 1999-2000**
ODI debut	**West Indies v India at Singapore 1999-2000**

THE PROFILE A loose-limbed left-hander with fast hands but slow feet, Wavell Hinds incinerated Pakistan's attack at Bridgetown in only his fourth Test in May 2000: his 165 and 52 included 33 boundaries. A fallow period followed, thanks partly to some harsh umpiring decisions in England, but the real problem was that lazy front foot. As opposition coaches caught on, edged drives and lbws abounded. It was therefore a surprise when Hinds was promoted to open for the last Test in Australia in 2000-01, and even more of a shock when he and Sherwin Campbell shared opening stands of 147 and 98. Then Chris Gayle came along, and that – along with West Indies' irritating tendency to chop and change after every series – meant that Hinds was dropped. But after three different opening combinations were tried during the one-dayers in England in 2004, Hinds was recalled for the Champions Trophy, to add experience and much-needed stability. He failed with the bat, but his bowling was effective in the semi-final and the final. He hammered 213 off South Africa on a featherbed at Georgetown early in 2005, sharing a huge stand with Shivnarine Chanderpaul, but in six subsequent matches his highest score was only 63, and – not helped by breaking a finger in Australia in 2005-06 – he lost his Test place again, although his handy medium-pacers ensure he is always in the one-day frame. Wavell is no relation of Ryan Hinds of Barbados, who has also played for West Indies.

THE FACTS Hinds's highest score of 213 against South Africa at Georgetown in 2004-05 included 146 in boundaries: he put on 284 with Shivnarine Chanderpaul, who also passed 200 for the first time in Tests ... Hinds made his first-class debut for Jamaica against Lancashire, who made a pre-season tour in April 1996 ... Five of his 17 first-class centuries have come against Indian teams, including one in Tests ... Hinds broke a finger fielding on the first day of West Indies' 2005-06 tour of Australia ...

THE FIGURES
Batting and fielding

	M	Inns	NO	Runs	HS	Avge	S/R	100	50	4s	6s	Ct	St
Tests *to 11.9.06*	45	80	1	2608	213	33.01	47.77	5	14	368	16	32	0
ODIs *to 11.9.06*	105	101	9	2795	127*	30.38	67.88	5	14	255	49	28	0
First-class *to 11.9.06*	117	201	6	6681	213	34.26	–	17	30	–	–	60	0

Bowling

	M	Balls	Runs	Wkts	BB	Avge	RpO	S/R	5i	10m
Tests *to 11.9.06*	45	1123	590	16	3–79	36.87	3.15	70.18	0	0
ODIs *to 11.9.06*	105	909	796	28	3–24	28.42	5.25	32.46	0	0
First-class *to 11.9.06*	117	2218	1078	28	3–9	38.50	2.91	79.21	0	0

BRAD HODGE

Full name	**Bradley John Hodge**
Born	**December 29, 1974, Sandringham, Victoria**
Teams	**Victoria, Lancashire**
Style	**Right-hand bat, occasional offspinner**
Test debut	**Australia v West Indies at Hobart 2005-06**
ODI debut	**Australia v New Zealand at Auckland 2005-06**

AUSTRALIA

THE PROFILE Brad Hodge was the unluckiest casualty of Australia's 2005-06 season of batting change. Picked for his first Test in November after being the reserve on three tours, he started with a fluent 60, and soon had 409 runs at the envious average of 58.42. That included a sumptuous 203 against South Africa at Perth. But two Tests later Hodge, a small right-hander who is more quiet and laid-back than his boyhood hero Dean Jones, was dropped amid whispers of a technical flaw against fast bowling, not helped by a brief drought in the Pura Cup. He missed the South African tour, as the selectors returned to Damien Martyn and Michael Clarke. Hodge picked himself up with a century in the Pura final loss to Queensland, but was again overlooked for the Bangladesh series and signed instead for Lancashire, his third English county. A regular and consistent domestic performer, he first played for Victoria in 1993-94 at 18, and threatened 1000 runs as he settled quickly at No. 4. The following years were more difficult, but he returned from dips in form a more complete player, with a classical technique and the ability to direct shots to all parts. Rewarded with his first central contract in 2004, Hodge toured India that year. He was considered for the opening Test, but missed the place grabbed spectacularly by Clarke. And now Hodge is again behind Clarke in the pecking order, although he remains in sight of resuming his short – and stunning – international career.

THE FACTS Hodge was the fifth Australian to turn his maiden Test century into a double, following Bob Simpson (who made 311), Sid Barnes, Syd Gregory and Hodge's boyhood idol Dean Jones: Jason Gillespie later joined their ranks ... In 2003 Hodge made 302 not out against Nottinghamshire, the highest score in Leicestershire's history: the following year he was the Man of the Match as Leicestershire won the Twenty20 Cup final ...

THE FIGURES

Batting and fielding

	M	Inns	NO	Runs	HS	Avge	S/R	100	50	4s	6s	Ct	St
Tests to 11.9.06	5	9	2	409	203*	58.42	51.77	1	1	47	0	9	0
ODIs to 11.9.06	5	5	0	79	59	15.80	58.08	0	1	9	0	1	0
First-class to 11.9.06	184	324	31	13970	302*	47.67	–	43	50	–	–	108	0

Bowling

	M	Balls	Runs	Wkts	BB	Avge	RpO	S/R	5i	10m
Tests to 11.9.06	5	12	8	0	–	–	4.00	–	0	0
ODIs to 11.9.06	5	18	16	0	–	–	5.33	–	0	0
First-class to 11.9.06	184	4857	2737	68	4–17	40.25	3.38	71.42	0	0

BRAD HOGG

Full name	**George Bradley Hogg**
Born	**February 6, 1971, Narrogin, Western Australia**
Teams	**Western Australia**
Style	**Left-hand bat, slow left-arm unorthodox spinner**
Test debut	**Australia v India at Delhi 1996-97**
ODI debut	**Australia v Zimbabwe at Colombo 1996-97**

THE PROFILE With his zooming flipper and hard-to-pick wrong'un, Brad Hogg is Australia's best chinaman bowler since Chuck Fleetwood-Smith in the 1930s. He announced himself with a stupendous flipper in the 2003 World Cup: Andy Flower leapt back, waited for the away-spin and then slumped, bamboozled, as the ball fizzed straight through onto his stumps. Until then, Hogg's progress had been anything but straightforward. Like Stuart MacGill, he spent years in Shane Warne's shadow. He went to that World Cup hoping to pick Warne's brains, and unexpectedly ended up filling his boots after Warne's drugs ban. Hogg's initial Test opportunity, at Delhi way back in October 1996, also came as Warne's stand-in. He took only one wicket – the story goes that he had long waited to hear Ian Healy growl "Bowled, Hoggy" from behind the stumps, but he performed so badly that the call never came. Seven years in the wilderness followed. Hogg began as a solid left-hand batsman, before flirting with chinamen in the nets. His batting has fallen away, although he did make a Pura Cup century in 2004-05, but his jack-in-a-box fielding makes up for it. Hogg used to be a postman – "I do my round like a Formula One driver," he once bragged – and has the ever-present smile of a postie who's never known yappy dogs or rainy days. He roared past 100 one-day wickets in Bangladesh early in 2006, and still makes important and energetic contributions. He is a youthful 35, but his days as an international are shortening – and in 2005-06 he was WA's second spin option behind Beau Casson.

THE FACTS There were seven years – and 78 matches – between Hogg's first and second Tests, an Australian record: Alan Hurst (30 matches) had the previous-longest wait for a second cap ... Hogg averages 14.38 with the ball in ODIs against Bangladesh, and 22.46 v England – but 80.66 v India ... He has taken more wickets in ODIs than any other Australian left-arm bowler, with a best of 5 for 32 v West Indies at Melbourne in January 2005 ... Hogg played county cricket for Warwickshire in 2004, making his highest score of 158 for them against Surrey at Edgbaston ...

THE FIGURES
Batting and fielding

	M	Inns	NO	Runs	HS	Avge	S/R	100	50	4s	6s	Ct	St
Tests *to 11.9.06*	4	5	1	38	17*	9.50	27.94	0	0	2	0	0	0
ODIs *to 11.9.06*	85	49	22	560	71*	20.74	78.21	0	2	29	1	25	0
First-class *to 11.9.06*	89	130	27	3571	158	34.66	–		4	24	–	–	50	0

Bowling

	M	Balls	Runs	Wkts	BB	Avge	RpO	S/R	5i	10m
Tests *to 11.9.06*	4	774	452	9	2–40	50.22	3.50	86.00	0	0
ODIs *to 11.9.06*	85	3960	2968	107	5–32	27.73	4.49	37.00	2	0
First-class *to 11.9.06*	89	11268	6145	145	6–44	42.37	3.27	77.71	5	0

MATTHEW HOGGARD

Full name	**Matthew James Hoggard**
Born	**December 31, 1976, Leeds, Yorkshire**
Teams	**Yorkshire**
Style	**Right-hand bat, right-arm fast-medium bowler**
Test debut	**England v West Indies at Lord's 2000**
ODI debut	**England v Zimbabwe at Harare 2001-02**

THE PROFILE Big and bustling, with the sort of energy coaches kill for, Matthew Hoggard shapes the ball away at pace and is surprisingly slippery off the pitch, although he can look innocuous when the ball refuses to move. Hoggard was one of Yorkshire's bright young things in the late '90s, but it was under Duncan Fletcher and Nasser Hussain that he grew into a senior bowler in the England quartet that swept all before them in 2004. His long apprenticeship was occasionally tortuous: after just two Tests, Hoggard was chosen to lead the attack in 2001-02 in India – he charged in obediently, and capped his winter with 7 for 63 against New Zealand at Christchurch. He did well at home in 2002, but suffered later Down Under, where his arcing inswing was meat and drink to Australia's left-handers, especially Matthew Hayden. To his credit, Hoggard retreated to the Adelaide Academy, and returned with a snappier run-up to contribute to the fifth-Test win at Sydney. Flashier colleagues consistently stole the limelight, but Hoggard's moments in the sun were worth waiting for: a brilliant hat-trick in Barbados in April 2004, then a phenomenal 12-wicket haul at Johannesburg the following winter, setting up a series-clinching 2–1 lead. The following summer, he did well after a quiet start as the Ashes were recaptured: satisfyingly, he nailed his old nemesis Hayden three times, including a first-baller at Edgbaston. Hoggard's batting is limited, but he has developed into a reliable blocker and an effective nightwatchman.

THE FACTS Hoggard became the third Englishman to take a Test hat-trick against West Indies, following Peter Loader (1957) and Dominic Cork (1995), at Bridgetown in March 2004 ... Rather surprisingly for a swing bowler he has a better bowling average overseas (28.30) than in England (31.06) ... Hoggard took 7 for 61 against South Africa at Johannesburg in 2003-04, and 12 for 205 in the match – the best return by an England bowler at the New Wanderers ground ... 76 (34%) of his Test wickets have been left-handers ... Hoggard rarely plays in ODIs now, but he did take 5 for 49 against Zimbabwe at Harare in October 2001 ...

THE FIGURES

Batting and fielding

	M	Inns	NO	Runs	HS	Avge	S/R	100	50	4s	6s	Ct	St
Tests to 11.9.06	58	79	26	414	38	7.81	22.18	0	0	36	0	23	0
ODIs to 11.9.06	26	6	2	17	7	4.25	56.66	0	0	0	0	5	0
First-class to 11.9.06	142	184	58	1112	89*	8.82	–	0	2	–	–	43	0

Bowling

	M	Balls	Runs	Wkts	BB	Avge	RpO	S/R	5i	10m
Tests to 11.9.06	58	12168	6607	222	7–61	29.76	3.25	54.81	6	1
ODIs to 11.9.06	26	1306	1152	32	5–49	36.00	5.29	40.81	1	0
First-class to 11.9.06	142	26916	13803	504	7–49	27.38	3.07	53.40	15	1

JAMIE HOW

NEW ZEALAND

Full name	**Jamie Michael How**
Born	**May 19, 1981, New Plymouth, Taranaki**
Teams	**Central Districts**
Style	**Right-hand bat, right-arm medium-pacer/offspinner**
Test debut	**New Zealand v West Indies at Auckland 2005-06**
ODI debut	**New Zealand v Sri Lanka at Queenstown 2005-06**

THE PROFILE Jamie How stepped up to the full New Zealand side in 2004-05 after some solid performances for Central Districts – 704, 682 and 592 runs in the three seasons from 2002-03. A well-organised opener, more of an accumulator than a dasher, How has a penchant for big scores: after taking a while to find his first-class feet, he scored 163 not out and 158 in consecutive innings in March 2003, against Northern Districts and Canterbury, and started the following season with 169 against Otago. Picked for his one-day debut against Sri Lanka at Queenstown on New Year's Eve, 2005, How ensured his celebrations would go well with a sparky 58, including eight fours and a six, as New Zealand won easily. His first encounter with West Indies resulted in 66 in an opening stand of 136 with Nathan Astle, but his other four one-day innings brought him only 17 runs. He played all three Tests against West Indies, and one in South Africa in May 2006 as a late replacement for the injured Peter Fulton. The rampant Dale Steyn removed him cheaply in both innings in that Test at Johannesburg, and 37 in his first match, against the Windies at Auckland, remains How's best in Tests so far. He is keen to develop his bowling, and although a knee injury has held him back recently, he wants to pick national coach John Bracewell's brains about offspin.

THE FACTS How's 58 against Sri Lanka at Queenstown in December 2005 was the highest score by a New Zealand opener on ODI debut ... He played in the 1999-2000 Under-19 World Cup in Sri Lanka, when his captain was James Franklin and the wicketkeeper was Brendon McCullum ... How also played soccer for New Zealand's youth sides, but eventually chose cricket ...

THE FIGURES
Batting and fielding

	M	Inns	NO	Runs	HS	Avge	S/R	100	50	4s	6s	Ct	St
Tests to 11.9.06	4	6	1	61	37	12.19	44.52	0	0	7	0	6	0
ODIs to 11.9.06	6	5	0	141	66	28.19	65.58	0	2	20	1	2	0
First-class to 11.9.06	51	84	6	2599	169	33.32	–	7	12	–	–	60	0

Bowling

	M	Balls	Runs	Wkts	BB	Avge	RpO	S/R	5i	10m
Tests to 11.9.06	4	–	–	–	–	–	–	–	–	–
ODIs to 11.9.06	6	0	–	–	–	–	–	–	–	–
First-class to 11.9.06	51	1362	787	16	3–55	49.18	3.46	85.12	0	0

MICHAEL HUSSEY

AUSTRALIA

Full name	**Michael Edward Killeen Hussey**
Born	**May 27, 1975, Morley, Western Australia**
Teams	**Western Australia**
Style	**Left-hand bat, occasional right-arm medium-pacer**
Test debut	**Australia v West Indies at Brisbane 2005-06**
ODI debut	**Australia v India at Perth 2003-04**

THE PROFILE English fans couldn't understand why Australia took so long to recognise Michael Hussey's claims. Bradmanesque in county cricket, he was less prolific in Australia, and seemed destined to remain unfulfilled unless the Langer-Hayden-Ponting top-order triumvirate cracked. Finally, late in 2005 Langer's fractured rib gave Hussey his break after 15,313 first-class runs, a record for an Australian before wearing baggy green. His first Test was a disappointment, but he relaxed for his second and made an attractive century. Three more hundreds followed, including a memorable 122 against South Africa at the MCG, when he and Glenn McGrath added 107 for the last wicket, and he currently averages in the mid-seventies in both Tests and ODIs. Like Langer and Graeme Wood, predecessors as left-hand Western Australian openers, Hussey has a tidy, compact style. Skilled off front foot and back, he is attractive to watch once set, which he was regularly at Northamptonshire, Gloucestershire and Durham. Only the third man to make three County Championship triple-centuries, he averaged 79, 72 and 89 in successive seasons from 2001, dipped to 36 in 2004, but soared back to 76 in 2005. At home he was less spectacular: 30 in 2000-01, rising to 55 in 2004-05. Reinventing himself in one-day cricket as an agile fielder and innovative batsman with cool head and loose wrists, once he made the national side Hussey underlined his credentials with some more Bradmanesque figures, and has now supplanted Michael Bevan as the Aussies' one-day "finisher".

THE FACTS Hussey scored 229 runs in ODIs before he was dismissed, and had an average of 100.22 after 32 matches ... He took only 166 days to reach 1000 runs in Tests, beating the 228-day record established by England's Andrew Strauss in 2005 ... Hussey's 331 not out against Somerset at Taunton in 2003 is the highest individual score for Northamptonshire ... He has had six innings in ODIs in New Zealand and has amassed 207 runs without being dismissed ...

THE FIGURES

Batting and fielding

	M	Inns	NO	Runs	HS	Avge	S/R	100	50	4s	6s	Ct	St
Tests to 11.9.06	11	19	4	1139	182	75.93	53.57	4	4	136	9	3	0
ODIs to 11.9.06	40	31	16	1156	88*	77.06	97.47	0	9	101	20	21	0
First-class to 11.9.06	187	336	31	16452	331*	53.94	–	43	71	–	–	203	0

Bowling

	M	Balls	Runs	Wkts	BB	Avge	RpO	S/R	5i	10m
Tests to 11.9.06	11	24	18	0	–	–	4.50	–	0	0
ODIs to 11.9.06	40	180	155	2	1–22	77.50	5.16	90.00	0	0
First-class to 11.9.06	187	1392	732	19	3–34	38.52	3.15	73.26	0	0

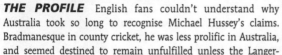

IFTIKHAR ANJUM

Full name	**Rao Iftikhar Anjum**
Born	**December 1, 1980, Khanewal, Punjab**
Teams	**Islamabad, Zarai Taraqiati Bank**
Style	**Right-hand bat, right-arm fast-medium bowler**
Test debut	**Pakistan v Sri Lanka at Kandy 2005-06**
ODI debut	**Pakistan v Zimbabwe at Multan 2004-05**

THE PROFILE With a high-arm action modelled on Glenn McGrath's, Iftikhar Anjum is another addition to Pakistan's seemingly endless production line of pace bowlers. Iftikhar, however, is more Aqib Javed than Wasim Akram or Waqar Younis, and his outswinger is considered by many to be just as lethal as Aqib's. He can bowl reverse-swing – a prerequisite for Pakistani bowlers – when the ball gets a bit rougher, and has good control over his yorkers. Iftikhar has performed consistently well on the domestic circuit, taking almost 300 wickets on Pakistan's generally lifeless pitches, including 73 in 2000-01, his first full season. Two years later, some stellar performances propelled him towards the national side: Iftikhar captained the Zarai Taraqiati Bank to victory in the Patron's Trophy final over WAPDA at Karachi, taking 7 for 85 in the first innings and ending with ten in the match. Not surprisingly, he was included in Pakistan's one-day squad for the series against India early in 2004, before making his debut in the Paktel Cup that September. He has since been a handy back-up bowler in one-dayers, although he rarely plays when everyone is fit. Pakistan's long injury list meant he won his first Test cap in Sri Lanka in April 2006: he was expensive at Kandy, and didn't take a wicket as Pakistan won inside three days. That probably led to his initial exclusion from the England tour in 2006, although he was called up later as injuries struck the squad again.

THE FACTS Iftikhar Anjum's best bowling figures are 7 for 59, for Zarai Taraqiati Bank against WAPDA at Hyderabad in February 2005 ... Two years previously he took 7 for 85 (10 for 116 in the match) against the same opposition in the Patron's Trophy final at Karachi ... Iftikhar took 7 for 94 – after a career-best innings of 78 – for Zarai Taraqiati Bank against Karachi Port Trust at Peshawar in December 2003 ...

THE FIGURES
Batting and fielding

	M	Inns	NO	Runs	HS	Avge	S/R	100	50	4s	6s	Ct	St
Tests to 11.9.06	1	1	1	9	9	–	23.07	0	0	2	0	0	0
ODIs to 11.9.06	19	10	9	73	19*	73.00	59.34	0	0	3	0	5	0
First-class to 11.9.06	72	114	26	1498	78	17.02	–	0	4	–	–	43	0

Bowling

	M	Balls	Runs	Wkts	BB	Avge	RpO	S/R	5i	10m
Tests to 11.9.06	1	84	62	0	–	–	4.42	–	0	0
ODIs to 11.9.06	19	888	675	13	2–13	51.92	4.56	68.30	0	0
First-class to 11.9.06	72	13286	7152	300	7–59	23.84	3.22	44.28	20	0

IMRAN FARHAT

Full name	**Imran Farhat**
Born	**May 20, 1982, Lahore, Punjab**
Teams	**Lahore, Habib Bank**
Style	**Left-hand bat, legspinner**
Test debut	**Pakistan v New Zealand at Auckland 2000-01**
ODI debut	**Pakistan v New Zealand at Auckland 2000-01**

THE PROFILE A gifted young left-hander who briefly threatened to solve Pakistan's perennial opening conundrum, Imran Farhat first made the Test side at 18, after success with the Under-19 and A teams. He bludgeons rather than times his runs, and was rather too cavalier in his early Test appearances: he was promptly dumped after touring New Zealand early in 2001, despite making 63 on his debut at Auckland. Back in domestic cricket, he tightened his game, tempering his shots with a better defensive technique, and returned a better batsman. Back in the Test side in 2003-04, he scored freely at home against South Africa and New Zealand. He notched his first centuries in Tests and ODIs, then went on to score a vital 101 in Pakistan's victory against India in the Lahore Test. He also shared four successive century opening stands – a record – in a clean sweep of the one-dayers against New Zealand. But he fell away after that, and – not helped by the emergence of another left-hand opener, Salman Butt – lost his place following mediocre displays against Sri Lanka and Australia. Butt was the only specialist opener named to play England at home at the end of 2005, but Farhat returned for the Sri Lankan tour that followed, and scored well in both Tests, ensuring that he went to England in 2006. There, he was unlucky enough to break a finger taking a sharp catch off Kevin Pietersen in the gully in the second Test, and missed the rest of the tour.

THE FACTS Imran Farhat's highest score is 242, for Habib Bank against Pakistan International Airlines in Karachi in December 2005: he shared a stand of 361 with Hasan Raza (178) ... He has made four other double-centuries, including one for Biman Airlines in Bangladesh ... Farhat scored 68, 91, 82 and 107 in successive ODIs against New Zealand at home in 2003-04, sharing opening stands of 115, 142, 134 and 197 with Yasir Hameed ... His brother, Humayun Farhat, is a wicketkeeper who played one Test, alongside Imran, against New Zealand at Hamilton in March 2001 ...

THE FIGURES
Batting and fielding

	M	Inns	NO	Runs	HS	Avge	S/R	100	50	4s	6s	Ct	St
Tests *to 11.9.06*	21	39	0	1287	128	33.00	53.69	2	8	204	1	28	0
ODIs *to 11.9.06*	27	27	1	823	107	31.65	71.25	1	4	92	10	9	0
First-class *to 11.9.06*	102	174	11	6860	242	42.08	–	15	29	–	–	102	0

Bowling

	M	Balls	Runs	Wkts	BB	Avge	RpO	S/R	5i	10m
Tests *to 11.9.06*	21	247	192	3	2–69	64.00	4.66	82.33	0	0
ODIs *to 11.9.06*	27	86	89	5	3–10	17.80	6.20	17.20	0	0
First-class *to 11.9.06*	102	4136	2322	82	7–31	28.31	3.36	50.43	2	0

INZAMAM-UL-HAQ

PAKISTAN

Full name	**Inzamam-ul-Haq**
Born	**March 3, 1970, Multan, Punjab**
Teams	**Multan**
Style	**Right-hand bat, occasional slow left-armer**
Test debut	**Pakistan v England at Birmingham 1992**
ODI debut	**Pakistan v West Indies at Lahore 1991-92**

THE PROFILE Inzamam-ul-Haq is a symbiosis of strength and subtlety. Power is no surprise, but sublime touch is remarkable for one of his bulk. He loathes exercise, and often looks a passenger in the field, but with bat in hand he is suddenly alive – strong off his legs, and unleashing ferocious pulls and drives. He sometimes plays across his front pad early on, but uses his feet well to spin. His hapless running is legendary, and most dangerous for his partners. Inzamam belted 329 against New Zealand at a boiling Lahore in May 2002, but struggled afterwards, making only 16 runs in the 2003 World Cup. He was briefly dropped, but roared back with a magnificent century to clinch a one-wicket victory over Bangladesh at Multan, his home town. He was rewarded with the captaincy, but faced criticism after losing at home to India. But he took a team thin on bowling to India early in 2005, and levelled the series with a rousing 184 in the final Test, his 100th. Since then, he has gone from strength to strength as captain – and premier batsman. A magnificent 2005 ended with victory over Ashes-winning England in arguably Inzamam's best series: he never failed to reach 50, made twin centuries for the first time, and passed Javed Miandad as Pakistan's leading century-maker – and he had never looked more of a leader. He slipped a little in England in 2006, losing the series then becoming embroiled in the ball-tampering row at The Oval, writing an unwanted note in history as the first captain to forfeit a Test match.

THE FACTS Inzamam-ul-Haq made 329 against New Zealand at Lahore in May 2002: the only higher score for Pakistan in Tests is Hanif Mohammad's 337 against West Indies at Bridgetown in 1957-58 ... He was the fifth man to score a century in his 100th Test, following Colin Cowdrey, Javed Miandad, Gordon Greenidge and Alec Stewart (Ricky Ponting later did it too) ... Inzamam averages 66.18 in Tests against New Zealand, but only 31.40 against Australia ... His record includes one Test for the World XI, and three ODIs for the Asia XI ...

THE FIGURES
Batting and fielding

	M	Inns	NO	Runs	HS	Avge	S/R	100	50	4s	6s	Ct	St
Tests to 11.9.06	1131	187	20	8498	329	50.88	54.26	25	44	1073	47	79	0
ODIs to 11.9.06	367	341	51	11549	137*	39.82	74.63	10	83	–	–	106	0
First-class to 11.9.06	234	374	55	16337	329	51.21	–	45	84	–	–	165	0

Bowling

	M	Balls	Runs	Wkts	BB	Avge	RpO	S/R	5i	10m
Tests to 11.9.06	113	9	8	0	–	–	5.33	–	0	0
ODIs to 11.9.06	367	58	64	3	1–0	21.33	6.62	19.33	0	0
First-class to 11.9.06	234	2704	1295	38	5–80	34.07	2.87	71.15	2	0

ANTHONY IRELAND

Full name	**Anthony John Ireland**
Born	**August 30, 1984, Masvingo**
Teams	**Midlands**
Style	**Right-hand bat, right-arm fast-medium bowler**
Test debut	**No Tests yet**
ODI debut	**Zimbabwe v New Zealand at Bulawayo 2005-06**

THE PROFILE Anthony Ireland is a tall allrounder from the Midlands area of Zimbabwe, a promising seam bowler who is also a useful batsman capable of playing a telling aggressive innings. He was underestimated at times, and decided to improve his game in club cricket in England (he returned there in 2006, to play for the Bristol club Thornbury). After the player rebellion of 2004, he was given more opportunities to perform in domestic cricket, and was duly promoted to the national squad the following year. He started his one-day career by dismissing Stephen Fleming and Chris Cairns but, like most of his team-mates, was then mauled by Lou Vincent. He took three more in his next game – Ganguly, Dhoni and Agarkar – and added six wickets in the first three matches of the series against Kenya early in 2006. But Ireland struggled on his first senior tour, to the West Indies in April 2006, not helped by breaking his left hand in practice at the start of the trip. When he was fit again, he struggled with his length, tending to bowl too short – which proved fatal against batsmen as adept with the pull as most West Indians are. But he is a hard-working bowler with a good attitude, and keeps himself very fit. He's also a good striker of the ball who has the potential to develop into an allrounder.

THE FACTS Ireland's two wickets on his ODI debut, at Bulawayo in August 2005, was rather overshadowed by Lou Vincent's 172 (a national record) as New Zealand ran up an impregnable 397 for 5 ... He dismissed Stephen Fleming in that match, and the next one he played against NZ ... Ireland took 4 for 16 for Zimbabwe A against Kenya in a one-day match in October 2005 ... He played for Gloucestershire's 2nd XI in 2006 before returning home to play against Bangladesh ...

THE FIGURES
Batting and fielding

	M	Inns	NO	Runs	HS	Avge	S/R	100	50	4s	6s	Ct	St
Tests to 11.9.06	0	–	–	–	–	–	–	–	–	–	–	–	–
ODIs to 11.9.06	14	6	3	13	8*	4.33	40.62	0	0	1	0	1	0
First-class to 11.9.06	8	14	2	39	15	3.25	29.54	0	0	–	–	2	0

Bowling

	M	Balls	Runs	Wkts	BB	Avge	RpO	S/R	5i	10m
Tests to 11.9.06	0	–	–	–	–	–	–	–	–	–
ODIs to 11.9.06	14	714	606	21	3–41	28.85	5.09	34.00	0	0
First-class to 11.9.06	8	903	571	16	4–87	35.68	3.79	56.43	0	0

WASIM JAFFER

INDIA

Full name	**Wasim Jaffer**
Born	**Feb 16, 1978, Bombay (now Mumbai), Maharashtra**
Teams	**Mumbai**
Style	**Right-hand batsman, occasional offspinner**
Test debut	**India v South Africa at Mumbai 1999-2000**
ODI debut	**No ODIs yet**

THE PROFILE A triple-century in only his second first-class game found Wasim Jaffer anointed as the great new hope of Mumbai cricket. He is a slightly built opening batsman with the style and panache of the young Mohammad Azharuddin, and much was expected of him on his Test debut in February 2000. But Allan Donald and Shaun Pollock proved too hot to handle – even though he showed glimpses of a steely and unflappable temperament – and his international career was put on hold. He continued to pile on the runs in domestic cricket, and a string of big scores in 2001-02 won him a place on the tour of the West Indies. Once there, he stroked his way to two elegant half-centuries, though a worrying tendency to give it away when well set resulted in him losing his place at the top of the order. He reminded the selectors of his quality with some superb batting for the A team in England in 2003, but spent three years in the domestic wilderness before being recalled to the squad in 2005-06. He made most of his first chance on return, against England at Nagpur in March 2006, following up a forthright 81 with his maiden Test hundred. He added 212 against West Indies in Antigua in June, and continued to score well as Virender Sehwag's opening partner in the Tests in the Caribbean, doing enough to keep Gautam Gambhir on the sidelines.

THE FACTS Jaffer scored 314 not out in only his second first-class match, for Mumbai against Saurashtra at Rajkot in November 1996: he shared an opening stand of 459 with Sulakshan Kulkarni (239) ... Jaffer made two more double-centuries, including 218 for India A against Warwickshire at Edgbaston in 2003, before making 212 in the first Test against West Indies at St John's in June 2006 ... He averages 44.91 in the second innings of Tests, against 24.57 in the first ...

THE FIGURES
Batting and fielding

	M	Inns	NO	Runs	HS	Avge	S/R	100	50	4s	6s	Ct	St
Tests *to 11.9.06*	14	26	0	883	212	33.96	45.82	2	6	121	1	15	0
ODIs *to 11.9.06*	0	–	–	–	–	–	–	–	–	–	–	–	–
First-class *to 11.9.06*	125	206	22	9482	314*	51.53	–	26	45	–	–	146	0

Bowling

	M	Balls	Runs	Wkts	BB	Avge	RpO	S/R	5i	10m
Tests *to 11.9.06*	14	66	18	2	2–18	9.00	1.63	33.00	0	0
ODIs *to 11.9.06*	0	–	–	–	–	–	–	–	–	–
First-class *to 11.9.06*	125	138	74	2	2–18	37.00	3.21	69.00	0	0

PHIL JAQUES

AUSTRALIA

Full name	**Philip Anthony Jaques**
Born	**May 3, 1979, Wollongong, New South Wales**
Teams	**New South Wales, Worcestershire**
Style	**Left-hand bat, occasional left-arm spinner**
Test debut	**Australia v South Africa at Melbourne 2005-06**
ODI debut	**Australia v South Africa at Melbourne 2005-06**

THE PROFILE   Phil Jaques was on holiday when the Test call finally came. It meant an early-career gamble had paid off: a British passport-holder, Jaques had been the subject of a national tug-of-war in 2003. He had scored 1409 runs for Northampton-shire, but refused to commit to England as "My heart says Australia". After that Jaques maintained such a consistent standard with New South Wales and Yorkshire that when Justin Langer was ruled out of the Boxing Day Test against South Africa in December 2005 Trevor Hohns admitted that he "virtually demanded selection". His Test debut was quiet – he walked after squirting Shaun Pollock to short leg for 2, and added 28 in the second innings – but he had been earmarked as a long-term prospect. Another opportunity came in Bangladesh, and he produced a capable 66. With an attacking mindset and a home-made left-handed technique, Jaques has shown the ability to score big runs on English greentops and hard-baked tracks in Australia and Pakistan, where he toured with Australia A in 2005. Another injury – to Simon Katich this time – led to a one-day call-up during the 2005-06 VB Series. He made a stunning impact with 94, but when Katich returned he was harshly dropped, amid suggestions that his fielding was substandard. Jaques had to introduce himself to Ricky Ponting before his debut, but his reputation had already excited the previous captain: "Australia is lucky to have a player like him coming through," said Steve Waugh. "He is the prototype for young players."

THE FACTS   Jaques's 94 against South Africa in Melbourne in January 2006 was the highest by any player making his ODI debut for Australia (beating Kepler Wessels's 79 in 1982-83), and the fifth-highest for all countries, behind four century-makers ... His second ODI was less memorable: out fourth ball for 0 as South Africa bowled Australia out for 93 ... Jaques was the first batsman to score double-centuries for and against Yorkshire, following 222 for Northamptonshire in 2003 with 243 for Yorkshire against Hampshire the following year ... He made 244 and 202 in successive matches for Worcestershire in 2006 ...

THE FIGURES

Batting and fielding

	M	Inns	NO	Runs	HS	Avge	S/R	100	50	4s	6s	Ct	St
Tests *to 11.9.06*	2	3	0	96	66	32.00	62.33	0	1	11	1	1	0
ODIs *to 11.9.06*	2	2	0	94	94	47.00	81.03	0	1	14	0	0	0
First-class *to 11.9.06*	86	151	8	8357	244	58.44	–	24	40	–	–	72	0

Bowling

	M	Balls	Runs	Wkts	BB	Avge	RpO	S/R	5i	10m
Tests *to 11.9.06*	2	0	–	–	–	–	–	–	–	–
ODIs *to 11.9.06*	2	0	–	–	–	–	–	–	–	–
First-class *to 11.9.06*	86	68	87	0	–	–	7.67	–	0	0

JAVED OMAR

BANGLADESH

Full name	**Mohammad Javed Omar Belim**
Born	**November 25, 1976, Dhaka**
Teams	**Dhaka**
Style	**Right-hand batsman, occasional legspinner**
Test debut	**Bangladesh v Zimbabwe at Bulawayo 2000-01**
ODI debut	**Bangladesh v India at Sharjah 1994-95**

THE PROFILE With a priceless ability to occupy the crease, Javed Omar Belim has developed into the closest thing to a Test-class opener that Bangladesh have produced in their torrid early years of senior international cricket. A glut of one-day internationals early in his career did not help his development, but all complaints that he scores his runs too slowly were offset by a historic Test debut n April 2001, when he carried his bat for 85 not out, only the third player in history to achieve this in his first match. "Gulla" underlined his limpet-like qualities later the same year with a painstaking 80, compiled over 100 overs, in his sixth Test, against Zimbabwe at Chittagong. His maiden international hundred, against Pakistan at Peshawar in August 2003, gave Bangladesh a first-innings lead for the first time and showed the first glimpse of a new steelier attitude from his side. He has chalked up a half-century of one-day caps, with a highest score of 85 not out against Sri Lanka back in the pre-Test days of 2000, but it is in the five-day arena that his obduracy is best received, and Omar was the only man to come to terms with England's early-season conditions on a traumatic tour in 2005. He reached double figures in all four innings of the Test series, including a brave 71 at the final attempt at Chester-le-Street. He remained in the Test frame, although big scores were elusive.

THE FACTS Javed Omar carried his bat for 85 on his Test debut, against Zimbabwe at Bulawayo in 2000-01: he was the first man to do this on debut since 1898-99, when Pelham Warner did it for England (Dr John Barrett also achieved the feat for Australia in 1890) ... He averages 40.18 in Tests against Zimbabwe, but his next-best is 25.66 against South Africa ... Omar's highest first-class score is 167, against the British Universities at Cambridge on the 2005 tour of England ... He made 106 and 151 for Dhaka against Barisal in Dhaka in 2005-06 ...

THE FIGURES
Batting and fielding

	M	Inns	NO	Runs	HS	Avge	S/R	100	50	4s	6s	Ct	St
Tests *to 11.9.06*	35	70	1	1525	119	22.10	36.69	1	6	207	0	7	0
ODIs *to 11.9.06*	53	53	4	1166	85*	23.79	52.21	0	9	125	3	10	0
First-class *to 11.9.06*	71	135	1	3761	167	28.06	–	7	17	–	–	23	0

Bowling

	M	Balls	Runs	Wkts	BB	Avge	RpO	S/R	5i	10m
Tests *to 11.9.06*	35	6	12	0	–	–	12.00	–	0	0
ODIs *to 11.9.06*	53	0	–	–	–	–	–	–	–	–
First-class *to 11.9.06*	71	222	145	2	2–75	72.50	3.91	111.00	0	0

SANATH JAYASURIYA

Full name **Sanath Teran Jayasuriya**
Born **June 30, 1969, Matara**
Teams **Bloomfield**
Style **Left-hand bat, slow left-arm orthodox spinner**
Test debut **Sri Lanka v New Zealand at Hamilton 1990-91**
ODI debut **Sri Lanka v Australia at Melbourne 1989-90**

THE PROFILE One of the most uncompromising strikers in world cricket, Sanath Jayasuriya found fame as a pinch-hitter at the 1996 World Cup, then showed he was also capable of massive scoring in Tests, collecting 340 in one innings against India and eventually becoming the first Sri Lankan to win 100 caps. He remains dizzily dangerous, especially on the subcontinent's slower surfaces. Short but powerfully built, he cuts and pulls with great power; his brutal bat-wielding is at odds with his shy, gentle nature. Streetwise opponents set traps in the gully and third man, but on song Jayasuriya can be virtually unstoppable, capable of scoring freely on both sides of the wicket. He is also a canny left-arm spinner, especially in ODIs, mixing his leg-stump darts with clever variations of pace. He had a successful stint as captain after Arjuna Ranatunga was dumped in 1999, but the responsibility took its toll. He stepped down after the 2003 World Cup, and a one-day slump immediately prompted calls for his retirement. But Jayasuriya was far from finished: he bounced back in 2004 with a blazing hundred that nearly levelled the series against Australia, and a marathon double-century against Pakistan. He added twin centuries in the Asia Cup, and sailed past 10,000 one-day runs the following year. He looked rusty at first in England in 2006 when summoned from Test retirement, but soon showed his old form in pyjamas, with 122 at The Oval then 152 and 157 in successive innings against England and Holland.

THE FACTS Jayasuriya made 340 against India in Colombo in August 1997, as Sri Lanka made the highest total in Test history, 952 for 6 declared ... In that innings he shared a world-record second-wicket partnership of 576 with Roshan Mahanama, who made 225 ... In the next Test Jayasuriya scored 199 ... He made his first-class debut for Sri Lanka B in Pakistan in 1988-89, and hit 203 and 207, both not out, in successive "Tests" there ... Jayasuriya played for Somerset in 2005 ... His record includes one ODI for the Asia XI ...

THE FIGURES

Batting and fielding

	M	Inns	NO	Runs	HS	Avge	S/R	100	50	4s	6s	Ct	St
Tests to 11.9.06	105	178	14	6745	340	41.12	–	14	30	882	56	78	0
ODIs to 11.9.06	364	354	15	11104	189	32.75	89.90	22	60	–	209	107	0
First-class to 11.9.06	246	388	33	14083	340	39.67	–	29	67	–	–	156	0

Bowling

	M	Balls	Runs	Wkts	BB	Avge	RpO	S/R	5i	10m
Tests to 11.9.06	105	7966	3271	96	5–34	34.07	2.46	82.97	2	0
ODIs to 11.9.06	364	12822	10238	278	6–29	36.82	4.79	46.12	4	0
First-class to 11.9.06	246	14246	6258	191	5–34	32.76	2.63	74.58	2	0

MAHELA JAYAWARDENE

SRI LANKA

Full name **Denagamage Proboth Mahela de Silva Jayawardene**
Born **May 27, 1977, Colombo**
Teams **Sinhalese Sports Club**
Style **Right-hand bat, occ. right-arm medium-pacer**
Test debut **Sri Lanka v India at Colombo 1997-98**
ODI debut **Sri Lanka v Zimbabwe at Colombo 1997-98**

THE PROFILE A fine technician with an excellent temperament, Mahela Jayawardene's exciting arrival in 1997 heralded the start of a new era for Sri Lanka's middle order. He was the best batsman they had produced since Sanath Jayasuriya, and his rich talent fuelled towering expectations. Perhaps mindful of his first Test, when he went in against India with the score at 790 for 4, he soon developed an appetite for big scores. His 66 then, in the world-record 952 for 6, was followed by a masterful 167 on a Galle minefield against New Zealand in only his fourth Test, and a marathon 242 against India in his seventh. However, after a purple patch from 2000, Jayawardene's form became more patchy in 2002. His declining one-day productivity was particularly alarming, although that was partly explained by his being shuffled up and down the order. He hardly scored a run in the 2003 World Cup, and was dropped afterwards. However, he soon regained his confidence, and benefited from a settled spot at No. 4 after Aravinda de Silva retired. A good Test series against England was followed by more runs in 2004. He was reappointed as the one-day vice-captain in 2003, and is clearly seen as the long-term successor to Marvan Atapattu, for whom he deputised admirably in England in 2006, producing a stunning double of 61 and 119 to lead the amazing rearguard which saved the Lord's Test. Later he put South Africa to the sword in Colombo, hitting a colossal 374, and sharing a world-record stand of 624 with Kumar Sangakkara.

THE FACTS Jayawardene made 374 against South Africa in Colombo in July 2006, sharing a world-record stand of 624 with Kumar Sangakkara (287) ... He has taken 59 catches off Muttiah Muralitharan in Tests, a record for a fielder-bowler combination, beating c Mark Taylor b Shane Warne (51) ... Jayawardene averages 67.84 in Tests against India, but only 27.33 against Pakistan ... His record includes two ODIs for the Asia XI ...

THE FIGURES

Batting and fielding

	M	Inns	NO	Runs	HS	Avge	S/R	100	50	4s	6s	Ct	St
Tests to 11.9.06	83	136	10	6250	374	49.60	52.25	16	29	775	31	111	0
ODIs to 11.9.06	221	205	22	5917	128	32.33	75.64	8	34	489	24	109	0
First-class to 11.9.06	160	252	19	11769	374	50.51	–	33	55	–	–	194	0

Bowling

	M	Balls	Runs	Wkts	BB	Avge	RpO	S/R	5i	10m
Tests to 11.9.06	83	458	228	4	2–32	57.00	2.98	114.50	0	0
ODIs to 11.9.06	221	568	539	7	2–56	77.00	5.69	81.14	0	0
First-class to 11.9.06	160	2858	1531	50	5–72	30.62	3.21	57.16	1	0

PRASANNA JAYAWARDENE

Full name	**Hewasandatchige Asiri Prasanna Wishvanath Jayawardene**
Born	**October 9, 1979, Colombo**
Teams	**Sebastianites**
Style	**Right-hand bat, wicketkeeper**
Test debut	**Sri Lanka v Pakistan at Kandy 2000**
ODI debut	**Sri Lanka v Pakistan at Sharjah 2002-03**

THE PROFILE A neat, unflashy wicketkeeper, Prasanna Jayawardene looked set for a long international career after touring England in 1998 at 19, but he became a bit of a back number after the rocket-fuelled arrival of Kumar Sangakkara in 2000. Waiting on the sidelines, in fact, had already been a feature of Jayawardene's career: he made his Test debut against Pakistan at Kandy in June 2000, but was confined to the dressing-room throughout, as Sri Lanka batted over the first three days before rain washed out play on the last two. The return of Romesh Kaluwitharana briefly pushed him even further down the pecking order, but with the Sri Lankan selectors voicing their concerns about overburdening Sangakkara, Jayawardene was recalled to the Test squad for the tour of Zimbabwe in April 2004. Sangakkara soon got the gloves back that time, but there was something of a sea-change after the 2006 tour of England, during which Jayawardene showed that his batting had improved. He was recalled for the visit of South Africa in July 2006, and this time the decision to lighten Sangakkara's load paid off spectacularly – he hammered 287, and shared a world-record stand of 642 with Mahela Jayawardene in the first Test in Colombo. Prasanna Jayawardene (no relation to Mahela) contented himself with a couple of catches and a stumping as the South Africans went down by an innings, but finally seemed to have booked in for a long run behind the stumps – at least in Tests.

THE FACTS Prasanna Jayawardene has scored three first-class centuries, the highest 143 for Sri Lanka A against Pakistan A at Dambulla in April 2005, when he shared an ninth-wicket stand of 171 with Malinga Bandara (79) ... All his ODIs were played in Sharjah in 2002-03 ... Jayawardene returned to Sebastianites (he spent three years in the St Sebastian's College XI) in 2005-06, after several years with Colombo's Nondescripts club ...

THE FIGURES
Batting and fielding

	M	Inns	NO	Runs	HS	Avge	S/R	100	50	4s	6s	Ct	St
Tests to 11.9.06	6	3	0	9	5	3.00	36.00	0	0	0	0	11	0
ODIs to 11.9.06	3	2	0	4	4	2.00	44.44	0	0	0	0	3	1
First-class to 11.9.06	122	187	22	3998	143	23.62	–	3	16	–	–	290	53

Bowling

	M	Balls	Runs	Wkts	BB	Avge	RpO	S/R	5i	10m
Tests to 11.9.06	6	0	–	–	–	–	–	–	–	–
ODIs to 11.9.06	3	0	–	–	–	–	–	–	–	–
First-class to 11.9.06	122	0	–	–	–	–	–	–	–	–

MITCHELL JOHNSON

Full name	**Mitchell Guy Johnson**
Born	**November 2, 1981, Townsville, Queensland**
Teams	**Queensland**
Style	**Left-hand bat, left-hand fast-medium bowler**
Test debut	**No Tests yet**
ODI debut	**Australia v New Zealand at Christchurch 2005-06**

THE PROFILE Mitchell Johnson is Australia's most exciting fast-bowling prospect since Brett Lee first dyed his roots. He's quick, he's tall, he's talented – but most of all, he's a left-armer. Only digging up a blond legspinner could create more excitement in Australia, which has seen only two of this style of diamond – Alan Davidson and Bruce Reid – reach 100 Test wickets. Johnson was picked in the one-day side after just 12 first-class games, and his future depends on whether he can stay fit. Dennis Lillee spotted him as a 17-year-old, calling him "a once-in-a-generation bowler". Lillee phoned Rod Marsh, then the Australian Academy's head coach, and Johnson was quickly on track for the national Under-19 team. Injuries kept interrupting his long-term plans, but he played a full season in 2004-05 and was a fixture with Queensland a year later, after being picked for the Australia A tour of Pakistan. Another representative catapult arrived in December 2005, when he was supersubbed into the final match of the one-day series in New Zealand. The following May he was given a central contract, only two years after driving a delivery truck and considering walking away from the game because of his fourth back stress injury. At 6ft 2ins (189cm), Johnson has the height to worry batsmen and is intent on scaring them as well. Shane Watson, his Queensland team-mate, is impressed: "He has just about the most talent I've ever seen in an allround athlete ... If he can keep improving the sky's the limit."

THE FACTS Johnson was the bowling star of the 2005-06 Pura Cup final, taking 6 for 51 – and ten wickets in the match – as Queensland followed up their mammoth total of 900 for 6 by routing a demoralised Victoria: "What a performance on a flat wicket," said his captain Jimmy Maher ... After five ODIs Johnson is yet to make a run or take a catch, but his three wickets have come without assistance (two bowled and one lbw) ...

THE FIGURES
Batting and fielding

	M	Inns	NO	Runs	HS	Avge	S/R	100	50	4s	6s	Ct	St
Tests to 11.9.06	0	–	–	–	–	–	–	–	–	–	–	–	–
ODIs to 11.9.06	5	1	1	0	0*	–	–	0	0	0	0	0	0
First-class to 11.9.06	17	22	6	317	51*	19.81	–	0	2	–	–	1	0

Bowling

	M	Balls	Runs	Wkts	BB	Avge	RpO	S/R	5i	10m
Tests to 11.9.06	0	–	–	–	–	–	–	–	–	–
ODIs to 11.9.06	5	198	174	3	2–24	58.00	5.27	66.00	0	0
First-class to 11.9.06	17	2739	1564	55	6–51	28.43	3.42	49.80	2	1

GERAINT JONES

Full name **Geraint Owen Jones**
Born **July 14, 1976, Kundiawa, Papua New Guinea**
Teams **Kent**
Style **Right-hand bat, wicketkeeper**
Test debut **England v West Indies at St John's 2003-04**
ODI debut **England v West Indies at Nottingham 2004**

THE PROFILE No player better encapsulated the fluctuating fortunes of the 2005 Ashes series than Geraint Jones. Fast-tracked into the Test team, Jones contributed vital runs – none more important than his 85 in a stand of 177 with Andrew Flintoff at Nottingham – but produced so many fumbles that every edge became a heart-in-the-mouth moment. He clung on, however, to the one chance that really mattered, to seal England's two-run win at Birmingham, and emerged from the series more or less in credit. Born in Papua New Guinea to Welsh parents, Jones learned his cricket in Australia, where he lived until he was 22. A qualified pharmacy technician, he was almost 27 when he came to the attention of the England selectors. In 2003 – Alec Stewart's last year – Jones scored 985 runs at 44 in his first full season for Kent, where he had displaced a former England tourist in Paul Nixon. Jones was rewarded with a West Indian tour, and after controversially replacing Chris Read (who had done little wrong behind the stumps, but scored few runs in front of them) for the final Test in Antigua, he cemented his place with a thrilling century against New Zealand at Headingley, where his sixth-wicket alliance with Flintoff had England fans smiling broadly. He improved his keeping in 2006, but his batting suffered – to the point where he lost his place against Pakistan, after 31 Tests in a row, to the resurgent Read, whose batting had come on.

THE FACTS Jones reached 100 dismissals in his 27th Test (in May 2006), the quickest by any England wicketkeeper: Alan Knott and Bob Taylor took 30 matches, while the overall record is 22 by Adam Gilchrist ... He averaged 31.88 in his first 15 Tests, but only 21.40 in his next 16 ... Jones made 71 (and won the Man of the Match award) to rescue England from 33 for 5 and tie the one-day NatWest Series final against Australia at Lord's in 2005 ... He scored 84 for Queensland Colts against New South Wales Colts in Sydney in March 1997, before being trapped in front by Brett Lee ...

THE FIGURES
Batting and fielding

	M	Inns	NO	Runs	HS	Avge	S/R	100	50	4s	6s	Ct	St
Tests to 11.9.06	31	47	4	1109	100	25.79	54.95	1	6	147	12	119	5
ODIs to 11.9.06	49	41	8	815	80	24.69	78.21	0	4	71	14	68	4
First-class to 11.9.06	71	105	13	2855	108*	31.03	–	4	16	–	–	223	14

Bowling

	M	Balls	Runs	Wkts	BB	Avge	RpO	S/R	5i	10m
Tests to 11.9.06	31	0	–	–	–	–	–	–	–	–
ODIs to 11.9.06	49	0	–	–	–	–	–	–	–	–
First-class to 11.9.06	71	6	4	0	–	–	4.00	–	–	–

SIMON JONES

Full name	**Simon Philip Jones**
Born	**December 25, 1978, Morriston, Swansea**
Teams	**Glamorgan**
Style	**Left-hand bat, right-arm fast-medium bowler**
Test debut	**England v India at Lord's 2002**
ODI debut	**England v Zimbabwe at Bulawayo 2004-05**

THE PROFILE Strapping and skiddy, Simon Jones recovered from career-threatening injury to become an integral member of the 2005 Ashes-winning team. His pace and mastery of reverse-swing brought him 18 wickets, before he was forced to sit out the nervy finale with an ankle problem. However, he had lasted much longer than in 2002-03: his tour ended abruptly on the first day of the series at Brisbane, when he slid awkwardly to prevent a boundary and ruptured a cruciate ligament in his right knee. He fought back courageously, spurred on by memories of the taunts he received while stricken on the Gabba outfield, and by early 2004 he was back to a good pace. Jones played in all four Tests in the Caribbean, but although he took 15 wickets he was very much the fourth member of the attack, forever fighting off the challenge of James Anderson. That began to change at Port Elizabeth in 2004-05, when his inspired fourth-day spell secured a notable victory over South Africa. By the time the Aussies arrived he had regained the yard of pace he had mislaid, and added a mysterious extra element ... reverse-swing. The bamboozling inswinger which plucked out Michael Clarke's off stump at Manchester was one of the images of the summer, as was a match-turning last-wicket stand of 51 with Andrew Flintoff at Birmingham. Sadly, injury struck again: a cartilage problem in his left knee kept him out for most of 2006, and forced him to miss the Ashes rematch too.

THE FACTS Jones averages 21.57 with the ball against Australia – and 39.41 against West Indies ... His best bowling is 6 for 45, for Glamorgan against Derbyshire at Cardiff in April 2002: he also took 6 for 53 for England against Australia at Manchester in August 2005 ... Like his England team-mates Marcus Trescothick and Alastair Cook, Jones was born on Christmas Day ... His father, Jeff, played 15 Tests for England as a feisty left-arm fast bowler in the 1960s ...

THE FIGURES

Batting and fielding

	M	Inns	NO	Runs	HS	Avge	S/R	100	50	4s	6s	Ct	St
Tests *to 11.9.06*	18	18	5	205	44	15.76	51.89	0	0	29	3	4	0
ODIs *to 11.9.06*	8	1	0	1	1	1.00	50.00	0	0	0	0	0	0
First-class *to 11.9.06*	75	90	30	716	46	11.93	–	0	0	–	–	17	0

Bowling

	M	Balls	Runs	Wkts	BB	Avge	RpO	S/R	5i	10m
Tests *to 11.9.06*	18	2821	1666	59	6–53	28.23	3.54	47.81	3	0
ODIs *to 11.9.06*	8	348	275	7	2–43	39.28	4.74	49.71	0	0
First-class *to 11.9.06*	75	11199	6900	217	6–45	31.79	3.69	51.60	11	1

MOHAMMAD KAIF

Full name **Mohammad Kaif**
Born **December 1, 1980, Allahabad, Uttar Pradesh**
Teams **Uttar Pradesh**
Style **Right-hand bat, occasional offspinner**
Test debut **India v South Africa at Bangalore 1999-2000**
ODI debut **India v England at Kanpur 2001-02**

INDIA

THE PROFILE An elegant batsman who evokes memories of the young Azharuddin, Mohammad Kaif comes from the cricket backwater of Uttar Pradesh. He first came to prominence with India's Under-19s: he captained the side, which also included Yuvraj Singh, Ajay Ratra and Reetinder Sodhi, that won the 2000 Youth World Cup. Kaif's assured strokeplay, and composure that belied his age, earned him a Test cap against South Africa soon after his 19th birthday. The selectors subsequently discarded him, but stints at the Australian Cricket Academy and its Indian equivalent in Bangalore helped iron out some of the kinks in his technique. Recalled to the one-day side during 2001-02, he made an impact with some steady and purposeful batting. But it was during the 2002 NatWest Series in England that he truly hit the high notes, culminating in a magnificent unbeaten 87 as India shocked England by successfully chasing 326 for victory in the final at Lord's. A superb century followed against Zimbabwe, but he struggled to kick on after that and had a quiet World Cup in 2003. Kaif's exceptional fielding, usually at cover, often compensated for his poor scores – but it wasn't enough to win him a permanent place in the Test team, although it usually ensured a one-day spot. Things may have changed after a good start to 2006, though: after a poor run he recovered with 91 against England at Nagpur in March, and followed that with a maiden Test century in St Lucia in June.

THE FACTS Kaif scored 100 in his second first-class match, for Uttar Pradesh against Haryana at Kanpur in April 1998, when he was 17 ... He averages 45.11 in ODIs against New Zealand, but only 5.00 against Australia ... Kaif's brother, Mohammad Saif, and his father, Mohammad Tarif, also played for Uttar Pradesh ... He has played county cricket for Derbyshire and Leicestershire ...

THE FIGURES
Batting and fielding

	M	Inns	NO	Runs	HS	Avge	S/R	100	50	4s	6s	Ct	St
Tests to 11.9.06	13	22	3	624	148*	32.84	40.31	1	3	64	2	14	0
ODIs to 11.9.06	119	104	23	2673	111*	33.00	72.55	2	17	220	9	54	0
First-class to 11.9.06	77	125	15	4397	148*	39.97	–	7	27	–	–	54	0

Bowling

	M	Balls	Runs	Wkts	BB	Avge	RpO	S/R	5i	10m
Tests to 11.9.06	13	18	4	0	–	–	1.33	–	0	0
ODIs to 11.9.06	119	0	–	–	–	–	–	–	–	–
First-class to 11.9.06	77	1166	524	17	3–4	30.82	2.69	68.58	0	0

JACQUES KALLIS

Full name	**Jacques Henry Kallis**
Born	**October 16, 1975, Pinelands, Cape Town**
Teams	**Cape Cobras**
Style	**Right-hand bat, right-arm fast-medium bowler**
Test debut	**South Africa v England at Durban 1995-96**
ODI debut	**South Africa v England at Cape Town 1995-96**

THE PROFILE In an era of fast scoring and high-octane entertainment, Jacques Kallis is a throwback – an astonishingly effective one – to a more sedate age, when your wicket was to be guarded with your life, and runs were an accidental by-product of crease-occupation. He blossomed after a quiet start into arguably the world's leading batsman, with the adhesive qualities of a Cape Point limpet. He nailed down the No. 3 position after several others had been tried, and his stock rose from then on. In 2005, he was the ICC's first Test Player of the Year, after a run of performances against West Indies and England that marked him out as the modern game's biggest scalp. His batting is not for the romantic: a Kallis century tends to be a soulless affair, with ruthless efficiency taking precedence over derring-do, and he has never quite dispelled the notion that he is a selfish batsman. But he has sailed to the top of South Africa's batting charts, and until Andrew Flintoff's emergence he was comfortably the world's leading allrounder, capable of swinging the ball sharply at a surprising pace off a relaxed run-up. Strong, with powerful shoulders and a deep chest, Kallis has the capacity to play a wide array of attacking strokes, if not always the inclination. He played his 100th Test in April 2006, not long after his 30th birthday, and has a batting average in the mid-50s and 200 wickets in both Tests and ODIs. He's a fine slip fielder too.

THE FACTS Kallis and Shaun Pollock were the first South Africans to play 100 Tests, reaching the mark at Centurion in April 2006 ... He averages 169.75 in Tests against Zimbabwe, and scored 388 runs against them in two Tests in 2001-02 without being dismissed ... Including his next innings he batted for a record 1241 minutes in Tests without getting out ... Kallis scored hundreds in five successive Tests in 2003-04 (only Don Bradman, with six, has done better) ... His record includes one Test and three ODIs for the World XI, and two ODIs for the Africa XI ...

THE FIGURES
Batting and fielding

	M	Inns	NO	Runs	HS	Avge	S/R	100	50	4s	6s	Ct	St
Tests *to 11.9.06*	102	172	28	8033	189*	55.78	42.83	24	40	898	55	98	0
ODIs *to 11.9.06*	231	221	39	7995	139	43.92	70.49	13	56	603	98	90	0
First-class *to 11.9.06*	188	306	42	14069	200	53.29	–	40	76	–	–	157	0

Bowling

	M	Balls	Runs	Wkts	BB	Avge	RpO	S/R	5i	10m
Tests *to 11.9.06*	102	13589	6342	200	6–54	31.71	2.80	67.94	4	0
ODIs *to 11.9.06*	231	8156	6564	203	5–30	32.33	4.82	40.17	2	0
First-class *to 11.9.06*	188	22168	10236	334	6–54	30.64	2.77	66.37	7	0

KAMRAN AKMAL

Full name **Kamran Akmal**
Born **January 13, 1982, Lahore, Punjab**
Teams **Lahore, National Bank**
Style **Right-hand bat, wicketkeeper**
Test debut **Pakistan v Zimbabwe at Harare 2002-03**
ODI debut **Pakistan v Zimbabwe at Bulawayo 2002-03**

THE PROFILE Kamran Akmal made his first-class debut at the age of 15 as a useful wicketkeeper and a hard-hitting batsman. Several good performances earned him an A-team spot in 2002, and after doing well against Sri Lanka A he was called up for the Zimbabwe tour ahead of the veteran Moin Khan. He was not expected to play in the Tests, but made his debut – and chipped in with a handy 38 – when Rashid Latif suffered a recurrence of an old back injury. Initially most of his matches came when Latif and Moin were unavailable: he stood in when Latif was suspended for five one-dayers against Bangladesh, and then again when Moin was injured for the last two Tests against India. However, from October 2004, with Latif out of favour and Moin no longer at his peak, Akmal became Pakistan's first-choice keeper. He responded with a magnificent showing with the gloves in Australia, despite repeated calls from home for a return to the old guard. In 2005, Akmal silenced those critics: as well as maintaining a high standard behind the stumps, he scored five international centuries. Three of them came while opening in one-dayers, and two in Tests, the first saving the match against India at Mohali, while the second, a blistering knock, came in the emphatic series-sealing win over England at Lahore. It seemed to have confirmed him as Pakistan's No. 1 – but a nightmare series in England in 2006, when he struggled with bat and gloves, set him back again.

THE FACTS Four of Kamran Akmal's eight first-class centuries have come in Tests: he scored five international hundreds in December 2005 and January 2006, including 154 in the Lahore Test against England, when he shared a sixth-wicket stand of 269 with Mohammad Yousuf (223) ... Moin Khan is the only other Pakistan wicketkeeper to score four Test hundreds ... Akmal averages 53.50 in ODIs against West Indies, but only 5.75 against Australia ... His brother Adnan has also played first-class cricket in Pakistan ...

THE FIGURES

Batting and fielding

	M	Inns	NO	Runs	HS	Avge	S/R	100	50	4s	6s	Ct	St
Tests to 11.9.06	27	45	2	1253	154	29.13	62.36	4	3	186	2	90	16
ODIs to 11.9.06	50	41	8	927	124	28.09	86.31	3	0	107	7	44	6
First-class to 11.9.06	112	172	22	4677	174	31.18	–	8	20	–	–	357	34

Bowling

	M	Balls	Runs	Wkts	BB	Avge	RpO	S/R	5i	10m
Tests to 11.9.06	27	0	–	–	–	–	–	–	–	–
ODIs to 11.9.06	50	0	–	–	–	–	–	–	–	–
First-class to 11.9.06	112	0	–	–	–	–	–	–	–	–

CHAMARA KAPUGEDERA

Full name	**Chamara Kantha Kapugedera**
Born	**February 24, 1987, Kandy**
Teams	**Colombo Cricket Club**
Style	**Right-hand bat, occasional right-arm medium-pacer**
Test debut	**Sri Lanka v England at Lord's 2006**
ODI debut	**Sri Lanka v Australia at Perth 2005-06**

THE PROFILE A naturally aggressive right-hander, Chamara Kapugedera is one of the few genuinely exciting batsmen the Sri Lankan selectors have unearthed from the Under-19 team in recent times. From his first appearances for Dharmaraja College in Kandy when he was 11, "Kapu" has rarely wasted an opportunity. After a prolific 2003-04 season, when he scored over 1000 runs at schoolboy level, he was picked for the following year's Under-19 tour of Pakistan. He made 112 in the first "Test", and bettered that with a stunning 131 in the third ODI against youth cricket's world champions at Karachi. He still rates that as his best innings, although he batted equally well for 70 on his first-class debut, for Sri Lanka A against the strong New Zealand A tourists in October 2005. The selectors eventually gambled, and fast-tracked him into the national squad after glowing reports from his youth coaches. Kapugedera was picked to tour India in November 2005, but injured his knee. However, he made his ODI debut, still only 18, against Australia at Perth early in 2006. A maiden fifty followed against Pakistan in March. He won his first Test cap at Lord's in May 2006, but was unlucky enough to receive the perfect inswinging yorker first ball from Sajid Mahmood. But he put that disappointment behind him with a composed 50 in the third Test, which Sri Lanka won to level the series. Kapugedera, who is also an excellent fielder, is very much one for the future.

THE FACTS Kapugedera scored 70 on his first-class debut, for Sri Lanka A against New Zealand A in Colombo in October 2005 ... He was selected for the 2006 tour of England after playing only three first-class matches, and made his maiden century – 134 not out against Sussex at Hove – the game after collecting a first-ball duck on his Test debut at Lord's ... Kapugedera played three Under-19 ODIs and finished them with a batting average of 154 ...

THE FIGURES

Batting and fielding

	M	Inns	NO	Runs	HS	Avge	S/R	100	50	4s	6s	Ct	St
Tests *to 11.9.06*	4	7	1	151	63	25.16	45.48	0	2	19	2	2	0
ODIs *to 11.9.06*	15	13	0	193	50	14.84	85.71	0	1	19	5	3	0
First-class *to 11.9.06*	12	20	5	645	134*	43.00	55.31	1	4	–	–	3	0

Bowling

	M	Balls	Runs	Wkts	BB	Avge	RpO	S/R	5i	10m
Tests *to 11.9.06*	4	0	–	–	–	–	–	–	–	–
ODIs *to 11.9.06*	15	0	–	–	–	–	–	–	–	–
First-class *to 11.9.06*	12	114	72	0	–	–	3.78	–	0	0

SIMON KATICH

AUSTRALIA

Full name	**Simon Mathew Katich**
Born	**August 21, 1975, Middle Swan, Western Australia**
Teams	**New South Wales**
Style	**Left-hand bat, slow left-arm unorthodox spinner**
Test debut	**Australia v England at Leeds 2001**
ODI debut	**Australia v Zimbabwe at Melbourne 2000-01**

THE PROFILE For Simon Katich 2005-06 was the most difficult season of his career. Lost from the Test radar after being bamboozled by Murali and failing against West Indies, he spent the summer clinging to his one-day spot – but the top of the limited-overs order will not be a safe seat. As Adam Gilchrist's rockets launch, Katich deflects arrows and absorbs punches. His batting is not pretty or powerful, but the side recognises his importance. In 1998-99 he amassed 1039 runs, including 115 as Western Australia won the Pura Cup final. He was on the brink of a Test debut when he contracted chicken-pox in Sri Lanka: associated health problems forced him to sit out much of the following summer, but after a stellar 2000-01 he was picked for his first Ashes tour. He replaced the injured Steve Waugh for the fourth Test, but had to wait two years for another opportunity, against Zimbabwe. Against India at the SCG, now his home ground, he registered his maiden Test century, and helped ensure that Waugh's final Test ended in stalemate rather than defeat. Later in 2004 he batted with eerie calmness in India: the highlight and lowlight came in the same innings, with 99 in the victory at Nagpur. An elegant display in New Zealand ensured another Ashes tour, but his troubles of the past year began in England, where he was upset by reverse-swing, and he was downgraded to a one-day-only role shortly after returning home.

THE FACTS In 2000-01 Katich's 1282 runs for NSW in domestic first-class cricket included a century against every other state ... Half of his 12 Test wickets came in one innings, during his 6 for 65 against Zimbabwe at Sydney in 2003-04 ... Katich's only ODI century, 107 not out against Sri Lanka at Brisbane, helped Australia win the 2005-06 VB Series finals after they lost the first match ... He played county cricket for Durham, Yorkshire and Hampshire, where he was captained by Shane Warne ...

THE FIGURES
Batting and fielding

	M	Inns	NO	Runs	HS	Avge	S/R	100	50	4s	6s	Ct	St
Tests to 11.9.06	23	38	3	1260	125	36.00	49.45	2	8	155	3	15	0
ODIs to 11.9.06	41	38	5	1232	107*	37.33	70.52	1	9	128	3	12	0
First-class to 11.9.06	148	253	34	10846	228*	49.52	–		29	57	–	–	139	0

Bowling

	M	Balls	Runs	Wkts	BB	Avge	RpO	S/R	5i	10m
Tests to 11.9.06	23	659	406	12	6–65	33.83	3.69	54.91	1	0
ODIs to 11.9.06	41	0	–	–	–	–	–	–	–	–
First-class to 11.9.06	148	4973	2986	78	7–130	38.28	3.60	63.75	3	0

JUSTIN KEMP

Full name	**Justin Miles Kemp**
Born	**October 2, 1977, Queenstown, Cape Province**
Teams	**Titans, Kent**
Style	**Right-hand bat, right-arm fast-medium bowler**
Test debut	**South Africa v Sri Lanka at Centurion 2000-01**
ODI debut	**South Africa v Sri Lanka at Bloemfontein 2000-01**

THE PROFILE Justin Kemp is tall and powerful, and the smiter of the biggest sixes in the world today. But Kemp, who also bowls at a handy fast-medium, has had a stop-start international career. He was tipped for great things when he broke into the South African side in 2000-01, taking five wickets in his first Test, against Sri Lanka at Centurion, and winning two more caps in the West Indies soon afterwards. Shortly after his Test debut, on his way to 188 in a domestic match, he smacked five sixes off one over, and the final ball fell two yards short of the man on the deep square-leg boundary. However, in the Caribbean he disappointed on the field and got into hot water off it, after admitting to smoking marijuana. After some undistinguished one-day outings the following season he disappeared until England toured in 2004-05. Filling the Lance Klusener one-day role to perfection, he clumped 80 from 50 balls in the series clincher at East London, and by the time New Zealand toured late in 2005 Kemp was looking like the genuine article. A crucial 73 off 64 balls in the first match, and a 19-ball 30 to clinch the series in the third, established him as one of the most dangerous hitters around. Although he is a back number in Tests – he has won only one more cap since his first season – he is an automatic selection in the one-day side, with almost a quarter of his runs coming in sixes.

THE FACTS Kemp hit 31 off an over (666661) from offspinner Morne Strydom during his career-best 188 for Eastern Province against North West at Port Elizabeth in February 2001 ... Kemp's father and grandfather also played first-class cricket, and his cousin is Dave Callaghan, who played 29 ODIs for South Africa in the 1990s ... His record includes three ODIs for the Africa XI ...

THE FIGURES
Batting and fielding

	M	Inns	NO	Runs	HS	Avge	S/R	100	50	4s	6s	Ct	St
Tests to 11.9.06	4	6	0	80	55	13.33	32.00	0	1	11	0	3	0
ODIs to 11.9.06	54	42	12	938	80	31.26	90.36	0	7	63	36	24	0
First-class to 11.9.06	87	141	17	4591	188	37.02	–	0	10	22	–	–	97	0

Bowling

	M	Balls	Runs	Wkts	BB	Avge	RpO	S/R	5i	10m
Tests to 11.9.06	4	479	222	9	3–33	24.66	2.78	53.22	0	0
ODIs to 11.9.06	54	983	746	22	3–20	33.90	4.55	44.68	0	0
First-class to 11.9.06	87	10029	4726	176	6–56	26.85	2.82	56.98	5	0

KHALED MASHUD

Full name	**Khaled Mashud**
Born	**February 8, 1976, Rajshahi**
Teams	**Rajshahi**
Style	**Right-hand bat, wicketkeeper**
Test debut	**Bangladesh v India at Dhaka 2000-01**
ODI debut	**Bangladesh v India at Sharjah 1994-95**

THE PROFILE A tidy, unflashy wicketkeeper, Khaled Mashud can also be a free-striking batsman whose matchwinning six against Kenya in the final of the 1997 ICC Trophy did much to raise his country's profile. But he is also capable of digging in, as shown by his stand of 93 with Aminul Islam in the inaugural Test against India in 2000-01, and, as Bangladesh's baptismal struggles continued, his doughty presence at No. 7 was often the saving grace of an innings. He is a good keeper standing up, and though he drops the odd ball off the seamers, he has been acclaimed by his coach, Dav Whatmore, as the best in Asia. Mashud – also known as "Pilot" – was saddled with the captaincy when Naimur Rahman was jettisoned after the home defeat by Zimbabwe late in 2001. However, he was powerless to halt Bangladesh's woeful run, and quit after their humiliations at the 2003 World Cup, but remained a pivotal figure in the side. His finest hour came in St Lucia in June 2004, when his unbeaten second-innings century secured Bangladesh a draw in their first Test in the Caribbean. He made an unbeaten 71 in the final match of the NatWest Series against Australia in England in 2005, but has now gone 24 Test innings without a half-century, although he did make 49 in Bangladesh's first Test win, over Zimbabwe in January 2005. But he's still only 30, and doesn't intend handing the gloves over to Mushfiqur Rahim just yet.

THE FACTS Khaled Mashud has missed only three of Bangladesh's 44 Tests to date – one match in Zimbabwe in 2000-01 (injured ankle) and two home Tests against South Africa in 2003, when he was out of favour after the World Cup ... He averages 30.75 in ODIs against New Zealand, but only 13 in 14 matches against Kenya ... He made 201 not out for Rajshahi against Khulna at Dhaka in 2001-02 ... Mashud and Mohammad Rafique are the last survivors in the current squad from the team that won the ICC Trophy in Kuala Lumpur in April 1997 ...

THE FIGURES
Batting and fielding

	M	Inns	NO	Runs	HS	Avge	S/R	100	50	4s	6s	Ct	St
Tests to 11.9.06	41	79	9	1361	103*	19.44	34.28	1	3	145	1	75	8
ODIs to 11.9.06	120	107	26	1777	71*	21.93	55.18	0	7	–	–	87	32
First-class to 11.9.06	77	139	16	3062	201*	24.89	–		3	12	–	–	128	13

Bowling

	M	Balls	Runs	Wkts	BB	Avge	RpO	S/R	5i	10m
Tests to 11.9.06	41	0	–	–	–	–	–	–	–	–
ODIs to 11.9.06	120	0	–	–	–	–	–	–	–	–
First-class to 11.9.06	77	7	14	0	–	–	12.00	–	0	0

ZAHEER KHAN

Full name	**Zaheer Khan**
Born	**October 7, 1978, Shrirampur, Maharashtra**
Teams	**Baroda, Worcestershire**
Style	**Right-hand bat, left-arm fast-medium bowler**
Test debut	**India v Bangladesh at Dhaka 1999-2000**
ODI debut	**India v Kenya at Nairobi 2000-01**

THE PROFILE Like Waqar Younis a decade before, left-armer Zaheer Khan yorked his way into the collective consciousness of the cricket world: his performances at the Champions Trophy in Kenya in September 2000 announced the arrival of an all-too-rare star in the Indian fast-bowling firmament. He might just as easily have come from the Pakistani pace stable – well-built, quick and unfazed by a batsman's reputation, Zaheer could move the ball both ways off the pitch and swing the old ball at a decent pace. After initially struggling to establish himself as a new-ball bowler, he came of age in the West Indies in 2002, when he led the line with great heart. His subsequent displays in England and New Zealand – not to mention some eye-catching moments at the 2003 World Cup – established him at the forefront of India's new pace generation, but a hamstring injury saw him relegated to bit-part performer while Indian cricket scripted some of its finest moments away in Australia and Pakistan. In a bid to jump the queue of left-armers vying for a national spot, Zaheer put in the hard yards for Worcestershire in 2006, bowling a lot of overs and, in the match against Essex, taking the first nine wickets to fall in the first innings before Darren Gough's flailing bat – and a dropped catch behind the stumps – spoilt his figures and his chances of a rare all-ten.

THE FACTS Zaheer Khan's 75 against Bangladesh at Dhaka in December 2004 is the highest score by a No. 11 in Tests: he dominated a last-wicket stand of 133 with Sachin Tendulkar ... He took 9 for 138 for Worcestershire v Essex at Chelmsford in June 2006 – it included a spell of 9 for 28, but a last-wicket stand of 97 cost him the chance of taking all ten wickets ... Khan averages 23.33 with the ball in Tests against New Zealand, but 92.66 against South Africa ... His record includes four ODIs for the Asia XI ...

THE FIGURES
Batting and fielding

	M	Inns	NO	Runs	HS	Avge	S/R	100	50	4s	6s	Ct	St
Tests to 11.9.06	42	54	14	507	75	12.67	55.83	0	1	55	12	10	0
ODIs to 11.9.06	107	58	24	453	34*	13.13	86.63	0	0	38	16	25	0
First-class to 11.9.06	94	120	27	1369	75	14.72	–	0	2	–	–	28	0

Bowling

	M	Balls	Runs	Wkts	BB	Avge	RpO	S/R	5i	10m
Tests to 11.9.06	42	7961	4398	121	5–29	36.34	3.31	65.79	3	0
ODIs to 11.9.06	107	5315	4335	155	4–19	27.96	4.89	34.29	0	0
First-class to 11.9.06	94	19166	10617	379	9–138	28.01	3.32	50.56	23	7

LANCE KLUSENER

Full name	**Lance Klusener**
Born	**September 4, 1971, Durban, Natal**
Teams	**Dolphins, Northamptonshire**
Style	**Right-hand bat, right-hand fast-medium bowler**
Test debut	**South Africa v India at Calcutta 1996-97**
ODI debut	**South Africa v England at East London 1995-96**

THE PROFILE Lance Klusener started as a tearaway for Natal in the mid-1990s, batting down the order. A childhood spent among Zulu children on a sugar-cane farm and three years in the army contributed to a straightforward approach to bowling: hit the batsman's head if you can't hit his stumps. He spent a while bowling just two lengths before an ankle injury in 1998 forced him to drop his pace and develop further skills. Later he tried medium-paced cutters off six paces, which many batsmen found impossible to get away. He was the standout player of the 1999 World Cup, averaging 140 and taking 17 wickets, and it was cruel luck that he was involved in the fatal run-out that cost South Africa a place in the final. Poor form later cost him his place, the 2003 World Cup failed to reignite his career, and he missed the subsequent tour of England. A recall was not a roaring success, and he seemed to be finished as an international player – until a fine season with Northamptonshire in 2006, under the eye of coach Kepler Wessels, raised hopes of a comeback for another tilt at the World Cup. Contrary to his reputation as an unrefined slogger, Klusener is one of the most skilful and adaptable players in the game. He is introspective by nature, and happiest holding a fishing rod. Not talking to the media is another hobby, although when he breaks his silence he does so with quiet intelligence and impressive clarity of thought.

THE FACTS Klusener took 8 for 64 against India at Calcutta in 1996-97, the best figures for South Africa on Test debut ... In all World Cup matches he averages 124 with the bat and 22.13 with the ball ... In 12 ODIs between February and June 1999 Klusener scored 400 runs without being dismissed ... He averages 68.28 with the bat in Tests against England, but only 14.10 against Australia ... After being omitted from the 2003 England tour Klusener sued the South African board for loss of earnings ...

THE FIGURES
Batting and fielding

	M	Inns	NO	Runs	HS	Avge	S/R	100	50	4s	6s	Ct	St
Tests *to 11.9.06*	49	69	11	1906	174	32.86	59.80	4	8	236	20	34	0
ODIs *to 11.9.06*	171	137	50	3576	103*	41.10	89.91	2	19	293	76	35	0
First-class *to 11.9.06*	158	221	48	6925	174	40.02	–	16	32	–	–	86	0

Bowling

	M	Balls	Runs	Wkts	BB	Avge	RpO	S/R	5i	10m
Tests *to 11.9.06*	49	6887	3033	80	8–64	37.91	2.64	86.08	1	0
ODIs *to 11.9.06*	171	7336	5751	192	6–49	29.95	4.70	38.20	6	0
First-class *to 11.9.06*	158	26387	12760	452	8–34	28.23	2.90	58.37	18	4

GARNETT KRUGER

Full name	**Garnett John-Peter Kruger**
Born	**January 5, 1977, Port Elizabeth, Cape Province**
Teams	**Lions**
Style	**Right-hand bat, right-arm fast bowler**
Test debut	**No Tests yet**
ODI debut	**South Africa v Australia at Brisbane 2005-06**

THE PROFILE Lanky, lithe and lively, Garnett Kruger oozes effortless pace and surprises many with his bouncer – but after almost four years on the fringe of the national side he remains a nearly man, with only three one-day caps, all in Australia early in

2006, to his name. Kruger, from Gelvandale, a coloured township north of Port Elizabeth, was first included in the squad for the first Test against West Indies at Johannesburg in December 2003, following a move to once-omnipotent, now-impotent Gauteng Lions after five years at Eastern Province. It started well: Kruger earned that Test-squad call-up on the back of 18 wickets in his first four SuperSport Series matches, and added five more in two first-class games for South Africa A against their Sri Lankan counterparts. But then a groin injury kept him out of a planned county stint with Leicestershire in 2004, and other pacemen, like Andre Nel and Dale Steyn, pressed their international claims. Consistent domestic performances ensured that Kruger's name was often mentioned, but he remained on the outer until earning a recall for the tour of Australia in 2005-06. Three one-day wickets against Queensland propelled him into the side for the early matches in the VB Series, but he managed only two wickets in three outings. He also toured West Indies with South Africa A in 2000-01, taking six wickets at 16.83 from just 33 overs and claiming an exotic career-best 58 against the Windward Islands at Arnos Vale.

THE FACTS Kruger's first international wicket was Australia's Michael Hussey, who had scored 292 runs in six ODIs since his previous dismissal ... He took 7 for 64 in only his third match for Eastern Province, against Border at East London in November 1999: these remained his best figures until he took 8 for 112 for Lions v Dolphins at Durban in October 2005 ... Kruger was voted South Africa's Domestic Player of the Year in 2005-06 by his fellow players ...

THE FIGURES
Batting and fielding

	M	Inns	NO	Runs	HS	Avge	S/R	100	50	4s	6s	Ct	St
Tests to 11.9.06	0	–	–	–	–	–	–	–	–	–	–	–	–
ODIs to 11.9.06	3	2	1	0	0*	0.00	0.00	0	0	0	0	1	0
First-class to 11.9.06	66	81	25	696	58	12.42	–	0	2	–	–	17	0

Bowling

	M	Balls	Runs	Wkts	BB	Avge	RpO	S/R	5i	10m
Tests to 11.9.06	0	–	–	–	–	–	–	–	–	–
ODIs to 11.9.06	3	138	139	2	1–43	69.50	6.04	69.00	0	0
First-class to 11.9.06	66	11876	6621	222	8–112	29.82	3.34	53.49	9	2

ANIL KUMBLE

Full name	**Anil Kumble**
Born	**October 17, 1970, Bangalore**
Teams	**Karnataka, Surrey**
Style	**Right-hand bat, legspinner**
Test debut	**India v England at Manchester 1990**
ODI debut	**India v Sri Lanka at Sharjah 1989-90**

THE PROFILE   No bowler has won more Test matches for India than Anil Kumble. Unorthodox, he trades the legspinner's usual yo-yo for a spear, as the ball hacks through the air rather than hanging in it, then comes off the pitch with a kick rather than a kink. He does not beat the bat as much as hit the splice, but has enjoyed stunning success, particularly on Indian soil, where his deliveries burst like water-bombs on the merest crack. Resilient and untiring, for most of his career Kumble struggled to make an impact outside India, but turned that around magnificently in Australia in 2003-04, with 24 wickets in three Tests. Then his 6 for 71 on a flat Multan track helped India win their first Test in Pakistan. Kumble is a handy batsman, although nervous running has hindered him in one-dayers. He catches well, usually in the gully, despite once being described as moving like "a man on stilts". In December 2001, at home at Bangalore, Kumble became the first Indian spinner to take 300 Test wickets. A year later he passed 300 in one-dayers too. Against Australia in 2004-05 he pushed his Test tally past 400 – also at Bangalore – then skittled the Aussies in the next Test at Chennai with 13 wickets. And in March 2006, he was India's first to 500. Superstardom has somehow eluded the low-profile Kumble, but his deeds – especially his "Perfect Ten" in an innings against Pakistan at Delhi in February 1999 – speak for themselves.

THE FACTS   Kumble was only the second bowler (after Jim Laker) to take all ten wickets in a Test innings, with 10 for 74 against Pakistan at Delhi in 1998-99 ... He has taken 325 wickets at 23.71 in Tests in India, and 208 at 36.44 overseas: he has taken 256 in Tests that India have won – the next-best is 128, by Harbhajan Singh ... Kumble has taken 88 Test wickets against Australia, and 78 against England ... His highest first-class score of 154 not out came for Karnataka against Kerala at Bijapur in November 1991 ... His record includes two ODIs for the Asia XI ...

THE FIGURES

Batting and fielding

	M	Inns	NO	Runs	HS	Avge	S/R	100	50	4s	6s	Ct	St
Tests to 11.9.06	110	140	27	2025	88	17.92	38.54	0	4	240	8	50	0
ODIs to 11.9.06	264	131	46	930	26	10.94	61.87	0	0	57	6	84	0
First-class to 11.9.06	216	277	56	5045	154*	22.82	–	6	16	–	–	106	–

Bowling

	M	Balls	Runs	Wkts	BB	Avge	RpO	S/R	5i	10m
Tests to 11.9.06	110	34890	15329	533	10–74	28.75	2.63	65.45	33	8
ODIs to 11.9.06	264	14117	10122	329	6–12	30.76	4.30	42.90	2	0
First-class to 11.9.06	216	59915	25771	1024	10–74	25.16	2.58	58.51	69	19

JUSTIN LANGER

Full name	**Justin Lee Langer**
Born	**November 21, 1970, Perth, Western Australia**
Teams	**Western Australia, Somerset**
Style	**Left-hand bat, occasional right-arm medium-pacer**
Test debut	**Australia v West Indies at Adelaide 1992-93**
ODI debut	**Australia v Sri Lanka at Sharjah 1993-94**

THE PROFILE Justin Langer is probably the first Test opener to average 45 yet always be scrabbling for his place. Or that's the perception: in a land of dashers Langer is seen as a grafter, only a couple of failures away from oblivion. The reality is rather different. Yesterday's ugly duckling is now a stroke-playing swan who amassed 1481 runs in 2004. Always an effective cutter and driver, he can now indulge in cross-batted hoicks from the start. Langer and his bludgeoning buddy Matthew Hayden have screwed up textbooks and record-books alike. It's a miraculous reinvention. Clanged on the helmet by Ian Bishop on his 1992-93 debut, Langer fought on for 54, but played only eight Tests in six years. He returned at No. 3, as the selectors sought the new David Boon. It worked: after Langer helped rescue the unrescueable Hobart Test of 1999-2000, then blistered 122 at Auckland, Steve Waugh dubbed him the world's best batsman. Langer may be short, but he is tall in enthusiasm, and boasts a black belt in taekwondo. His strong-willed batting was a rare highlight in England in 2005, when he was Australia's leading scorer: he also took blows to the helmet and body, which are a common theme. In his 100th Test, at Johannesburg in April 2006, he turned into a Makhaya Ntini bouncer before he'd scored. Taken to hospital with concussion, he spent the rest of the match off the field, and considered quitting altogether before opting for another shot at the Ashes.

THE FACTS Langer played only eight ODIs, something that bugs him no end, despite a Gilchristian strike rate of 88.88 runs per 100 balls ... Langer and Hayden are Australia's most prolific opening pair, putting on a total of 5741 runs together: only Gordon Greenidge and Desmond Haynes (6482 for West Indies) have shared more runs in partnership ... Langer averages 62.94 against New Zealand – and only 20.00 against Zimbabwe ... He scored 342 for Somerset against Surrey at Guildford in 2006 ...

THE FIGURES
Batting and fielding

	M	Inns	NO	Runs	HS	Avge	S/R	100	50	4s	6s	Ct	St
Tests to 11.9.06	100	173	10	7393	250	45.35	53.71	22	29	873	40	68	0
ODIs to 11.9.06	8	7	2	160	36	32.00	88.88	0	0	13	4	2	1
First-class to 11.9.06	291	511	48	23511	342	50.77	–		72	90	–	–	241	0

Bowling

	M	Balls	Runs	Wkts	BB	Avge	RpO	S/R	5i	10m
Tests to 11.9.06	100	6	3	0	–	–	3.00	–	0	0
ODIs to 11.9.06	8	0	–	–	–	–	–	–	–	–
First-class to 11.9.06	291	374	204	5	2–17	40.79	3.27	74.79	0	0

CHARL LANGEVELDT

Full name	**Charl Kenneth Langeveldt**
Born	**December 17, 1974, Stellenbosch, Cape Province**
Teams	**Lions**
Style	**Right-hand bat, right-arm fast-medium bowler**
Test debut	**South Africa v England at Cape Town 2004-05**
ODI debut	**South Africa v Kenya at Kimberley 2001-02**

THE PROFILE For much of the early part of his career, Charl Langeveldt combined his first-class cricket with his job as a prison warder at Drakenstein prison, not far from the headquarters of Boland, his provincial home, a short drive north of Cape Town. Langeveldt first came to prominence with his ability to swing the ball at genuine pace, and further work on his action in recent seasons allowed him to generate even more movement, bringing him to the attention of the national selectors. He made his one-day international debut against Kenya at Kimberley in 2001-02, taking two top-order wickets. He followed that with career-best figures of 4 for 21 when the two sides met again at Cape Town shortly afterwards. Langeveldt was included in South Africa's 15-man squad for their ill-starred World Cup campaign in 2003, but played only in the pool match against Kenya. He returned to favour after South Africa experienced a dramatic slump in the middle of 2004, taking 3 for 31 in Sri Lanka and 3 for 17 against Bangladesh in the Champions Trophy in England. He made his Test debut in style against England at Cape Town in 2004-05, breaking his hand while batting but nonetheless taking 5 for 46. It was enough to win him selection for the series in the Caribbean which followed, and he came into his own there. In the third one-dayer in Barbados, he produced one of the most sensational finales in one-day international history, plucking a last-over hat-trick out of thin air to steal a one-run victory over West Indies and give his team victory in the series. Test success proved more elusive, and he featured in only two of South Africa's matches in 2005-06.

THE FACTS Langeveldt's hat-trick against West Indies at Bridgetown in May 2005 was South Africa's first in ODIs ... He averages 22.45 with the ball in ODIs against West Indies, but 130 against Australia ... Langeveldt took 5 for 7 when the SA Board President's XI bowled out the touring Bangladeshis for 51 at Pietermaritzburg in October 2000 ...

THE FIGURES

Batting and fielding

	M	Inns	NO	Runs	HS	Avge	S/R	100	50	4s	6s	Ct	St
Tests *to 11.9.06*	6	4	2	16	10	8.00	30.76	0	0	3	0	2	0
ODIs *to 11.9.06*	29	5	1	7	3	1.75	50.00	0	0	0	0	1	0
First-class *to 11.9.06*	59	71	24	681	56	14.48	–	0	1	–	–	16	0

Bowling

	M	Balls	Runs	Wkts	BB	Avge	RpO	S/R	5i	10m
Tests *to 11.9.06*	6	999	593	16	5–46	37.06	3.56	62.43	1	0
ODIs *to 11.9.06*	29	1352	1102	38	5–62	29.00	4.89	35.57	1	0
First-class *to 11.9.06*	59	10257	5121	174	5–19	29.43	2.99	58.94	5	1

SOUTH AFRICA

BRIAN LARA

WEST INDIES

Full name **Brian Charles Lara**
Born **May 2, 1969, Cantaro, Santa Cruz, Trinidad**
Teams **Trinidad & Tobago**
Style **Left-hand bat, occasional legspinner**
Test debut **West Indies v Pakistan at Lahore 1990-91**
ODI debut **West Indies v Pakistan at Karachi 1990-91**

THE PROFILE No-one since Bradman has built big scores as
often and as fast as Brian Lara at his best. Even his stance is
thrilling: bat raised high, weight poised on bent front knee, eyes
low and level. In the space of two months in 1994, Lara's 375 and
501 broke the records for the highest Test and first-class scores. During an inventive but
largely fruitless first spell as captain of a fading team, Lara defied the 1998-99 Australians
with successive innings of 213, 8, 153 not out and 100. For a while, excess weight and
hamstring problems hampered his once-lightning footwork, and the torrent of runs became
an occasional spurt. Garry Sobers suggested a tweak to that flourishing backlift, and Lara
returned to his best in Sri Lanka late in 2001. He reclaimed the captaincy the following year,
but it was just as tough: another defeat in South Africa, then crushed by England at home.
But Lara responded to the prospect of a whitewash with an unbeaten 400 in Antigua,
becoming the first man to reclaim the world Test batting record. He skippered in England in
2004, losing all four Tests, before surprise victory in the Champions Trophy sparked hopes of
a West Indian resurgence. However, after a bitter contracts dispute his next big moment came
under Shivnarine Chanderpaul's leadership, at Adelaide in November 2005, when he became
Test cricket's leading run-scorer. When Chanderpaul stood down Lara had a third shot at the
captaincy, but narrow defeat by India left him considering his options again.

THE FACTS Lara's 375 and 400 not out were both scored at St John's, Antigua, ten
years apart ... His 501 not out for Warwickshire v Durham at Edgbaston in 1994 remains
the highest first-class score ... Lara has been on the losing side in a record 61 Tests, beating
Alec Stewart's old mark of 54 ... In Sri Lanka in 2001-02 Lara scored 688 runs in three Tests
(all lost), a record 42% of West Indies' output ... He averages 86.53 in Tests against Sri
Lanka, but 34.55 v India ... Only Don Bradman (12) has scored more than Lara's eight Test
double-centuries ... His record includes one Test and four ODIs for the World XI ...

THE FIGURES
Batting and fielding

	M	Inns	NO	Runs	HS	Avge	S/R	100	50	4s	6s	Ct	St
Tests *to 11.9.06*	128	227	6	11505	400*	52.02	60.31	32	47	1501	81	161	0
ODIs *to 11.9.06*	270	262	27	9661	169	41.11	79.37	19	59	965	117	111	0
First-class *to 11.9.06*	256	432	11	21523	501*	51.12	–		62	86	–	–	314	0

Bowling

	M	Balls	Runs	Wkts	BB	Avge	RpO	S/R	5i	10m
Tests *to 11.9.06*	128	60	28	0	–	–	2.80	–	0	0
ODIs *to 11.9.06*	270	49	61	4	2-5	15.25	7.46	12.25	0	0
First-class *to 11.9.06*	256	514	416	4	1-1	104.02	4.85	128.50	0	0

108

JERMAINE LAWSON

WEST INDIES

Full name	**Jermaine Jay Charles Lawson**
Born	**January 13, 1982, Spanish Town, St Catherine, Jamaica**
Teams	**Jamaica**
Style	**Right-hand bat, right-arm fast bowler**
Test debut	**West Indies v India at Chennai 2002-03**
ODI debut	**West Indies v Sri Lanka at Colombo 2001-02**

THE PROFILE In the space of an extraordinary fortnight in May 2003, Jermaine Lawson ran the full gamut of emotions as an international cricketer. A tall, rangy fast bowler capable of searing pace and high accuracy, Lawson had burst into Test cricket six months before, blasting out six wickets for three runs against the hapless Bangladeshis in only his third match. If that was good, even better was to follow against the Australians. After recovering from chicken-pox, he picked up a hat-trick in the dying stages of the third Test, before demolishing Australia in Antigua with 7 for 78, figures that set West Indies on their way to what became an historic victory. By now, however, Lawson's ragged bowling action had come under scrutiny from the match officials, and he was reported to the ICC for investigation. He was subsequently cleared after undergoing remedial action. His return to Test cricket was a little bumpy, however, with match figures of 2 for 126 against Bangladesh in June 2004. He got through the unsuccessful 2004 England tour without any adverse comment, but picked up a spinal stress fracture that sidelined him for the Champions Trophy at the end of that season. Though he returned with some success at first in 2005, his action was back under the spotlight in Sri Lanka in July, although he was again given the all-clear by the ICC. He toured Australia in 2005-06, but played only in the first Test before disappearing from the radar. He was then no-balled for throwing in a club game in Jamaica in April 2006, putting his career in doubt again.

THE FACTS Lawson completed his Test hat-trick against Australia at Bridgetown in May 2003 by trapping Justin Langer lbw with the first ball of the second innings, after bowling Brett Lee and Stuart MacGill with the last two balls of the first ... Lawson took 6 for 3 against Bangladesh at Dhaka in December 2002, in only his third Test ... His 7 for 78 against Australia in May 2003 remain the best figures in any Test at the Antigua Recreation Ground in St John's ...

THE FIGURES

Batting and fielding

	M	Inns	NO	Runs	HS	Avge	S/R	100	50	4s	6s	Ct	St
Tests to 11.9.06	13	21	6	52	14	3.46	29.37	0	0	6	0	3	0
ODIs to 11.9.06	13	5	2	18	8	6.00	112.50	0	0	2	0	0	0
First-class to 11.9.06	44	61	29	345	29	8.02	–	0	0	–	–	12	0

Bowling

	M	Balls	Runs	Wkts	BB	Avge	RpO	S/R	5i	10m
Tests to 11.9.06	13	2364	1512	51	7–78	29.64	3.83	46.35	2	0
ODIs to 11.9.06	13	558	498	17	4–57	29.29	5.35	32.82	0	0
First-class to 11.9.06	44	6911	4109	134	7–78	30.66	30.66	51.57	3	0

VVS LAXMAN

Full name	**Vangipurappu Venkata Sai Laxman**
Born	**November 1, 1974, Hyderabad, Andhra Pradesh**
Teams	**Hyderabad**
Style	**Right-hand bat, occasional offspinner**
Test debut	**India v South Africa at Ahmedabad 1996-97**
ODI debut	**India v Zimbabwe at Cuttack 1997-98**

THE PROFILE At his sublime best, VVS Laxman is a sight for the gods. Wristy, willowy and sinuous, he can match – sometimes even better – Tendulkar for strokeplay. His on-side game is comparable to his idol Azharuddin's, and yet he is decidedly more assured on the off side, and has the rare gift of being able to hit the same ball to either side. The Australians, who have suffered more than most, paid him the highest compliment after India's 2003-04 tour Down Under by admitting they did not know where to bowl to him. Laxman, a one-time medical student, finally showed signs of coming to terms with his considerable gifts in March 2001, as he tormented Steve Waugh's thought-to-be-invincible Aussies with a majestic 281 to stand the Kolkata Test on its head. But then he returned to mortality, suffering the frustrations of numerous twenties and thirties, and struggling to hold his one-day place. An uncharacteristic grinding century in Antigua in May 2002 marked his second coming, and he has been a picture of consistency since, often dazzling, but less prone to collaborating in his own dismissal. After the acute disappointment of being left out of the 2003 World Cup he made an emphatic return with a string of hundreds in Australia the next season, and followed that with a matchwinning 107 in the deciding one-dayer of India's ice-breaking tour of Pakistan in March 2004. By 2006, though, he was again confined to the five-day arena, and collected his tenth Test ton in St Kitts.

THE FACTS Laxman's 281 against Australia at Kolkata in March 2001 was the highest Test score by an Indian at the time (since passed by Virender Sehwag), and included a Indian-record stand of 376 for the fifth wicket with Rahul Dravid ... He averages 52.03 against Australia, and his highest three scores (281, 178 and 167) have all come against them ... Laxman has scored two first-class triple-centuries for Hyderabad – 353 v Karnataka at Bangalore in April 2000, and 301 not out v Bihar at Jamshedpur in February 1998 ...

THE FIGURES

Batting and fielding

	M	Inns	NO	Runs	HS	Avge	S/R	100	50	4s	6s	Ct	St
Tests *to 11.9.06*	77	124	14	4698	281	42.70	49.06	10	25	658	4	81	0
ODIs *to 11.9.06*	85	82	7	2338	131	31.17	71.25	6	10	222	4	39	0
First-class *to 11.9.06*	174	279	30	13279	353	53.32	–		40	56	–	–	184	1

Bowling

	M	Balls	Runs	Wkts	BB	Avge	RpO	S/R	5i	10m
Tests *to 11.9.06*	77	252	100	1	1–32	100.00	2.38	252.00	0	0
ODIs *to 11.9.06*	85	42	40	0	–	–	5.71	–	0	0
First-class *to 11.9.06*	174	1583	659	18	3–11	36.61	2.49	87.94	0	0

AUSTRALIA

BRETT LEE

Full name	**Brett Lee**
Born	**November 8, 1976, Wollongong, New South Wales**
Teams	**New South Wales**
Style	**Right-hand bat, right-arm fast bowler**
Test debut	**Australia v India at Melbourne 1999-2000**
ODI debut	**Australia v Pakistan at Brisbane 1999-2000**

THE PROFILE If Brett Lee were a Ferrari ... No. There is no if. He's already the fastest in the world, equal with Shoaib Akhtar at a flicker above or below 100mph. When Lee releases the throttle and begins that smooth acceleration, anything could happen: that leaping, classical delivery might produce a devastating yorker, a devilish slower ball or a young-Donald outswinger. Add a dash of peroxide, a fruity vocabulary, a trademark jump for joy, and a pop group (Six And Out), and you have the 21st century's first designer cricketer. Steve Waugh unleashed Lee at first, but Ricky Ponting gave him a blueprint for lasting success that doesn't rely solely on speed. Lee's career hasn't always been easy. He struggled with injury and accusations of throwing, and had a strangely barren first Ashes series in 2001. Three years later he overcame ankle surgery, but was 12th man for nine successive Tests. He returned for the 2005 Ashes, and earned plaudits for his never-say-die attitude with ball and bat, nearly conjuring victory at Edgbaston with a battling 43. Andrew Flintoff's consoling of Lee at the end was the defining image of that epic series. His 2006 brightened further when he partnered Michael Kasprowicz in a nailbiting win at Johannesburg that eased the pain of that previous near-miss. And when Glenn McGrath first struggled for impact then withdrew to care for his sick wife, Lee became leader of the attack – a position he had craved since first crashing onto the Test scene.

THE FACTS Lee took a hat-trick against Kenya in 2002-03, one of only four in the World Cup ... His older brother Shane played 45 ODIs for Australia between 1995 and 2001 ... Lee averages 22.71 with the ball against West Indies, but almost double that (44.14) against England ... He was on the winning side in each of his first ten Tests, a sequence ended by England's win at Leeds in 2001 ... Lee took 5 for 47 in his first Test innings, but did not improve on that until his 44th match ...

THE FIGURES
Batting and fielding

	M	Inns	NO	Runs	HS	Avge	S/R	100	50	4s	6s	Ct	St
Tests *to 11.9.06*	54	60	11	1033	64	21.08	56.38	0	3	123	15	15	0
ODIs *to 11.9.06*	135	60	24	694	57	19.27	83.41	0	2	33	22	34	0
First-class *to 11.9.06*	89	103	18	1579	79	18.57	55.73	0	5	–	–	26	0

Bowling

	M	Balls	Runs	Wkts	BB	Avge	RpO	S/R	5i	10m
Tests *to 11.9.06*	54	11098	6636	211	5–30	31.45	3.58	52.59	7	0
ODIs *to 11.9.06*	135	6902	5414	237	5–22	22.84	4.70	29.12	5	0
First-class *to 11.9.06*	89	17681	10180	372	7–114	27.36	3.45	47.52	16	2

JON LEWIS

Full name	**Jonathan Lewis**
Born	**August 26, 1975, Aylesbury, Buckinghamshire**
Teams	**Gloucestershire**
Style	**Right-hand bat, right-arm medium-pacer**
Test debut	**England v Sri Lanka at Nottingham 2006**
ODI debut	**England v Bangladesh at The Oval 2005**

THE PROFILE Jon Lewis, a consistent county wicket-taker with his skiddy medium-paced awayswingers, seemed destined to be a no-cap wonder after frequently being called up by England only to be left out at the last minute. It started in South Africa early in 2005, when Lewis, a late addition to an injury-hit squad, was congratulated by his team-mates ahead of the rain-delayed start of the final Test at Centurion. It seemed that a first cap was imminent: but it didn't happen then, or at home during 2005, even though Lewis rocked the Australians with four wickets in the Twenty20 international pipe-opener at the Rose Bowl early in that famous tour, ripping out Symonds, Clarke and Ponting for ducks. His ODI career also started well, with three wickets against Bangladesh, but the Aussies seemed to work him out after that. Suspicions remained that he just wasn't quick enough to be an international force, and although Lewis did finally get a Test cap against Sri Lanka at Trent Bridge in 2006 – and again started well, the first of his three wickets coming with his third ball – he was sidelined when Pakistan visited later that summer. At 31 that might have been it, except as England's one-day attack continued to struggle with injuries and lack of form Lewis was the only quicker bowler to do the basics right – and he retained his knack of grabbing early wickets. He's an old-fashioned tailender with the bat, capable of the odd mighty blow, and captained Gloucestershire in 2006.

THE FACTS Lewis took a wicket (Michael Vandort of Sri Lanka) with his third ball in Test cricket, at Nottingham in 2006 ... In 2005 he had taken a wicket with his seventh ball in a Twenty20 international (Michael Clarke at the Rose Bowl) and one with his 11th ball in ODIs (Javed Omar of Bangladesh at The Oval) ... Lewis took 8 for 95 for Gloucestershire against the Zimbabwean tourists at Gloucester in 2000: his best Championship figures are 7 for 38 (10 for 75 in the match) against Somerset at Bristol in 2006 ...

THE FIGURES
Batting and fielding

	M	Inns	NO	Runs	HS	Avge	S/R	100	50	4s	6s	Ct	St
Tests *to 11.9.06*	1	2	0	27	20	13.50	60.00	0	0	5	0	0	0
ODIs *to 11.9.06*	7	3	1	16	7*	8.00	76.19	0	0	1	0	0	0
First-class *to 11.9.06*	158	222	47	2513	62	14.36	–	0	5	–	–	38	0

Bowling

	M	Balls	Runs	Wkts	BB	Avge	RpO	S/R	5i	10m
Tests *to 11.9.06*	1	246	122	3	3–68	40.66	2.97	82.00	0	0
ODIs *to 11.9.06*	7	372	241	11	3–32	21.90	3.88	33.81	0	0
First-class *to 11.9.06*	158	29767	15200	574	8–95	26.48	3.06	51.85	30	5

BRENDON McCULLUM

Full name	**Brendon Barrie McCullum**
Born	**September 27, 1981, Dunedin, Otago**
Teams	**Canterbury, Glamorgan**
Style	**Right-hand bat, wicketkeeper**
Test debut	**New Zealand v South Africa at Hamilton 2003-04**
ODI debut	**New Zealand v Australia at Sydney 2001-02**

THE PROFILE Brendon McCullum has stepped up to the national side as a wicketkeeper-batsman after an outstanding career in international youth cricket, where he proved capable of dominating opposition attacks. He found it hard to replicate that at the highest level at first, although there were occasional fireworks at domestic level. But he finally made his mark in England in 2004, with 200 runs in the Test series, including an entertaining 96 at Lord's. After that near-miss he finally brought up his maiden century in Bangladesh in October, with 143 at Dhaka. He added another hundred in the two-day victory over Zimbabwe in August 2005, and now needs to reproduce that form against the stronger teams. McCullum first made the New Zealand one-day side as a batsman, in the 2001-02 VB Series in Australia, where he made the acquaintance of Brett Lee, who has since let him have more than one beamer, to widespread outrage. Two years later McCullum, by now keeping wicket, forced his way past Robbie Hart into the Test side for the 2003-04 series against South Africa. At Napier in April 2005 he narrowly missed another Test century, falling lbw to Lasith Malinga for 99 in the match where Malinga's low-slung action caused several batsmen to complain that they were "losing" the ball in the umpires' trousers. But McCullum biffed two sixes and ten fours in that innings, and had onlookers murmuring the name Gilchrist, which bodes well for New Zealand's prospects, especially in the 2007 World Cup.

THE FACTS McCullum has made five dismissals in an ODI innings three times: the only other New Zealander to do this is Adam Parore (once) ... His 101 against the Rest of South Africa at Benoni in April 2006 included seven sixes ... McCullum hit 186 (out of 311) in an Under-19 Test against South Africa at Lincoln in 2000-01, and made 160 against Leicestershire on his debut for Glamorgan in July 2006 ... His father Stuart and brother Nathan have also played for Otago ...

THE FIGURES
Batting and fielding

	M	Inns	NO	Runs	HS	Avge	S/R	100	50	4s	6s	Ct	St
Tests to 11.9.06	23	35	2	1083	143	32.81	62.56	2	6	135	9	56	5
ODIs to 11.9.06	84	65	14	1120	56*	21.96	77.24	0	4	91	22	104	8
First-class to 11.9.06	55	90	5	2815	160	33.11	–		6	14	–	–	130	11

Bowling

	M	Balls	Runs	Wkts	BB	Avge	RpO	S/R	5i	10m
Tests to 11.9.06	23	0	–	–	–	–	–	–	–	–
ODIs to 11.9.06	84	0	–	–	–	–	–	–	–	–
First-class to 11.9.06	55	0	–	–	–	–	–	–	–	–

STUART MacGILL

Full name	**Stuart Charles Glyndwr MacGill**
Born	**February 25, 1971, Mount Lawley, Perth, W Australia**
Teams	**New South Wales**
Style	**Right-hand bat, legspinner**
Test debut	**Australia v South Africa at Adelaide 1997-98**
ODI debut	**Australia v Pakistan at Sydney 1999-2000**

THE PROFILE The praise lavished on his decision to boycott Zimbabwe in 2004 continued an unwelcome pattern for Stuart MacGill: he has long generated headlines for being out of the Australian team rather than for his performances in it. An old-fashioned operator with a gargantuan legbreak and a majestic wrong'un, MacGill has the best strike rate and worst luck of any modern spinner. His misfortune has been to play alongside Shane Warne. After showing they could work in tandem with 13 wickets against Pakistan at Sydney in January 2005, MacGill hoped – almost pleaded – for more double-act opportunities. In seven Tests in 2005-06, he dismantled the World XI, and finished with 16 wickets in two games against Bangladesh. He has stayed philosophical, eagerly running in and usually running amok. A batting duffer and increasingly feckless fielder, he has played only three ODIs despite collecting his domestic scalps at a stupefying rate of one every 27 balls. MacGill seldom smiles after taking a wicket: instead he lets out a roar of accomplishment. It is only one of his quirks. He is a wine buff who only recently learned to enjoy beer, and he once read 24 novels on tour in Pakistan. The son and grandson of Western Australian players, he socialises with non-cricketers, and is often portrayed as a thinker, the odd man out. It's something he plays down – although, tellingly, no other Aussie declined to tour Zimbabwe. Australia's next scheduled Test trip is back there in 2007, and MacGill's mind has not changed.

THE FACTS MacGill collected 53 wickets in 11 Tests during Shane Warne's 2003-04 drugs ban, yet was often maligned for bowling one boundary-ball per over – rather unfair, considering that was standard for all leggies pre-Warne ... In 16 Tests in which they have played together, MacGill has taken 82 wickets at 22.4, to Warne's 74 at 29.57 ... MacGill has taken 55 wickets against West Indies, 39 (in only six Tests) against England, and 33 at 15.75 against Bangladesh: 53 of his wickets have come in eight Tests at Sydney ... He is married to the former *Neighbours* actress and TV presenter Rachel Friend ...

THE FIGURES

Batting and fielding

	M	Inns	NO	Runs	HS	Avge	S/R	100	50	4s	6s	Ct	St
Tests *to 11.9.06*	40	45	11	347	43	10.20	49.43	0	0	38	2	16	0
ODIs *to 11.9.06*	3	2	1	1	1	1.00	33.33	0	0	0	0	2	0
First-class *to 11.9.06*	164	194	51	1421	53	9.93	_	0	1	–	–	70	0

Bowling

	M	Balls	Runs	Wkts	BB	Avge	RpO	S/R	5i	10m
Tests *to 11.9.06*	40	10211	5387	198	8–108	27.20	3.16	51.57	12	2
ODIs *to 11.9.06*	3	180	105	6	4–19	17.50	3.50	30.00	0	0
First-class *to 11.9.06*	164	36581	20704	700	8–108	29.57	3.39	52.25	40	6

AUSTRALIA

GLENN McGRATH

Full name	**Glenn Donald McGrath**
Born	**February 9, 1970, Dubbo, New South Wales**
Teams	**New South Wales**
Style	**Right-hand bat, right-arm fast-medium bowler**
Test debut	**Australia v New Zealand at Perth 1993-94**
ODI debut	**Australia v South Africa at Melbourne 1993-94**

THE PROFILE The young Glenn McGrath was described as "thin – but Ambrose-thin, not Bruce Reid-thin". Later, Mike Atherton compared McGrath to Ambrose on a vaster scale. He became, after a faltering start, the great Australian paceman of his time: only Dennis Lillee threatens his title as the greatest of all time – even if he never delivers another ball. "Whenever people have written me off, I have always proved them wrong," warned McGrath as the press box prepared its playing obituaries early in 2006. He still bowls an unremitting off-stump line and an immaculate length, gains off-cut and bounce, and specialises in the opposition's biggest wickets. His bulging trophy cabinet includes World Cup winners' medals from 1999 and 2003. An ankle injury threatened to derail his quest for 500 Test wickets, but after briefly contemplating retirement he returned with yet another five-wicket haul against Sri Lanka in July 2004. Three months later, at Nagpur, he became the first paceman to play 100 matches in the baggy green, and his greatness was further confirmed as he demolished the brittle Pakistanis at Perth with 8 for 24. Adept at picking his moments, he chose the first day at Lord's in 2005 to reach 500, and his subsequent ankle and arm injuries were crucial to the Ashes defeat. The following summer was also painfully disrupted with the recurrence of his wife Jane's cancer. He withdrew temporarily, but at 36 still wants to right the wrongs of that 2005 Ashes campaign.

THE FACTS McGrath started as a batting rabbit – he was out to his first ball in both Tests and ODIs – but eventually made 61 against New Zealand in 2004-05, the third-highest score by a No. 11 in a Test ... His 7 for 15 against the outclassed Namibians in 2003 are the best figures in World Cup history ... Against the World XI in October 2005 McGrath passed Courtney Walsh's record of 519 Test wickets by a fast bowler ... McGrath has taken 136 Test wickets against England, at 20.47, and 110 at 19.38 against West Indies ... His record includes one ODI for the World XI ...

THE FIGURES
Batting and fielding

	M	Inns	NO	Runs	HS	Avge	S/R	100	50	4s	6s	Ct	St
Tests to 11.9.06	119	133	49	631	61	7.51	41.48	0	2	51	1	37	0
ODIs to 11.9.06	221	60	32	104	11	3.71	48.82	0	0	7	0	34	0
First-class to 11.9.06	184	188	65	967	61	7.86	–	0	2	–	–	53	0

Bowling

	M	Balls	Runs	Wkts	BB	Avge	RpO	S/R	5i	10m
Tests to 11.9.06	119	27993	11684	542	8–24	21.55	2.50	51.64	28	3
ODIs to 11.9.06	221	11563	7425	331	7–15	22.43	3.85	34.93	7	0
First-class to 11.9.06	184	40504	16912	814	8–24	20.77	2.50	49.75	41	7

FARVEEZ MAHAROOF

Full name	**Mohamed Farveez Maharoof**
Born	**September 7, 1984, Colombo**
Teams	**Bloomfield**
Style	**Right-hand bat, right-arm fast-medium bowler**
Test debut	**Sri Lanka v Zimbabwe at Harare 2003-04**
ODI debut	**Sri Lanka v Zimbabwe at Harare 2003-04**

THE PROFILE Farveez Maharoof is a young fast-bowling allrounder of exciting potential, and bowls lively seamers from an upright, open-chested action. The selectors, impressed by his performances as Sri Lanka's Under-19 captain, fast-tracked him into the national squad for the Zimbabwe tour early in 2004, as they looked towards the future, especially the 2007 World Cup. Faced with weak opposition, the 19-year-old Maharoof picked up a bunch of wickets – including 3 for 3 in his first ODI – but then came up against better players during the Asia Cup. He still performed reasonably well, and made a mark with his swinging deliveries when South Africa toured. He had worked his way up through the representative ranks, playing for Sri Lanka's Under-15, U17 and U19 teams, and enjoyed a prolific school career for Wesley College, with a highest score of 243 and best bowling figures of 8 for 20. He has found Test wickets hard to come by, but his occasionally ferocious hitting has helped him cement a place in the one-day side. A mean display during the Champions Trophy in England in 2004, when he exploited the end-of-summer conditions expertly, suggested that he could be especially useful when Sri Lanka play in seamer-friendly conditions, although his major contribution to the 5-0 clean sweep of the one-dayers in England in 2006 was a rapid half-century at Headingley. Most importantly, he has also shown that he is comfortable under pressure, all too often the Achilles heel of Sri Lanka's recent fast-bowling allrounders.

THE FACTS Maharoof took 4 for 20, his best one-day figures, to help Sri Lanka to victory over India at Ahmedabad in November 2005 after coming on as the supersub ... He had figures of 3-1-3-3 on his ODI debut, as Zimbabwe were bowled out for 35 at Harare in April 2004 ... Maharoof captained Sri Lanka in the 2004 Under-19 World Cup, and won the Man of the Match award against Australia ... He played for Middlesex 2nd XI in 2003 ...

THE FIGURES

Batting and fielding

	M	Inns	NO	Runs	HS	Avge	S/R	100	50	4s	6s	Ct	St
Tests to 11.9.06	15	23	4	449	72	23.63	39.48	0	3	56	2	5	0
ODIs to 11.9.06	46	29	9	404	58*	20.20	88.20	0	1	34	10	9	0
First-class to 11.9.06	31	44	5	828	72	21.23	41.64	0	4	–	–	12	0

Bowling

	M	Balls	Runs	Wkts	BB	Avge	RpO	S/R	5i	10m
Tests to 11.9.06	15	1944	1095	20	4–52	54.75	3.37	97.20	0	0
ODIs to 11.9.06	46	1864	1438	52	4–20	27.65	4.62	35.84	0	0
First-class to 11.9.06	31	3923	2114	69	4–12	30.63	3.23	56.85	0	0

SAJID MAHMOOD

Full name	**Sajid Iqbal Mahmood**
Born	**December 21, 1981, Bolton, Lancashire**
Teams	**Lancashire**
Style	**Right-hand bat, right-arm fast-medium bowler**
Test debut	**England v Sri Lanka at Lord's 2006**
ODI debut	**England v New Zealand at Bristol 2004**

THE PROFILE A former supermarket shelf-stacker, Sajid Mahmood was spotted in the Bolton League and joined Lancashire on a scholarship in 2002. From there, he rose rapidly through the ranks, and, despite having only six first-class wickets to his name, he was selected for the England A tour of India in 2003-04. In unhelpful conditions, his wholehearted performances on that trip meant his full England debut was only a matter of time, although it was a chastening experience – his seven overs disappeared for 56 against New Zealand in a one-dayer at Bristol. Mahmood is tall and decidedly rapid, and bowls a fuller length than many of his pace-bowling peers. For a while, he made his name at the expense of his team-mates – in 2003, he put Andrew Flintoff out of action with a beamer in the Old Trafford nets, and later broke Alex Gidman's hand at the Academy. But three years later, he was inflicting the damage on his opponents instead, as he announced his Test arrival against Sri Lanka at Lord's with a fiery three-wicket burst, including another debutant, Chamara Kapugedera, who received the perfect inswinger first ball. But it got harder after that: he tended to fire one down the leg side every over, and proved horrendously expensive in the one-dayers against Sri Lanka that followed. Another injury to Flintoff (not Mahmood-induced this time) gave him another chance against Pakistan, and after failing to take a wicket in front of his home crowd he got it right at Headingley, with four wickets on the final day.

THE FACTS Mahmood took a wicket (Kumar Sangakkara) in his second over in Tests, at Lord's in May 2006, and soon had 3 for 6 – but finished with 3 for 50 ... His figures of 7-0-80-2 against Sri Lanka at The Oval in June 2006 were among England's most expensive in ODIs (Steve Harmison claimed the record with 10-0-97-0 a few days later) ... Mahmood struck 94 from 66 balls for Lancashire v Sussex at Manchester in June 2004 ... Amir Khan, the young boxer who won a silver medal at the 2004 Athens Olympics, is his cousin ...

THE FIGURES

Batting and fielding

	M	Inns	NO	Runs	HS	Avge	S/R	100	50	4s	6s	Ct	St
Tests *to 11.9.06*	5	5	1	63	33	15.75	57.27	0	0	8	0	0	0
ODIs *to 11.9.06*	12	8	1	53	22*	7.57	91.37	0	0	5	1	0	0
First-class *to 11.9.06*	40	50	7	655	94	15.23	63.34	0	2	–	–	7	0

Bowling

	M	Balls	Runs	Wkts	BB	Avge	RpO	S/R	5i	10m
Tests *to 11.9.06*	5	822	498	15	4–22	33.20	3.63	54.80	0	0
ODIs *to 11.9.06*	12	528	562	12	3–37	46.83	6.38	44.00	0	0
First-class *to 11.9.06*	40	5613	3450	115	5–37	30.00	3.68	48.80	3	0

BLESSING MAHWIRE

Full name	**Ngonidzashe Blessing Mahwire**
Born	**July 31, 1982, Bikita, Masvingo**
Teams	**Manicaland**
Style	**Right-hand bat, right-arm fast-medium bowler**
Test debut	**Zimbabwe v Pakistan at Harare 2002-03**
ODI debut	**Zimbabwe v Australia at Melbourne 2003-04**

THE PROFILE A brisk awayswing bowler and a handy lower-order batsman, Blessing Mahwire was the first international player to emerge from the Masvingo area of Zimbabwe, where he turned in some impressive schoolboy performances, especially with the bat. He attended the CFX Academy in 2001 and was posted to Manicaland, where he developed more as a bowler, although without losing his ability with the bat – he made a maiden Test half-century against New Zealand in August 2005, after scoring 42 in the first innings. He had won his first Test cap against Pakistan at Harare three years earlier, but struggled to make an impact at first. He was recalled for the tour of Australia late in 2003, and although he was lucky enough to miss Matthew Hayden's 380 at Perth he did play in the second Test at Sydney, but went wicketless. He nevertheless impressed with his whole-hearted attitude, and stayed for the home series against West Indies in November 2003. But six months later his bowling action came under scrutiny, and he was reported to the ICC after the first Test against Sri Lanka at Harare. With assistance from coach Kevin Curran, he remodelled his action, getting more side-on, and returned against India and New Zealand later in 2005, doing well with both bat and ball, although he struggled for consistency in the West Indies early in 2006. By then he had emerged as an unofficial spokesman for the players in their ongoing dispute with the board.

THE FACTS Mahwire's modest batting record does include one first-class century – 115 for Manicaland against Matabeleland at Bulawayo in March 2004 ... His best bowling figures of 7 for 64 also came against Matabeleland at Bulawayo, the following season ... Mahwire took seven wickets (including three in the final) as Zimbabwe won the tri-nations tournament against Bermuda and Canada in Trinidad in May 2006 ...

THE FIGURES
Batting and fielding

	M	Inns	NO	Runs	HS	Avge	S/R	100	50	4s	6s	Ct	St
Tests to 11.9.06	10	17	6	147	50*	13.36	42.48	0	1	21	2	1	0
ODIs to 11.9.06	22	19	8	117	22*	10.63	46.98	0	0	5	2	6	0
First-class to 11.9.06	46	77	12	997	115*	15.33	–	1	2	–	–	16	0

Bowling

	M	Balls	Runs	Wkts	BB	Avge	RpO	S/R	5i	10m
Tests to 11.9.06	10	1287	915	18	4–92	50.83	4.26	71.50	0	0
ODIs to 11.9.06	22	855	747	21	3–29	35.57	5.24	40.71	0	0
First-class to 11.9.06	46	6785	3929	131	7–64	29.99	3.47	51.79	3	0

LASITH MALINGA

Full name	**Separamadu Lasith Malinga Swarnajith**
Born	**August 28, 1983, Galle**
Teams	**Nondescripts**
Style	**Right-hand bat, right-arm fast bowler**
Test debut	**Sri Lanka v Australia at Darwin 2004**
ODI debut	**Sri Lanka v United Arab Emirates at Dambulla 2004**

THE PROFILE   A rare Sri Lankan cricketer from the south, Lasith Malinga hardly played any proper cricket until he was 17, preferring the softball version in the coconut groves near his home in Rathgama, a village near Galle. But after he was spotted by the former Test fast bowler Champaka Ramanayake, he was hurried into the Galle team, took 4 for 40 and 4 for 37 on his first-class debut against Colombo Cricket Club, and has hardly looked back since. He bowls with a distinctive and explosive round-arm action – which earned him the nickname "Slinga Malinga" – and generates genuine pace, often disconcerting batsmen who struggle to pick up the ball's trajectory. In New Zealand in 2005 the home batsmen complained that the ball was getting lost in the umpires' trousers, and unsuccessfully tried to persuade them to wear white ones. Malinga was a surprise selection for the 2004 tour of Australia, despite a fearsome reputation at home. He soon showed his speed, starting with 6 for 90 against the Northern Territory Chief Minister's XI at Darwin. That paved the way for his inclusion in the Test team, and he acquitted himself well, with six wickets in his first match and four in the second: he added 5 for 80 (nine in the match) against New Zealand at Napier in April 2005. With a propensity for no-balls he is usually seen as too erratic for the one-day side, but belied that reputation with 13 wickets in the 5-0 whitewash of England in 2006.

THE FACTS   After Malinga took a Test-best 5 for 80 (9 for 210 in the match) with his low-slung action against New Zealand at Napier in April 2005, Stephen Fleming unsuccessfully asked the umpires to change their clothing: "There's a period there where the ball gets lost in their trousers" ... He took 6 for 17, his best first-class figures, as Galle bowled out the Police for 51 in Colombo in November 2003 ... In 2004 Malinga told Cricinfo: "My hero was Waqar Younis. I loved the way he bowled fast inswinging yorkers" ...

THE FIGURES
Batting and fielding

	M	Inns	NO	Runs	HS	Avge	S/R	100	50	4s	6s	Ct	St
Tests *to 11.9.06*	19	24	10	125	26	8.92	38.81	0	0	16	1	7	0
ODIs *to 11.9.06*	15	8	5	30	15	10.00	49.18	0	0	2	0	1	0
First-class *to 11.9.06*	64	80	35	377	30	8.37	37.14	0	0	–	–	21	0

Bowling

	M	Balls	Runs	Wkts	BB	Avge	RpO	S/R	5i	10m
Tests *to 11.9.06*	19	3165	2034	62	5–80	32.80	3.85	51.04	1	0
ODIs *to 11.9.06*	15	734	580	20	4–44	29.00	4.74	36.70	0	0
First-class *to 11.9.06*	64	9002	5963	193	6–17	30.89	3.97	46.64	5	0

HAMISH MARSHALL

NEW ZEALAND

Full name	**Hamish John Hamilton Marshall**
Born	**February 15, 1979, Warkworth, Auckland**
Teams	**Northern Districts, Gloucestershire**
Style	**Right-hand bat, occasional right-arm medium-pacer**
Test debut	**New Zealand v South Africa at Jo'burg 2000-01**
ODI debut	**New Zealand v Pakistan at Lahore 2003-04**

THE PROFILE A stylish middle-order batsman, curly-haired Hamish Marshall made his Test debut against South Africa in December 2000. The match was disrupted by rain, but Marshall, only 21, made an unbeaten 40 from No. 7, showing great maturity and promise. However, he had to wait another three years for a second chance: he was called up for a one-day series in Pakistan late in 2003. He made 55 in the first match, and an impressive 101 not out in the third, but New Zealand were still whitewashed 5-0. But when Pakistan made the return tour immediately afterwards, Marshall contributed 64 and 84, and this time his team won. More one-day runs followed against South Africa, and in England in 2004, including 44 as West Indies were beaten in the final of the NatWest Series. His maiden Test century followed in March 2005, against Australia, no less – a fine 146 at Christchurch, in which he was unshakeable against pace, although admittedly Brett Lee wasn't playing. Another big hundred – 160 – followed next month against Sri Lanka ... not bad going for someone whose highest score when he made his Test debut was only 58. But lean times followed, and although coach John Bracewell remained an admirer, not least because of Marshall's fine fielding, the critics were collecting a lot of ammunition – 279 runs in 18 one-day innings in 2005-06, with a highest score of 50 and eight single-figure dismissals, and a similar drought of 102 runs in eight Test innings during the season.

THE FACTS Marshall did not make a first-class hundred until his 81st innings, in December 2004 – and his next two centuries were in Tests early in 2005, including his career-best 160 against Sri Lanka at Napier ... Against Australia in 2004-05 Marshall played alongside his identical twin James – a Test first – forcing Ricky Ponting to ponder how to tell them apart ... While on a scholarship to Lord's in 1998 Marshall fielded as substitute in the Princess Diana Memorial match, and caught Mike Atherton off Chris Cairns ...

THE FIGURES
Batting and fielding

	M	Inns	NO	Runs	HS	Avge	S/R	100	50	4s	6s	Ct	St
Tests *to 11.9.06*	13	19	2	652	160	38.35	47.34	2	2	83	3	1	0
ODIs *to 11.9.06*	55	51	8	1310	101*	30.46	72.85	1	11	88	6	15	0
First-class *to 11.9.06*	74	123	8	3761	168	32.70	–	8	17	–	–	34	0

Bowling

	M	Balls	Runs	Wkts	BB	Avge	RpO	S/R	5i	10m
Tests *to 11.9.06*	13	6	4	0	–	–	4.00	–	0	0
ODIs *to 11.9.06*	55	0	–	–	–	–	–	–	–	–
First-class *to 11.9.06*	74	300	160	2	1–12	80.00	3.20	150.00	0	0

CHRIS MARTIN

NEW ZEALAND

Full name	**Christopher Stewart Martin**
Born	**December 10, 1974, Christchurch, Canterbury**
Teams	**Auckland**
Style	**Right-hand bat, right-arm fast-medium bowler**
Test debut	**New Zealand v S Africa at Bloemfontein 2000-01**
ODI debut	**New Zealand v Zimbabwe at Taupo 2000-01**

THE PROFILE Chris Martin is an angular fast-medium bowler who receives almost as much attention for his inept batting as for his nagging bowling, which has produced 99 Test wickets, including 11 in the match as New Zealand whipped South Africa at Auckland in March 2004. Seven more scalps followed in the next game. It was all the more remarkable as they were his first Tests in almost two years – he had been overlooked since Pakistan piled up 643 at Lahore in May 2002 (Martin 1 for 108). He got his original chance after a crop of injuries, but did not disgrace himself in the first portion of his Test career, taking 34 wickets at 34 in his first 11 Tests, including six as Pakistan were crushed by an innings at Hamilton in 2000-01. Since his return he has maintained that average of 34, happy to bowl long spells *à la* Ewen Chatfield – he took 5 for 152 at Brisbane in November 2004, after a surprisingly unproductive England tour. He remained in the frame throughout 2005-06, rounding the season off with 5 for 37 as South Africa struggled in the first innings of the final Test at Johannesburg, which they eventually squeaked by four wickets. But Martin is likely to be remembered more for his clueless batting: after 41 Test innings he has 17 ducks and is yet to reach double figures, although he did once manage 25 for his former province, Canterbury, sharing a stand of 75 with Chris Harris.

THE FACTS Very few Test players approach Martin's negative ratio of runs (48) to wickets (99): two that do are the England pair of Bill Bowes (28 runs, 68 wickets) and David Larter (15 runs, 37 wickets) ... Martin shares the Test record of four pairs of ducks, with Marvan Atapattu, Bhagwat Chandrasekhar, Merv Dillon and Courtney Walsh ... He has played only two ODIs since 2000-01, but took six of his 11 wickets in those two games ... In Tests Martin averages 23.13 with the ball against South Africa, but 102.12 against Australia ...

THE FIGURES
Batting and fielding

	M	Inns	NO	Runs	HS	Avge	S/R	100	50	4s	6s	Ct	St
Tests to 11.9.06	31	41	18	48	7	2.08	18.60	0	0	6	0	9	0
ODIs to 11.9.06	9	6	1	6	3	1.19	25.00	0	0	0	0	3	0
First-class to 11.9.06	102	128	58	294	25	4.20	–	0	0	–	–	22	0

Bowling

	M	Balls	Runs	Wkts	BB	Avge	RpO	S/R	5i	10m
Tests to 11.9.06	31	5806	3413	99	6–54	34.47	3.52	58.64	7	1
ODIs to 11.9.06	9	438	397	11	3–62	36.09	5.43	39.81	0	0
First-class to 11.9.06	102	19380	9702	305	6–54	31.80	3.00	63.54	13	1

DAMIEN MARTYN

AUSTRALIA

Full name	**Damien Richard Martyn**
Born	**October 21, 1971, Darwin, Northern Territory**
Teams	**Western Australia**
Style	**Right-hand bat, right-arm medium-pace bowler**
Test debut	**Australia v West Indies at Brisbane 1992-93**
ODI debut	**Australia v West Indies at Sydney 1992-93**

THE PROFILE No contemporary cricketer, Tendulkar aside, makes batting look as simple as Damien Martyn. But it was not always so. For the brash youngster, batting was an exercise in extravagance: to defend was to display weakness, a policy that backfired in January 1994, when an airy square-drive at Sydney triggered a five-run defeat by South Africa and a seven-year hitch to his own career. By the time Western Australia made him captain at 23, Martyn looked a tormented man. All the more remarkable, then, that he blossomed into a relaxed, feathery artist. He is an old-style batsman whose first movement is back. Elbow high, head still, he has a golfer's deft touch, and all the shots, including a brutal reverse-sweep. Mostly, though, Martyn sticks to the textbook, and composes pristine hundreds which, like the best wicketkeepers, pass almost unnoticed. He was the quiet man of the 2003 World Cup until spanking 88 in the final despite a broken finger. From March 2004 a magnificent 13-month streak of 1608 Test runs at 61, with seven varied hundreds, finally moved him from the shadows into the more uncomfortable limelight. The flood ended in England: after only 178 runs – and a couple of horrid umpiring decisions – he was the major casualty of the Ashes defeat. He was reprieved when experience was wanted for South Africa early in 2006. Just as returning to a 34-year-old looked dubious, Martyn repaid the selectors with a nerveless 101 that led to victory in the final Test at Johannesburg.

THE FACTS Martyn averages 61.57 against Pakistan, and 40 or more against all the other Test sides except Bangladesh (5.50) … In ODIs his *lowest* average is against Pakistan (28.31), but he averages 118 from 15 matches against Zimbabwe … Martyn has been on the winning side in 147 of his 200 ODIs … He is the only Test cricketer who was born in Darwin, but missed out (broken finger) when the Northern Territory capital staged its first Test in 2003 …

THE FIGURES
Batting and fielding

	M	Inns	NO	Runs	HS	Avge	S/R	100	50	4s	6s	Ct	St
Tests *to 11.9.06*	65	106	14	4361	165	47.40	51.48	13	23	509	10	33	0
ODIs *to 11.9.06*	200	174	49	5030	144*	40.24	78.50	5	34	401	21	65	0
First-class *to 11.9.06*	201	338	46	14522	238	49.73	–		44	73	–	–	155	2

Bowling

	M	Balls	Runs	Wkts	BB	Avge	RpO	S/R	5i	10m
Tests *to 11.9.06*	65	348	168	2	1–1	84.00	2.89	174.00	0	0
ODIs *to 11.9.06*	200	794	704	12	2–21	58.66	5.31	66.16	0	0
First-class *to 11.9.06*	201	3365	1563	37	4–30	42.24	2.78	90.94	0	0

HAMILTON MASAKADZA

Full name	**Hamilton Masakadza**
Born	**August 9, 1983, Harare**
Teams	**Manicaland**
Style	**Right-hand bat, occasional legspinner**
Test debut	**Zimbabwe v West Indies at Harare 2001**
ODI debut	**Zimbabwe v South Africa at Bulawayo 2001-02**

THE PROFILE Hamilton Masakadza was still a schoolboy when he set the record – since beaten by Bangladesh's Mohammad Ashraful – as the youngest man to score a century on Test debut. That was against West Indies in July 2001, when he made a composed 119 from No. 3 – driving well, and showing few signs of nerves in the nineties – that was largely responsible for Zimbabwe saving the match after trailing by 216 on first innings. A year later, though, he put his professional cricket career on hold to study at the University of the Free State. Although it was agreed that he would still be available for Zimbabwe if required, he could not maintain his form playing against South African clubs, and the selectors initially decided to await his return in 2005. But the various disputes that have bedevilled Zimbabwe's cricket led to his early recall for the one-dayers against England in December 2004: not surprisingly, he struggled at first, before registering his maiden ODI fifty in the final match. His return to the Test team brought mixed results, but he was the best batsman, technically, on Zimbabwe's tour of South Africa early in 2005, showing an application lacking in his team-mates. He added a polished 71 against India at Harare in September. Masakadza declined a contract early in 2006, saying that he wanted to concentrate on his studies, but he remained in the frame despite that, and played against Bangladesh later in the year, after missing the tour of West Indies.

THE FACTS Masakadza was only the second Zimbabwean, after Dave Houghton in 1992-93, to make a century on Test debut: he made 119 against West Indies in July 2001, 11 days short of his 18th birthday ... He was the youngest to score a Test-debut century at the time, a record later beaten by Mohammad Ashraful of Bangladesh: only Ashraful, Mushtaq Mohammad and Sachin Tendulkar have made Test hundreds at a more tender age ... In February 2001 Masakadza had become not only the youngest Zimbabwean ever to score a first-class century, but also the first black Zimbabwean to make one, with 100 for Mashonaland against the CFX Academy ...

THE FIGURES
Batting and fielding

	M	Inns	NO	Runs	HS	Avge	S/R	100	50	4s	6s	Ct	St
Tests to 11.9.06	15	30	1	785	119	27.06	43.95	1	3	107	4	8	0
ODIs to 11.9.06	23	23	1	355	66	16.13	61.10	0	3	37	0	11	0
First-class to 11.9.06	40	70	3	2287	142	34.13	–	5	12	–	–	20	0

Bowling

	M	Balls	Runs	Wkts	BB	Avge	RpO	S/R	5i	10m
Tests to 11.9.06	15	126	39	2	1–9	19.50	1.85	63.00	0	0
ODIs to 11.9.06	23	146	143	5	2–26	28.60	5.87	29.20	0	0
First-class to 11.9.06	40	776	427	8	1–8	53.37	3.30	97.00	0	0

MASHRAFE MORTAZA

Full name	**Mashrafe bin Mortaza**
Born	**October 5, 1983, Norail, Jessore, Khulna**
Teams	**Khulna**
Style	**Right-hand bat, right-arm fast-medium bowler**
Test debut	**Bangladesh v Zimbabwe at Dhaka 2001-02**
ODI debut	**Bangladesh v Zimbabwe at Chittagong 2001-02**

THE PROFILE Young, quick and aggressive, Mashrafe Mortaza has emerged as the leader of Bangladesh's pack of upcoming young pacemen, although fitness remains a problem. He made great strides under the tutelage of Andy Roberts, working on his stamina, and he was given his first Test cap against Zimbabwe at Dhaka in 2001-02, in what was his first-class debut – indeed by mid-2006 he had played only seven first-class matches outside the Test arena. Though banging it in is his preferred style, Mashrafe proved adept at reining in his attacking instincts to concentrate on line and length. He excelled in the second Test against England in 2003-04, taking 4 for 60 in the first innings to keep Bangladesh in touch, but suffered a twisted knee towards the end of the game that kept him out of Tests for over a year. He was recalled towards the end of 2004, and subsequently enhanced his reputation on the inaugural tour of England, standing head and shoulders above his team-mates in a torrid series. He is not a complete mug with the bat. A persistent back injury caused him to return home early and miss the Test series in Sri Lanka in September 2005 – the sixth time he had failed to last throughout a tour – but he was back to face the Australians in April 2006, and removed Matthew Hayden early on to start the Aussies' embarrassment in the first Test at Fatullah.

THE FACTS Mashrafe Mortaza was the first Bangladeshi (Nazmul Hossain in 2004-05 was the second) to make his first-class debut in a Test match: only three others have done this since 1899 – Graham Vivian of New Zealand (1964-65), Zimbabwe's Ujesh Ranchod (1992-93) and Yasir Ali of Pakistan in 2003-04 ... He started the famous ODI victory over Australia at Cardiff in 2005 by dismissing Adam Gilchrist second ball for 0 ... Mortaza's 6 for 26 against Kenya in Nairobi in August 2006 are Bangladesh's best bowling figures in ODIs ... He scored 132 not out for Khulna to help stave off defeat after following on against Sylhet at Khulna in 2004-05 ...

THE FIGURES

Batting and fielding

	M	Inns	NO	Runs	HS	Avge	S/R	100	50	4s	6s	Ct	St
Tests to 11.9.06	20	37	4	283	48	63.73	62.50	0	0	33	7	5	0
ODIs to 11.9.06	41	33	7	396	44*	15.23	97.53	0	0	38	11	11	0
First-class to 11.9.06	27	48	6	640	132*	15.23	71.50	1	2	–	–	7	0

Bowling

	M	Balls	Runs	Wkts	BB	Avge	RpO	S/R	5i	10m
Tests to 11.9.06	20	3560	1871	50	4–60	37.42	3.15	71.20	0	0
ODIs to 11.9.06	41	2115	1684	54	6–26	31.18	4.77	39.16	1	0
First-class to 11.9.06	27	4721	2465	69	4–60	35.72	3.13	68.42	0	0

STUART MATSIKENYERI

Full name	**Stuart Matsikenyeri**
Born	**May 3, 1983, Harare**
Teams	**Manicaland**
Style	**Right-hand bat, offspinner**
Test debut	**Zimbabwe v West Indies at Harare 2003-04**
ODI debut	**Zimbabwe v Pakistan at Bulawayo 2002-03**

THE PROFILE A talented batsman and a modest, hard-working character, Stuart Matsikenyeri followed his Churchill High School friends Hamilton Masakadza and Tatenda Taibu into the national team. He's on the short side, with a ready smile, a good eye and a penchant for the screaming cut and the pull – but his impulsive streak sometimes finds him out, as does high-quality fast bowling, and he is yet to improve on the 57 he made in his first Test innings, against West Indies at Harare in November 2003. He had played a few one-day games before that, including one in the 2003 World Cup, and also made a vital 44 at Trent Bridge later that year – putting on 96 with Grant Flower after his side had lurched to 11 for 4 – to take Zimbabwe to a rare victory over England. Also a useful offspinner, Matsikenyeri learned his cricket in the black township of Highfield on the outskirts of Harare. He represented Zimbabwe's Under-16 and U-19 teams, and also played club cricket in Australia, an important step in his development. He is an impressive fielder in a variety of positions, especially the gully. In 2006 he declined to sign a new contract with the board, but, like several others, subsequently returned to the fold as the lure of the 2007 World Cup grew closer. After missing the West Indian tour early in 2006, he made a run-a-ball 89 in his first match back, to help Zimbabwe to a one-day victory over Bangladesh.

THE FACTS Matsikenyeri made 150 against the Bangladesh Board President's XI at Chittagong in January 2005, putting on 241 with Vusi Sibanda (122) ... He made 57 (and 46 not out) on his Test debut, against West Indies at Harare in November 2003, but passed 50 only once in his seven subsequent Tests ... Matsikenyeri's highest ODI score of 89, against Bangladesh at Harare in July 2006, helped Zimbabwe to their first win over a Test-playing country since January 2005 (also Bangladesh) ... He took 5 for 41 for Manicaland against Midlands at Mutare in October 2004 ...

THE FIGURES
Batting and fielding

	M	Inns	NO	Runs	HS	Avge	S/R	100	50	4s	6s	Ct	St
Tests to 11.9.06	8	16	1	351	57	23.40	50.57	0	2	46	3	7	0
ODIs to 11.9.06	47	45	2	793	89	18.44	63.59	0	3	86	4	15	0
First-class to 11.9.06	55	100	9	2504	150	27.51	–	0	3	13	–	38	0

Bowling

	M	Balls	Runs	Wkts	BB	Avge	RpO	S/R	5i	10m
Tests to 11.9.06	8	483	345	2	1–58	172.50	4.28	241.50	0	0
ODIs to 11.9.06	47	666	585	11	2–33	53.18	5.27	60.54	0	0
First-class to 11.9.06	55	2810	2079	48	5–41	43.31	4.43	58.54	1	0

KYLE MILLS

NEW ZEALAND

Full name	**Kyle David Mills**
Born	**March 15, 1979, Auckland**
Teams	**Auckland**
Style	**Right-hand bat, right-arm fast-medium**
Test debut	**New Zealand v England at Nottingham 2004**
ODI debut	**New Zealand v Pakistan at Sharjah 2000-01**

THE PROFILE Injuries at an inopportune time affected Kyle Mills's prospects of making a more significant start to his international career. While he was recovering, Shane Bond, Ian Butler and Jacob Oram seized their opportunities, making it harder for Mills to force his way back. In and out of the team after the 2003 World Cup in which he made only one fleeting, wicketless appearance – he marked another comeback, against Pakistan in 2003-04, by picking up a reprimand for excessive appealing. However, he did enough to earn a call-up for the tour of England in 2004, and made his Test debut in the third match at Trent Bridge. But he picked up a side strain during the game, and was forced to fly home and miss the NatWest Series. That was a shame, as one-day cricket is really his forte: he played throughout the 2005-06 season, chipping in with wickets in almost every game, even if his once-promising batting had diminished to the point that he managed double figures only once in 16 matches. A feisty temper remains, though: Stephen Fleming had to pull him away from Graeme Smith during a bad-tempered one-day series towards the end of 2005. Mills returned to South Africa for the Tests early in 2006, and picked up eight wickets in the two matches he played, almost doubling his career tally.

THE FACTS Mills spanked his only first-class century from No. 9 at Wellington in 2000-01, helping Auckland recover from 109 for 7 to reach 347 ... He averages 20.42 with the ball against Sri Lanka in ODIs, but 44.71 against Australia ... Mills achieved the first ten-wicket haul of his career, and in the process notched up 100 first-class wickets, for Auckland against Canterbury in December 2004 ...

THE FIGURES
Batting and fielding

	M	Inns	NO	Runs	HS	Avge	S/R	100	50	4s	6s	Ct	St
Tests *to 11.9.06*	7	12	3	120	31	13.33	41.95	0	0	17	2	2	0
ODIs *to 11.9.06*	60	34	17	230	44*	13.52	61.33	0	0	12	6	19	0
First-class *to 11.9.06*	47	67	19	1488	117*	31.00	–	1	9	–	–	18	0

Bowling

	M	Balls	Runs	Wkts	BB	Avge	RpO	S/R	5i	10m
Tests *to 11.9.06*	7	1041	534	17	4-43	31.41	3.07	61.23	0	0
ODIs *to 11.9.06*	60	2996	2321	78	4-14	29.75	4.64	38.41	0	0
First-class *to 11.9.06*	47	7571	3689	140	5-33	26.35	2.92	54.07	3	1

MOHAMMAD ASHRAFUL

Full name	**Mohammad Ashraful**
Born	**July 7, 1984, Dhaka**
Teams	**Dhaka**
Style	**Right-hand bat, legspinner**
Test debut	**Bangladesh v Sri Lanka at Colombo 2001-02**
ODI debut	**Bangladesh v Zimbabwe at Bulawayo 2000-01**

THE PROFILE   On September 8, 2001, at the Sinhalese Sports Club in Colombo, Mohammad Ashraful turned a terrible mismatch into a slice of history by becoming the youngest man – or boy – to make a Test century. Bangladesh still crashed to heavy defeat, but "Matin" brought hope and consolation with a sparkling hundred, repeatedly dancing down to hit the Sri Lankan spinners, including Muralitharan, back over their heads ... and on his debut, too. It was the day before his 17th birthday according to some sources, and 63 days after it according to most others: either way, he broke the long-standing record set by Mushtaq Mohammad (17 years 82 days) when he made 101 for Pakistan against India in 1960-61. Inevitably, such a heady early achievement proved hard to live up to, and after a prolonged poor run Ashraful was dropped for England's first visit in October 2003. He returned to the side a better player, but no less flamboyant, as he demonstrated with a glorious unbeaten 158 in defeat against India at Chittagong late in 2004. Still not 21 when Bangladesh made their maiden tour of England the following year, Ashraful confirmed his status as one for the future at Cardiff, when his brilliantly paced century set Bangladesh up for their astonishing victory over Australia in the NatWest Series. But Ashraful didn't fulfil his evident potential on the tour of Sri Lanka that followed, often getting out to loose shots, and made little impact against the Australians early in 2006 either.

THE FACTS   Only 12 players have made their Test debuts at a younger age than Mohammad Ashraful: four of them are from Bangladesh (Mohammad Sharif, Talha Jubair, Mushfiqur Rahim and Enamul Haque junior) ... Ashraful's 100 against Australia at Cardiff in 2005 was only Bangladesh's second ODI century, after Mehrab Hossain's 101 not out against Zimbabwe at Dhaka in 1998-99 ... He averages 110.50 in Tests against India – and only 5.75 against England ... Ashraful took the catch off Enamul Haque junior that sealed Bangladesh's first Test win, against Zimbabwe at Chittagong in January 2005 ...

THE FIGURES
Batting and fielding

	M	Inns	NO	Runs	HS	Avge	S/R	100	50	4s	6s	Ct	St
Tests to 11.9.06	33	65	3	1511	158*	24.37	44.85	3	6	177	17	10	0
ODIs to 11.9.06	76	72	3	1391	100*	20.15	72.29	1	9	145	17	12	0
First-class to 11.9.06	67	126	4	3429	158*	28.10	–	9	14	–	–	28	0

Bowling

	M	Balls	Runs	Wkts	BB	Avge	RpO	S/R	5i	10m
Tests to 11.9.06	33	834	623	9	2–42	69.22	4.48	92.66	0	0
ODIs to 11.9.06	76	340	344	10	3–26	34.40	6.07	34.00	0	0
First-class to 11.9.06	67	4327	2565	80	7–99	32.06	3.55	54.08	5	0

PAKISTAN

MOHAMMAD ASIF

Full name	**Mohammad Asif**
Born	**December 20, 1982, Sheikhupura, Punjab**
Teams	**Sialkot, National Bank, Leicestershire**
Style	**Left-hand bat, right-arm fast-medium bowler**
Test debut	**Pakistan v Australia at Sydney 2004-05**
ODI debut	**Pakistan v England at Rawalpindi 2005-06**

THE PROFILE When Mohammad Asif made his debut at Sydney in January 2005, there was little to suggest that Pakistan's long and happy tradition of unearthing blitzing fast bowlers was about to continue: he bowled 18 innocuous overs as Australia completed a whitewash. He did make a running catch at long-on look easier than it actually was, and resisted stubbornly for over 100 minutes without being dismissed. Towards the end of 2005, though, Pakistan's coach Bob Woolmer called Asif the most improved player around the national squad, and he responded with ten wickets as Pakistan A embarrassed England at the start of their tour in November 2005. Asif didn't feature in the Tests, but did make an impressive one-day debut the day after his 23rd birthday, dismissing Marcus Trescothick with his third ball and ending up with 2 for 14 from seven incisive overs. Tall and lean, and slightly more muscular than when he made his debut, he generates good pace. His action isn't pure, and now involves a Shoaib Akhtar-ish position of the left arm in his jump, but it earned him seven plum wickets at Karachi as Pakistan clinched a famous win over India early in 2006, then he was the Man of the Series in Sri Lanka, with 17 wickets, including 11 for 71 in the three-day win at Kandy. An elbow injury kept him out of the first three Tests in England in 2006, but he looked dangerous when he returned at The Oval, taking four wickets in England's first innings before the ball-tampering row blew up.

THE FACTS Mohammad Asif took 11 for 71 (6 for 44 and 5 for 27) against Sri Lanka at Kandy in April 2006 ... For Pakistan A against the England tourists in Lahore in November 2005 he took 7 for 62 in the first innings (10 for 106 in the match) ... At The Oval in 2006 Asif collected his fifth consecutive Test duck, equalling the unwanted record of Australia's Bob Holland and Ajit Agarkar of India ...Asif took 7 for 35 as Sialkot bowled Multan out for 67 at Multan in October 2004 ... He played county cricket for Leicestershire in 2006, taking 5 for 56 against Essex in his second match ...

THE FIGURES
Batting and fielding

	M	Inns	NO	Runs	HS	Avge	S/R	100	50	4s	6s	Ct	St
Tests *to 11.9.06*	6	8	3	18	12*	3.60	16.36	0	0	2	0	2	0
ODIs *to 11.9.06*	17	4	2	13	6	6.50	41.93	0	0	1	0	2	0
First-class *to 11.9.06*	64	85	34	426	42	8.35	–	0	0	–	–	26	0

Bowling

	M	Balls	Runs	Wkts	BB	Avge	RpO	S/R	5i	10m
Tests *to 11.9.06*	6	1159	635	30	6–44	21.16	3.28	38.63	2	1
ODIs *to 11.9.06*	17	856	562	19	3–28	29.57	3.93	45.05	0	0
First-class *to 11.9.06*	64	11350	6347	259	7–35	24.50	3.35	43.82	15	5

MOHAMMAD HAFEEZ

Full name	**Mohammad Hafeez**
Born	**October 17, 1980, Sargodha, Punjab**
Teams	**Faisalabad, Sui Gas Pipelines**
Style	**Right-hand bat, offspinner**
Test debut	**Pakistan v Bangladesh at Karachi 2003-04**
ODI debut	**Pakistan v Zimbabwe at Sharjah 2002-03**

THE PROFILE Mohammad Hafeez was one of the young players the selectors tried after Pakistan's abysmal display in the 2003 World Cup. Some good one-day performances followed, in Sharjah, Sri Lanka and England: he showed good technique and temperament at the top of the order and bowled his Saqlainish offspinners tidily, but was arguably at his most impressive in the field. Patrolling the point-cover region with feverish alertness, he saved plenty of runs and also caught well. His organised approach to batting earned him a Test cap when Bangladesh toured shortly afterwards, and Hafeez started brightly, scoring a half-century on debut then stroking a maiden hundred in his second Test. However, his form dipped alarmingly in the ODIs that followed against South Africa – only 33 runs in five innings. He lost his Test place, and was then dumped from the one-day team as well. Consistent domestic performances kept him in contention, but he seemed to be a back number after being dropped again early in 2005. He was not originally chosen for the 2006 tour of England, but a spanking 180 against Australia A at Darwin in July, while Pakistan struggled to find an opening combination worth the name in England, led to a surprise call-up for the final Test at The Oval. Before the ball-tampering row overshadowed everything, Hafeez contributed a tidy 95, then spanked 46 in the Twenty20 bunfight that followed. From nowhere, a World Cup place seemed to be his for the taking.

THE FACTS Mohammad Hafeez scored 50 in his first Test, against Bangladesh at Karachi in August 2003, and added 102 not out in his second, at Peshawar a week later ... He averages 41 with the bat in ODIs against Sri Lanka – but only 1.00 in three matches against New Zealand ... Hafeez took 8 for 57 (10 for 87 in the match) for Faisalabad against Quetta at Faisalabad in December 2004 ...

THE FIGURES
Batting and fielding

	M	Inns	NO	Runs	HS	Avge	S/R	100	50	4s	6s	Ct	St
Tests to 11.9.06	4	7	1	309	102*	51.50	50.82	1	2	41	3	2	0
ODIs to 11.9.06	35	35	1	608	69	17.88	52.82	0	3	70	5	16	0
First-class to 11.9.06	80	134	5	4250	180*	32.94	–	8	22	–	–	64	0

Bowling

	M	Balls	Runs	Wkts	BB	Avge	RpO	S/R	5i	10m
Tests to 11.9.06	4	228	74	1	1–14	74.00	1.94	228.00	0	0
ODIs to 11.9.06	35	1265	933	29	3–17	32.17	4.42	43.62	0	0
First-class to 11.9.06	80	5323	2356	78	8–57	30.20	2.65	68.24	3	1

MOHAMMAD RAFIQUE

Full name	**Mohammad Rafique**
Born	**May 9, 1970, Dhaka**
Teams	**Dhaka**
Style	**Left-hand bat, slow left-arm orthodox spinner**
Test debut	**Bangladesh v India at Dhaka 2000-01**
ODI debut	**Bangladesh v India at Sharjah 1994-95**

THE PROFILE An accurate, rhythmical slow left-armer, Rafique played in Bangladesh's inaugural Test in November 2000, and was far from outclassed, producing his side's most economical figures. His career hit the rocks shortly afterwards, when his bowling action was reported as suspect, but he bounced back in May 2003, with 6 for 77 against South Africa at Dhaka. It was the best bowling performance by a Bangladeshi in 19 Tests at the time – and only their third five-wicket haul – and it spurred Rafique on to greater things. Later in 2003 he was the leading wicket-taker in the series against England. He can bat a bit too, usually employing the long handle. His 77 at Hyderabad in May 1998 was instrumental in Bangladesh's victory over Kenya – surprisingly, their first in seven attempts – while in May 2004 he carved an astonishing 111 from No. 9 to help secure a precious first-innings lead against West Indies in St Lucia. His 5 for 65 helped Bangladesh win their first Test, against Zimbabwe at Chittagong early in 2005, and he also played a vital role in turning around the one-day series that followed. He was named Bangladesh's Cricketer of the Year for 2004-05, and survived a public training-ground argument with coach Dav Whatmore to play a role in the national side past his 36th birthday. Nine wickets as Bangladesh almost upset Australia at Fatullah in April 2006 edged him towards a notable double of 1000 runs and 100 wickets in Tests. He's almost there in ODIs, too.

THE FACTS Mohammad Rafique has taken 17 wickets at 23.82 against India, but only 11 at 51.54 against England ... He had played only one first-class match before his Test debut in 2000-01 ... 26 (30%) of his 87 Test wickets have been left-handers ... Rafique and Khaled Mashud are the last survivors in the current squad from the team that won the ICC Trophy in Kuala Lumpur in April 1997 ...

THE FIGURES

Batting and fielding

	M	Inns	NO	Runs	HS	Avge	S/R	100	50	4s	6s	Ct	St
Tests to 11.9.06	26	50	5	982	111	21.82	65.55	1	4	101	33	6	0
ODIs to 11.9.06	100	90	13	1049	77	13.62	72.44	0	2	103	24	22	0
First-class to 11.9.06	47	81	9	1464	111	20.33	_		1	8	–	–	18	0

Bowling

	M	Balls	Runs	Wkts	BB	Avge	RpO	S/R	5i	10m
Tests to 11.9.06	26	7233	3184	87	6–77	36.59	2.64	83.13	7	0
ODIs to 11.9.06	100	5060	3787	95	5–47	39.86	4.49	53.26	1	0
First-class to 11.9.06	47	12702	4966	195	7–52	25.46	2.34	65.13	12	2

MOHAMMAD SAMI

Full name	**Mohammad Sami**
Born	**February 24, 1981, Karachi, Sind**
Teams	**Karachi, National Bank**
Style	**Right-hand bat, right-arm fast-medium bowler**
Test debut	**Pakistan v New Zealand at Auckland 2000-01**
ODI debut	**Pakistan v Sri Lanka at Sharjah 2000-01**

THE PROFILE Mohammad Sami shouldered his way into Test cricket side with outstanding domestic performances, and had an immediate impact on his debut with eight wickets against New Zealand in March 2001. Then, in only his third match, he took a hat-trick, prising out the last three Sri Lankans in the Asian Test Championship final: he has a one-day hat-trick too. But since that promising start, and especially after the 2003 World Cup, when he was expected to become Pakistan's spearhead after the retirements of Wasim Akram and Waqar Younis, his story has been a fitful and disappointing one, as several promising pacemen have overtaken him after various uninspiring performances. He is occasionally threatening, as he was against India early in 2005, especially in the Kolkata Test and some of the ODIs. But mostly he has been surprisingly ineffective, and prone to leaking runs. Sami was finally dropped after a poor home series against India early in 2006, missed the Sri Lankan tour, and was lucky to be recalled for the trip to England – but he was wayward there too, and only stayed in the side as others were injured. Nobody is sure where the problem lies: he's fit; he's athletic; he generates surprising pace from a shortish run-up; he does outswing, reverse-swing and yorkers; he has been given licence to attack with the new ball ... but still that Test average is nudging 50. Some say it's a confidence thing, but opportunities will be limited when other fast bowlers regain fitness.

THE FACTS Mohammad Sami took a hat-trick against Sri Lanka in the Asian Test Championship final at Lahore in March 2002 ... He had also taken a hat-trick in an ODI against West Indies at Sharjah the previous month: neither one involved a fielder, as all the victims were bowled or lbw ... Among bowlers who have taken more than 50 Test wickets, only Carl Hooper (49.42) has a worse average ... Sami's 5 for 36 on debut, against New Zealand at Auckland in March 2001, remain his best figures in Tests ... He has played county cricket for Kent, and took his career-best figures of 8 for 64 for them against Nottinghamshire at Maidstone in 2003 ...

THE FIGURES
Batting and fielding

	M	Inns	NO	Runs	HS	Avge	S/R	100	50	4s	6s	Ct	St
Tests to 11.9.06	28	43	11	337	49	10.53	29.90	0	0	38	2	6	0
ODIs to 11.9.06	76	41	19	227	23	10.31	61.85	0	0	7	8	18	0
First-class to 11.9.06	75	98	32	905	49	13.71	–	0	0	–	–	27	0

Bowling

	M	Balls	Runs	Wkts	BB	Avge	RpO	S/R	5i	10m
Tests to 11.9.06	28	5982	3531	73	5–36	48.36	3.54	81.94	2	0
ODIs to 11.9.06	76	3764	3093	109	5–10	28.37	4.93	34.53	1	0
First-class to 11.9.06	75	13913	8099	257	8–64	31.51	3.49	54.13	13	2

PAKISTAN

MOHAMMAD YOUSUF

Full name	**Mohammad Yousuf**
Born	**August 27, 1974, Lahore, Punjab**
Teams	**Lahore, WAPDA**
Style	**Right-hand bat**
Test debut	**Pakistan v South Africa at Durban 1997-98**
ODI debut	**Pakistan v Zimbabwe at Harare 1997-98**

THE PROFILE Until his conversion to Islam in 2005, Mohammad Yousuf (formerly Yousuf Youhana) was one of the rare Christians to play for Pakistan. After a difficult debut in 1997-98, he quickly established himself as a stylish world-class batsman, and a middle-order pillar alongside Inzamam-ul-Haq: latterly he has shared some big stands with Younis Khan too, and is equally adept in the one-day arena. Yousuf gathers his runs through composed, orthodox strokeplay, unlike some of his colleagues. He is particularly strong driving through the covers and flicking wristily off his legs, and has a backlift as decadent and delicious as any, although a tendency to overbalance when playing across his front leg can get him into trouble. He is quick between the wickets, although not the best judge of a single, and there were signs in England in 2006 of increasing sluggishness in the field. Some initially questioned his temperament under pressure, but he began to silence those critics at the end of 2004. First came a spellbindingly languid century against Australia at Melbourne, as stand-in captain, when he ripped into Shane Warne as few Pakistanis have done before or since. A century followed in the Kolkata cauldron, and he ended 2005 with possibly his most important knock, an easy-on-the-eye 223 against England at Lahore, eschewing the waftiness that had previously blighted him. He followed that with 461 runs in three Tests against India, then another double-century at Lord's in July 2006, as his batting burgeoned along with an impressive new beard.

THE FACTS Since becoming a Muslim in September 2005 Mohammad Yousuf has averaged 81.38 in 11 Tests: in 59 matches beforehand he averaged 47.46 ... He made double-centuries in successive matches against England, 223 at Lahore in December 2005, and 202 at Lord's in July 2006: he has scored two more double-hundreds in Tests (against New Zealand and Bangladesh), but no others in first-class cricket, where his highest score is 163 ... Against India at home early in 2006 Yousuf shared successive stands of 319, 142, 242, 0 and 158 with Younis Khan, with whom he averages 83.29 overall ... His record includes four ODIs for the Asia XI ...

THE FIGURES
Batting and fielding

	M	Inns	NO	Runs	HS	Avge	S/R	100	50	4s	6s	Ct	St
Tests *to 11.9.06*	70	117	9	5737	223	53.12	51.97	19	25	743	44	58	0
ODIs *to 11.9.06*	223	211	30	7455	141*	41.18	74.14	11	50	592	78	50	0
First-class *to 11.9.06*	109	179	16	8008	223*	49.12	–	23	40	–	–	74	0

Bowling

	M	Balls	Runs	Wkts	BB	Avge	RpO	S/R	5i	10m
Tests *to 11.9.06*	70	6	3	0	–	–	3.00	–	0	0
ODIs *to 11.9.06*	223	1	1	0	–	–	6.00	–	0	0
First-class *to 11.9.06*	109	18	24	0	–	–	8.00	–	0	0

DINESH MONGIA

Full name	**Dinesh Mongia**
Born	**April 17, 1977, Chandigarh**
Teams	**Punjab, Leicestershire**
Style	**Left-hand bat, slow left-arm orthodox spinner**
Test debut	**No Tests yet**
ODI debut	**India v Australia at Pune 2000-01**

THE PROFILE Dinesh Mongia has quietly gone about accumulating runs without ever being showered with the plaudits reserved for flashier but less effective players. He first played for Punjab in 1995-96, and was a steady if unspectacular performer until 2000-01, when he forced his way into the national squad with a string of big scores, including a triple-century and two doubles. Pugnacious and dogged, he lacks the natural grace of some left-handers, but does possess a wide range of attacking strokes. He has done a sterling job when given a one-day chance, and hammered 159 in the series decider against Zimbabwe in March 2002. Suspicions lingered that kinks in his technique might be exposed on more challenging tracks abroad, and some indifferent displays in England in 2002 found him sidelined for a while. He forced his way back into the side for the 2003 World Cup, and played in the final, which India lost. The following year Mongia played club cricket in England in an attempt to cement his international place, and ended up deputising for Carl Hooper at Old Trafford. He was popular in the Lancashire dressing-room, and made a mark too at Leicester, who he joined in 2005: some solid displays for them the following year – including successive scores of 160-plus in the Championship – resulted in a recall to Indian colours for the Champions Trophy at home late in 2006. Despite a first-class average of over 50, Mongia seems to have been pigeonholed as a one-day player by the Indian selectors.

THE FACTS There have been only four higher scores for India in ODIs than Mongia's 159 not out against Zimbabwe at Guwahati in March 2002 ... Mongia made 309 not out for Punjab against Jammu & Kashmir at Jalandhar in November 2000, sharing a stand of 388 with Pankaj Dharmani (176) after Punjab had been 36 for 3: later that season Mongia made 201 and 208 for North Zone in the Duleep Trophy ... He averages 84 in ODIs against South Africa – and 4.66 against New Zealand ...

THE FIGURES

Batting and fielding

	M	Inns	NO	Runs	HS	Avge	S/R	100	50	4s	6s	Ct	St
Tests to 11.9.06	0	–	–	–	–	–	–	–	–	–	–	–	–
ODIs to 11.9.06	51	45	6	1073	159*	27.51	73.39	1	3	107	8	21	0
First-class to 11.9.06	118	179	19	8004	308*	50.02	–		27	28	–	–	118	0

Bowling

	M	Balls	Runs	Wkts	BB	Avge	RpO	S/R	5i	10m
Tests to 11.9.06	0	–	–	–	–	–	–	–	–	–
ODIs to 11.9.06	51	400	370	8	3–31	46.25	5.55	50.00	0	0
First-class to 11.9.06	118	3755	1611	45	4–34	35.80	2.57	83.44	0	0

RUNAKO MORTON

Full name	**Runako Shakur Morton**
Born	**July 22, 1978, Nevis**
Teams	**Leeward Islands**
Style	**Right-hand bat, occasional offspinner**
Test debut	**West Indies v Sri Lanka at Colombo 2005**
ODI debut	**West Indies v Pakistan at Sharjah 2001-02**

THE PROFILE Runako Morton is fiery on and off the pitch. His career looked to be over before it had properly started when he was expelled from the West Indian Academy in 2001 for a series of disciplinary breaches. He refused to be bowed, and continued to accumulate runs for the Leeward Islands. In February 2002, his penance complete, he was called into an injury-plagued squad. But he threw away his opportunity when he pulled out of the Champions Trophy in September 2002, pretending that his grandmother had died. His career slipped further down the pan when he was arrested in January 2004, in connection with a stabbing incident, but he was given a third chance at redemption in May 2005, when he was recalled to the one-day squad when South Africa toured, although he didn't actually play. After moving to live in Trinidad – and calming down, he says – he finally made his debut (becoming only the fifth Test player from the tiny island of Nevis) in Sri Lanka in 2005, in a side decimated by a damaging contracts dispute, and also toured New Zealand early in 2006, making two handy scores in the Tests, and adding a defiant one-day century at Napier. He struggled against spin, though, and was pushed up to open in the home one-day series against Zimbabwe, helping himself to 79 and 109. But the Indians were an altogether stiffer proposition, and he was dropped after innings of 23, 1 and 0 against them in May 2006.

THE FACTS The highest of Morton's seven first-class centuries is only 114, for West Indies A against Sri Lanka A in Colombo in June 2005, although he did make 126 in a one-day game for West Indies A against Kent at Canterbury in June 2002 ... Morton withdrew from the 2002 Champions Trophy in Sri Lanka, claiming that his grandmother had died: it later turned out that one of his grandmothers had been dead for 16 years, and the other was still alive ...

THE FIGURES

Batting and fielding

	M	Inns	NO	Runs	HS	Avge	S/R	100	50	4s	6s	Ct	St
Tests *to 11.9.06*	4	7	1	193	70*	32.16	48.61	0	2	25	2	6	0
ODIs *to 11.9.06*	20	19	1	656	110*	36.44	63.81	2	4	64	4	8	0
First-class *to 11.9.06*	59	97	6	3185	114	35.00	–	7	20	–	–	71	0

Bowling

	M	Balls	Runs	Wkts	BB	Avge	RpO	S/R	5i	10m
Tests *to 11.9.06*	4	36	22	0	–	–	3.66	–	0	0
ODIs *to 11.9.06*	20	6	2	0	–	–	2.00	–	0	0
First-class *to 11.9.06*	59	437	261	8	3–17	32.62	3.58	54.62	0	0

TAWANDA MUPARIWA

Full name	**Tawanda Mupariwa**
Born	**April 16, 1985, Bulawayo**
Teams	**Matabeleland**
Style	**Right-hand bat, right-arm fast-medium bowler**
Test debut	**Zimbabwe v Sri Lanka at Bulawayo 2003-04**
ODI debut	**Zimbabwe v Sri Lanka at Harare 2003-04**

THE PROFILE Tawanda Mupariwa, a product of the Bulawayo development programme, is an accurate pace bowler with a slender build. He relies on accuracy, has a good inswinger, and a deceptive slower ball. He started off as a wicketkeeper, but Wisdom Siziba claimed that position in the local development team. When Mupariwa joined the Bulawayo Athletic Club (which is associated with the development side), the former umpire Chuck Coventry encouraged him to develop his pace bowling. After being controversially omitted from Zimbabwe's Under-19 team in 2003-04, Mupariwa showed outstanding form as a pace bowler for Matabeleland in the Logan Cup, and forced the national selectors to fast-track him into the national squad when several "rebel" players withdrew from the series against Sri Lanka after a contracts dispute. He began the West Indies tour of 2006 as a fringe player – he hadn't established himself before, although he did have the knack of picking up wickets – but made such outstanding progress that he finished as Zimbabwe's first-choice new-ball bowler, with 15 wickets in his seven ODIs on the trip, including Brian Lara twice in successive matches. His batting also developed as he worked hard at it, and he is an outstanding fielder. Coach Kevin Curran says he is a good learner with the right attitude, and perhaps the player who made more progress than any other on that tough tour.

THE FACTS Mupariwa's Test debut was a chastening one – he finished with 0 for 136 as Sri Lanka ran up 713 for 3 declared ... He's had more luck in ODIs, where he averages just under two wickets per match, with a best return of 3 for 19 against Bermuda at Port-of-Spain in May 2006 ... Mupariwa's best first-class bowling, 5 for 48, came in his first match of 2004-05, for Matabeleland against Mashonaland at Bulawayo ...

THE FIGURES

Batting and fielding

	M	Inns	NO	Runs	HS	Avge	S/R	100	50	4s	6s	Ct	St
Tests to 11.9.06	1	2	1	15	14	15.00	33.33	0	0	2	0	0	0
ODIs to 11.9.06	16	15	5	127	33	12.70	74.70	0	0	10	1	5	0
First-class to 11.9.06	19	32	8	294	37	12.25	–	0	0	–	–	7	0

Bowling

	M	Balls	Runs	Wkts	BB	Avge	RpO	S/R	5i	10m
Tests to 11.9.06	1	204	136	0	–	–	4.00	–	0	0
ODIs to 11.9.06	16	879	710	32	4–61	22.18	4.84	27.46	0	0
First-class to 11.9.06	19	2974	1532	58	5–48	26.41	3.09	51.27	2	0

MUTTIAH MURALITHARAN

SRI LANKA

Full name	**Muttiah Muralitharan**
Born	**April 17, 1972, Kandy**
Teams	**Tamil Union**
Style	**Right-hand bat, offspinner**
Test debut	**Sri Lanka v Australia at Colombo 1992-93**
ODI debut	**Sri Lanka v India at Colombo 1993-94**

THE PROFILE Muttiah Muralitharan is one of the most successful bowlers the game has seen, Sri Lanka's greatest player ... and without doubt the most controversial cricketer of the modern age. Murali's rise from humble beginnings – the Tamil son of a hill-country confectioner – to the top of the wicket-taking lists has divided opinion because of his weird bent-armed delivery. From a loose-limbed, open-chested action, his chief weapons are the big-turning offbreak and two top-spinners, one of which goes straight on and the other, his doosra, which spins from a rubbery wrist in the opposite direction to his stock ball. However, suspicions about his action became widespread after he was no-balled for throwing in Australia in 1995-96, first on Boxing Day at Melbourne, then in the subsequent one-day series. He was cleared by ICC after biomechanical analysis concluded that his action, and a congenitally deformed elbow which he can't fully straighten, create the "optical illusion of throwing". But the controversy did not die: Murali was called again in Australia in 1998-99, sent for more tests, and cleared again. Then his new doosra prompted further suspicion, and he was sent for more high-tech tests in 2004, which ultimately forced ICC to revise their rules on chucking. On the field, Murali continued to pile up the wickets, overtaking Courtney Walsh's Test-record 519 in May 2004: only shoulder trouble, which required surgery, allowed Shane Warne to pass him. Murali returned, potent as ever, and flummoxed England with 8 for 70 at Nottingham to square the 2006 series.

THE FACTS Muralitharan was the second bowler (after Shane Warne) to take 600 Test wickets, and the first to take 1,000 in all international cricket (Tests and ODIs), reaching that landmark in March 2006 ... His 56 Test five-wicket hauls is easily a record (next come Warne and Richard Hadlee with 36), while 18 ten-wicket matches is also unapproached (Warne has 10) ... Murali has taken nine wickets in a Test innings twice, and his 16 for 220 at The Oval in 1998 is the fifth-best haul in all Tests ... His record includes one Test and three ODIs for the World XI, and four ODIs for the Asia XI ...

THE FIGURES

Batting and fielding

	M	Inns	NO	Runs	HS	Avge	S/R	100	50	4s	6s	Ct	St
Tests *to 11.9.06*	108	140	49	1095	67	12.03	69.30	0	1	125	24	59	0
ODIs *to 11.9.06*	276	128	49	456	27	5.77	67.75	0	0	28	5	111	0
First-class *to 11.9.06*	199	245	71	1968	67	11.31	–	0	1	–	–	109	0

Bowling

	M	Balls	Runs	Wkts	BB	Avge	RpO	S/R	5i	10m
Tests *to 11.9.06*	108	36139	14432	657	9–51	21.96	2.39	55.00	56	18
ODIs *to 11.9.06*	276	15067	9685	416	7–30	23.28	3.85	36.21	8	0
First-class *to 11.9.06*	199	56678	22297	1180	9–51	18.89	2.36	48.03	103	30

MUSHFIQUR RAHIM

Full name	**Mohammad Mushfiqur Rahim**
Born	**September 1, 1988, Bogra**
Teams	**Has not played domestic first-class cricket**
Style	**Right-hand bat, wicketkeeper**
Test debut	**Bangladesh v England at Lord's 2005**
ODI debut	**Bangladesh v Zimbabwe at Harare 2006**

THE PROFILE A wild-card inclusion for Bangladesh's maiden tour of England in 2005, Mushfiqur Rahim was just 16 when he was selected for that daunting trip – two Tests in May, followed by six ODIs against England and Australia – even though he hadn't been named in the preliminary squad of 20. Mushfiqur was principally selected as an understudy to the ever-present wicketkeeper, Khaled Mashud, but his inclusion was further evidence of Bangladesh's determination to build for a better future. He had done well on an A-team tour of Zimbabwe earlier in 2005, scoring a century in the first Test at Bulawayo, and also enjoyed some success in England the previous year with the Under-19s, making 88 in the second Test at Taunton. He showed more evidence of grit with the full team, with a maiden first-class half-century to soften the pain of defeat against Sussex, followed by a career-best 115 against Northamptonshire. That earned him a call-up – as a batsman – to become the youngest player to appear in a Test match at Lord's. He was one of only three players to reach double figures in a disappointing first innings, but a twisted ankle kept him out of the second Test. After captaining Bangladesh's Under-19s to fifth place in the Youth World Cup in February 2006, he also featured in Bogra's inaugural Test, against Sri Lanka the following month, but could make little of the spin of Murali and Malinga Bandara. The experience can only stand him in good stead for the future.

THE FACTS Mushfiqur Rahim's hundred for Bangladesh against Northamptonshire in 2005 made him the youngest century-maker in English first-class cricket, beating Sachin Tendulkar's record: Rahim was 16 years 261 days old, 211 days younger than Tendulkar was in 1990; the youngest Englishman was 17-year-old Stephen Peters for Essex in 1996 ... Before the 2006-07 season started in Bangladesh, Mushfiqur had not appeared in domestic first-class cricket there ...

THE FIGURES
Batting and fielding

	M	Inns	NO	Runs	HS	Avge	S/R	100	50	4s	6s	Ct	St
Tests to 11.9.06	2	4	0	24	19	6.00	28.23	0	0	3	0	1	0
ODIs to 11.9.06	1	0	–	–	–	–	–	–	–	–	–	0	0
First-class to 11.9.06	10	18	3	514	115*	34.26	45.16	2	3	–	–	12	1

Bowling

	M	Balls	Runs	Wkts	BB	Avge	RpO	S/R	5i	10m
Tests to 11.9.06	2	0	–	–	–	–	–	–	–	–
ODIs to 11.9.06	1	0	–	–	–	–	–	–	–	–
First-class to 11.9.06	10	0	–	–	–	–	–	–	–	–

NAFEES IQBAL

BANGLADESH

Full name	**Mohammad Nafees Iqbal Khan**
Born	**October 31, 1985, Chittagong**
Teams	**Chittagong**
Style	**Right-hand bat, occasional right-arm medium-pacer**
Test debut	**Bangladesh v New Zealand at Dhaka 2004-05**
ODI debut	**Bangladesh v England at Chittagong 2003-04**

THE PROFILE A young, crowd-pleasing opener, Nafees Iqbal is not one of nature's shrinking violets. A nephew of Bangladesh's larger-than-life former captain Akram Khan, Nafees shot to prominence in the second warm-up match of England's inaugural tour in 2003-04. After slapping a giddy century for Bangladesh A in Dhaka, he dismissed England's spinners as "ordinary", an assessment that attracted more column inches than the innings itself. Had he not been about to lead Bangladesh's Under-19 team in Pakistan, he might have had the opportunity to expand on that statement in the subsequent Test series. Instead, he waited for a late summons to the one-day squad, and made his debut in front of his home fans at Chittagong. His Test debut followed the following year, and in January 2005 he produced his maiden hundred, an invaluable match-saving 121 against Zimbabwe at Dhaka, which secured Bangladesh their maiden series victory, after making 56 in the historic win at Chittagong. Indifferent form after that cost Nafees his place, and he did not feature in the Tests against Australia in April 2006: he had lost his one-day place nearly a year before, after a poor start to the NatWest Series in England.

THE FACTS Nafees Iqbal was still two months short of his 16th birthday when he made 75 on his first-class debut, for Chittagong against Biman Bangladesh at Savar in November 2000 ... He averages 51.25 in Tests against Zimbabwe, and 8.25 against England ... Nafees's uncle, Akram Khan, played eight Tests and 44 ODIs for Bangladesh, captaining them in pre-Test days ...

THE FIGURES
Batting and fielding

	M	Inns	NO	Runs	HS	Avge	S/R	100	50	4s	6s	Ct	St
Tests to 11.9.06	11	22	0	518	121	23.54	38.88	1	2	72	1	2	0
ODIs to 11.9.06	16	16	0	309	58	19.31	54.40	0	2	32	2	2	0
First-class to 11.9.06	51	92	6	2705	147	31.45	–	5	14	–	–	10	0

Bowling

	M	Balls	Runs	Wkts	BB	Avge	RpO	S/R	5i	10m
Tests to 11.9.06	11	0	–	–	–	–	–	–	–	–
ODIs to 11.9.06	16	0	–	–	–	–	–	–	–	–
First-class to 11.9.06	51	61	33	0	–	–	3.24	–	0	0

NAVED-UL-HASAN

Full name	**Rana Naved-ul-Hasan**
Born	**February 28, 1978, Sheikhupura, Punjab**
Teams	**Sialkot, Sussex**
Style	**Right-hand bat, right-arm fast-medium bowler**
Test debut	**Pakistan v Sri Lanka at Karachi 2004-05**
ODI debut	**Pakistan v Sri Lanka at Sharjah 2002-03**

THE PROFILE Naved-ul-Hasan made his debut in Sharjah immediately after the disastrous 2003 World Cup, when he seemed to be competing with Abdul Razzaq, Azhar Mahmood and Shoaib Malik for the allrounder's spot. Few backed him then, despite some impressive early performances, and he was dropped soon after, supposedly because of some unspecified disciplinary problems. But, helped by the continuing doubts about Shoaib Akhtar's fitness and injuries to other bowlers, Naved has worked his way up to become the one-day team's spearhead. As with most Pakistan pace bowlers, he can bowl a reverse-swinging yorker almost at will, and his change of pace, as Virender Sehwag would testify, is another useful weapon. But his nous, his control over line and length, and his refusal to give anything less than his all in the field have stood out. He was Pakistan's leading one-day bowler in 2005, impressing first in the VB Series in Australia and then on the flatter, less responsive pitches of India and the Caribbean. So far it has been a different story in Tests, although he was badly missed in 2006 in England – where he had starred in county cricket for Sussex – when he missed the entire Test series with a troublesome groin injury. He is a hard-hitting lower-order batsman, with centuries for Sheikhupura and Sussex, although he hasn't had much chance to display this skill at international level yet, despite his insistence that he is, in fact, a natural wicketkeeper/batsman. He gave up his first love, hockey, for cricket.

THE FACTS Naved-ul-Hasan has taken 31 wickets at 23.67 in ODIs against India – and seven at 42.00 against Australia ... He took 6 for 27 against India at Jamshedpur in April 2005 ... Naved made his highest score of 139 for Sussex against Middlesex at Lord's in 2005, and then took seven wickets, including four in one over in the second innings ... He took 91 wickets in Pakistan in 2000-01: the following season he took 7 for 49, still his best figures, for Sheikhupura against Sialkot at Muridke ...

THE FIGURES
Batting and fielding

	M	Inns	NO	Runs	HS	Avge	S/R	100	50	4s	6s	Ct	St
Tests to 11.9.06	8	13	3	176	42*	17.60	82.24	0	0	24	3	3	0
ODIs to 11.9.06	50	33	13	302	29	15.10	78.23	0	0	25	6	11	0
First-class to 11.9.06	81	118	14	2452	139	23.57	–	2	8	–	–	45	0

Bowling

	M	Balls	Runs	Wkts	BB	Avge	RpO	S/R	5i	10m
Tests to 11.9.06	8	1421	931	16	3–30	58.18	3.93	88.81	0	0
ODIs to 11.9.06	50	2401	2182	81	6–27	26.93	5.45	29.64	1	0
First-class to 11.9.06	81	16032	8805	387	7–49	22.75	3.29	41.42	23	4

ANDRE NEL

Full name	**Andre Nel**
Born	**July 15, 1977, Germiston, Transvaal**
Teams	**Titans**
Style	**Right-hand bat, right-arm fast bowler**
Test debut	**South Africa v Zimbabwe at Harare 2001-02**
ODI debut	**South Africa v West Indies at Port-of-Spain 2000-01**

THE PROFILE   Andre Nel is a muscular fast bowler who has belied his conservative Afrikaans upbringing by amassing a chequered disciplinary record. He was sent home from the A-team tour of Australia in 2003 after being found to be driving under the influence of alcohol in Tasmania. It was only his latest misdemeanour, but he was nonetheless chosen for the one-day portion of the 2003 tour of England, where he was already playing for Northamptonshire. Nel was tipped early on as a future international, and he first made the headlines in February 2001 when he felled Allan Donald – his hero – with a fierce bouncer. Nel burst into tears as Donald tottered off, and it later emerged that he was following instructions from his coach, Ray Jennings, to target South Africa's premier fast bowler. Further controversy followed when Nel was one of five players caught smoking marijuana during a tour of the Caribbean. However, it was during the home West Indies series of 2003-04, during which he got married, that Nel established himself – and he was only in trouble once, for making facial gestures at Chris Gayle. Back trouble curtailed his progress, but he returned with wickets – and more gurning – against England in 2004-05. He came into his own in Australia in 2005-06, where he was an intimidating presence with 14 wickets and an attacking approach. Four Boxing Day dismissals preceded a strong showing at Sydney, and the Aussie crowds – sensing a kindred spirit to their own Merv Hughes – loved to hate him.

THE FACTS   Nel has taken 39 of his 84 wickets in seven Tests against West Indies, at an average of 20.61: against New Zealand he averages 76.00 ... He took 10 for 88 in the match in South Africa's innings win over West Indies at Bridgetown in April 2005 ... Nel has dismissed Brian Lara eight times in Tests (and three more times in ODIs) ... He played once for Essex in 2005, taking wickets with his first and third balls against Somerset ... Nel has never made a first-class fifty, but did hit 64 in a three-day game against a Western Australia XI in December 2005, sharing a ninth-wicket stand of 175 with Jacques Rudolph ...

THE FIGURES

Batting and fielding

	M	Inns	NO	Runs	HS	Avge	S/R	100	50	4s	6s	Ct	St
Tests to 11.9.06	23	25	6	135	18*	7.10	35.15	0	0	18	1	9	0
ODIs to 11.9.06	45	7	5	12	4*	6.00	42.85	0	0	1	0	12	0
First-class to 11.9.06	83	93	32	844	44	13.83	–	0	0	–	–	30	0

Bowling

	M	Balls	Runs	Wkts	BB	Avge	RpO	S/R	5i	10m
Tests to 11.9.06	23	4959	2503	84	6–32	29.79	3.02	59.03	3	1
ODIs to 11.9.06	45	2184	1716	58	4–39	29.58	4.71	37.65	0	0
First-class to 11.9.06	83	16460	7582	295	6–25	25.70	2.76	55.79	12	1

MAKHAYA NTINI

Full name	**Makhaya Ntini**
Born	**July 6, 1977, Mdingi, Cape Province**
Teams	**Warriors**
Style	**Right-hand bat, right-arm fast bowler**
Test debut	**South Africa v Sri Lanka at Cape Town 1997-98**
ODI debut	**South Africa v New Zealand at Perth 1997-98**

THE PROFILE   Makhaya Ntini has had a fair bit to contend with during his young life. A product of the United Cricket Board's development programme, Ntini was discovered as a cattleherd in the Eastern Cape, given a pair of boots and packed off to Dale College, one of South Africa's best-regarded cricketing nurseries. With an action consciously modelled on Malcolm Marshall's, Ntini found himself touring Australia in 1997-98 when Roger Telemachus failed a fitness test. He made his one-day international debut on that tour, bowling well in helpful conditions at Perth, and his Test debut – the first black African to play for South Africa – came later the same year. He was then convicted of rape, but cleared on appeal. After that ordeal he returned for the Sharjah tournament in 2000, impressing observers with greater control than before. Although he is a little short of the genuine pace of a Brett Lee or a Shoaib Akhtar, he steadily improved, getting closer to the stumps but maintaining his high pace and occasional dangerous late inswing, and in 2003 became the first South African to take ten wickets in a Test at Lord's, before devastating West Indies in Trinidad in 2005 with 13 for 132, the best match figures for South Africa. Ntini steamed on, relishing his new role as the pace spearhead, and 46 Test wickets in 2005-06 hoisted him past 250. He also ruined Justin Langer's 100th Test by clanging him on the head and forcing him out of the match at the Wanderers in April 2006.

THE FACTS   Ntini's 13 for 132 (6 for 95 and 7 for 37) at Port-of-Spain in April 2005 are South Africa's best match figures in Tests, surpassing Hugh Tayfield's 13 for 165 at Melbourne in 1952-53 ... He has taken 54 Test wickets against England, and 53 against West Indies ... Ntini has taken 176 (64%) of his Test wickets in 35 matches at home ... Only 18 (7%) of his Test wickets have been lbws ... Ntini's record includes one ODI for the World XI ...

THE FIGURES
Batting and fielding

	M	Inns	NO	Runs	HS	Avge	S/R	100	50	4s	6s	Ct	St
Tests to 11.9.06	69	78	23	572	32*	10.40	55.58	0	0	87	8	18	0
ODIs to 11.9.06	129	31	17	147	42*	10.50	66.51	0	0	11	5	25	0
First-class to 11.9.06	134	156	47	1060	34*	9.72	–	0	0	–	–	32	0

Bowling

	M	Balls	Runs	Wkts	BB	Avge	RpO	S/R	5i	10m
Tests to 11.9.06	69	14597	7751	274	7-37	28.28	3.18	53.27	14	4
ODIs to 11.9.06	129	6462	4772	206	6-22	23.16	4.43	31.36	3	0
First-class to 11.9.06	134	24916	13619	465	7-37	29.28	3.27	53.58	19	4

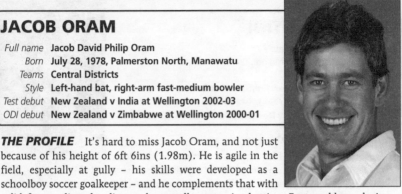

JACOB ORAM

NEW ZEALAND

Full name	**Jacob David Philip Oram**
Born	**July 28, 1978, Palmerston North, Manawatu**
Teams	**Central Districts**
Style	**Left-hand bat, right-arm fast-medium bowler**
Test debut	**New Zealand v India at Wellington 2002-03**
ODI debut	**New Zealand v Zimbabwe at Wellington 2000-01**

THE PROFILE It's hard to miss Jacob Oram, and not just because of his height of 6ft 6ins (1.98m). He is agile in the field, especially at gully – his skills were developed as a schoolboy soccer goalkeeper – and he complements that with solid fast-medium bowling and naturally aggressive batting. Foot problems during 2001-02 cost him a season at a vital stage, but he came back strongly the following year and sealed a place in both the Test and one-day sides. He narrowly missed a century against Pakistan in the Boxing Day Test at Wellington in 2003, but made up for that in the next match by carving 119 not out against South Africa, then 90 in the second Test, which earned him a spot for the England tour of 2004. Oram was consistent with the bat there, making 67 at Lord's, but his bowling was starting to lose its sting, and he went down with a back injury shortly after pounding 126, again not out, against Australia at Brisbane in November. A stress reaction to the injury kept him on the sidelines when Australia toured early in 2005, although he helped New Zealand win a triangular series in Zimbabwe with four wickets in the final against India in September. After nearly 18 months out of the Test side Oram showed in April 2006 what New Zealand's middle order had been missing, coming in at 38 for 4 in the first match at Centurion and making his highest score of 133.

THE FACTS Oram averages 62.00 in Tests against Australia, 60.50 against South Africa – and 10.25 against India ... With the ball he averages 19.69 against India, and 106.00 against Australia ... Oram scored his maiden century in only his fourth first-class match, for Central Districts against Canterbury at Christchurch in 1998-99, and his 155 remains his highest score ...

THE FIGURES
Batting and fielding

	M	Inns	NO	Runs	HS	Avge	S/R	100	50	4s	6s	Ct	St
Tests to 11.9.06	20	35	7	1203	133	42.96	51.19	3	4	134	16	12	0
ODIs to 11.9.06	83	62	6	1034	81	18.46	74.92	0	3	86	27	21	0
First-class to 11.9.06	61	96	14	3129	155	38.15	–	6	16	–	–	31	0

Bowling

	M	Balls	Runs	Wkts	BB	Avge	RpO	S/R	5i	10m
Tests to 11.9.06	20	3250	1384	38	4–41	36.42	2.55	85.52	0	0
ODIs to 11.9.06	83	3676	2812	94	5–26	29.91	4.58	39.10	2	0
First-class to 11.9.06	61	7271	2911	101	6–45	28.82	2.40	71.99	2	0

MONTY PANESAR

ENGLAND

Full name **Mudhsuden Singh Panesar**
Born **April 25, 1982, Luton, Bedfordshire**
Teams **Northamptonshire**
Style **Left-hand bat, slow left-arm orthodox spinner**
Test debut **England v India at Nagpur 2006**
ODI debut **No ODIs yet**

THE PROFILE Monty Panesar made his Test debut early in 2006, and by the middle of the year had made himself a cult hero to English crowds enchanted by his enthusiastic wicket celebrations and his endearingly erratic fielding. That, and equally amateurish batting, had threatened to hold him back at Test level, but when Ashley Giles was ruled him out of the 2005-06 Indian tour Panesar received a late summons. He's a throwback to an earlier Northamptonshire slow left-armer, Bishan Bedi, who also twirled away in a patka at the County Ground, teasing and tempting with flight and guile. After playing for England Under-19s, Panesar took eight wickets on his first-class debut, against Leicestershire in 2001, including 4 for 11 in the second innings. University intruded, but despite only two first-class games in 2001, and six in 2002, he did enough to earn a place in the Academy squad in Australia during the winter. Finally free from studies, he had a fine season in 2005, with 46 Championship wickets at 21.54, and his county coach Kepler Wessels led the calls for an England tour spot. Panesar made his debut at Nagpur, picking up Sachin Tendulkar as his first Test wicket, then adding the scalps of Mohammad Kaif and Rahul Dravid. Duncan Fletcher's known preference for allround excellence threatened his place when Pakistan arrived in 2006 – but Panesar's fine performances at Manchester and Leeds, when he ripped the ball sharply and teased out 14 wickets in two big wins, put an end to such talk.

THE FACTS Panesar's best figures are 7 for 181, for Northamptonshire against Essex at Chelmsford in July 2005 ... He was the first Sikh to play Test cricket for anyone other than India: when Panesar opposed Harbhajan Singh during his debut at Nagpur in 2005-06 it was the first instance of one Sikh bowling to another in a Test ... Panesar was the first Luton-born Test cricketer, and only the seventh to have been born in Bedfordshire, the previous one being Wayne Larkins ...

THE FIGURES

Batting and fielding

	M	Inns	NO	Runs	HS	Avge	S/R	100	50	4s	6s	Ct	St
Tests to 11.9.06	10	13	8	51	26	10.20	33.33	0	0	6	1	2	0
ODIs to 11.9.06	0	–	–	–	–	–	–	–	–	–	–	–	–
First-class to 11.9.06	48	60	26	269	39*	7.91	32.10	0	0	–	–	13	0

Bowling

	M	Balls	Runs	Wkts	BB	Avge	RpO	S/R	5i	10m
Tests to 11.9.06	10	2408	1037	32	5–72	32.40	2.58	75.25	2	0
ODIs to 11.9.06	0	–	–	–	–	–	–	–	–	–
First-class to 11.9.06	48	11312	5251	175	7–181	30.00	2.78	64.64	9	1

JEETAN PATEL

Full name	**Jeetan Shashi Patel**
Born	**May 7, 1980, Wellington**
Teams	**Wellington**
Style	**Right-hand bat, offspinner**
Test debut	**New Zealand v South Africa at Cape Town 2005-06**
ODI debut	**New Zealand v Zimbabwe at Harare 2005-06**

THE PROFILE The son of Indian parents, but born and brought up in Wellington's eastern suburbs, offspinner Jeetan Patel was fast-tracked into the New Zealand one-day side after John Bracewell, the coach, identified him as the sort of slow bowler who could be effective at the death. Patel first played for Wellington in 1999-2000, bowling 59 overs and taking 5 for 145 against Auckland on his debut. Three middling seasons followed, and he seemed to be heading nowhere, with an average in the mid-forties. But then he took 6 for 32 against Otago in the last State Championship match of 2004-05, propelling Wellington into the final against Auckland, which they lost. Suddenly good judges were noting his ability to make the ball loop and drift, not unlike a right-handed Daniel Vettori. Bracewell took him to Zimbabwe for a one-day tournament in August 2005, and he played nine ODIs during the season, in eight being either the super-sub or the subbed-out player, as his batting – although better than when he began – is underwhelming. At home his 2 for 23 from ten overs throttled Sri Lanka at Wellington, and won him the match award, then three wickets at Christchurch helped subdue West Indies too. All this put Patel in line for a first Test cap, which came against South Africa at Cape Town in April 2006. And he had a nice long bowl, wheeling down 42 overs and removing Graeme Smith, Boeta Dippenaar and AB de Villiers at a cost of 117 runs.

THE FACTS Patel won the Man of the Match award for his tight spell of 2 for 23 against Sri Lanka at Wellington in 2005-06 after being super-subbed into the game ... He also won the match award in his first international Twenty20 match, after taking 3 for 20 against South Africa at Johannesburg in October 2005 ... Patel hit his highest score of 58 not out for Wellington against Otago at Dunedin in 2000-01, after going in as a nightwatchman ...

THE FIGURES
Batting and fielding

	M	Inns	NO	Runs	HS	Avge	S/R	100	50	4s	6s	Ct	St
Tests to 11.9.06	1	1	1	27	27*	–	87.09	0	0	3	0	1	0
ODIs to 11.9.06	9	0	–	–	–	–	–	–	–	–	–	–	0
First-class to 11.9.06	54	66	28	745	58*	19.60	–	0	2	–	–	18	0

Bowling

	M	Balls	Runs	Wkts	BB	Avge	RpO	S/R	5i	10m
Tests to 11.9.06	1	252	117	3	3–117	39.00	2.78	84.00	0	0
ODIs to 11.9.06	9	453	392	13	3–42	30.15	5.19	34.84	0	0
First-class to 11.9.06	54	9082	4218	106	6–32	39.79	2.78	85.67	3	0

MUNAF PATEL

Full name	**Munaf Musa Patel**
Born	**July 12, 1983, Ikhar, Gujarat**
Teams	**Maharashtra**
Style	**Right-hand bat, right-arm fast-medium bowler**
Test debut	**India v England at Mohali 2005-06**
ODI debut	**India v England at Goa 2005-06**

THE PROFILE Few medium-pacers generated as much hype before bowling a ball in first-class – let alone international – cricket as Munaf Patel, the young boy from the little town of Ikhar in Gujarat, did early in 2003. Kiran More spotted him in the nets and sent him straight to Chennai to train under Dennis Lillee. Soon he was being hailed as the fastest man in Indian cricket. Then, as Baroda and Gujarat jostled for his signature, Patel chose Mumbai, after Sachin Tendulkar had a word with the authorities there. Even then Patel's first-class career was anything but smooth, as he spent more time recovering from various injuries than actually playing, and he later moved to play for Maharashtra. He's strongly built, though not overly tall; a wild mane flows behind him as he bustles up to the bowling crease, gathering momentum before releasing the ball with a windmill-whirl of hands. Patel's priority is to bowl quick, which is what caught More's eye in the first place. Now he has added reverse swing to his repertoire, and also has a well-directed yorker. In March 2006 he finally received a call from the selectors – now chaired by Patel's old pal More – for the second Test against England, after taking 10 for 91 against them for the Board President's XI. And things kept getting better: he ended the Mohali Test with 7 for 97, the best performance by an Indian fast bowler on debut, and continued to take wickets consistently in the West Indies later in 2006.

THE FACTS Patel's match figures of 7 for 97 were the best on Test debut by an Indian fast bowler, beating Mohammad Nissar's 6 for 135 in India's inaugural Test, against England at Lord's in 1932 (Abid Ali, more of a medium-pacer, took 7 for 116 on debut against Australia at Adelaide in 1967-68) ... Patel's best first-class figures are 6 for 50, for Maharashtra against Railways at Delhi in January 2006 ...

THE FIGURES

Batting and fielding

	M	Inns	NO	Runs	HS	Avge	S/R	100	50	4s	6s	Ct	St
Tests to 11.9.06	6	7	2	32	13	6.40	32.32	0	0	3	1	3	0
ODIs to 11.9.06	6	3	2	3	2*	3.00	33.33	0	0	0	0	0	0
First-class to 11.9.06	30	34	9	385	78	15.40	–	0	1	–	–	8	0

Bowling

	M	Balls	Runs	Wkts	BB	Avge	RpO	S/R	5i	10m
Tests to 11.9.06	6	1374	680	24	4–25	28.33	2.96	57.25	0	0
ODIs to 11.9.06	6	246	235	2	1–48	117.50	5.73	123.00	0	0
First-class to 11.9.06	30	5535	2535	112	6–50	22.63	2.76	49.17	4	1

IRFAN PATHAN

Full name	**Irfan Khan Pathan**
Born	**October 27, 1984, Baroda, Gujarat**
Teams	**Baroda**
Style	**Left-hand bat, left-arm medium-fast bowler**
Test debut	**India v Australia at Adelaide 2003-04**
ODI debut	**India v Australia at Melbourne 2003-04**

THE PROFILE Left-armer Irfan Pathan was initially rated the most talented swing and seam bowler to emerge from India since Kapil Dev. Within a couple of years in international cricket, he was being thought of as a possible successor for Kapil in the allround department, too. When he made his Test debut in Australia late in 2003, it was with the energy of a 19-year-old, but with a composed air striking even for one who had been specifically readied for the purpose via the A-team and age-group sides. His instinct is not just what to bowl to who and when, but also to keep learning new tricks. Already he possesses perhaps the most potent left-armer's outswinger in world cricket – which helped him to a Test hat-trick in the first over of the Karachi Test in January 2006 – he's adept at reverse-swinging the ball, and enjoys long spells. He played a big part in India's one-day and Test series wins in Pakistan early in 2004. His batting also took off, and he was regularly pushed up the order, sometimes even opening in one-dayers. His first stint at No. 3 produced a spectacular 83 against Sri Lanka at Nagpur – and he has often bailed India out in the Test arena as well, with successive innings of 93 and 82 against Sri Lanka late in 2005, and 90 as India piled up 603 against Pakistan at Faisalabad early in 2006. He had a quiet tour of the Caribbean later that year, but remains a fine long-term prospect.

THE FACTS Pathan was the first bowler to take a hat-trick in the first over of a Test match, when he dismissed Salman Butt, Younis Khan and Mohammad Yousuf at Karachi in January 2006: from 0 for 3, Pakistan recovered to win the match by 341 runs ... He took 12 for 126 in the match against Zimbabwe at Harare in September 2005 ... Pathan has also played for Middlesex ... His brother Yusuf Pathan bowls offspin for Baroda ...

THE FIGURES

Batting and fielding

	M	Inns	NO	Runs	HS	Avge	S/R	100	50	4s	6s	Ct	St
Tests to 11.9.06	25	32	2	835	93	27.83	49.97	0	6	99	13	8	0
ODIs to 11.9.06	64	46	13	858	83	26.00	80.48	0	4	84	21	10	0
First-class to 11.9.06	60	75	15	1495	93	24.91	–	0	9	–	–	19	0

Bowling

	M	Balls	Runs	Wkts	BB	Avge	RpO	S/R	5i	10m
Tests to 11.9.06	25	5078	2802	91	7–59	30.79	3.31	55.80	7	2
ODIs to 11.9.06	64	3231	2651	108	5–27	24.54	4.92	29.92	1	0
First-class to 11.9.06	60	11495	6156	193	7–59	31.89	3.21	59.55	10	3

RUCHIRA PERERA

Full name	**Panagodage Don Ruchira Laksiri Perera**
Born	**April 6, 1977, Colombo**
Teams	**Colts**
Style	**Left-hand bat, left-arm fast-medium bowler**
Test debut	**Sri Lanka v India at Colombo 1998-99**
ODI debut	**Sri Lanka v England at Perth 1998-99**

THE PROFILE Ruchira Perera is a lively and hard-working left-arm fast bowler who can swing the ball back in to the right-hander. He lost form and confidence after his action was labelled suspect in England early in 2002: after advice from Daryl Foster, a bowling coach and biomechanics expert, Perera modified his wrist position just before the point of delivery, which cleared up the problem with his elbow to the satisfaction of the Sri Lankan authorities. He returned to international duty against South Africa later in 2002, but self-belief had seeped away. During the next two years he battled hard, but gradually became disillusioned, and prior to the 2003-04 provincial tournament was considering an offer to play league cricket as a professional in England. But he regained form during the competition – he took 45 wickets in all that season, at 20.35 – and caught the eye of the selectors again. Perera's last Test to date was in South Africa in November 2002, but more recently he has been something of a one-day regular, playing throughout the VB Series in Australia in 2005-06, although without much to show for it in the wickets column. He was called up for the one-day leg of the 2006 tour of England, but was expensive and wicketless in his one outing, at The Oval. He is occasionally hot-headed, and while that has made him a frequent visitor to the referee's office, he is generally good for team spirit, bringing great humour to the dressing-room, and is respected for his commitment with ball in hand.

THE FACTS Perera's best first-class bowling figures of 7 for 40 came for Sinhalese Sports Club against Burgher RC in Colombo in April 2001 ... He also took 7 for 90 for Central against Southern Province at Kandy in January 2004 ... Perera has not yet played an ODI at home in Sri Lanka – 10 of his 16 matches have been in Australia ...

THE FIGURES
Batting and fielding

	M	Inns	NO	Runs	HS	Avge	S/R	100	50	4s	6s	Ct	St
Tests to 11.9.06	8	9	6	33	11*	11.00	26.61	0	0	4	0	2	0
ODIs to 11.9.06	16	5	2	8	4*	2.66	53.33	0	0	0	0	2	0
First-class to 11.9.06	84	89	40	402	33*	8.20	–	0	0	–	–	34	0

Bowling

	M	Balls	Runs	Wkts	BB	Avge	RpO	S/R	5i	10m
Tests to 11.9.06	8	1130	661	17	3–40	38.88	3.50	66.47	0	0
ODIs to 11.9.06	16	762	689	16	3–23	43.06	5.42	47.62	0	0
First-class to 11.9.06	84	10820	6531	257	7–40	25.41	3.62	42.10	8	0

KEVIN PIETERSEN

Full name **Kevin Peter Pietersen**
Born **June 27, 1980, Pietermaritzburg, Natal, South Africa**
Teams **Hampshire**
Style **Right-hand bat, offspinner**
Test debut **England v Australia at Lord's 2005**
ODI debut **England v Zimbabwe at Harare 2004-05**

ENGLAND

THE PROFILE Expansive with bat and explosive with bombast, Kevin Pietersen is not one for the quiet life. Bold-minded and big-hitting, he first ruffled feathers by quitting South Africa – he was disenchanted with the race-quota system – in favour of England, his eligibility coming courtesy of an English mother. He never doubted he would play Test cricket: he has self-confidence in spades but, fortunately, sackfuls of talent too. Sure enough, as soon as he was eligible for England, in September 2004, he was chosen for a one-day series in Zimbabwe, where he averaged 104, earning him a late call-up to play ... South Africa. Undeterred by hostile crowds, he announced his arrival (loudly, of course) with a robust century in the second match at Bloemfontein. On reaching his ton, he kissed the England badge with unreserved fervour. Test cricket was next on the to-do list, and it was only a matter of time. Overlooked for the two early-season Bangladesh Tests in 2005, he replaced Graham Thorpe, against Australia, at Lord's ... and coolly blasted a couple of fifties in a losing cause. Six dropped catches might have dented his confidence, but with the Ashes at stake, he again showed his eye for the limelight by clubbing 158 on the final day at The Oval, to secure the draw England needed. "KP" had arrived – and how. He played for the World XI less than a year after his one-day debut, then added another Test century in India before hammering 158 and 142 in successive home Tests against Sri Lanka in 2006.

THE FACTS Pietersen reached his hundred against South Africa at East London in February 2005 from 69 balls, the fastest for England in ODIs ... He averages 151.33 in ODIs against South Africa – and 23 v Bangladesh ... Pietersen has scored three double-centuries, all for Nottinghamshire before moving to Hampshire in 2005: his highest is 254 not out against Middlesex at Trent Bridge in August 2002 ... Five of his 25 first-class centuries were made against Derbyshire ... His record includes two ODIs for the World XI ...

THE FIGURES
Batting and fielding

	M	Inns	NO	Runs	HS	Avge	S/R	100	50	4s	6s	Ct	St
Tests to 11.9.06	18	34	1	1597	158	48.39	72.22	5	6	192	32	11	0
ODIs to 11.9.06	38	32	7	1382	116	55.28	95.64	3	9	138	34	19	0
First-class to 11.9.06	98	161	13	7584	254*	51.24	–		26	31	–	–	91	0

Bowling

	M	Balls	Runs	Wkts	BB	Avge	RpO	S/R	5i	10m
Tests to 11.9.06	18	84	76	1	1–11	76.00	5.42	84.00	0	0
ODIs to 11.9.06	38	84	91	1	1–4	91.00	6.50	84.92	0	0

LIAM PLUNKETT

Full name	**Liam Edward Plunkett**
Born	**April 6, 1985, Middlesbrough, Yorkshire**
Teams	**Durham**
Style	**Right-hand bat, right-arm fast-medium bowler**
Test debut	**England v Pakistan at Lahore 2005-06**
ODI debut	**England v Pakistan at Lahore 2005-06**

THE PROFILE Liam Plunkett's selection for England's tours of Pakistan and India in 2005-06 represented the culmination of a two-year rise to prominence. He had made his first-class debut for Durham in 2003, taking on immediate responsibilities in the absence of Steve Harmison and the injured Mark Davies, and in 2005 reached 50 wickets in a season for the first time. Not dissimilar to the young Harmison in build or bowling style, Plunkett also has the makings of a useful allrounder, as he demonstrated with a composed half-century in only his second one-day international in Pakistan. Earlier on that tour, following the withdrawal of Simon Jones with an ankle injury, Plunkett also made his Test debut, acquitting himself well in the ruins of a thumping defeat at Lahore. His second Test, against India at Mohali in March 2006, was less successful, but at the age of 20, he had undoubtedly marked himself out as one for the future. Injuries to Jones, Andrew Flintoff and James Anderson meant that Plunkett was in the frame throughout the 2006 home season, but although he picked up a few wickets – six of them in the demolition of Sri Lanka at Birmingham late in May – there was a frustrating looseness about some of his bowling, and he looked overplaced at No. 8 in the batting order. He was expensive in the embarrassing 5–0 one-day defeat by the Sri Lankans, then, after an undistinguished Lord's Test against Pakistan, joined England's growing injury list himself with a side strain.

THE FACTS Plunkett took three wickets in his first ODI, and scored 56 in his second, both against Pakistan in December 2005 ... He took 5 for 53 on his County Championship debut, for Durham v Yorkshire at Leeds in 2003 ... Plunkett's best bowling figures are 6 for 74, for Durham v Hampshire at Chester-le-Street in August 2004 ... His highest score is 74 not out, for Durham v Somerset at Stockton in May 2005, when he shared a ninth-wicket stand of 124 with Mark Davies ... Plunkett took 13 wickets in three Under-19 Tests in Australia in 2002-03, when England lost a closely contested series 2–1 ...

THE FIGURES

Batting and fielding

	M	Inns	NO	Runs	HS	Avge	S/R	100	50	4s	6s	Ct	St
Tests to 11.9.06	6	9	1	69	28	8.62	28.99	0	0	7	0	2	0
ODIs to 11.9.06	16	15	5	200	56*	20.00	81.96	0	1	15	4	4	0
First-class to 11.9.06	40	60	14	887	74*	19.28	40.74	0	2	–	–	13	0

Bowling

	M	Balls	Runs	Wkts	BB	Avge	RpO	S/R	5i	10m
Tests to 11.9.06	6	1004	601	16	3–17	37.56	3.59	62.75	0	0
ODIs to 11.9.06	16	734	727	16	3–51	45.43	5.94	45.87	0	0
First-class to 11.9.06	40	6233	3917	123	6–74	31.84	3.77	50.67	4	0

SHAUN POLLOCK

Full name	**Shaun Maclean Pollock**
Born	**July 16, 1973, Port Elizabeth, Cape Province**
Teams	**Dolphins**
Style	**Right-hand bat, right-arm fast-medium bowler**
Test debut	**South Africa v England at Centurion 1995-96**
ODI debut	**South Africa v England at Cape Town 1995-96**

THE PROFILE It would have been surprising if Shaun Pollock had not been an international cricketer. Father Peter led the South African attack through the 1960s, while uncle Graeme was arguably the finest left-hand batsman of them all. It is as an immaculate line-and-length seamer that Shaun will be remembered. At first he was slippery and aggressive, and his Natal team-mates totted up the number of batsmen he pinned. He was brought into the Test side against England in 1995-96 by his father, the chairman of selectors at the time. Pollock junior settled in quickly, and his testing new-ball partnership with Allan Donald was the springboard of much of South Africa's success during the late 1990s. Pollock moves the ball both ways, and also has stamina and courage, as he proved in 1997-98 when he toiled in blazing heat to take 7 for 87 in 41 overs on a flat Adelaide track. He was handed the captaincy in 2000 when Hansie Cronje was booted out, and faced the huge challenge of lifting a shocked and demoralised side. However, he lost credibility after a drubbing in Australia, and was later blamed for South Africa's disastrous 2003 World Cup, when they failed to qualify for the Super Sixes by one run: Pollock was replaced by Graeme Smith. With 100 Test caps under his belt, "Polly" is now approaching the veteran stage; his nagging brilliance around off stump remains, but his pace and ability to take top-order wickets has dipped, relegating him to first change.

THE FACTS Pollock and Jacques Kallis were the first South Africans to play 100 Tests, reaching the mark at Centurion in April 2006 ... He is South Africa's leading wicket-taker in Tests and ODIs ... 82 (21%) of his Test wickets have been lbws ... Pollock's father Peter took 116 wickets in 28 Tests in the 1960s, while his uncle Graeme averaged 60.97 from 23 matches ... On his debut for Warwickshire, in a Benson & Hedges Cup match in 1996, Pollock took four wickets in four balls v Leicestershire ... His record includes three ODIs for the World XI, and three for the Africa XI ...

THE FIGURES
Batting and fielding

	M	Inns	NO	Runs	HS	Avge	S/R	100	50	4s	6s	Ct	St
Tests to 11.9.06	102	147	37	3515	111	31.95	51.94	2	15	377	33	68	0
ODIs to 11.9.06	259	171	59	2805	75	25.04	85.59	0	11	184	47	96	0
First-class to 11.9.06	178	256	53	6686	150*	32.93	–		6	33	–	–	125	0

Bowling

	M	Balls	Runs	Wkts	BB	Avge	RpO	S/R	5i	10m
Tests to 11.9.06	102	23172	9253	395	7–87	23.42	2.39	58.66	16	1
ODIs to 11.9.06	259	13486	8456	348	6–35	24.29	3.76	38.75	4	0
First-class to 11.9.06	178	37508	14923	635	7–33	23.50	2.38	59.06	22	2

RICKY PONTING

AUSTRALIA

Full name	**Ricky Thomas Ponting**
Born	**December 19, 1974, Launceston, Tasmania**
Teams	**Tasmania**
Style	**Right-hand bat, right-arm medium-pace bowler**
Test debut	**Australia v Sri Lanka at Perth 1995-96**
ODI debut	**Australia v South Africa at Wellington 1994-95**

THE PROFILE Ricky Ponting began with Tasmania at 17 and Australia at 20, and was unluckily given out for 96 on his Test debut. He remains the archetypal modern cricketer, playing all the shots with a full flourish and knowing only attack – and his dead-eye fielding is a force by itself. A gambler and a buccaneer, Ponting is a one-day natural. He has had setbacks, against probing seam and high-class finger-spin, which he plays with hard hands when out of form. In the '90s there were off-field indiscretions that forced him to address an alcohol problem, but his growing maturity was acknowledged when he succeeded Steve Waugh as one-day captain in 2002. It was a seamless transition: Ponting led the 2003 World Cup campaign from the front, clouting a coruscating century in the final, and acceded to the Test crown when Waugh finally stepped down early in 2004. But things changed in 2005. A humiliating one-day defeat by Bangladesh caused the first ripples of dissent against his leadership style, and more followed as the Ashes series progressed. A heroic 156 saved the Manchester Test, but he couldn't save the urn. The result hurt, and the pain lingered. Ponting's record in charge is tainted – although he recovered to win 11 of 12 Tests in 2005-06 – but his batting remains untarnished. He finished 2005 with 1544 runs, including two hundreds in a Test three times. He now has more centuries than anyone but Sachin, Sunny and Steve, and in his 32nd year is far from finished.

THE FACTS The only Australian with a higher Test batting average than Ponting's 58.82 is Don Bradman (99.94) ... Ponting is the only player to score two hundreds in his 100th Test, against South Africa at Sydney in January 2006 ... His 140 not out in 2003 is the highest score in the World Cup final, but his 242 at Adelaide in 2003-04, also against India, is the highest by a player on the losing side in a Test (in the next game he made 257, and they won) ... When he was 8, Ponting's grandmother gave him a T-shirt that read "Under this shirt is a Test player" ... His record includes one ODI for the World XI ...

THE FIGURES

Batting and fielding

	M	Inns	NO	Runs	HS	Avge	S/R	100	50	4s	6s	Ct	St
Tests to 11.9.06	105	175	24	8792	257	58.22	58.86	31	34	999	57	120	0
ODIs to 11.9.06	252	246	29	9210	164	42.44	79.25	20	52	776	119	104	0
First-class to 11.9.06	199	336	49	17123	257	59.66	–	64	68	–	–	203	0

Bowling

	M	Balls	Runs	Wkts	BB	Avge	RpO	S/R	5i	10m
Tests to 11.9.06	105	527	231	5	1–0	46.20	2.62	105.40	0	0
ODIs to 11.9.06	252	150	104	3	1–12	34.66	4.16	50.06	0	0
First-class to 11.9.06	199	1422	757	14	2–10	54.07	3.19	101.57	0	0

RAMESH POWAR

INDIA

Full name	**Ramesh Rajaram Powar**
Born	**May 20, 1978, Bombay**
Teams	**Mumbai**
Style	**Right-hand bat, offspinner**
Test debut	**No Tests yet**
ODI debut	**India v Pakistan at Rawalpindi 2003-04**

THE PROFILE A stocky offspinner who is more than handy with the bat, Ramesh Powar has been a consistent performer in domestic cricket, and was crucial to Mumbai's 2002-03 Ranji Trophy success. His 20 wickets with his flighted stuff was useful enough, but even more crucial were his runs. He never batted higher than No. 7 – sometimes going in as low as No. 10 – but ended up with Mumbai's second-highest aggregate, scoring 418 runs at more than 46, most of those coming when his team was in trouble. His domestic exploits soon caught the selectors' attention, and he made the Indian squad for the Pakistan tour early in 2004. His offspin and his batting both stood up in the couple of ODIs he played, but even more impressive was his combative attitude, as he bravely tossed the ball up on batting shirtfronts, and didn't bat an eyelid while striking some lusty blows against the pace of Shoaib Akhtar and Mohammad Sami. An ideal bits-and-pieces player, Powar returned to the one-day side early in 2006, now armed with a new delivery – a drifter – which helped him to 63 domestic wickets in 2005-06, after 54 the previous season. Again he impressed with both bat and ball, although some critics made disparaging remarks about his waistline, causing him to tempt fate: "I've never missed a game owing to fitness problems." Almost inevitably, he then twisted an ankle and missed the first two ODIs in the West Indies in June 2006.

THE FACTS Powar has made four hundreds in first-class cricket, the highest of them 131 against Railways at Mumbai in December 2003 ... His best bowling figures of 7 for 44 came for West Zone against South Zone at Hyderabad in February 2005 ... Powar made 54 in the Jamshedpur ODI against England in April 2006 ...

THE FIGURES

Batting and fielding

	M	Inns	NO	Runs	HS	Avge	S/R	100	50	4s	6s	Ct	St
Tests to 11.9.06	0	–	–	–	–	–	–	–	–	–	–	–	–
ODIs to 11.9.06	15	9	4	107	54	21.40	67.29	0	1	10	1	0	0
First-class to 11.9.06	69	87	12	2494	131	33.25	–	4	14	–	–	34	0

Bowling

	M	Balls	Runs	Wkts	BB	Avge	RpO	S/R	5i	10m
Tests to 11.9.06	0	–	–	–	–	–	–	–	–	–
ODIs to 11.9.06	15	700	544	16	3–34	34.00	4.66	43.75	0	0
First-class to 11.9.06	69	13981	6493	249	7–44	26.07	2.78	56.14	13	2

DAREN POWELL

Full name	**Daren Brentlyle Powell**
Born	**April 15, 1978, Jamaica**
Teams	**Jamaica**
Style	**Right-hand bat, right-arm fast bowler**
Test debut	**West Indies v New Zealand at Bridgetown 2001-02**
ODI debut	**West Indies v Bangladesh at Dhaka 2002-03**

THE PROFILE Daren Powell began his cricketing life at school in Jamaica as a No. 3 batsman and offspinner, but then came across a concrete pitch that he thought wouldn't suit his spin bowling, so decided to try some medium-pace instead. Seam-up turned out to be the way forward for Powell, and he has developed into a slippery fast bowler with a rhythmic, high action. But his international career has been less smooth. A solitary Test against New Zealand at home in 2002 was followed by one in India and two in Bangladesh, but pitches in the subcontinent were never going to suit his style of bowling, and he was dropped – without really doing much wrong – and sat on the sidelines for two years. Powell continued to pick up wickets in domestic cricket, and returned for the first Test against South Africa in March 2005, when several players were unavailable owing to a bitter contracts dispute, and did enough to retain his place throughout that season when the others returned. He picked up 5 for 25 on the first day of the second Test against Sri Lanka at Kandy later that year (West Indies still lost heavily), and retained his place for the tour of Australia at the end of 2005. He slipped down the pecking order after the tour of New Zealand that followed, and was kept out by the Barbados boys – Pedro Collins, Fidel Edwards and Corey Collymore – and his Jamaican team-mate Jerome Taylor during the 2006 home season.

THE FACTS Powell cemented his place in the side for the first Test of West Indies' tour of Australia late in 2006 by taking four wickets in the warm-up game against Queensland, including Test opener Matthew Hayden for a duck: in the Test Hayden made 118 ... Powell's best bowling figures of 6 for 49 were for Derbyshire against Durham University at Derby in 2004 ... He has also played for Gauteng in South Africa ...

THE FIGURES

Batting and fielding

	M	Inns	NO	Runs	HS	Avge	S/R	100	50	4s	6s	Ct	St
Tests to 11.9.06	17	26	0	157	16	6.03	30.07	0	0	15	3	1	0
ODIs to 11.9.06	9	5	1	14	6	3.50	46.66	0	0	0	0	1	0
First-class to 11.9.06	63	87	14	983	62	13.46	–	0	3	–	–	19	0

Bowling

	M	Balls	Runs	Wkts	BB	Avge	RpO	S/R	5i	10m
Tests to 11.9.06	17	3142	1756	43	5–25	40.83	3.35	73.06	1	0
ODIs to 11.9.06	9	456	337	5	2–28	67.40	4.43	91.20	0	0
First-class to 11.9.06	63	10036	5404	184	6–49	29.36	3.23	54.54	6	0

ASHWELL PRINCE

Full name	**Ashwell Gavin Prince**
Born	**May 28, 1977, Port Elizabeth, Cape Province**
Teams	**Cape Cobras**
Style	**Left-hand bat, occasional left-arm spinner**
Test debut	**South Africa v Australia at Johannesburg 2001-02**
ODI debut	**South Africa v Bangladesh at Kimberley 2002-03**

THE PROFILE A crouching left-hander with a high-batted stance and a Gooch-like grimace, Ashwell Prince was helped into the national team by South Africa's controversial race-quota system, although he quickly justified his selection by top-scoring on debut with a gutsy 49 against Australia in 2001-02. That, and a matchwinning 48 in the third Test, seemed to have buried his reputation as a one-day flasher. But by the start of the following season his form had fallen away horribly, and he failed in four successive Tests against Bangladesh and Sri Lanka. Domestic runs got his place back, and valuable knocks against West Indies and England at home also made him a more regular member of the one-day side. Test hundreds followed, against outclassed Zimbabwe and almost-outclassed West Indies, but his 119 against Australia at Sydney in January 2006 was an altogether better performance. Prince had struggled against Shane Warne, falling to him in his first four innings of the series, and although he eventually succumbed again it was only after an important stand of 219 with Jacques Kallis. Warne troubled him again in the return series, when Prince's only substantial contribution was a splendid 93 in the third Test at Johannesburg. Free of Warne's wiles, Prince smacked a cathartic century against New Zealand in April 2006. Shortly after that an ankle injury to Graeme Smith meant that Prince was named as South Africa's first black captain, for the Test tour of Sri Lanka. Long rated highly by Ali Bacher, Prince is strong through the off side, and although his throwing from the deep has been hampered by a long-term shoulder injury, he remains a brilliant shot-stopping fielder in the covers.

THE FACTS Prince averages 66.33 in Test against West Indies – and 1.00 v Bangladesh ... In 18 Test innings against Australia, Prince has been dismissed 11 times by Shane Warne ... Prince's highest first-class score is 184 for Western Province Boland against the Lions at Paarl in 2004-05 ... His record includes three ODIs for the Africa XI ...

THE FIGURES
Batting and fielding

	M	Inns	NO	Runs	HS	Avge	S/R	100	50	4s	6s	Ct	St
Tests to 11.9.06	23	36	3	1254	139*	38.00	41.03	4	3	135	3	9	0
ODIs to 11.9.06	37	33	11	870	89*	39.54	66.21	0	3	67	3	20	0
First-class to 11.9.06	111	172	18	6294	184	41.13	–	15	30	–	–	65	0

Bowling

	M	Balls	Runs	Wkts	BB	Avge	RpO	S/R	5i	10m
Tests to 11.9.06	23	78	31	1	1-2	31.00	2.38	78.00	0	0
ODIs to 11.9.06	27	0	–	–	–	–	–	–	–	–
First-class to 11.9.06	111	186	93	2	1-2	46.50	3.00	93.00	0	0

SURESH RAINA

Full name	**Suresh Kumar Raina**
Born	**November 27, 1986, Ghaziabad, Uttar Pradesh**
Teams	**Uttar Pradesh**
Style	**Left-hand bat, occasional offspinner**
Test debut	**No Tests yet**
ODI debut	**India v Sri Lanka at Dambulla 2005**

THE PROFILE An aggressive young batsman who has dismantled bowling attacks across the country, the prodigious Suresh Raina puts people in mind of Yuvraj Singh, another powerful left-hander. A string of fine performances at junior level – where he frequently bullied his way to double-hundreds – landed him a spot in the India Under-19 squad. In April 2005, in the final of the Ranji Trophy one-day tournament at Mumbai, Raina strolled in, spanked nine fours and a six in 48 from 33 balls as Uttar Pradesh tied with Tamil Nadu and shared the title, then left to catch the flight home for his school exams. Later his 620 runs in six matches in 2005-06 propelled Uttar Pradesh to the senior Ranji Trophy title, while a couple of composed knocks, when given the opportunity in one-dayers, persuaded Rahul Dravid to gush: "Raina has shown what a phenomenal player he can turn into." His electric fielding added zing to India's one-day side, and it came as no surprise when, even before he'd managed an ODI fifty, he was fast-tracked into the Test squad against England in March 2006, although he didn't actually play. Definitely one to watch.

THE FACTS Raina has so far scored two first-class centuries, both for Uttar Pradesh – 106 against Andhra at Kanpur in December 2003, and 127 against Punjab at Lucknow two years later ... All three of his ODI half-centuries came against England early in 2006, including 81 not out at Faridabad ... Raina scored 72 in the first Under-19 Test and 63 in the third in England in 2002, when Irfan Pathan was a team-mate ...

THE FIGURES

Batting and fielding

	M	Inns	NO	Runs	HS	Avge	S/R	100	50	4s	6s	Ct	St
Tests *to 11.9.06*	0	–	–	–	–	–	–	–	–	–	–	–	–
ODIs *to 11.9.06*	26	19	4	481	81*	32.06	73.43	0	3	43	3	10	0
First-class *to 11.9.06*	23	40	3	1827	127	49.37	53.86	2	14	–	–	28	–

Bowling

	M	Balls	Runs	Wkts	BB	Avge	RpO	S/R	5i	10m
Tests *to 11.9.06*	0	–	–	–	–	–	–	–	–	–
ODIs *to 11.9.06*	26	32	37	1	1–23	37.00	6.93	32.00	0	0
First-class *to 11.9.06*	23	432	183	1	1–41	183.00	2.54	432.00	0	0

ED RAINSFORD

ZIMBABWE

Full name	**Edward Charles Rainsford**
Born	**December 14, 1984, Kadoma**
Teams	**Midlands**
Style	**Right-hand bat, right-arm fast-medium bowler**
Test debut	**No Tests yet**
ODI debut	**Zimbabwe v Australia at Harare 2003-04**

THE PROFILE Ed Rainsford is a tall fast-medium bowler who has developed an excellent yorker, which works best to left-handers, as his stock delivery swings into them. He won early selection for the Zimbabwe national squad against Sri Lanka in 2004, when several "rebel" players withdrew after a contracts dispute. He played five one-day internationals as that row rumbled on, without making much impression – except perhaps on Michael Vaughan and Andrew Strauss, dismissed by Rainsford in the Champions Trophy match at Edgbaston in September 2004. But Zimbabwe's continuing player drain led to his recall, after some problems with spinal stress fractures, in 2006. He clinched selection for the West Indies tour with three wickets in the third one-dayer against Kenya at Harare in February, and was one of the few to enhance his reputation in the Caribbean before leaving early to fulfil a club contract in London. He grew up in the Midlands town of Kadoma, but showed little interest in cricket until he was 11, when his father, who had played at school himself, coached him and fired his enthusiasm. After five years in the first team at Jameson High in Kadoma, Rainsford was so hungry for cricket that he would get a lift three times a week to Kwekwe, 45 miles away, to practise with the National League club team there. This led to Logan Cup selection for Midlands, as well as the Under-19 World Cup and the Academy in 2004.

THE FACTS Rainsford's best ODI bowling figures of 3 for 16 came against Kenya at Bulawayo in February 2006 ... He removed both openers (Ian Bell and Matt Prior) in the fourth match of England's 2004-05 tour, at Bulawayo ... One of his brothers played for Midlands in the early '90s before the Logan Cup acquired first-class status ...

THE FIGURES

Batting and fielding

	M	Inns	NO	Runs	HS	Avge	S/R	100	50	4s	6s	Ct	St
Tests *to 11.9.06*	0	–	–	–	–	–	–	–	–	–	–	–	–
ODIs *to 11.9.06*	15	9	5	33	9*	8.25	44.00	0	0	1	0	1	0
First-class *to 11.9.06*	21	34	11	264	50*	11.47	–	0	1	–	–	10	0

Bowling

	M	Balls	Runs	Wkts	BB	Avge	RpO	S/R	5i	10m
Tests *to 11.9.06*	0	–	–	–	–	–	–	–	–	–
ODIs *to 11.9.06*	15	804	567	16	3–16	35.43	4.23	50.25	0	0
First-class *to 11.9.06*	21	2674	1424	58	6–67	24.55	3.19	46.10	2	0

BANGLADESH

RAJIN SALEH

Full name	**Khondokar Mohammad Rajin Saleh Alam**
Born	**November 20, 1983, Sylhet, Bangladesh**
Teams	**Sylhet**
Style	**Right-hand bat, occasional offspinner**
Test debut	**Bangladesh v Pakistan at Karachi 2003-04**
ODI debut	**Bangladesh v Pakistan at Multan 2003-04**

THE PROFILE   Rajin Saleh is one of the most talented batsmen in Bangladesh, and, as a man who takes pride in his physical fitness as well, he has also become a favourite of his coach, Dav Whatmore. Saleh, a No. 3 batsman on the domestic circuit, first attracted attention when he averaged 56 in the National League in 2000-01. He had played only five matches for Sylhet when he was included in the Bangladesh Cricket Board XI which took on the Australian Cricket Academy the following year, but made 81 in the first match, a knock which drew high praise from the Aussie press. Technically sound, Saleh is equally solid forward or back, and has rapidly become a mainstay of the Bangladesh batting line-up. And before he had turned 21 he was elevated to the captaincy for the Champions Trophy in England in 2004, after Habibul Bashar broke his thumb. Back in the ranks, he cracked 89 in the historic victory over Zimbabwe at Chittagong early in 2005, but lost his place after making only 2 and 7 against England at Chester-le-Street. An undefeated 108 against Kenya at Fatullah in March 2006 – on the 35th anniversary of Bangladesh's independence from Pakistan – forced Saleh back into the Test reckoning, and he distinguished himself with innings of 67, 33 and 71 against the Australians.

THE FACTS   Rajin Saleh captained Bangladesh in the Champions Trophy in England in 2004 when only 20 ... His 108 not out against Kenya at Fatullah in March 2006 was Bangladesh's third century in ODIs (the others were scored by Mehrab Hossain in 1998–99 and Mohammad Ashraful in 2005), and their highest score at the time ... Saleh averages 35.57 in ODIs against Pakistan, and 0.00 against South Africa ... He has two brothers who have also played first-class cricket ...

THE FIGURES

Batting and fielding

	M	Inns	NO	Runs	HS	Avge	S/R	100	50	4s	6s	Ct	St
Tests *to 11.9.06*	17	33	1	930	89	29.06	36.75	0	6	111	5	11	0
ODIs *to 11.9.06*	42	42	1	999	108*	24.36	55.04	1	6	93	3	9	0
First-class *to 11.9.06*	49	88	8	2874	130*	35.92	–		6	13	–	–	41	0

Bowling

	M	Balls	Runs	Wkts	BB	Avge	RpO	S/R	5i	10m
Tests *to 11.9.06*	17	402	244	2	1–9	122.00	3.64	201.00	0	0
ODIs *to 11.9.06*	42	527	451	15	4–16	30.06	5.13	35.13	0	0
First-class *to 11.9.06*	49	1016	598	5	2–44	119.59	3.53	203.19	0	0

DENESH RAMDIN

Full name	**Denesh Ramdin**
Born	**March 13, 1985, Couva, Trinidad**
Teams	**Trinidad & Tobago**
Style	**Right-hand bat, wicketkeeper**
Test debut	**West Indies v Sri Lanka at Colombo 2005**
ODI debut	**West Indies v India at Dambulla 2005**

THE PROFILE Denesh Ramdin is a wicketkeeper-batsman of great potential, viewed by many in the Caribbean as the long-term solution to the void which has never really been satisfactorily filled since the retirement of Jeff Dujon in 1991. Originally a fast bowler who then kept wicket when he had finished his stint with the ball, Ramdin decided at 13 to concentrate on keeping, honing his reflexes and working on his agility. He led both the Trinidad & Tobago and West Indies Under-19 sides before being selected, still only 19 and with just 13 first-class games behind him, as the first-choice keeper for the senior squad's tour of Sri Lanka in 2005. He impressed everyone with his work behind and in front of the stumps, and continued to do so in the series in Australia later in 2005. A plucky 71 – he shared a fine partnership of 182 in the second Test at Hobart with his fellow Trinidadian Dwayne Bravo, just after they'd heard that T&T had qualified for the soccer World Cup – was his best moment Down Under. A slight shortage of Ramdin runs meant that Carlton Baugh was preferred for some of the home one-dayers early in 2006, and it was something of a surprise when Ramdin returned for the Tests against India. But he justified his selection with some smooth keeping, and a gritty unbeaten 62 that took West Indies frustratingly close to victory in the series-deciding fourth Test in Jamaica.

THE FACTS Ramdin played in the West Indies side that won the Under-15 World Challenge in 2000, beating Pakistan in the final at Lord's: four years later he captained West Indies in the Under-19 World Cup, when they lost the final at Dhaka – to Pakistan ... His highest score is 125 not out for Trinidad & Tobago against Jamaica at St Augustine in January 2006 ... Ramdin was one of only eight players offered central contracts by the cash-strapped West Indian board in June 2006 ...

THE FIGURES
Batting and fielding

	M	Inns	NO	Runs	HS	Avge	S/R	100	50	4s	6s	Ct	St
Tests to 11.9.06	12	22	4	478	71	26.55	45.30	0	3	62	1	29	0
ODIs to 11.9.06	14	12	4	264	74*	33.00	81.48	0	1	25	0	16	0
First-class to 11.9.06	33	56	6	1312	125*	26.24	–	2	7	–	–	80	12

Bowling

	M	Balls	Runs	Wkts	BB	Avge	RpO	S/R	5i	10m
Tests to 11.9.06	12	0	–	–	–	–	–	–	–	–
ODIs to 11.9.06	14	0	–	–	–	–	–	–	–	–
First-class to 11.9.06	33	0	–	–	–	–	–	–	–	–

CHRIS READ

Full name	**Christopher Mark Wells Read**
Born	**August 10, 1978, Paignton, Devon**
Teams	**Nottinghamshire**
Style	**Right-hand bat, wicketkeeper**
Test debut	**England v New Zealand at Birmingham 1999**
ODI debut	**England v South Africa at Bloemfontein 1999-2000**

THE PROFILE Born in Devon, reared in Bristol and an England A tourist before he had even played a first-class game, Chris Read soon established himself as the tidiest wicketkeeper in English cricket, although, like Jack Russell before him, he found that that is no longer a guarantee of international selection. A back-foot scrapper with a productive whip-pull, he bats as high as No. 6 for Nottinghamshire, and was given a Test debut against New Zealand at 20 in 1999, embarrassingly ducking into a Chris Cairns slower ball which shattered his stumps. He made England's one-day team that winter in South Africa and, despite a below-par performance with the gloves, showed composure with the bat, memorably mowing Shaun Pollock for six to reignite one run-chase. Read then fell behind James Foster in the race to become England's next keeper, but he was a more rounded player by the time Alec Stewart finally retired. Back came Read, but, after keeping immaculately in the first three Tests in the Caribbean early in 2004, he was controversially dumped in favour of Geraint Jones, the better batsman. Two months later, Read was out of the one-day side as well, despite some combative performances down the order. He went back to county cricket to work on his batting – at the expense of his keeping, some said – and an impressive unbeaten 150 for England A against Pakistan in July 2006 won him back his Test place shortly afterwards, with Jones ironically jettisoned after improving his keeping but struggling with the bat.

THE FACTS Read's first first-class match was for England A, on tour in Kenya in January 1998 ... His highest score is 160, for Nottinghamshire against Warwickshire at Trent Bridge in June 1999 ... Read played for Devon in the NatWest Trophy against Sussex in 1995, when he was only 16: the following year, he opened for Devon against Essex ... He started on the Gloucestershire staff, but moved to Nottinghamshire to escape the shadow of Jack Russell ... Read has yet to play a Test or an ODI against Australia, or India ...

THE FIGURES
Batting and fielding

	M	Inns	NO	Runs	HS	Avge	S/R	100	50	4s	6s	Ct	St
Tests to 11.9.06	13	19	3	325	55	20.31	41.03	0	1	34	4	37	5
ODIs to 11.9.06	33	21	7	294	30*	21.00	74.61	0	0	21	6	40	2
First-class to 11.9.06	171	258	40	6790	160	31.14	–	9	37	–	–	495	23

Bowling

	M	Balls	Runs	Wkts	BB	Avge	RpO	S/R	5i	10m
Tests to 11.9.06	13	0	–	–	–	–	–	–	–	–
ODIs to 11.9.06	33	0	–	–	–	–	–	–	–	–
First-class to 11.9.06	171	36	33	0	–	–	5.50	–	0	0

PIET RINKE

Full name	**Harry Peter Rinke**
Born	**November 5, 1981, Marondera**
Teams	**Manicaland**
Style	**Right-hand bat, right-arm medium-pace bowler**
Test debut	**No Tests yet**
ODI debut	**Zimbabwe v Kenya at Bulawayo 2005-06**

THE PROFILE Piet Rinke (it's pronounced "Rinky") is a stocky medium-pacer who can swing the ball both ways, and an aggressive one-day opener. He was rather surprisingly called up by Zimbabwe early in 2006, even though he had not played first-class cricket locally since September 2003 (however, he had toured Bangladesh with the A team for a one-day series early in 2004). Rinke was a graduate of the CFX Academy in 2002, but confined himself to club cricket, and the occasional provincial one-day game, after his national contract was not renewed. Although by no means an opening batsman in first-class cricket, he has made a reputation as a one-day biffer, with powerful hitting capable of shredding wayward attacks within a few overs. After Zimbabwe's player rebellion, Rinke offered his services to coach Kevin Curran, saying he wanted to return to full-time cricket, and soon proved his value locally. He scored well against Kenya early in 2006, then tonked two centuries in warm-up matches in the West Indies ... but his limited technique was cruelly exposed when the real thing started, and he managed only 23 runs in six ODI innings. A tendency to play across the line got him into trouble, especially against the quicker bowlers. However, his attitude won him some friends, and he is working to overcome his technical deficiencies. He was not fully fit in the West Indies, but has since lost weight and is trying hard to improve his fielding.

THE FACTS Rinke has scored 72 twice in ODIs – once against Kenya and once against Canada ... He averages 42 against Kenya, but only 3.83 against West Indies – his scores there early in 2006 were 1, 6, 0, 0, 4 and 12 ... Rinke's highest first-class score is 84 not out, for the CFX Academy against Mashonaland A at Harare in March 2002, while he took 6 for 43 for Midlands against Manicaland at Mutare in September 2003, in his last first-class match for three years ...

THE FIGURES
Batting and fielding

	M	Inns	NO	Runs	HS	Avge	S/R	100	50	4s	6s	Ct	St
Tests to 11.9.06	0	–	–	–	–	–	–	–	–	–	–	–	–
ODIs to 11.9.06	15	15	0	312	72*	20.80	86.18	0	3	41	2	0	0
First-class to 11.9.06	9	16	2	346	84*	24.71	39.18	0	1	–	–	6	0

Bowling

	M	Balls	Runs	Wkts	BB	Avge	RpO	S/R	5i	10m
Tests to 11.9.06	0	–	–	–	–	–	–	–	–	–
ODIs to 11.9.06	15	223	217	6	2–11	36.16	5.83	37.16	0	0
First-class to 11.9.06	9	1328	658	26	6–43	25.30	2.97	51.07	2	0

JACQUES RUDOLPH

Full name	**Jacobus Andries Rudolph**
Born	**May 4, 1981, Springs, Transvaal**
Teams	**Eagles**
Style	**Left-hand bat, occasional legspinner**
Test debut	**South Africa v Bangladesh at Chittagong 2002-03**
ODI debut	**South Africa v India at Dhaka 2002-03**

THE PROFILE Jacques Rudolph is seen by many as a victim of reverse discrimination in South African cricket. His debut double-century – and his record-breaking 429-run stand with Boeta Dippenaar – against Bangladesh in April 2003 came 18 months after he had forced his way into the squad through sheer weight of runs. Twice before he had been expecting to win his first cap, and twice politics intervened. His first international experience came at Centurion in November 2001, when the Indians were in dispute with referee Mike Denness and ICC ruled the match unofficial. Then two months later he was named to face Australia at Sydney, but the South African board president Percy Sonn vetoed his selection, saying there were not enough "players of colour" in the side, and Justin Ontong debuted instead. Since then, however, Rudolph has become a middle-order fixture, accumulating his runs undemonstratively. A left-hander who stands tall at the point of delivery, bat upraised, he has pleasing footwork and balance, and favours the cover-drive. Rudolph's unbeaten 102 – a classic rearguard lasting more than seven hours – saved the Perth Test in December 2005. That was his fifth Test century, but his highest score in five more matches against the Aussies in 2005-06 was only 41. After that he had a shoulder operation, which put paid to plans for a season with Derbyshire, and he was miffed to be left out of South Africa's preliminary squad for the 2007 World Cup, after an indifferent run – only two half-centuries in his last 20 ODIs.

THE FACTS Rudolph was the fifth man to score a double-century on Test debut, with 222 not out against Bangladesh at Chittagong in April 2003: he followed "Tip" Foster, Lawrence Rowe, Brendon Kuruppu and Mathew Sinclair ... In that innings he put on 429 for the third wicket with Boeta Dippenaar, a South African Test record ... Occasional legspinner Rudolph took a wicket with his second ball in Tests, dismissing Nasser Hussain for 42 at Leeds in 2003 ... His record includes two ODIs for the Africa XI ...

THE FIGURES
Batting and fielding

	M	Inns	NO	Runs	HS	Avge	S/R	100	50	4s	6s	Ct	St
Tests to 11.9.06	35	63	7	2028	222*	36.21	42.95	5	8	288	6	22	0
ODIs to 11.9.06	45	39	6	1174	81	35.57	68.05	0	7	109	5	11	0
First-class to 11.9.06	93	167	10	6521	222*	41.53	–	18	30	–	–	66	0

Bowling

	M	Balls	Runs	Wkts	BB	Avge	RpO	S/R	5i	10m
Tests to 11.9.06	35	664	432	4	1–1	108.00	3.90	166.00	0	0
ODIs to 11.9.06	45	24	26	0	–	–	6.50	–	0	0
First-class to 11.9.06	93	3248	1833	44	5–87	41.65	3.38	73.81	2	0

SALMAN BUTT

PAKISTAN

Full name	**Salman Butt**
Born	**October 7, 1984, Lahore, Punjab**
Teams	**Lahore, National Bank**
Style	**Left-hand bat, occasional offspinner**
Test debut	**Pakistan v Bangladesh at Multan 2003-04**
ODI debut	**Pakistan v West Indies at Southampton 2004**

THE PROFILE   Because he's left-handed, with supple wrists, it is easy to compare Salman Butt with the delectable Saeed Anwar. His drives and cuts through extra cover and backward point are flicked or scooped: it is a high-scoring region for him, as it was for Anwar. He doesn't mind pulling, and off his toes he's efficient, rather than whippy as Anwar was. But in attitude and temperament he is more like Anwar's long-time opening partner, Aamer Sohail. He has a confident air, a certain spikiness, and is a rare young Pakistan player at ease when speaking English. Butt first made headlines by smashing 233 against the South African Academy during an Under-19 tour, and his breakthrough at the highest level came late in 2004. First came a maiden one-day century, at Eden Gardens, then he did it in Tests too, with 70 at Melbourne and 108 in the New Year Test at Sydney. Then came the fall: he failed to build on that during 2005, despite another one-day hundred against India, and found himself dropped as doubts crept in about his defence and his dash. He responded by unveiling startling restraint against England late in the year, grinding out a hundred and two fifties in the Tests, followed by another ton at India's expense. His strokemaking was never really in doubt, but with the tightening of his defence, Salman Butt could be one half of the solution to the opening conundrum that has haunted Pakistan since ... well, since Anwar and Sohail retired.

THE FACTS   All three of Salman Butt's ODI hundreds to date have been scored against India: he averages 45.70 against them, but only 14.83 against West Indies (and 1.00 v Scotland) ... Butt's highest score is 206, for Lahore Whites against Karachi Whites at Lahore in November 2004 ... He captained Pakistan in the Under-19 World Cup in New Zealand early in 2002 ... All of Butt's first-class wickets came in the same innings – he took 4 for 82 for Lahore against Faisalabad in Lahore in April 2004 ...

THE FIGURES

Batting and fielding

	M	Inns	NO	Runs	HS	Avge	S/R	100	50	4s	6s	Ct	St
Tests to 11.9.06	14	26	0	777	122	29.88	51.42	2	4	109	1	7	0
ODIs to 11.9.06	33	33	1	962	108*	30.66	71.25	3	3	124	1	9	0
First-class to 11.9.06	47	82	3	2745	206*	34.74	–		7	13	–	–	16	0

Bowling

	M	Balls	Runs	Wkts	BB	Avge	RpO	S/R	5i	10m
Tests to 11.9.06	14	24	18	0	–	–	4.50	–	0	0
ODIs to 11.9.06	33	36	42	0	–	–	7.00	–	0	0
First-class to 11.9.06	47	520	354	4	4–82	88.50	4.08	130.00	0	0

THILAN SAMARAWEERA

Full name	**Thilan Thusara Samaraweera**
Born	**September 22, 1976, Colombo**
Teams	**Sinhalese Sports Club**
Style	**Right-hand bat, offspinner**
Test debut	**Sri Lanka v India at Colombo 2001-02**
ODI debut	**Sri Lanka v India at Sharjah 1998-99**

THE PROFILE As an offspinner, Thilan Samaraweera lived in the shadow of Muttiah Muralitharan early on in his career, only occasionally getting a one-day outing. But since scoring 103 not out on Test debut against India in August 2001, an innings that helped Sri Lanka to a 2-1 series win, he has carved out a reputation as a specialist batsman, and the departure of Aravinda de Silva and Hashan Tillakaratne allowed him to cement a place in the middle order, where his patient no-risks approach makes him a very valuable foil for some of his more flamboyant colleagues. An adhesive and well-organised player, he took a particular liking to his home ground, the Sinhalese Sports Club in Colombo, where he scored three centuries in his first six Tests. Until Sri Lanka toured India at the end of 2005 he maintained a Test batting average of over 50, but a low-key run – including difficulties against the moving ball in England in 2006 – pushed that down a few points. He has been branded a Test specialist by the selectors, and seldom features in ODIs. His steady offspin is rarely used now, although he has a developing reputation as a partnership-breaker and clearly has the talent to become a useful support bowler. Although Mahela Jayawardene and Kumar Sangakkara are the main contenders for the captaincy when Marvan Atapattu steps down, Samaraweera has also impressed while leading the A team, and could be an outside bet as skipper a few years down the line.

THE FACTS Samaraweera was the third Sri Lankan, after Brendon Kuruppu and Romesh Kaluwitharana, to score a century on Test debut, against India in August 2001 ... That innings, and his next two Test centuries as well, was scored at the Sinhalese Sports Club, his home ground in Colombo, where he averages 77.90 in Tests ... Only one of his five Test centuries was scored outside Colombo: 100 v Pakistan at Faisalabad in October 2004 ... Samaraweera's brother Dulip played seven Tests for Sri Lanka in the early 1990s ...

THE FIGURES
Batting and fielding

	M	Inns	NO	Runs	HS	Avge	S/R	100	50	4s	6s	Ct	St
Tests to 11.9.06	39	58	8	2089	142	41.78	41.53	5	13	223	1	30	0
ODIs to 11.9.06	17	13	1	199	33	16.58	52.50	0	0	15	0	3	0
First-class to 11.9.06	166	220	46	7422	206	42.65	–	15	44	–	–	135	0

Bowling

	M	Balls	Runs	Wkts	BB	Avge	RpO	S/R	5i	10m
Tests to 11.9.06	39	1285	671	14	4–49	47.49	3.13	91.78	0	0
ODIs to 11.9.06	17	672	509	10	3–34	50.90	4.54	67.20	0	0
First-class to 11.9.06	166	17415	8102	347	6–55	23.34	2.79	50.18	15	2

MARLON SAMUELS

Full name	**Marlon Nathaniel Samuels**
Born	**January 5, 1981, Kingston, Jamaica**
Teams	**Jamaica**
Style	**Right-hand bat, offspinner**
Test debut	**West Indies v Australia at Adelaide 2000-01**
ODI debut	**West Indies v Sri Lanka at Nairobi 2000-01**

THE PROFILE Marlon Samuels is a classy right-hander whose composed start in Tests prompted comparisons with Viv Richards. When he flew into Australia for the third Test of the 2000-01 series, Samuels was only 19 and had played just one first-class match for his native Jamaica. But he showed a beautifully balanced technique, standing still at the crease and moving smoothly into his strokes off either foot. His undistinguished offspin also claimed a couple of wickets. Samuels exudes a bull-headed confidence – he used to skip his schoolwork, saying that exams were irrelevant for future Test cricketers. That confidence/arrogance almost got him sent home from India late in 2002, after he defied a team curfew – but he was kept on, and responded with a disciplined maiden Test century at Kolkata, and followed that with 91 against Bangladesh. But he struggled with both form and injury, and was dropped after two poor home Tests against Sri Lanka in 2003. Then he tweaked his knee, and spent a frustrating time on the sidelines. He was back for the 2005-06 Australian tour, and warmed up for the first Test by hammering 257 against Queensland, and followed that with 5 for 86 with the ball, another career-best. But just as he seemed to have cemented his place in the side he injured his knee again, and had to fly home. He returned for the third Test against India in June 2006, making a composed 87. Knees permitting, he could be back for a long time.

THE FACTS Samuels scored 257 and then took 5 for 87 – both career-bests – for the West Indians against Queensland in Brisbane in October 2005 ... He scored his maiden first-class century in a Test – 104 v India at Kolkata in October 2002: he was the fifth West Indian to do this, following Clifford Roach, Clairmonte Depeiaza, Gerry Alexander and Bernard Julien ... His brother Robert Samuels, older by ten years, played six Tests and eight ODIs as a left-hand opener, and scored 125 against New Zealand in his second Test ...

THE FIGURES

Batting and fielding

	M	Inns	NO	Runs	HS	Avge	S/R	100	50	4s	6s	Ct	St
Tests to 11.9.06	23	41	4	1044	104	28.21	44.76	1	7	142	5	9	0
ODIs to 11.9.06	65	61	8	1512	108*	28.52	73.39	1	10	151	20	20	0
First-class to 11.9.06	57	96	7	3168	257	35.59	–	5	20	–	–	31	0

Bowling

	M	Balls	Runs	Wkts	BB	Avge	RpO	S/R	5i	10m
Tests to 11.9.06	23	1308	703	5	2–49	140.60	3.22	261.60	0	0
ODIs to 11.9.06	65	2052	1667	42	3–25	39.69	4.87	48.85	0	0
First-class to 11.9.06	57	3987	1974	33	5–87	59.81	2.97	120.81	1	0

KUMAR SANGAKKARA

Full name	**Kumar Chokshanada Sangakkara**
Born	**October 27, 1977, Matale**
Teams	**Nondescripts**
Style	**Left-hand bat, wicketkeeper**
Test debut	**Sri Lanka v South Africa at Galle 2000**
ODI debut	**Sri Lanka v Pakistan at Galle 2000**

THE PROFILE Within months of making the side at 22, Kumar Sangakkara had become one of Sri Lanka's most influential players: a talented left-hand strokemaker, a slick wicketkeeper, a sharp-eyed strategist and an even sharper-tongued sledger, capable of riling even the most unflappable. His success was unexpected, for his domestic performances had been relatively modest, but the selectors' judgment was immediately justified as he starred in his first one-day tournament, in July 2000. Early on his keeping could be ragged, but his effortless batting oozed class from the start. He possesses the grace of David Gower, but the attitude of an Australian. His greatest weakness is a tendency to over-react when the adrenaline really starts to pump. At the outset he was happier on the back foot, but a fierce work ethic and a deep interest in the theory of batsmanship helped him, and he is now as comfortable driving through the covers as cutting behind point. He was briefly relieved of keeping duties after the 2003 World Cup: he made more runs, but the team was unbalanced, and he got the gloves back when Australia visited early in 2004. This time the extra burden had no discernible effect on his batting: he made 185 against Pakistan in March 2006, and scored consistently in England too. A charismatic personality and an astute thinker – he is training as a lawyer – Sangakkara is tipped as a future captain. He played for the World XI in the Super Series one-dayers in Australia in October 2005.

THE FACTS Sangakkara scored 287, and shared a partnership of 624 – the highest-ever in first-class cricket – with Mahela Jayawardene (374) against South Africa in Colombo in July 2006 ... He also made 270, putting on 438 with Marvan Atapattu, against Zimbabwe at Bulawayo in May 2004 ... Sangakkara averages 82.66 in Tests against Pakistan, but 25.40 against Australia ... His record includes three ODIs for the World XI and four for the Asia XI ...

THE FIGURES

Batting and fielding

	M	Inns	NO	Runs	HS	Avge	S/R	100	50	4s	6s	Ct	St
Tests to 11.9.06	62	103	5	4796	287	48.93	53.96	10	22	652	14	142	20
ODIs to 11.9.06	174	160	21	4974	138*	35.78	73.99	5	33	496	20	146	45
First-class to 11.9.06	135	214	14	8098	287	40.49	–	14	43	–	–	289	33

Bowling

	M	Balls	Runs	Wkts	BB	Avge	RpO	S/R	5i	10m
Tests to 11.9.06	62	6	4	0	–	–	4.00	–	0	0
ODIs to 11.9.06	174	0	–	–	–	–	–	–	–	–
First-class to 11.9.06	135	108	66	1	1–13	66.00	3.66	108.00	0	0

RAMNARESH SARWAN

Full name	**Ramnaresh Ronnie Sarwan**
Born	**June 23, 1980, Wakenaam Island, Essequibo, Guyana**
Teams	**Guyana**
Style	**Right-hand bat, legspinner**
Test debut	**West Indies v Pakistan at Bridgetown 1999-2000**
ODI debut	**West Indies v England at Nottingham 2000**

THE PROFILE A light-footed right-hander, Ramnaresh Sarwan was brought up in the South American rainforest around the Essequibo River. After his first Test innings – 84 against Pakistan – the former England captain Ted Dexter was moved to predict a Test average of 50, an unfair millstone to hang around any young player's neck. But on his first tour, to England in 2000, Sarwan lived up to the hype by topping the averages: his footwork was strikingly confident and precise. It was a surprise when a horror run of three runs in five innings followed in Australia, but he did better against India at home in 2002. It still took him 28 matches to post his maiden Test century, 119 against Bangladesh in December 2002. But, as Graham Gooch and Steve Waugh can testify, the first time is often the hardest, and he has scored consistently since. He made 392 runs in four Tests against South Africa in 2003-04 then, after a lean run at home against England, stroked a stunning unbeaten 261 against Bangladesh at Kingston in June 2004. Then came another England tour: he began and ended it on a low note, but was prolific in between. He also played a big part as West Indies reached the final of the one-day NatWest Series then won the Champions Trophy in England in 2004, and carried on his good form in Australia the following year. That average is still under 40, ten points shy of Dexter's prediction, but time is on Sarwan's side.

THE FACTS Sarwan's 261 not out at Kingston in June 2004 is the highest score against Bangladesh, and also the highest Test score by a Guyanese batsman, beating Rohan Kanhai's 256 for West Indies against India at Calcutta in 1958-59 ... In ODIs Sarwan averages 74 against India – but only 21.83 against Sri Lanka ... He was out for 199 when Guyana played Kenya at Georgetown in February 2004 ... Sarwan made 100 and 111 for the West Indies Board President's XI against the touring Zimbabweans at Pointe-à-Pierre in March 2000 ... He has played county cricket for Gloucestershire ...

THE FIGURES

Batting and fielding

	M	Inns	NO	Runs	HS	Avge	S/R	100	50	4s	6s	Ct	St
Tests *to 11.9.06*	63	114	7	4207	261*	39.31	44.81	9	26	552	8	45	0
ODIs *to 11.9.06*	102	96	22	3465	115*	46.82	77.44	3	23	278	35	29	0
First-class *to 11.9.06*	154	261	18	9119	261*	37.52	–		21	51	–	–	117	0

Bowling

	M	Balls	Runs	Wkts	BB	Avge	RpO	S/R	5i	10m
Tests *to 11.9.06*	63	1747	970	21	4-37	46.19	3.33	83.19	0	0
ODIs *to 11.9.06*	102	358	357	8	3-31	44.62	5.98	44.75	0	0
First-class *to 11.9.06*	154	3772	1929	49	6-62	39.36	3.06	76.97	1	0

VIRENDER SEHWAG

INDIA

Full name	**Virender Sehwag**
Born	**October 20, 1978, Delhi**
Teams	**Delhi**
Style	**Right-hand bat, offspinner**
Test debut	**India v South Africa at Bloemfontein 2001-02**
ODI debut	**India v Pakistan at Mohali 1998-99**

THE PROFILE Virender Sehwag is a primal talent whose rough edges make him all the more appealing. By the time he had scored his first centuries in ODIs (off 70 balls, against New Zealand) and Tests (on debut, against South Africa, from 68 for 4), he was already eliciting comparisons with his idol Sachin Tendulkar. It is half-true. Like Tendulkar, he is short and square with curly hair, and plays the straight drive, back-foot punch and whip off the hips identically – but he leaves Tendulkar standing when it comes to audacity. Asked to open in England in 2002, Sehwag proved an instant hit, cracking 84 and 106 in the first two Tests. And he kept conjuring up pivotal innings, none as significant as India's first triple-century (brought up, characteristically, with a six), against Pakistan at Multan early in 2004. Sehwag bowls effective, loopy offspin, and is a reliable catcher in the slips. Surprisingly, he struggled in one-day cricket after his electric start, and endured a run of 60 games from January 2004 in which he averaged below 30. His fitness levels also dropped, but he continued to sparkle in Tests, with a magnificent 254 – and an opening stand of 410 with Rahul Dravid – against Pakistan at Lahore in January 2006. Then, in June, he came excruciatingly close to scoring a century before lunch on the first day in St Lucia, a feat never yet accomplished by an Indian. If anyone's going to do it, Sehwag is likely to be the one.

THE FACTS Sehwag's 309 against Pakistan at Multan in March 2004 was India's highest score (and first triple-century) in Tests ... He made 105 on his Test debut, against South Africa at Bloemfontein in November 2001 ... Sehwag averages 91.14 in Tests against Pakistan, with three double-centuries, but only 11.50 against Bangladesh ... His record includes one Test and three ODIs for the World XI, and four ODIs for the Asia XI ...

THE FIGURES
Batting and fielding

	M	Inns	NO	Runs	HS	Avge	S/R	100	50	4s	6s	Ct	St
Tests to 11.9.06	49	81	3	4066	309	52.12	75.78	12	12	598	41	38	0
ODIs to 11.9.06	153	149	7	4608	130	32.45	96.76	7	23	633	64	64	0
First-class to 11.9.06	103	166	7	8229	309	51.75	–	25	30	–	–	94	0

Bowling

	M	Balls	Runs	Wkts	BB	Avge	RpO	S/R	5i	10m
Tests to 11.9.06	49	1192	628	12	3–33	52.33	3.16	99.33	0	0
ODIs to 11.9.06	153	3110	2753	69	3–25	39.89	5.31	45.07	0	0
First-class to 11.9.06	103	5216	2727	67	4–32	40.70	3.13	77.85	0	0

SHAHADAT HOSSAIN

Full name	Kazi Shahadat Hossain
Born	August 7, 1986, Dhaka
Teams	Dhaka
Style	Right-hand bat, right-arm fast-medium bowler
Test debut	Bangladesh v England at Lord's 2005
ODI debut	Bangladesh v Kenya at Bogra 2005-06

THE PROFILE Shahadat Hossain was discovered during a talent-spotting camp in Narayanganj, and whisked away to the Bangladesh Institute of Sports (BKSP) for refinement. He was picked for the 2004 Under-19 World Cup, where he stood out as a promising fast bowler in a tournament which generally lacked firepower, and was rapidly called up for Bangladesh A. Shahadat – who's also known as "Rajib" – has all the necessary attributes for a genuine fast bowler. He is tall, comes in off a smooth run-up, and doesn't put unnecessary pressure on his body with a slightly open-chested delivery position. He has a strong frame, and endurance in abundance. He is naturally aggressive and, above everything, has raw pace. His Test debut at Lord's in 2005 was a chastening experience, as he conceded 101 runs in just 12 overs. But he was still only 18: since then he impressed against Sri Lanka, taking four wickets in an innings in Colombo and again at Chittagong, before going one better in Bogra's inaugural Test: his 5 for 86 confirmed him as the leading fast bowler on either side. He struggled against the Australians in April 2006, having only the wicket of Ricky Ponting to show for 67 overs of effort, but if he continues to progress, along with the left-armer Syed Rasel, he could be a force for Bangladesh in the years to come.

THE FACTS Shahadat Hossain's 5 for 86 against Sri Lanka at Bogra in 2005-06 was only the second five-wicket haul by a Bangladesh fast bowler in Tests, following Manjural Islam's 6 for 81 against Zimbabwe at Bulawayo in 2000-01 ... He took only two wickets – both against Kenya – in his first six ODIs ... Shahadat took 5 for 63 and 5 for 53 (his first-class career-best) in successive A-team Tests in Zimbabwe in February 2005 ...

THE FIGURES
Batting and fielding

	M	Inns	NO	Runs	HS	Avge	S/R	100	50	4s	6s	Ct	St
Tests to 11.9.06	7	14	5	55	13	6.11	30.38	0	0	6	0	3	0
ODIs to 11.9.06	10	4	3	9	5*	9.00	56.25	0	0	0	0	0	0
First-class to 11.9.06	21	36	16	223	37	11.15	46.16	0	0	–	–	6	0

Bowling

	M	Balls	Runs	Wkts	BB	Avge	RpO	S/R	5i	10m
Tests to 11.9.06	7	1071	793	16	5–86	49.56	4.44	66.93	1	0
ODIs to 11.9.06	10	376	311	11	3–34	28.27	4.96	34.18	0	0
First-class to 11.9.06	21	3230	2179	61	5–53	35.72	4.04	52.95	4	0

SHAHID AFRIDI

Full name	**Sahibzada Mohammad Shahid Khan Afridi**
Born	**March 1, 1980, Khyber Agency**
Teams	**Karachi, Habib Bank**
Style	**Right-hand bat, legspinner**
Test debut	**Pakistan v Australia at Karachi 1998-99**
ODI debut	**Pakistan v Kenya at Nairobi 1996-97**

THE PROFILE A flamboyant allrounder introduced to international cricket as a 16-year-old legspinner, Shahid Afridi astonished everyone except himself by pinch-hitting the fastest one-day hundred in his maiden innings. He's a compulsive shot-maker, and although until 2004 that was too often his undoing, a combination of growing maturity and a sympathetic coach has seen him blossom into one of the most dangerous players around. A string of incisive contributions culminated in a violent century against India in April 2005: the only faster ODI hundred was Afridi's own. A few weeks before, he had smashed 58 in 34 balls, and also grabbed three crucial wickets, as Pakistan memorably squared the Test series at Bangalore. And so it continued: a Test ton against West Indies, important contributions against England, then, early in 2006, he went berserk on some flat pitches against India. An Afridi virtuoso is laced with lofted drives and short-arm jabs over midwicket. He's at his best when forcing straight, and at his weakest pushing at the ball just outside off. But perhaps the biggest improvement has been in his legspin: it is now integral in one-dayers, and curiously effective at key moments in Tests. When conditions suit, he gets turn as well as lazy drift, but variety is the key: there's a vicious faster ball and an offbreak too. He's also an agile fielder, and possesses the firmest handshake in international cricket. He shocked everyone when, after finally establishing himself, he announced his retirement from Tests early in 2006. To less surprise, he retracted his retirement a fortnight later.

THE FACTS In his second match (he hadn't batted in the first) Shahid Afridi hit the fastest hundred in ODIs, from only 37 balls, against Sri Lanka in Nairobi in October 1996 ... Afridi has the fastest strike rate – 107.83 runs per 100 balls – of anyone who has batted more than 20 times in ODIs ... In successive matches against India early in 2006 he hit 103 (from 80 balls) at Lahore, and 156, from 128 balls with six sixes, at Faisalabad ... Afridi has hit more ODI sixes than anyone else ... His record includes three ODIs for the Asia XI and two for the World XI ...

THE FIGURES
Batting and fielding

	M	Inns	NO	Runs	HS	Avge	S/R	100	50	4s	6s	Ct	St
Tests to 11.9.06	26	46	1	1683	156	37.40	86.13	5	8	216	50	10	0
ODIs to 11.9.06	230	218	9	4860	109	23.25	107.83	4	26	458	216	83	0
First-class to 11.9.06	89	151	4	4686	164	31.87	–	11	22	–	–	55	0

Bowling

	M	Balls	Runs	Wkts	BB	Avge	RpO	S/R	5i	10m
Tests to 11.9.06	26	3092	1640	47	5–52	34.89	3.18	65.78	1	0
ODIs to 11.9.06	230	8949	6891	192	5–11	35.89	4.62	46.60	2	0
First-class to 11.9.06	89	10783	5614	189	6–101	29.70	3.12	57.05	6	0

SHAHRIAR NAFEES

Full name	**Shahriar Nafees Ahmed**
Born	**January 25, 1986, Dhaka**
Teams	**Barisal**
Style	**Left-hand bat**
Test debut	**Bangladesh v Sri Lanka at Colombo 2005-06**
ODI debut	**Bangladesh v England at Nottingham 2005**

THE PROFILE As a left-hand opening batsman, Shahriar Nafees is a rarity among Bangladesh cricketers, and at the age of 19 he was thrust into the Test squad for their maiden tour of England with just five first-class matches behind him. He hadn't fared too badly in those, however, with 350 runs at 35, and his Under-19 coach Richard McInness reckoned he had the talent and temperament to become a future Test captain. With Nafees Iqbal and Javed Omar established as Bangladesh's opening pair, the England trip was a case of watching and learning for Shahriar. He did get an opportunity in the NatWest Series, and cashed in with 75 in the final one-dayer against Australia. He made his Test debut in Sri Lanka in September 2005, and made 51 in his second match. He also got starts in all the one-day games, but converted only one into a fifty. Then in April 2006 he exploded in sensational fashion against the might of Australia, stroking his way to a brilliant hundred, his maiden first-class ton as well as his first in Tests, at Fatullah. His stunning 138, with 19 fours, set up a scarcely believable first-day total of 355 for 5 as the Aussies reeled. He added 33 in the second innings, and a brisk 79 in the second Test to show that this was no flash in the pan.

THE FACTS Shahriar Nafees's 138 against Australia at Fatullah in 2005-06 was his maiden century in first-class cricket: his previous-highest score was 97, for the Board President's XI against the touring Zimbabweans in January 2005 ... Shahriar's 118 not out against Zimbabwe at Harare in August 2006 was Bangladesh's highest score in ODIs ... He averages less in ODIs at home (24.20) than he does in Sri Lanka (37.00) and England (35.75) ... Shahriar captained Bangladesh Under-19 in a one-day game against England Under-19, skippered by Alastair Cook, in 2004 ...

THE FIGURES

Batting and fielding

	M	Inns	NO	Runs	HS	Avge	S/R	100	50	4s	6s	Ct	St
Tests to 11.9.06	6	12	0	402	138	33.50	55.60	1	2	55	0	6	0
ODIs to 11.9.06	25	25	1	787	118*	32.79	66.52	1	5	94	1	6	0
First-class to 11.9.06	21	41	1	1408	138	35.20	62.19	1	12	–	–	13	0

Bowling

	M	Balls	Runs	Wkts	BB	Avge	RpO	S/R	5i	10m
Tests to 11.9.06	6	0	–	–	–	–	–	–	–	–
ODIs to 11.9.06	25	0	–	–	–	–	–	–	–	–
First-class to 11.9.06	21	18	20	0	–	–	6.66	–	0	0

SHOAIB AKHTAR

Full name	**Shoaib Akhtar**
Born	**August 13, 1975, Rawalpindi, Punjab**
Teams	**Rawalpindi**
Style	**Right-hand bat, right-arm fast bowler**
Test debut	**Pakistan v West Indies at Rawalpindi 1997-98**
ODI debut	**Pakistan v Zimbabwe at Harare 1997-98**

THE PROFILE Shoaib Akhtar electrified the 1999 World Cup with his spectacular run-up and blistering speed. Star status was sealed by a flop of unruly hair, a talent for showboating and a vivid nickname – "The Rawalpindi Express". But it was too much, too young. Breaking the 100mph barrier seemed to matter more than cementing his place. He was twice sidelined after throwing allegations, and although his action was cleared – tests showed a hyper-extensible elbow – injuries then impinged. He was back in 2002, shaking up the Aussies with five-fors in Brisbane and Colombo. He promised much in the 2003 World Cup, but came a cropper, especially in a needle encounter with Sachin Tendulkar. That was followed by a forgettable series against India: Shoaib struggled for wickets, and left the field at a crucial stage of the third Test, citing wrist and back trouble, though neither seemed to bother him later when he batted. Pakistan lost, and Shoaib felt the heat as his commitment was questioned: a difficult relationship with captain and coach didn't help. He blew hot and cold in Australia in 2004-05, by turns Pakistan's most incisive threat and their most disinterested player. Worries about fitness and attitude kept him out for most of 2005, but he bounced back at the end with 17 England wickets, mixing yorkers and bouncers with lethal slower balls – and looked, importantly, a team man to the core. But just when he seemed to be back there were further whispers about his action, then he missed most of the 2006 England tour with ankle trouble.

THE FACTS Shoaib Akhtar was clocked at 100.04mph by an unofficial speed-gun during a one-dayer against New Zealand in April 2002: he also recorded 100.23mph (161.3kph) at the 2003 World Cup ... His best figures in Tests (6 for 11 at Lahore in May 2002) and ODIs (6 for 16 at Karachi the previous month) both came against New Zealand ... Against England at Cape Town in the 2003 World Cup Shoaib was the fifth No. 11 to top-score in an ODI innings, with 43 ... His record includes three ODIs for the Asia XI and two for the World XI ...

THE FIGURES

Batting and fielding

	M	Inns	NO	Runs	HS	Avge	S/R	100	50	4s	6s	Ct	St
Tests to 11.9.06	42	62	12	537	47	10.74	42.08	0	0	52	22	11	0
ODIs to 11.9.06	133	65	31	344	43	10.11	73.50	0	0	22	10	17	0
First-class to 11.9.06	120	168	47	1503	59*	12.42	–	0	1	–	–	37	0

Bowling

	M	Balls	Runs	Wkts	BB	Avge	RpO	S/R	5i	10m
Tests to 11.9.06	42	7490	4240	165	6–11	25.69	3.39	45.39	12	2
ODIs to 11.9.06	133	6276	4854	208	6–16	23.33	4.64	30.17	4	0
First-class to 11.9.06	120	18696	11294	428	6–11	26.38	3.62	43.68	28	2

SHOAIB MALIK

Full name	**Shoaib Malik**
Born	**February 1, 1982, Sialkot, Punjab**
Teams	**Sialkot, Pakistan International Airlines**
Style	**Right-hand bat, offspinner**
Test debut	**Pakistan v Bangladesh at Multan 2001-02**
ODI debut	**Pakistan v West Indies at Sharjah 1999-2000**

THE PROFILE Short of wicketkeeping, there are few roles that Shoaib Malik hasn't tried. He has batted everywhere from 1 to 10 in one-dayers, though since the arrival of Bob Woolmer as coach he has settled at 3 or 4. He began in Tests in the lower order, but lately has been opening. As an offspinner, everything about his bowling, from the short-stepping run-up to the doosra, bears a striking similarity to Saqlain Mushtaq's. His action isn't clean, though: he has been reported twice, first in October 2004, after which he played primarily as a batsman for the next six months before undergoing elbow surgery. He was reported again in November 2005, and had another operation early in 2006, which kept him out of the Tests in England. But his versatility and intelligence mark him out as vital to Pakistan's future, possibly even as captain. Under Woolmer, Shoaib became a one-day linchpin, regularly marshalling run-chases or setting up platforms for big totals. He is an uncomplicated batsman, free with checked drives and cuts, or slogging when needed. Against India, in both the 2005 and 2006 series, he produced all these – but he can still come in at No. 6, as he did against South Africa in October 2003, and blast 82 from 41 balls. He finally made the Test side, and started opening in the Caribbean in 2005. He struggled against England later that year, but defied Murali with an unbeaten eight-hour 148 to earn a draw in Colombo in March 2006.

THE FACTS Shoaib Malik extended his first Test century, against Sri Lanka in Colombo in March 2006, to 148 not out in 448 minutes as Pakistan forced a draw ... He made 90, 95 and 106 in successive one-day innings against India in February 2006 ... Shoaib has batted in every position except No. 11 in ODIs, averaging 56.11 from No. 4 and 40.53 at No. 3 (and 7.50 at No. 10) ... His best bowling figures are 7 for 81, for Pakistan International Airlines against WAPDA at Faisalabad in February 2001 ... Shoaib has played county cricket for Gloucestershire ...

THE FIGURES
Batting and fielding

	M	Inns	NO	Runs	HS	Avge	S/R	100	50	4s	6s	Ct	St
Tests *to 11.9.06*	15	24	4	798	148*	39.90	43.41	1	4	110	7	5	0
ODIs *to 11.9.06*	122	107	11	3118	143	32.47	77.98	5	18	266	34	42	0
First-class *to 11.9.06*	67	101	13	2468	148*	28.04	–		6	10	–	–	31	0

Bowling

	M	Balls	Runs	Wkts	BB	Avge	RpO	S/R	5i	10m
Tests *to 11.9.06*	15	1303	748	13	4–42	57.53	3.44	100.23	0	0
ODIs *to 11.9.06*	122	4532	3340	98	4–19	34.08	4.42	46.24	0	0
First-class *to 11.9.06*	67	9554	4749	162	7–81	29.31	2.98	58.97	5	1

VUSI SIBANDA

Full name	**Vusimuzi Sibanda**
Born	**October 10, 1983, Highfields, Harare**
Teams	**Midlands**
Style	**Right-hand bat, occasional right-arm medium-pacer**
Test debut	**Zimbabwe v West Indies at Harare 2003-04**
ODI debut	**Zimbabwe v West Indies at Bulawayo 2003-04**

THE PROFILE Vusi Sibanda is a contemporary of Tatenda Taibu, Hamilton Masakadza and Stuart Matsikenyeri. Like them, he comes from the Harare black township of Highfield, and earned a Zimbabwe Cricket Union scholarship to Churchill High School. An opening batsman and occasional medium-pacer, Sibanda was a student at the CFX Academy in 2002. His selection for Zimbabwe came too early, but although he failed to live up to his potential, the crisis in the national side meant that he kept his place long after others would have been jettisoned. He is a superb timer of the ball, predominantly off the front foot, but was slow to acquire the ability to build a big innings, and his continued selection was down almost entirely to his outstanding potential rather than actual performance. He has a very sound technique, but poor shot-selection often brought about his downfall; however, the coach Kevin Curran said that he matured well on the West Indian tour early in 2006. He suffered a hand injury at the start, but took his opportunities when given them, and ended with 78 and a superb 116 against Bermuda in the tri-series in Trinidad in May. Consistent performances against top-class opposition are long overdue, but nobody doubts that he has the ability to achieve them.

THE FACTS Sibanda finally hit his maiden first-class century in January 2005, hitting 122 against the Bangladesh Board President's XI at Chittagong – he put on 241 with Stuart Matsikenyeri, who made 150 ... He has failed to reach double figures in 19 of his 33 innings in ODIs, including three successive ducks in 2004 ... Sibanda toured England in 2003, but was out for 0 in his only first-class innings, against Middlesex at Shenley ...

THE FIGURES
Batting and fielding

	M	Inns	NO	Runs	HS	Avge	S/R	100	50	4s	6s	Ct	St
Tests to 11.9.06	3	6	0	48	18	8.00	52.74	0	0	10	0	4	0
ODIs to 11.9.06	39	38	1	748	116	20.21	57.49	1	4	83	7	14	0
First-class to 11.9.06	40	77	1	1646	122	21.60	–		1	10	–	–	33	0

Bowling

	M	Balls	Runs	Wkts	BB	Avge	RpO	S/R	5i	10m
Tests to 11.9.06	0	–	–	–	–	–	–	–	–	–
ODIs to 11.9.06	39	90	87	2	1–12	43.50	5.80	45.00	0	0
First-class to 11.9.06	40	702	514	11	4–30	46.72	4.39	63.81	0	0

MATHEW SINCLAIR

Full name	**Mathew Stuart Sinclair**
Born	**November 9, 1975, Katherine, Australia**
Teams	**Central Districts**
Style	**Right-hand bat, occasional right-arm medium-pacer**
Test debut	**New Zealand v West Indies at Wellington 1999-2000**
ODI debut	**New Zealand v Australia at Christchurch 1999-2000**

THE PROFILE Two double-centuries in his first 12 Tests, including one on debut, suggested that Mathew Sinclair should be a fixture in the New Zealand side – but he has been inconsistent since, and was close to leaving the country for good until he regained a central contract for 2006-07 after another fine domestic season (723 runs at 51.64). A correct right-hander, Sinclair made 214 against West Indies at Wellington in 1999-2000, and followed that with an unbeaten 204 against Pakistan at Christchurch in March 2001. In between there was 150 against South Africa at Port Elizabeth. But he struggled after that fine start, and lost his place. He was recalled for the third Test against South Africa at Wellington in March 2004, but an impressive 74 wasn't enough to get him picked for the tour of England later that year, although he was called up from club cricket in East Anglia after Craig McMillan broke a finger. Similarly, that October he was rushed to Bangladesh when Michael Papps dislocated his shoulder, and collected 76 in the first Test, followed by a dogged 69 against Australia at Brisbane – but after one more Test he was out of the side, then lost the central contract he has only just regained. Sinclair might have been in the other dressing-room at the Gabba: he was born in Australia's Northern Territory, but his mother moved to New Zealand after Sinclair's father was killed in a car crash when he was only five.

THE FACTS Sinclair is one of only five people to score a double-century on Test debut: the others are "Tip" Foster, Lawrence Rowe, Brendon Kuruppu and Jacques Rudolph ... He averages 108.33 in Tests against Pakistan, but 5.25 against Sri Lanka ... Sinclair has not played a Test or an ODI against England ... His highest first-class score is 268 for New Zealand A v South Africa A at Potchefstroom in 2004-05 ...

THE FIGURES

Batting and fielding

	M	Inns	NO	Runs	HS	Avge	S/R	100	50	4s	6s	Ct	St
Tests to 11.9.06	25	42	5	1365	214	36.89	43.79	3	4	161	7	22	0
ODIs to 11.9.06	45	44	2	1180	118*	28.09	60.76	2	7	101	4	15	0
First-class to 11.9.06	123	208	22	8869	268*	47.68	–	21	48	–	–	117	1

Bowling

	M	Balls	Runs	Wkts	BB	Avge	RpO	S/R	5i	10m
Tests to 11.9.06	25	24	13	0	–	–	3.25	–	0	0
ODIs to 11.9.06	45	0	–	–	–	–	–	–	–	–
First-class to 11.9.06	123	696	306	5	2–42	61.20	2.63	139.19	0	0

RUDRA PRATAP SINGH

INDIA

Full name	**Rudra Pratap Singh**
Born	**December 6, 1985, Rae Bareli, Uttar Pradesh**
Teams	**Uttar Pradesh**
Style	**Right-hand bat, left-arm fast-medium bowler**
Test debut	**India v Pakistan at Faisalabad 2005-06**
ODI debut	**India v Zimbabwe at Harare 2005-06**

THE PROFILE Rudra Pratap Singh first made the headlines in the Under-19 World Cup in Bangladesh in 2004, taking eight wickets at 24.75 apiece and bowling well in the slog overs at the end of the innings. Later that year he joined the conveyor belt of Indian left-arm seamers, taking 34 wickets in six Ranji Trophy games for Uttar Pradesh, the joint-highest for the summer. He made the national one-day squad at the end of 2005, and took two wickets in his second over of international cricket, against Zimbabwe at Harare in September. He took four wickets (and the match award) against Sri Lanka in his third game, and three more in his fourth, before a run of four wicketless matches cost him his place after the first match of the West Indies tour in May 2006. He also won a couple of Test caps, winning the match award on his debut for some persistent bowling on a shirtfront at Faisalabad, where Pakistan ran up 588. He drifted out of contention after that, but he is still young, and well respected in the Indian set-up, as Virender Sehwag confirmed: "RP is a very talented bowler – his specialty is that he can bring the ball into the right-handers and swing it both ways."

THE FACTS RP Singh won the Man of the Match award on his Test debut – even though there were six centuries in the match, at Faisalabad in January 2006: Singh took 4 for 89 in Pakistan's first innings of 588 ... He averages 15.25 with the ball in ODIs against Sri Lanka, and 17.62 against Pakistan ... Singh took 2 for 25 in the semi-final of the Under-19 World Cup in February 2004 – but Pakistan still won by two wickets ...

THE FIGURES
Batting and fielding

	M	Inns	NO	Runs	HS	Avge	S/R	100	50	4s	6s	Ct	St
Tests to 11.9.06	2	3	2	6	6	6.00	18.18	0	0	0	0	0	0
ODIs to 11.9.06	15	5	4	20	9*	20.00	60.60	0	0	1	0	4	0
First-class to 11.9.06	17	22	7	106	23*	7.06	–	0	0	–	–	7	0

Bowling

	M	Balls	Runs	Wkts	BB	Avge	RpO	S/R	5i	10m
Tests to 11.9.06	2	522	345	9	4–89	38.33	3.96	58.00	0	0
ODIs to 11.9.06	15	683	561	19	4–35	29.52	4.92	35.94	0	0
First-class to 11.9.06	17	3238	1640	59	5–33	27.79	3.03	54.88	4	1

175

VRV SINGH

Full name	**Vikram Raj Vir Singh**
Born	**September 17, 1984, Chandigarh, Punjab**
Teams	**Punjab**
Style	**Right-hand bat, right-arm fast-medium bowler**
Test debut	**India v West Indies at St John's 2005-06**
ODI debut	**India v West Indies at Gros Islet 2005-06**

THE PROFILE A product of India's Under-19 system, Vikram Singh first turned heads when he played for Punjab in 2005. A fresh burst of energy in a country teeming with workhorse medium-pacers, VRV, a tall, open-chested bowler, insisted that he would never compromise on speed. Though he struggles to locate his radar at times, he is undoubtedly a genuine fast bowler in the making. In his first year of domestic cricket for Punjab, he took 34 Ranji Trophy wickets at 20.67 apiece, with a best of 7 for 75. In the 2005 Challenger Trophy – amounting to trial matches for the national squad – VRV stood out, along with Sreesanth, among the fast-bowling prospects. He was called up for the one-dayers against Sri Lanka late in 2005, but failed a fitness test and was promptly dumped. Then, as selection loomed again, he injured his landing foot and had to undergo rehabilitation. But the selectors kept faith, and named him for the one-day series against England early in 2006. He played in the last two games, but was wicketless and expensive. Then came the EurAsia Cup in Abu Dhabi, where he bowled impressively for the A team, collecting 11 wickets in four matches to stay in the reckoning. He made his Test debut in Antigua, and picked up two wickets in the first innings of a drawn game, and impressed the watching Ian Bishop: "VRV is only a baby; to me he is starting to bowl better with every game."

THE FACTS For India A in the EurAsia Cup in Abu Dhabi in April 2006, VRV Singh took 5 for 38 – and Rudra Pratap Singh 5 for 30 – as the United Arab Emirates were bowled out for 70 ... He took 7 for 75 and 6 for 40 in only his fourth first-class match, for Punjab against Hyderabad at Secunderabad in December 2004: then he took 5 for 40 against Tamil Nadu in his next match ...

THE FIGURES

Batting and fielding

	M	Inns	NO	Runs	HS	Avge	S/R	100	50	4s	6s	Ct	St
Tests to 11.9.06	2	1	0	2	2	2.00	25.50	0	0	0	0	0	0
ODIs to 11.9.06	2	1	0	8	8	8.00	61.53	0	0	1	0	3	0
First-class to 11.9.06	10	10	1	167	47	18.55	100.60	0	0	–	–	1	0

Bowling

	M	Balls	Runs	Wkts	BB	Avge	RpO	S/R	5i	10m
Tests to 11.9.06	2	282	158	2	2–61	79.00	3.36	141.00	0	0
ODIs to 11.9.06	2	72	150	0	–	–	8.75	–	0	0
First-class to 11.9.06	10	1685	969	37	7–75	26.18	3.45	45.54	3	1

DWAYNE SMITH

Full name	**Dwayne Romel Smith**
Born	**April 12, 1983, Storey Gap, St Michael, Barbados**
Teams	**Barbados**
Style	**Right-hand bat, right-arm medium-pace bowler**
Test debut	**West Indies v South Africa at Cape Town 2003-04**
ODI debut	**West Indies v South Africa at Cape Town 2003-04**

THE PROFILE   Tall, aggressive and powerful, Dwayne Smith shares his name with the wide receiver for the Wisconsin Badgers, and the 2002 world champion of Public Speaking – and when he was called up to join the West Indian Test squad in South Africa in December 2003, he was about as well known in cricket circles as either of them. All that changed, however, on the final day of the third Test at Cape Town, where he put the calypso back into Caribbean cricket with a wonderful debut century. Smith had been given a surprise opportunity – ahead of his Grenadian namesake Devon – when Marlon Samuels flew home with a knee injury. It was rumoured that Viv Richards had recognised something of himself in the stance of the young Barbadian and, sure enough, he needed just 93 balls to justify his selection, bringing up only the second century of his first-class career with a crashing cover-drive. It was enough to stem West Indies' run of seven consecutive defeats in South Africa. His batting reflects both his temperament and his youth: he's still inclined to lose his wicket through careless strokeplay, and he made starts, but no more, in his next few Tests before the selectors lost patience. He has had more one-day opportunities, maintaining a strike rate that is healthier than his average. But his one-day case is boosted by his athletic fielding, and his handy medium-pacers, with which he grabbed 5 for 45 against New Zealand at Auckland in March 2006.

THE FACTS   Smith was the 11th West Indian to make a century on his Test debut, but only the third from Barbados (after Conrad Hunte and Gordon Greenidge) and the first to do it against South Africa ... He has the best strike rate (103.20) of any West Indian who has scored more than 500 runs in ODIs, and is surpassed overall only by Shahid Afridi, Andy Blignaut and Lance Cairns ... Smith hit 103 not out off just 70 balls for the West Indies Board XI against the touring Bangladeshis in Grenada in May 2004 ...

THE FIGURES
Batting and fielding

	M	Inns	NO	Runs	HS	Avge	S/R	100	50	4s	6s	Ct	St
Tests *to 11.9.06*	10	14	1	320	105*	24.61	70.02	1	0	47	6	9	0
ODIs *to 11.9.06*	42	35	2	611	68	18.51	103.20	0	2	46	29	15	0
First-class *to 11.9.06*	51	83	5	2154	114	27.61	–	5	6	–	–	48	0

Bowling

	M	Balls	Runs	Wkts	BB	Avge	RpO	S/R	5i	10m
Tests *to 11.9.06*	10	651	344	7	3–71	49.14	3.17	93.00	0	0
ODIs *to 11.9.06*	42	1136	937	27	5–45	34.70	4.94	42.07	1	0
First-class *to 11.9.06*	51	3831	1877	62	4–45	30.27	2.93	61.79	0	0

GRAEME SMITH

Full name	**Graeme Craig Smith**
Born	**February 1, 1981, Johannesburg, Transvaal**
Teams	**Cape Cobras**
Style	**Left-hand bat, occasional offspinner**
Test debut	**South Africa v Australia at Cape Town 2001-02**
ODI debut	**South Africa v Australia at Bloemfontein 2001-02**

THE PROFILE In March 2003, at just 22, Graeme Smith became South Africa's youngest-ever captain, when Shaun Pollock was dumped after a disastrous World Cup campaign. A tall, aggressive left-hand opener, Smith had few leadership credentials – and only a handful of caps – but the selectors' faith was instantly justified: in England in 2003 he collected back-to-back double-centuries – 277 at Edgbaston, and a matchwinning 259 at Lord's. Reality bit back in 2004, when his declining side lost Test series to India and Sri Lanka. There was also a run of 11 defeats in 12 ODIs, the start of an ultimately fruitless Test series with England, and personal humiliation after some Stephen Fleming mind games in Auckland. Yet Smith continued to crunch runs aplenty, and there was one minor epic, an unbeaten 125 to square the series in New Zealand. He yields to no-one physically, but he can be subdued by more insidious means: by the end of 2004, as Matthew Hoggard's inswinger had him frequently fumbling around his front pad, even the runs had started to dry up. But he roared back in the West Indies in 2005, with hundreds in three successive Tests. Then, early in 2006, he orchestrated a 3-2 home win over Australia in probably the greatest one-day series ever played. Smith kick-started his side's reply to Australia's 434 for 4 in the decider at Johannesburg with 90 from 55 balls, adding 187 with Herschelle Gibbs in just 20.1 overs. South Africa eventually won with a ball to spare.

THE FACTS In the first Test against England in 2003 Smith scored 277 at Birmingham, the highest score by a South African in Tests: in the second he made 259, the highest Test score by a visiting player at Lord's, beating Don Bradman's 254 in 1930 ... Smith and Herschelle Gibbs are the only opening pair to share three stands of 300 or more in Tests ... He averages 76.91 in Tests against West Indies – but only 22.25 against Australia ... Smith played four matches for Somerset in 2005, scoring 311 against Leicestershire in one of them ... His record includes one Test for the World XI (as captain), and one ODI for the Africa XI ...

THE FIGURES
Batting and fielding

	M	Inns	NO	Runs	HS	Avge	S/R	100	50	4s	6s	Ct	St
Tests to 11.9.06	48	84	5	3891	277	49.25	59.84	11	14	505	13	59	0
ODIs to 11.9.06	91	90	5	3389	134*	39.87	78.97	6	19	391	14	36	0
First-class to 11.9.06	83	144	10	6720	311	50.14	–	19	23	–	–	113	0

Bowling

	M	Balls	Runs	Wkts	BB	Avge	RpO	S/R	5i	10m
Tests to 11.9.06	48	1247	724	8	2–145	90.50	3.48	155.87	0	0
ODIs to 11.9.06	91	686	655	10	3–30	65.50	5.72	68.59	0	0
First-class to 11.9.06	83	1615	971	11	2–145	88.27	3.60	146.81	0	0

SREESANTH

Full name **Shanthakumaran Sreesanth**
Born **February 6, 1983, Kothamangalam, Kerala**
Teams **Kerala**
Style **Right-hand bat, right-arm fast-medium bowler**
Test debut **India v England at Nagpur 2005-06**
ODI debut **India v Sri Lanka at Nagpur 2005-06**

INDIA

THE PROFILE For three seasons, Sreesanth was little more than an answer to a trivia question: who's the only Kerala bowler to have taken a Ranji Trophy hat-trick? He started as a legspinner, idolising Anil Kumble, then once he turned to pace his rise was rapid but, since he played for a weak side, unnoticed. Not too many bowlers are selected for the Duleep Trophy in their first season, but Sreesanth was, in 2002-03 after taking 22 wickets in his first seven games. His progress was halted by a hamstring injury the following year, but he returned stronger, with a more side-on action and increased pace, and a superb display at the 2005 Challenger Trophy – trial matches for the national squad – propelled him into the side for the Sri Lanka series. Later he snapped up 6 for 55 against England, the best one-day figures by an Indian fast bowler at home. Idiosyncratic, with an aggressive approach – to the stumps and the game – he can be expensive in one-dayers, but is also a wicket-taking bowler. He does it in Tests, too – in Antigua in June 2006 he fired out Ramnaresh Sarwan and Brian Lara (for 0) in successive overs. "People think I am high-strung," he says of his whole-hearted approach. "I keep saying things to calm myself and perk myself up, but I don't see it or feel it as draining at all. In fact, it's been a habit with me for a long time, this constant revving-up, something like brushing my teeth."

THE FACTS Sreesanth took a hat-trick for Kerala against Himachal Pradesh at Palakkad in the Ranji Trophy in November 2004 ... He is only the second man from Kerala to play for India, after Tinu Yohannan, another fast-medium bowler ... Sreesanth did not score a run in ODIs until his 16th match, although that was only his fourth innings ... His best first-class figures of 5 for 57 came in only his second match, for Kerala against Saurashtra at Rajkot in November 2002 ...

THE FIGURES
Batting and fielding

	M	Inns	NO	Runs	HS	Avge	S/R	100	50	4s	6s	Ct	St
Tests to 11.9.06	5	7	3	75	29*	18.75	54.34	0	0	7	1	1	0
ODIs to 11.9.06	18	5	3	3	2*	1.50	60.00	0	0	0	0	2	0
First-class to 11.9.06	28	36	14	177	29*	8.04	36.12	0	0	–	–	6	0

Bowling

	M	Balls	Runs	Wkts	BB	Avge	RpO	S/R	5i	10m
Tests to 11.9.06	5	1019	566	19	4–70	29.78	3.33	53.63	0	0
ODIs to 11.9.06	18	913	869	24	6–55	36.20	5.71	38.04	1	0
First-class to 11.9.06	28	4854	2589	81	5–57	31.96	3.20	59.92	2	0

DALE STEYN

Full name	**Dale Willem Steyn**
Born	**June 27, 1983, Phalaborwa, Limpopo Province**
Teams	**Titans**
Style	**Right-hand bat, right-arm fast bowler**
Test debut	**South Africa v England at Port Elizabeth 2004-05**
ODI debut	**Africa XI v Asia XI at Centurion 2005-06**

THE PROFILE Dale Steyn's rise to the South African side was as rapid as his bowling: he was picked for the first Test against England in December 2004 little more than a season after his first-class debut. He is genuinely fast, if slightly raw, and moves the ball away from the right-hander. He sprints up to the wicket and hurls the ball down aggressively, often following up with a snarl for the batsman, *à la* Allan Donald. He took eight wickets in three Tests against England before returning to the finishing school of domestic cricket. He missed the massacres that followed against Zimbabwe, and the West Indian tour. He was recalled in April 2006, and responded with his first five-wicket haul as New Zealand were routed in the first Test at Centurion. Seven more wickets followed in the third match at Johannesburg, which South Africa also won, as the partnership of Steyn and Makhaya Ntini looked ever more promising. He had half a season of county cricket with Essex in 2005, after being recommended by Darren Gough, and although his wickets were expensive (14 at 59.85) he took the chance to polish his previously negligible batting, improving his highest score from 11 to 82 after going in as a nightwatchman against Durham. Steyn is a rare first-class cricketer from the far north of South Africa, close to the Zimbabwean border – he was born in Phalaborwa, just two miles from the Kruger National Park in Limpopo Province.

THE FACTS Steyn improved his highest first-class score by 745% when he scored 82 for Essex against Durham at Chester-le-Street in July 2005: his previous-highest was 11 ... He was the leading wicket-taker in South African first-class cricket in 2005-06, with 68 at 20.95 ... Steyn made his official ODI debut for the Africa XI, and his record includes two matches for them ...

THE FIGURES

Batting and fielding

	M	Inns	NO	Runs	HS	Avge	S/R	100	50	4s	6s	Ct	St
Tests to 11.9.06	8	13	4	70	13	7.77	34.31	0	0	9	1	2	0
ODIs to 11.9.06	4	2	0	3	21	2.00	26.66	0	0	0	0	0	0
First-class to 11.9.06	35	44	12	317	82	9.90	44.08	0	1	–	–	7	0

Bowling

	M	Balls	Runs	Wkts	BB	Avge	RpO	S/R	5i	10m
Tests to 11.9.06	8	1631	1124	32	5–47	35.12	4.13	50.96	2	0
ODIs to 11.9.06	4	109	132	3	1–2	44.00	7.26	36.33	0	0
First-class to 11.9.06	35	6845	3997	133	5–27	30.05	3.50	51.46	6	1

ANDREW STRAUSS

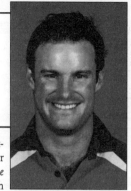

Full name	**Andrew John Strauss**
Born	**March 2, 1977, Johannesburg, South Africa**
Teams	**Middlesex**
Style	**Left-hand bat**
Test debut	**England v New Zealand at Lord's 2004**
ODI debut	**England v Sri Lanka at Dambulla 2003-04**

THE PROFILE Andrew Strauss, a fluid and attractive left-hand opener, had a rapid rise to prominence. His stock rose after Angus Fraser stood down as Middlesex's captain to write for *The Independent*. Strauss filled the breach admirably: 1400 runs in 2003, his first full season in charge, proved he was unfazed by responsibility. He was born in Johannesburg, but – schooled at Radley College and Durham University – is a very English product. At the crease, there is something of Graham Thorpe about his ability to accumulate runs without recourse to big shots, and it was this that first earned him a one-day place in 2003-04. He confirmed his star quality – and his affinity for Lord's – with a century on Test debut against New Zealand (hastening Nasser Hussain's retirement) in May 2004, and added another in his first ODI there, against West Indies two months later. But that was only a warm-up: in South Africa that winter, Strauss won the first Test almost single-handedly with 126 and 94 not out, and added two further hundreds on his way to 656 runs in the series. In 2005 he overcame initial uncertainties against McGrath and, especially, Warne to record two more tons in England's historic Ashes victory. The following summer he became England's captain almost by default, after Michael Vaughan and Andrew Flintoff were injured. He started with a traumatic 5-0 one-day whitewash against Sri Lanka, but a hundred against Pakistan in his first Test as captain – at Lord's, naturally – helped settle him into the role.

THE FACTS Strauss was the 15th Englishman (but the first for 11 years) to score a century on Test debut, with 112 against New Zealand at Lord's in May 2004: he was run out for 83 in the second innings ... In July 2006 he became only the third man to make a century on debut as England captain, following Archie MacLaren (1897-98) and Allan Lamb (1989-90) ... England have never lost a Test in which Strauss has scored a century ... Strauss has opened with Ben Hutton – who was also born in Johannesburg – for school (Radley), university (Durham) and county (Middlesex) ...

THE FIGURES

Batting and fielding

	M	Inns	NO	Runs	HS	Avge	S/R	100	50	4s	6s	Ct	St
Tests *to 11.9.06*	31	58	2	2597	147	46.37	51.99	10	7	335	6	39	0
ODIs *to 11.9.06*	61	60	7	1847	152	34.84	78.13	2	11	205	4	19	0
First-class *to 11.9.06*	121	215	12	8544	176	42.08	–		22	37	–	–	89	0

Bowling

	M	Balls	Runs	Wkts	BB	Avge	RpO	S/R	5i	10m
Tests *to 11.9.06*	31	0	–	–	–	–	–	–	–	–
ODIs *to 11.9.06*	61	6	3	0	–	–	3.00	–	0	0
First-class *to 11.9.06*	121	48	58	1	1-27	58.02	7.25	48.00	0	0

ZIMBABWE

GREGORY STRYDOM

Full name	**Gregory Mark Strydom**
Born	**March 26, 1984, Pretoria, South Africa**
Teams	**Matabeleleland**
Style	**Right-hand bat, right-arm medium-pacer/offspinner**
Test debut	**No Tests yet**
ODI debut	**Zimbabwe v Kenya at Bulawayo 2005-06**

THE PROFILE Greg Strydom is a clean hitter of the ball who loves to hit the bowlers – especially medium-pacers and spinners – out of the park. He scores runs quickly in both versions of the game, and is a reliable bowler who mixes up medium-pace with some offbreaks. He was consistently overlooked by the Zimbabwean selectors despite some fine domestic performances, until he was finally named in the squad to take on Kenya in February 2006. His major weakness is that he has limited footwork, which leaves him vulnerable to genuinely quick bowlers. He also tends to concentrate on the boundary shots and forget the need to work the singles. His preferred method can be divined from his efforts for Matabeleland against Manicaland at Mutare in April 2004: he scored 128 from 78 balls in the first innings, with 12 fours and ten sixes, and 104 from 90 in the second, with six more sixes and eight fours. That came three weeks after he pummelled the same opposition for 216 – 35 fours, six sixes – at Bulawayo. He struggled when he came up against better bowlers, but has been learning to build an innings and work the ball around for those singles. Short and of average build, he has powerful forearms that are responsible for most of his big leg-side hits. He can be an abrasive character at times, but has settled down under coach Kevin Curran.

THE FACTS Strydom's best score in ODIs is 58, against Bangladesh at Harare in August 2006: he also made 48, against West Indies in St Lucia in March 2006 ... In six of his other seven ODI innings he has failed to reach double figures ... Strydom's 16 sixes in the match between Matabeleland and Manicaland at Mutare in 2003-04 has been bettered only twice in first-class cricket, by Andrew Symonds (20 in 1995) and Warwickshire's Jim Stewart (17 in 1959) ...

THE FIGURES
Batting and fielding

	M	Inns	NO	Runs	HS	Avge	S/R	100	50	4s	6s	Ct	St
Tests to 11.9.06	0	–	–	–	–	–	–	–	–	–	–	–	–
ODIs to 11.9.06	11	9	0	143	58	15.88	70.44	0	1	17	3	4	0
First-class to 11.9.06	27	50	4	1772	216	38.52	–	4	9	–	–	21	0

Bowling

	M	Balls	Runs	Wkts	BB	Avge	RpO	S/R	5i	10m
Tests to 11.9.06	0	–	–	–	–	–	–	–	–	–
ODIs to 11.9.06	11	66	61	1	1–28	61.00	5.54	66.00	0	0
First-class to 11.9.06	27	2307	1479	33	4–48	44.81	3.84	69.90	0	0

182

SCOTT STYRIS

Full name	**Scott Bernard Styris**
Born	**July 10, 1975, Brisbane, Australia**
Teams	**Auckland, Middlesex**
Style	**Right-hand bat, right-arm medium-pacer**
Test debut	**New Zealand v West Indies at St George's 2001-02**
ODI debut	**New Zealand v India at Rajkot 1999-2000**

THE PROFILE Scott Styris, who was born in Australia but moved to New Zealand when he was six, had a long apprenticeship in domestic cricket, playing almost ten years for Northern Districts before finally making the Test side. By the time of his debut, in Grenada in June 2002, he had been a one-day regular for three years, and had done nothing to suggest that he was a Test batsman – he had 418 runs at 16 in 40 ODIs, and was regarded more as a containing medium-pacer. But he thumped an uncomplicated 107 in his first Test innings, added 69 not out in the second, and has been a fixture ever since, latterly adding solidity at the giddy heights of No. 4 – from where, in March 2004, his 170 set up a winning total against South Africa at Auckland. On that 2002 tour of the Caribbean Styris took 6 for 25 at Port-of-Spain, New Zealand's best ODI bowling analysis at the time (since beaten by Shane Bond, twice). Coach John Bracewell has encouraged him to work on his offspin, as an option that would put less strain on his body than his energetic military mediums, but this has yet to be unveiled outside the nets. Styris continued to score consistently – for Middlesex, for his new province Auckland, and for New Zealand: his thrilling 101 set up the successful pursuit of Australia's 331 at Christchurch in December 2005, and he signed off the 2005-06 season with 90 against West Indies at Auckland.

THE FACTS Styris was the seventh New Zealander to score a century on Test debut, following Jackie Mills, Bruce Taylor, Rodney Redmond, Mark Greatbatch, Mathew Sinclair and Lou Vincent ... He averages only 16.83 in ODIs against Australia, despite making 101 against them at Christchurch in 2005-06 ... Styris was actually awarded his first cap on the eve of the Karachi Test against Pakistan in May 2002, only for it to be taken back when the match was cancelled after a bomb blast ...

THE FIGURES
Batting and fielding

	M	Inns	NO	Runs	HS	Avge	S/R	100	50	4s	6s	Ct	St
Tests to 11.9.06	27	44	4	1527	170	38.17	51.83	5	6	196	13	23	0
ODIs to 11.9.06	116	99	12	2503	141*	28.77	78.12	3	14	186	45	45	0
First-class to 11.9.06	109	179	18	5183	212*	32.19	–	9	26	–	–	88	0

Bowling

	M	Balls	Runs	Wkts	BB	Avge	RpO	S/R	5i	10m
Tests to 11.9.06	27	1906	981	20	3–28	49.04	3.08	95.29	0	0
ODIs to 11.9.06	116	4287	3365	106	6–25	31.74	4.70	40.44	1	0
First-class to 11.9.06	109	12130	6006	199	6–32	30.18	2.97	60.95	9	1

BANGLADESH

SYED RASEL

Full name	**Syed Rasel**
Born	**July 3, 1984, Jessore, Khulna**
Teams	**Khulna**
Style	**Left-hand bat, left-arm fast-medium bowler**
Test debut	**Bangladesh v Sri Lanka at Colombo 2005-06**
ODI debut	**Bangladesh v Sri Lanka at Colombo 2005-06**

THE PROFILE   A sensational spell of swing bowling for Bangladesh A against Kent at Canterbury in August 2005 propelled Syed Rasel into the international reckoning at the age of 21. He had missed the senior tour earlier in the season, but, having steadily developed his trade on a difficult five-week trip, Rasel tore through Kent's defences with 7 for 50 in the first innings, and finished with 10 for 91 in the match. It wasn't enough to win the game, but he was immediately drafted into the senior squad for the tour of Sri Lanka that followed in September, and he made his Test and one-day debuts there. With shades of Chaminda Vaas in his left-arm approach, he took six wickets in his first two matches, including 4 for 129 in the second Test in Colombo, a match that Bangladesh lost by an innings. Nevertheless, he soon had his revenge on home soil, taking 2 for 28 at Bogra the following February, as Sri Lanka slumped to their first-ever one-day defeat at Bangladesh's hands. Rasel rose through the ranks from divisional cricket in his home province of Khulna, and his ability to swing the ball at a good pace sets him apart from many of his rivals: he seems set for a promising career.

THE FACTS   Fourteen of Syed Rasel's ODI wickets have come against Kenya, and eight against Sri Lanka ... He took 7 for 55 (11 for 109 in the match) for Khulna against Dhaka in Dhaka, and 8 for 67 against Barisal at Barisal, both in 2003-04 ... All four of his Tests so far have been against Sri Lanka ...

THE FIGURES
Batting and fielding

	M	Inns	NO	Runs	HS	Avge	S/R	100	50	4s	6s	Ct	St
Tests to 11.9.06	4	4	2	30	19	5.00	44.11	0	0	5	0	0	0
ODIs to 11.9.06	15	6	1	26	15	5.20	61.90	0	0	3	0	3	0
First-class to 11.9.06	32	47	11	374	33	10.38	44.73	0	0	–	–	6	0

Bowling

	M	Balls	Runs	Wkts	BB	Avge	RpO	S/R	5i	10m
Tests to 11.9.06	4	551	360	9	4–129	40.00	3.92	61.22	0	0
ODIs to 11.9.06	15	783	523	23	4–22	22.73	4.00	34.04	0	0
First-class to 11.9.06	32	5292	2584	87	8–67	29.70	2.92	60.82	3	2

ANDREW SYMONDS

Full name	**Andrew Symonds**
Born	**June 9, 1975, Birmingham, Warwickshire, England**
Teams	**Queensland**
Style	**Right-hand bat, right-arm medium-pace or offbreaks**
Test debut	**Australia v Sri Lanka at Galle 2004**
ODI debut	**Australia v Pakistan at Lahore 1998-99**

THE PROFILE   Andrew Symonds brings gusto to whatever he
does, whether firing down offbreaks or medium-pacers, hurling
his bulk around the outfield, or ruffling the bowler's hair after a
wicket. He saves his loudest grunt for batting, where he is an
unabashed six-hitter. For Gloucestershire, when only 20, he scythed a world-record 16 in
an innings against Glamorgan, and 20 in the match (another record). He has been
demolishing attacks ever since, but his flaw has been to attempt one six too many. During
four years in and out of the one-day side he wasted opportunities galore. But one day
changed everything: striding out with Australia sinking against Pakistan during the 2003
World Cup – a game and a tournament he never expected to play in – Symonds sculpted a
masterly 143 from 125 balls. Until then, he had mustered just 762 one-day runs at 23: ever
since he has averaged around 50. Symonds could have played for England, but dreamed
only of wearing the baggy green. In 2004 his fantasy was fulfilled on Sri Lanka's spinning
minefields. He batted gamely without looking comfortable, and was dumped after two
Tests. Almost two years later he received an extended run as Australia tried to find a
Flintoff, but couldn't reproduce his one-day consistency. Faced with the axe, he cracked a
huge six – the first of five – against South Africa at the MCG to open his account in a
pressure-relieving 72, but he was dropped again early in 2006. However he remains an
automatic one-day pick.

THE FACTS   Birmingham-born Symonds was voted *England's* Young Cricketer of the
Year in 1995, but turned down a place on an England A tour that winter and pledged his
future to Australia, where he grew up ... He played 71 ODIs before winning his first Test
cap, a record at the time ...   Symonds has played county cricket for Gloucestershire, Kent
and Lancashire ... He first came to public notice in Queensland as a 13-year-old, after a
partnership of 466 with Matthew Mott, who also went on to play first-class cricket ...

THE FIGURES
Batting and fielding

	M	Inns	NO	Runs	HS	Avge	S/R	100	50	4s	6s	Ct	St
Tests *to 11.9.06*	10	15	0	286	72	19.06	57.31	0	2	27	11	10	0
ODIs *to 11.9.06*	146	116	22	3697	156*	39.32	92.21	5	18	328	74	65	0
First-class *to 11.9.06*	198	329	28	12819	254*	42.58	–		38	53	–	–	141	0

Bowling

	M	Balls	Runs	Wkts	BB	Avge	RpO	S/R	5i	10m
Tests *to 11.9.06*	10	894	409	9	3–50	45.44	2.74	99.33	0	0
ODIs *to 11.9.06*	146	5023	4148	114	5–18	36.38	4.95	44.06	1	0
First-class *to 11.9.06*	198	15413	7703	211	6–105	36.50	2.99	73.04	2	0

TATENDA TAIBU

Full name	**Tatenda Taibu**
Born	**May 14, 1983, Harare**
Teams	**Mashonaland**
Style	**Right-hand bat, wicketkeeper, occ. offspinner**
Test debut	**Zimbabwe v West Indies at Bulawayo 2001**
ODI debut	**Zimbabwe v West Indies at Harare 2001**

THE PROFILE Barely five feet tall and light on his feet, Tatenda Taibu is a throwback to the traditional style of wicketkeeper, and he was earmarked as the long-term successor to Andy Flower at an early age. He was plucked from school at 16 to tour the West Indies early in 2000. He hadn't even played domestic first-class cricket then – his Mashonaland debut was delayed after he went to the wrong ground – but he toured South Africa with the Under-19s, and was later one of Zimbabwe's few bright spots in the 2003 World Cup and the tour of England that followed. He was vice-captain there, despite being only 19, and in April 2004 became Test cricket's youngest-ever captain after Heath Streak resigned. Taibu led a woefully inexperienced side by personal example, such as when his double of 85 and 153 – cutting out the cross-bat strokes that had earlier dogged him – prevented defeat by Bangladesh at Dhaka in January 2005. In his first Test in charge he even took the pads off and took a wicket. But the pressure began to tell, and soon he found himself caught up in another players' revolt, against the board's mismanagement. Taibu was vilified in the press, and his personal safety was threatened: in November 2005 he announced his retirement from international cricket, and went off to play club cricket in Bangladesh. He remains a popular figure, and must surely play for Zimbabwe again – although it probably won't happen while the current office-holders run the board.

THE FACTS Taibu's 153 against Bangladesh at Dhaka in 2004-05 is the most recent of Zimbabwe's 42 Test centuries ... In his first Test as captain, against Sri Lanka at Harare in May 2004, he took off the pads and took the first wicket to fall, ending an opening stand of 281 by dismissing Sanath Jayasuriya ... For Mashonaland against Midlands at Kwekwe in 2003-04 Taibu scored a career-best 175 not out (after bagging a pair in the previous game) and then took 8 for 43 ... His record includes one ODI for the African XI ...

THE FIGURES
Batting and fielding

	M	Inns	NO	Runs	HS	Avge	S/R	100	50	4s	6s	Ct	St
Tests to 11.9.06	24	46	3	1273	153	29.60	40.93	1	9	154	5	48	4
ODIs to 11.9.06	84	71	15	1410	96*	25.17	61.81	0	7	94	14	73	8
First-class to 11.9.06	71	118	14	3260	175*	31.34	–	5	17	–	–	176	15

Bowling

	M	Balls	Runs	Wkts	BB	Avge	RpO	S/R	5i	10m
Tests to 11.9.06	24	48	27	1	1–27	27.00	3.37	48.00	0	0
ODIs to 11.9.06	84	84	61	2	2–42	30.50	4.35	42.00	0	0
First-class to 11.9.06	71	924	431	22	8–43	19.59	2.79	42.00	1	0

BRENDAN TAYLOR

Full name	**Brendan Ross Murray Taylor**
Born	**February 6, 1986, Harare**
Teams	**Mashonaland**
Style	**Right-hand bat, wicketkeeper, occ. offspinner**
Test debut	**Zimbabwe v Sri Lanka at Harare 2003-04**
ODI debut	**Zimbabwe v Sri Lanka at Harare 2003-04**

THE PROFILE Beatle-haired Brendan Taylor, who was fast-tracked into the Zimbabwe team at 18 against Sri Lanka in April 2004 after several "rebel" players withdrew in a contracts dispute, had long been regarded as a potential Test player. Usually an opener – although his one-day best of 98 came from No. 4 – he certainly has the ability to build an innings, although he often gets himself out overdoing the aggression. Opponents admire some of his shots, especially his full-blooded front-foot cover drive, but poor footwork (which he is trying to improve) lets him down at times, and leads to dismissals when he is well set. Taylor was nurtured by Iain Campbell, the father of the former Test captain Alistair, at the Lilfordia primary school near Harare, and was a regular choice for national age-group teams, playing in two Under-19 World Cups. He made his first-class debut for Mashonaland A at the age of 16, scoring 47, and the following year hit an unbeaten 200 in the B Division of the Logan Cup. He appears to be well regarded by the Zimbabwean board, and was picked for the national side even though he did not sign a new contract at the start of 2006, and despite a recent suspension for misconduct. Taylor kept wicket in his schooldays, and when Tatenda Taibu retired he took over the gloves again for the one-dayers against Kenya early in 2006, and did a sound job then and on the tour of West Indies that followed. In August 2006 his last-ball six at Harare carried Zimbabwe to a spine-tingling win over Bangladesh.

THE FACTS Taylor's highest score of 193 was for Mashonaland v Matabeleland at Harare in April 2005: he shared a third-wicket stand of 261 with Stuart Carlisle, who made 205 ... Taylor scored 100 not out in the plate final of the 2001-02 Under-19 World Cup, against Nepal ... He averages 41.66 in ODIs against Australia, but only 13 against England ... Taylor averages 45.78 in ODIs in which he has kept wicket, but only 23.58 as a specialist batsman ... His highest score in ODIs is 98, v Bermuda at Port-of-Spain in May 2006 ...

THE FIGURES
Batting and fielding

	M	Inns	NO	Runs	HS	Avge	S/R	100	50	4s	6s	Ct	St
Tests *to 11.9.06*	10	20	0	422	78	21.10	45.96	0	3	60	2	7	0
ODIs *to 11.9.06*	47	47	4	1325	98	30.81	65.33	0	9	122	19	25	6
First-class *to 11.9.06*	38	74	2	2188	193	30.38	–	4	10	–	–	34	0

Bowling

	M	Balls	Runs	Wkts	BB	Avge	RpO	S/R	5i	10m
Tests *to 11.9.06*	10	42	38	0	–	–	5.42	–	0	0
ODIs *to 11.9.06*	47	210	224	8	3–54	28.00	6.40	26.25	0	0
First-class *to 11.9.06*	38	258	161	3	2–36	53.66	3.74	86.00	0	0

JEROME TAYLOR

Full name	**Jerome Everton Taylor**
Born	**June 22, 1984, St Elizabeth, Jamaica**
Teams	**Jamaica**
Style	**Right-hand bat, right-arm fast bowler**
Test debut	**West Indies v Sri Lanka at Gros Islet 2002-03**
ODI debut	**West Indies v Sri Lanka at Kingstown 2002-03**

THE PROFILE Jerome Taylor was just 18, with a solitary limited-overs game for Jamaica to his name, when he was called into the squad for the final one-dayer of West Indies' home series against Sri Lanka in June 2003. It was the culmination of an explosive first season for Taylor, who was named the most promising fast bowler in the 2003 Carib Beer Series after picking up 21 wickets at 20.14 in six first-class matches. That haul included a second-innings spell of 8 for 59 in Jamaica's five-wicket victory over Trinidad & Tobago, a match in which he took ten wickets for the first time. After a persistent back injury, he bounced back with 26 more wickets at 16.61 in the 2004-05 Carib Beer Cup, which – along with the prolonged contracts dispute which opened up places in the squad – helped him force his way back into international contention. He had a quiet tour of New Zealand early in 2006, bowling tightly in the one-dayers but playing only one Test. However, the inexperienced Zimbabweans found Taylor's pace too hot to handle in the Caribbean shortly afterwards: he took 2 for 19 and 4 for 24 in the first two games, winning the match award in both. He continued his good form when the Indians arrived, taking three wickets as West Indies picked up a consolation victory at the end of the one-day series, then collecting nine – including his first five-wicket haul – in vain in the deciding Test at Kingston in July 2006.

THE FACTS Taylor was 18 years 363 days old when he made his Test debut in June 2003: only six men have played for West Indies at a younger age, the most recent of them Garry Sobers in 1953-54 and Alfie Roberts two years later ... Taylor took 8 for 59 (10 for 81 in the match) in only his third first-class game, for Jamaica against Trinidad & Tobago at Port-of-Spain in March 2003 ... He also took 10 for 104 (4 for 46 and 6 for 58) as the West Indians drew with Zimbabwe A in Harare in 2003-04 ...

THE FIGURES
Batting and fielding

	M	Inns	NO	Runs	HS	Avge	S/R	100	50	4s	6s	Ct	St
Tests *to 11.9.06*	7	11	3	90	23	11.25	52.94	0	0	12	1	0	0
ODIs *to 11.9.06*	12	3	1	19	9	9.50	111.76	0	0	2	0	3	0
First-class *to 11.9.06*	31	45	11	321	35	9.44	–	0	0	–	–	8	0

Bowling

	M	Balls	Runs	Wkts	BB	Avge	RpO	S/R	5i	10m
Tests *to 11.9.06*	7	1006	612	18	5–50	34.00	3.65	55.88	1	0
ODIs *to 11.9.06*	12	564	429	17	4–24	25.23	4.56	33.17	0	0
First-class *to 11.9.06*	31	4315	2175	94	8–59	23.13	3.02	45.90	6	2

ROSS TAYLOR

Full name	**Ross Luteru Taylor**
Born	**March 8, 1984, Lower Hutt, Wellington**
Teams	**Central Districts**
Style	**Right-hand bat, offspinner**
Test debut	**No Tests yet**
ODI debut	**New Zealand v West Indies at Napier 2005-06**

THE PROFILE Ross Taylor was singled out for attention from an early age – he captained New Zealand in the 2001-02 Under-19 World Cup – but it was only in 2005 that he made the breakthrough to the senior ranks. He started the year by extending his maiden first-class century to 184, for Central Districts against Wellington at Palmerston North, then began the following season with such a bang that the selectors were bound to come calling. An innings of 107 – with five sixes – in a warm-up game against Otago was followed by an identical score in a State Shield one-dayer, also against Otago, in January 2006. He then cracked 121 against Wellington in the same competition, 114 – yes, versus Otago again – in the semi-final, then hit 50 in the final against Canterbury. Taylor rounded off a fine season with 106 as CD won the State Championship final at Wellington. He finished with 537 first-class runs at 38, and 649 in one-dayers at an average of 59 and a breakneck strike rate. "The way he's batting he could bludgeon any attack," said Mathew Sinclair, a provincial team-mate. It all led to a call-up for the final two one-dayers of West Indies' tour early in 2006, and innings of 15 (run out) and 31 (with seven fours) hinted at a rosy future if he can bring his new-found maturity to the international arena.

THE FACTS Taylor has scored three of his four limited-overs centuries against Otago, and averages 87.20 against them ... He hit 66 from 22 balls in a Twenty20 match – against Otago again – in January 2006 ... Taylor won the 2002 New Zealand Young Player to Lord's scholarship, following the likes of Martin Crowe and Ken Rutherford ...

THE FIGURES

Batting and fielding

	M	Inns	NO	Runs	HS	Avge	S/R	100	50	4s	6s	Ct	St
Tests to 11.9.06	0	–	–	–	–	–	–	–	–	–	–	–	–
ODIs to 11.9.06	2	2	0	46	31	23.00	117.94	0	9	0	0	0	0
First-class to 11.9.06	31	47	2	1566	184	34.80	–	2	11	–	–	25	0

Bowling

	M	Balls	Runs	Wkts	BB	Avge	RpO	S/R	5i	10m
Tests to 11.9.06	0	–	–	–	–	–	–	–	–	–
ODIs to 11.9.06	2	0	–	–	–	–	–	–	–	–
First-class to 11.9.06	31	312	177	3	2–34	59.00	3.40	104.00	0	0

SACHIN TENDULKAR

Full name	**Sachin Ramesh Tendulkar**
Born	**April 24, 1973, Bombay**
Teams	**Mumbai**
Style	**Right-hand bat, occasional medium-pace/legspin**
Test debut	**India v Pakistan at Karachi 1989-90**
ODI debut	**India v Pakistan at Gujranwala 1989-90**

THE PROFILE You only have to attend a one-dayer at the Wankhede Stadium, and watch the lights flicker and the floor tremble as the massive wave of applause echoes around the ground when he comes in, to realise what Sachin Tendulkar means to Mumbai ... and India. Age, and troublesome elbow and shoulder injuries, may have dimmed the light a little, but he's still a light-footed dancing genius with bat in hand, the nearest thing to Bradman, as The Don himself recognised before his death. Sachin seems to have been around for ever: that's because he made his Test debut at 16 in 1989, shrugging off a blow on the head against Pakistan; captivated England in 1990, with a maiden Test century; and similarly enchanted Australians in 1991-92. He leads the list of ODI and World Cup run-scorers by a country mile, and owns the records for most centuries in Tests and one-dayers too. Fitness and desire permitting, he could reach 100 hundreds in international cricket before he's done. Until he throttled back in his thirties, he usually looked to attack, but although Dravid may average more now, and Sehwag is more explosive, Tendulkar's is the wicket the opposition want. Small, steady at the crease before a decisive move forward or back, he remains a master, and his whipped flick to fine leg remains an object of wonder. He could have starred as a bowler, as he can do offbreaks, legbreaks, or dobbly medium-pacers, and remains a handy option for the captain, especially in one-dayers.

THE FACTS Tendulkar passed his childhood idol Sunil Gavaskar's record of 34 Test centuries in December 2005, with 109 v Sri Lanka at Delhi: in seven Tests afterwards his highest score was 34 ... No one is close to his record of 39 ODI centuries – Sourav Ganguly is next with 22 ... Tendulkar's first mark on the record books came when he was 14, in an unbroken stand of 664 (a record for all cricket) with another future Test batsman, Vinod Kambli, in a school game ... He was Yorkshire's first official overseas player, in 1992 ...

THE FIGURES
Batting and fielding

	M	Inns	NO	Runs	HS	Avge	S/R	100	50	4s	6s	Ct	St
Tests *to 11.9.06*	132	211	22	10469	248*	55.39	–	35	41	–	41	82	0
ODIs *to 11.9.06*	363	354	34	14148	186*	44.21	85.97	39	72	1508	149	107	0
First-class *to 11.9.06*	228	353	37	18872	248*	59.72	–	59	87	–	–	149	0

Bowling

	M	Balls	Runs	Wkts	BB	Avge	RpO	S/R	5i	10m
Tests *to 11.9.06*	132	3330	1893	37	3–10	51.16	3.41	90.00	0	0
ODIs *to 11.9.06*	363	7349	6194	142	5–32	43.61	5.05	51.75	2	0
First-class *to 11.9.06*	228	6617	3748	61	3–10	61.44	3.39	108.47	0	0

UPUL THARANGA

Full name	**Warushavithana Upul Tharanga**
Born	**February 2, 1985, Balapitiya**
Teams	**Nondescripts**
Style	**Left-hand bat, occasional wicketkeeper**
Test debut	**Sri Lanka v India at Ahmedabad 2005-06**
ODI debut	**Sri Lanka v West Indies at Dambulla 2005-06**

THE PROFILE Upul Tharanga's call-up to Sri Lanka's one-day squad in July 2005 brightened a year marred by the Indian Ocean tsunami, which washed away his family home in Ambalangoda, a fishing town on the west coast. From an early age Tharanga, a wispy left-hander blessed with natural timing, had been tipped for the big time, playing premier-league cricket at 15 and passing seamlessly through the various national age-group squads. He first caught the eye during the Under-19 World Cup in Bangladesh early in 2004, with 117 against South Africa and 61 in 42 balls against India in the next game. Then, after a successful Under-19 tour of Pakistan, the Sri Lankan board sent him to play league cricket in Essex, where he did well for Loughton. In August 2005 he won his first one-day cap, and hit 105 against Bangladesh in only his fifth match – he celebrated modestly, aware that stiffer challenges lay ahead – and then pummelled 165 against them in his third Test. Another one-day hundred followed at Christchurch in January 2006, then he lit up Lord's with 120 in the first of what became five successive defeats of England: he added 109 in the fifth of those, at Headingley, sharing an ODI record opening stand with Sanath Jayasuriya. The feature of those innings was the way he made room to drive through the off side. Other opponents might not be so accommodating, but a bright future beckons for Tharanga, who is also a useful wicketkeeper.

THE FACTS Tharanga and Sanath Jayasuriya put on 286 in 31.5 overs against England at Leeds in July 2006, a new first-wicket record for all ODIs: Tharanga made 109, his fourth one-day century ... He averages 69.40 in ODIs against England, but 14.60 against India ... Tharanga made 165 and 71 not out in the ten-wicket defeat of Bangladesh at Bogra in March 2006 ... That helped boost his average against Bangladesh to 99 ...

THE FIGURES
Batting and fielding

	M	Inns	NO	Runs	HS	Avge	S/R	100	50	4s	6s	Ct	St
Tests to 11.9.06	10	19	1	591	165	32.83	51.12	1	3	84	4	10	0
ODIs to 11.9.06	29	27	0	946	120	35.03	76.16	4	3	112	1	6	0
First-class to 11.9.06	43	74	1	2227	165	30.50	–	4	11	–	–	41	0

Bowling

	M	Balls	Runs	Wkts	BB	Avge	RpO	S/R	5i	10m
Tests to 11.9.06	10	0	–	–	–	–	–	–	–	–
ODIs to 11.9.06	29	0	–	–	–	–	–	–	–	–
First-class to 11.9.06	43	0	–	–	–	–	–	–	–	–

MARCUS TRESCOTHICK

Full name	**Marcus Edward Trescothick**
Born	**December 25, 1975, Keynsham, Somerset**
Teams	**Somerset**
Style	**Left-hand bat, right-arm medium-pace bowler**
Test debut	**England v West Indies at Manchester 2000**
ODI debut	**England v Zimbabwe at The Oval 2000**

THE PROFILE There was something biblical about Marcus Trescothick's early career: seven years of schoolboy plenty, seven years of famine when he started with Somerset. And lo, it came to pass that he batted on a pacy pitch at Taunton while Duncan Fletcher was Glamorgan's coach in 1999, and stormed to 167. When England needed a one-day opener in 2000, Fletcher remembered Trescothick. Hefty, knock-kneed and genial, he was described by Nasser Hussain as a left-handed Gooch, but his ease on the big stage and his blazing strokeplay – a mixture of expert leaves, crisp cover-drives, spanking pulls and fearless slog-sweeps – are just as reminiscent of David Gower. All that stands between him and the top drawer is a tendency to get out when well set. He seemed to have conquered this at home in 2002, but it reappeared – like so many English frailties – in Australia the following winter: Trescothick still has not made a Test hundred against them. He showed glimpses of his blazing best against South Africa in 2003, biffing 219 in the astonishing series-levelling victory at The Oval, but he struggled in the Caribbean that winter. The selectors never lost faith, and Trescothick repaid them with twin tons against West Indies at Birmingham, and a brutal 180 at Johannesburg early in 2005. After bullying the Bangladeshis he spearheaded the batting against Australia with 431 runs. A mystery virus drove him home from India early in 2006, and after underperforming at home he opted out of a return visit for the Champions Trophy in order to focus on the Ashes rematch.

THE FACTS Trescothick averages 59.16 in Tests against India, but 33.76 v Australia ... Six of his 12 one-day hundreds have come in matches which England lost ... Like his England team-mates Simon Jones and Alastair Cook, Trescothick was born on Christmas Day ... Trescothick made 206 for England Under-19 v India at Birmingham in September 1994: his opening partner, Michael Vaughan, was out for 6 ... He scored 322 for Somerset's 2nd XI v Warwickshire at Taunton in 1997 ... Trescothick's modest bowling haul includes a first-class hat-trick, for Somerset v Young Australia at Taunton in 1995: the first victim was Adam Gilchrist ...

THE FIGURES

Batting and fielding

	M	Inns	NO	Runs	HS	Avge	S/R	100	50	4s	6s	Ct	St
Tests *to 11.9.06*	76	143	10	5825	219	43.79	54.51	14	29	831	42	95	0
ODIs *to 11.9.06*	123	122	6	4335	137	37.37	85.21	12	21	528	41	49	0
First-class *to 11.9.06*	207	360	18	12227	219	35.75	–	24	63	–	–	240	0

Bowling

	M	Balls	Runs	Wkts	BB	Avge	RpO	S/R	5i	10m
Tests *to 11.9.06*	76	300	155	1	1–34	155.00	3.10	300.00	0	0
ODIs *to 11.9.06*	123	232	219	4	2–7	54.75	5.66	58.00	0	0
First-class *to 11.9.06*	207	2674	1541	36	4–36	42.80	2.53	74.27	0	0

TUSHAR IMRAN

Full name	**Sheikh Tushar Imran**
Born	**December 20, 1983, Kharki, Jessore, Khulna**
Teams	**Khulna**
Style	**Right-hand bat, occasional right-arm medium-pacer**
Test debut	**Bangladesh v Sri Lanka at Colombo 2002**
ODI debut	**Bangladesh v Zimbabwe at Chittagong 2001-02**

THE PROFILE A dashing striker of the ball, Tushar Imran established himself as one of the rising stars of Bangladesh cricket at the age of just 17, when he cracked 131 from 106 balls in a domestic league match in 2000-01 – the same season in which his country was granted Test status. His one-day debut came the following year, against Zimbabwe, and when new blood was demanded to help revive Bangladesh's flagging Test fortunes, he was thrust into the fray against Sri Lanka in July 2002. He struggled, making 8 and 28 in a 288-run defeat, but the selectors clearly believed he had what it takes: three former captains – Naimur Rahman, Akram Khan and Aminul Islam – were axed to make way for him. By his own admission he can be too impetuous for his own good, and although he continued as a regular member of the one-day team his Test career stalled after three more fruitless outings. But the Bangladesh A tour of England in the summer of 2005 provided an opportunity to press for a comeback, and after impressing in patches – not least with a run-a-ball 70 against Surrey – Tushar returned to the squad for the tour of Sri Lanka that September. He played in two of the three ODIs against Australia in April 2006: he failed with the bat but had the consolation of his first international wicket when he dismissed Brad Hogg.

THE FACTS Tushar Imran has only reached double figures once in his eight Test innings, with 28 against Sri Lanka in Colombo in his first match ... He has also failed to reach double figures in 18 of his 35 ODI innings ... Tushar made 198 for Khulna against Dhaka in Dhaka in March 2006, being run out while the last man was at the crease ...

THE FIGURES
Batting and fielding

	M	Inns	NO	Runs	HS	Avge	S/R	100	50	4s	6s	Ct	St
Tests to 11.9.06	4	8	0	55	28	6.87	30.21	0	0	7	0	1	0
ODIs to 11.9.06	36	35	0	547	65	15.62	61.52	0	2	63	1	5	0
First-class to 11.9.06	53	96	6	2705	198	30.05	–	7	12	–	–	28	0

Bowling

	M	Balls	Runs	Wkts	BB	Avge	RpO	S/R	5i	10m
Tests to 11.9.06	4	0	–	–	–	–	–	–	–	–
ODIs to 11.9.06	36	90	66	1	1–24	66.00	4.40	90.00	0	0
First-class to 11.9.06	53	760	479	14	3–22	34.21	3.78	54.28	0	0

UMAR GUL

Full name	**Umar Gul**
Born	**April 14, 1984, Peshawar, North-Western Frontier Province**
Teams	**Peshawar, Pakistan International Airlines**
Style	**Right-hand bat, right-arm fast-medium bowler**
Test debut	**Pakistan v Bangladesh at Karachi 2003-04**
ODI debut	**Pakistan v Zimbabwe at Sharjah 2002-03**

THE PROFILE Umar Gul had played only nine first-class games when he was drafted into the Pakistan side at 19, in the wake of a miserable 2003 World Cup campaign. He performed admirably on Sharjah's flat tracks, maintaining good discipline and obtaining appreciable outswing with the new ball. He can also nip the ball back from outside off. He had a gentle introduction to Test cricket, collecting 15 wickets against Bangladesh later in 2003, including four in each innings at Multan. Sterner challenges followed, and he starred in his only Test of India's historic "comeback" tour of Pakistan, at Lahore in April 2004. Gul, who had been disparaged by some as the "Peshawar Rickshaw" to Shoaib Akhtar's "Rawalpindi Express", tore through India's imposing top order, moving the ball both ways off the seam at a sharp pace. His 5 for 31 in the first innings – he dismissed Sehwag, Tendulkar, Laxman, Dravid and Parthiv Patel as they slipped from 69 for 1 to 127 for 6 – gave Pakistan the early initiative, which they drove home to level the series. Stress fractures in the back kept him out of the third Test, and it was two years before he returned, after a good domestic season. He managed only two wickets in the Tests in Sri Lanka, but was retained for the subsequent tour of England – where, in the absence of several senior seamers, he looked the best of the rest, particularly enjoying the conditions at Headingley, taking five wickets in the first innings as the others struggled.

THE FACTS Umar Gul took 5 for 17 against Bangladesh at Lahore in September 2003: he hasn't taken more than two wickets in any other ODI ... His best bowling figures are 8 for 78, for Peshawar against Karachi Urban at Peshawar in October 2005 ... Gul claimed 5 for 46 on his first-class debut, for Pakistan International Airlines against ADBP at Karachi in his only match in 2000-01, then took 45 wickets at 18.62 in 2001-02, his first full season of domestic cricket ...

THE FIGURES

Batting and fielding

	M	Inns	NO	Runs	HS	Avge	S/R	100	50	4s	6s	Ct	St
Tests *to 11.9.06*	11	14	1	67	14	5.15	30.45	0	0	8	2	4	0
ODIs *to 11.9.06*	19	2	1	19	17*	19.00	55.88	0	0	3	0	1	0
First-class *to 11.9.06*	35	38	6	349	46	10.90	–	0	0	–	–	10	0

Bowling

	M	Balls	Runs	Wkts	BB	Avge	RpO	S/R	5i	10m
Tests *to 11.9.06*	11	2390	1440	45	5–31	32.00	3.61	53.11	2	0
ODIs *to 11.9.06*	19	848	664	22	5–17	30.18	4.69	38.54	1	0
First-class *to 11.9.06*	35	7073	4102	162	8–78	25.32	3.47	43.66	11	1

ROBIN UTHAPPA

Full name	**Aiyudda Robin Uthappa**
Born	**November 11, 1985, Coorg, Karnataka**
Teams	**Karnataka**
Style	**Right-hand bat, occ. right-arm medium-pacer**
Test debut	**No Tests yet**
ODI debut	**India v England at Indore 2005-06**

THE PROFILE The son of Venu Uthappa, an international hockey referee, the tall and robust Robin Uthappa was long spoken of as a batsman with an international future. Although his record in domestic cricket – a first-class average of 32 from 20 matches, with just one hundred – is modest, his limited-overs figures stack up better: he averages a touch under 40, with a highest score of 160, and his runs come at a strike rate of over 90. Originally a wicketkeeper-batsman, Uthappa gave up the big gloves to concentrate on batting, and now occasionally bowls some medium-pace. As a batsman he has always been attractive to watch – hard-hitting, with all the shots and unafraid to hit the ball in the air. Uthappa first caught the eye with a brilliant 66 in a losing cause for India B against India A in the Challenger Trophy (trial matches for the national squad) at Mumbai early in 2005, against an attack that included Zaheer Khan, Murali Kartik and Rudra Pratap Singh. But it was in the next edition of the same tournament, at Mohali in October 2005, when he really arrived in the big league. After VVS Laxman made a century for India A, Uthappa cracked a matchwinning 116 from only 93 balls. It won him a place instead of Virender Sehwag in the final one-dayer against England early in 2006, and he capitalised with a well-paced 86 at Indore. His next two outings were less spectacular, but time is on his side.

THE FACTS Uthappa's 86 against England at Indore in April 2006 was the highest score by an Indian making his ODI debut, beating Brijesh Patel's 82 against England at Leeds in 1974 ... His only first-class century was 162 for Karnataka against Madhya Pradesh at Bangalore in November 2004: he also thumped 160 in a one-day game against Kerala at Margao in January 2005 ... For India B against India A at Mohali in October 2005 Uthappa sped from 61 to 101 in the space of 14 balls ...

THE FIGURES

Batting and fielding

	M	Inns	NO	Runs	HS	Avge	S/R	100	50	4s	6s	Ct	St
Tests to 11.9.06	0	–	–	–	–	–	–	–	–	–	–	–	–
ODIs to 11.9.06	3	3	0	98	86	32.66	79.67	0	1	13	1	1	0
First-class to 11.9.06	22	36	1	1163	162	33.22	–	1	8	–	–	26	0

Bowling

	M	Balls	Runs	Wkts	BB	Avge	RpO	S/R	5i	10m
Tests to 11.9.06	0	–	–	–	–	–	–	–	–	–
ODIs to 11.9.06	3	0	–	–	–	–	–	–	–	–
First-class to 11.9.06	22	84	54	1	1–15	54.00	3.85	84.00	0	0

PROSPER UTSEYA

ZIMBABWE

Full name	**Prosper Utseya**
Born	**March 26, 1985, Harare**
Teams	**Manicaland**
Style	**Right-hand bat, offspinner**
Test debut	**Zimbabwe v Sri Lanka at Harare 2003-04**
ODI debut	**Zimbabwe v Sri Lanka at Bulawayo 2003-04**

THE PROFILE A diminutive offspinner of real promise, Prosper Utseya was unexpectedly thrust into the Zimbabwe national team at 19, against Sri Lanka in April 2004, after several "rebel" players withdrew in a contracts dispute. He made 45 in his first Test, but failed to take a wicket, and it soon became clear that the selectors considered him more of a one-day specialist. He was given a long run in the limited-overs side, but failed to make a consistent mark with either bat or ball – until the tour of the West Indies early in 2006, when his mature bowling was a rare highlight. His flight and ability to turn the ball was widely praised, and his economy rate was remarkable at times. A good team man, he was vice-captain of that side and certainly led the bowling. Quick in the field, he was also responsible for several run-outs, but needs to do some work on his batting. He succeeded Terry Duffin as captain for the home one-dayers against Bangladesh later in 2006, and led his side to an exciting 3–2 victory. Utseya was first introduced to cricket at Chipembere Primary School in the Harare township of Highfield, and won a Zimbabwe Cricket Union scholarship to Churchill High School. He played for Takashinga from an early age, and made his first-class debut for Mashonaland A just before his 17th birthday, scoring 58 in a tight situation against Manicaland in only his second match. He later played for Manicaland, before returning to play for Midlands.

THE FACTS Utseya's ODI economy rate of 3.79 runs per over is the best for Zimbabwe in all ODIs: among current bowlers worldwide only Shaun Pollock (3.76) is more thrifty ... Utseya has yet to make a first-class century, but has scores of 89 not out, 89 and 88 to his name ... He took 5 for 32 for Midlands against Manicaland at Mutare in October 2004 ...

THE FIGURES

Batting and fielding

	M	Inns	NO	Runs	HS	Avge	S/R	100	50	4s	6s	Ct	St
Tests *to 11.9.06*	1	2	0	45	45	22.50	77.58	0	0	5	1	2	0
ODIs *to 11.9.06*	44	34	13	189	31*	9.00	54.46	0	0	15	1	15	0
First-class *to 11.9.06*	28	52	4	955	89*	19.89	–	0	6	–	–	15	0

Bowling

	M	Balls	Runs	Wkts	BB	Avge	RpO	S/R	5i	10m
Tests *to 11.9.06*	1	72	55	0	–	–	4.58	–	0	0
ODIs *to 11.9.06*	44	2235	1413	31	3–35	45.58	3.79	72.09	0	0
First-class *to 11.9.06*	28	3966	2231	44	5–32	50.70	3.37	90.13	1	0

CHAMINDA VAAS

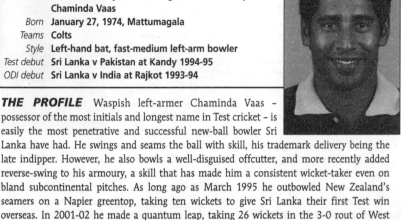

Full name	**Warnakulasuriya Patabendige Ushantha Joseph Chaminda Vaas**
Born	**January 27, 1974, Mattumagala**
Teams	**Colts**
Style	**Left-hand bat, fast-medium left-arm bowler**
Test debut	**Sri Lanka v Pakistan at Kandy 1994-95**
ODI debut	**Sri Lanka v India at Rajkot 1993-94**

THE PROFILE Waspish left-armer Chaminda Vaas – possessor of the most initials and longest name in Test cricket – is easily the most penetrative and successful new-ball bowler Sri Lanka have had. He swings and seams the ball with skill, his trademark delivery being the late indipper. However, he also bowls a well-disguised offcutter, and more recently added reverse-swing to his armoury, a skill that has made him a consistent wicket-taker even on bland subcontinental pitches. As long ago as March 1995 he outbowled New Zealand's seamers on a Napier greentop, taking ten wickets to give Sri Lanka their first Test win overseas. In 2001-02 he made a quantum leap, taking 26 wickets in the 3-0 rout of West Indies, and becoming only the second fast bowler, after Imran Khan, to take 14 wickets in a match on the subcontinent. He's consistent in one-dayers too, and given to spectacular bursts of wicket-taking: he was the first to take eight in an ODI, as Zimbabwe were blown away for 38 in Colombo in December 2001, and also uniquely claimed a hat-trick with the first three balls of the match against Bangladesh in the 2003 World Cup. Vaas has taken 300 wickets in both Tests and one-dayers, and is easily Sri Lanka's most successful bowler after Muttiah Muralitharan. His approach to his batting is equally whole-hearted: he has scored well over 2000 runs in Tests without making a century, and faced more balls in the Tests in England in 2006 than any of Sri Lanka's specialist batsmen.

THE FACTS Vaas's figures of 8 for 19 against Zimbabwe in Colombo in December 2001 are the best in all ODIs ... That included a hat-trick, and he took another with the first three balls of the match against Bangladesh at Pietermaritzburg in the 2003 World Cup: at the end of the first over they were 5 for 4 ... Vaas has made 2503 runs in Tests – only Shane Warne (2958) has scored more without making a century ... Vaas has played county cricket for Hampshire and Worcestershire ... His record includes one ODI for the Asia XI ...

THE FIGURES
Batting and fielding

	M	Inns	NO	Runs	HS	Avge	S/R	100	50	4s	6s	Ct	St
Tests *to 11.9.06*	94	136	26	2503	74*	22.75	42.61	0	11	315	14	28	0
ODIs *to 11.9.06*	281	194	62	1814	50*	13.74	73.17	0	1	112	21	55	0
First-class *to 11.9.06*	163	219	44	4064	134	23.22	–	3	16	–	–	49	0

Bowling

	M	Balls	Runs	Wkts	BB	Avge	RpO	S/R	5i	10m
Tests *to 11.9.06*	94	20374	9062	307	7–71	29.51	2.66	66.36	11	2
ODIs *to 11.9.06*	281	13791	9698	354	8–19	27.39	4.21	38.95	4	0
First-class *to 11.9.06*	163	31707	14378	583	7–54	24.66	2.72	54.38	25	3

JOHAN VAN DER WATH

SOUTH AFRICA

Full name	**Johannes Jacobus van der Wath**
Born	**January 10, 1978, Newcastle, Natal**
Teams	**Eagles**
Style	**Right-hand bat, right-arm fast-medium bowler**
Test debut	**No Tests yet**
ODI debut	**South Africa v Australia at Melbourne 2005-06**

THE PROFILE   He's been described as looking like a cross between Sylvester Stallone and Billy Joel, while in Australia Ian Healy managed to call him "Johan Volkswagen", but Johan van der Wath is a versatile allrounder, capable of lively pace bowling and powerful hitting. After ten years of domestic cricket, he had a short county stint with Sussex during 2005, and then gained a spot in the South Africa A side for the tour of Sri Lanka and an accompanying tri-series. An impressive 2005-06 domestic season for the Eagles, which included the Man of the Match award in the one-day Standard Bank Cup final, made the selectors take note, and he was duly called up when Jacques Kallis was forced home from the 2005-06 VB Series in Australia with an elbow injury. van der Wath impressed with his whole-hearted approach, and picked up ten wickets in six matches. He overcame a six-ball debut duck by thumping an unbeaten 37 – with four sixes – off 16 balls against Australia at Sydney. He didn't return until the famous match at the Wanderers in March 2006, when South Africa somehow overhauled Australia's record total of 434: he played his part with 35 from 18 balls. van der Wath is pragmatic about his prospects: "I am not even looking at Test selection yet, I am just trying to focus on finding my feet for the Proteas at one-day level and to try to book a World Cup place."

THE FACTS   Johan van der Wath has hit two first-class centuries – 113 not out for Free State against KwaZulu-Natal at Bloemfontein in October 2001, and 100 for Eagles against Titans, also at Bloemfontein, in March 2005 ... His best bowling is 6 for 37 for Free State against Boland at Bloemfontein in March 2002 ... van der Wath has hit eight sixes – and only three fours – in ODIs ...

THE FIGURES
Batting and fielding

	M	Inns	NO	Runs	HS	Avge	S/R	100	50	4s	6s	Ct	St
Tests *to 11.9.06*	0	–	–	–	–	–	–	–	–	–	–	–	–
ODIs *to 11.9.06*	7	6	2	80	37*	20.00	140.35	0	0	3	8	2	0
First-class *to 11.9.06*	53	83	14	1734	113*	25.13	–	2	10	–	–	20	0

Bowling

	M	Balls	Runs	Wkts	BB	Avge	RpO	S/R	5i	10m
Tests *to 11.9.06*	0	–	–	–	–	–	–	–	–	–
ODIs *to 11.9.06*	7	376	399	10	2–21	39.90	6.36	37.60	0	0
First-class *to 11.9.06*	53	9134	4413	153	6–37	28.84	2.89	59.69	8	0

MICHAEL VANDORT

Full name	**Michael Graydon Vandort**
Born	**January 19, 1980, Colombo**
Teams	**Colombo Cricket Club**
Style	**Left-hand bat, occasional right-arm medium-pacer**
Test debut	**Sri Lanka v Bangladesh at Colombo 2001-02**
ODI debut	**Sri Lanka v Australia at Melbourne 2005-06**

THE PROFILE Michael Vandort, a 6ft 5ins tall left-hander fond of the off-drive, emerged in 2001 after a string of impressive performances for Colombo Cricket Club and Sri Lanka A. A late developer, he played only once for his school, St Joseph's College, but nonetheless quickly made an impression in first-class cricket. He was picked for the Board XI against the Indians in August 2001, and earned himself a berth in the Test squad with an impressive 116 against the proven new-ball attack of Javagal Srinath and Venkatesh Prasad. He sat on the sidelines throughout that series, but was given a chance against Bangladesh when the selectors rested some senior players. He duly scored a century in the second Test, but with the Jayasuriya-Atapattu opening combination seemingly unassailable he had to wait more than three years before another sniff. An injury to Jayasuriya paved the way for his one-day debut, at Melbourne in February 2006: he top-scored with a gritty 48, but Jayasuriya returned and Vandort missed the rest of the VB Series, although he did play two Tests against Bangladesh shortly afterwards. With Jayasuriya in short-lived retirement Vandort got his chance in England in 2006, and starred in defeat at Edgbaston, last out for a dogged 105 in the second innings. He failed to reach double figures in his other three knocks, though, and missed the one-day demolitions that followed – he's a good slip fielder but is rather ponderous in the field, and this counts against him in the one-day arena.

THE FACTS Vandort's first four Tests, spread over four-and-a-half years, were all against Bangladesh: he averaged 68.20 in them ... He scored 100 on his first-class debut, for Colombo Cricket Club against Kurunegala in Colombo in March 1999 ... When still only 18 Vandort made 226 and 225 in successive matches for Colombo Cricket Club in 1998-99, against Panadura and Singha ...

THE FIGURES

Batting and fielding

	M	Inns	NO	Runs	HS	Avge	S/R	100	50	4s	6s	Ct	St
Tests to 11.9.06	6	11	2	461	140	51.22	51.73	2	2	55	1	2	0
ODIs to 11.9.06	1	1	0	48	48	48.00	41.02	0	0	3	0	0	0
First-class to 11.9.06	91	149	13	4940	226	36.32	–	10	24	–	–	77	0

Bowling

	M	Balls	Runs	Wkts	BB	Avge	RpO	S/R	5i	10m
Tests to 11.9.06	6	0	–	–	–	–	–	–	–	–
ODIs to 11.9.06	1	0	–	–	–	–	–	–	–	–
First-class to 11.9.06	91	61	53	1	1–46	53.00	5.21	61.00	0	0

MICHAEL VAUGHAN

Full name **Michael Paul Vaughan**
Born **October 29, 1974, Manchester, Lancashire**
Teams **Yorkshire**
Style **Right-hand bat, offspinner**
Test debut **England v South Africa at Johannesburg 1999-2000**
ODI debut **England v Sri Lanka at Dambulla 2000-01**

THE PROFILE In September 2005 Michael Vaughan secured his place in English cricket's hall of fame, becoming the first captain to lift the Ashes since Mike Gatting in 1986-87. It was the culmination of a five-year journey for Vaughan, whose captaincy had become as classy and composed as the batting technique that briefly carried him to the top of the world rankings. Vaughan had faced his first ball in Test cricket with England 2 for 4 on a damp flyer at Johannesburg late in 1999, and drew immediate comparisons with Michael Atherton for his calm aura at the crease. But he soon demonstrated he was more than just a like-for-like replacement. He blossomed magnificently, playing with a freedom Atherton never dared to approach. He conjured 900 runs in seven Tests against Sri Lanka and India in 2002, the prelude to a formidable series in Australia – three tons, 633 runs. He became one-day skipper early in 2003, and inherited the Test captaincy shortly afterwards when Nasser Hussain abdicated, having spotted Vaughan's burgeoning man-management abilities. After a stutter in Sri Lanka, he confirmed the arrival of a new era by routing West Indies in the Caribbean. Returning home, England swept seven out of seven Tests in 2004, won in South Africa, then triumphed in the greatest Ashes series of them all. Sadly, Vaughan has been unable to press on. An old knee injury flared up, culminating in a series of operations that wrecked his 2006 season, kept him out of the Ashes rematch, and even threatened his career.

THE FACTS Vaughan made 633 runs in the 2002-03 Ashes series: the last Englishman to score as many in Australia was Geoff Boycott, with 657 in 1970-71 ... Vaughan averages 90.12 in Tests against India, but only 14 against Zimbabwe: he averaged 50.98 before he was captain, and only 35.89 since ... He has never reached 200 in first-class cricket, but has passed 150 on 14 occasions, the last six of them in Tests ... Born in Manchester, Vaughan was the first Lancastrian to play for Yorkshire after the home-grown-only policy was relaxed in the mid 1990s ...

THE FIGURES

Batting and fielding

	M	Inns	NO	Runs	HS	Avge	S/R	100	50	4s	6s	Ct	St
Tests to 11.9.06	64	115	8	4595	197	42.94	52.40	15	14	600	22	37	0
ODIs to 11.9.06	74	71	10	1730	90*	28.36	68.46	0	15	173	11	20	0
First-class to 11.9.06	230	407	25	14549	197	38.08	–	39	61	–	–	107	0

Bowling

	M	Balls	Runs	Wkts	BB	Avge	RpO	S/R	5i	10m
Tests to 11.9.06	64	936	537	6	2-71	89.50	3.44	156.00	0	0
ODIs to 11.9.06	74	664	562	12	4-22	46.83	5.07	55.33	0	0
First-class to 11.9.06	230	9210	5142	114	4-39	45.10	3.34	80.78	0	0

DANIEL VETTORI

Full name	**Daniel Luca Vettori**
Born	**January 27, 1979, Aucklandy**
Teams	**Northern Districts, Warwickshire**
Style	**Left-hand bat, left-arm orthodox spinner**
Test debut	**New Zealand v England at Wellington 1996-97**
ODI debut	**New Zealand v Sri Lanka at Christchurch 1996-97**

THE PROFILE Daniel Vettori is probably the best left-arm spinner around – an assessment reinforced by his selection in the World XI for the ICC Super Series in Australia late in 2005 – and the only cloud on his horizon is a susceptibility to injury, particularly in the bowler's danger area of the back. He seemed to have recovered from one stress fracture, which led to a dip in form in 2003, but after just a couple of matches in 2006 for Warwickshire, his second English county, Vettori was on the plane home nursing another one. When fit, he still exhibits the enticing flight and guile that made him New Zealand's youngest Test player, ten days past his 18th birthday, in 1996-97. There were signs on the tour of England in 2004 that he was back to his best after his mini-slump, although a hamstring injury impinged, then he butchered the Bangladeshis shortly afterwards, taking 20 wickets in the two Tests. After starting at No. 11, blinking nervously through his glasses, he has improved his batting, to the point that he has made two centuries – one of them New Zealand's fastest in Tests, an 82-ball effort against the admittedly hopeless Zimbabweans at Harare in August 2005. He helped himself to his 200th Test wicket in the same two-day massacre. The selectors gave a sign of their future plans by making him captain in Stephen Fleming's absence for the Chappell-Hadlee one-day series against Australia in December 2005. As long as the back holds out ...

THE FACTS Vettori made his first-class debut in 1996-97, for Northern Districts against the England tourists: his maiden first-class victim was Nasser Hussain ... Three weeks later Vettori made his Test debut, New Zealand's youngest-ever player at 18 years 10 days – and his first wicket was Hussain again ... Vettori has taken 52 Test wickets against Australia, but only four against Pakistan, costing 100.25 each ... His record includes one Test and four ODIs for the World XI ...

THE FIGURES

Batting and fielding

	M	Inns	NO	Runs	HS	Avge	S/R	100	50	4s	6s	Ct	St
Tests to 11.9.06	71	102	16	2136	137*	24.83	54.48	2	11	279	6	35	0
ODIs to 11.9.06	173	108	34	1043	83	14.09	79.01	0	2	74	6	43	0
First-class to 11.9.06	115	157	22	3289	137*	24.36	–	3	17	–	–	53	0

Bowling

	M	Balls	Runs	Wkts	BB	Avge	RpO	S/R	5i	10m
Tests to 11.9.06	71	17234	7658	219	7–87	34.96	2.66	78.69	12	2
ODIs to 11.9.06	173	7979	5608	167	5–30	33.58	4.21	47.77	1	0
First-class to 11.9.06	115	26642	11963	365	7–87	32.77	2.69	72.99	22	2

LOU VINCENT

Full name	**Lou Vincent**
Born	**November 11, 1978, Warkworth, Auckland**
Teams	**Auckland, Worcestershire**
Style	**Right-hand bat, occasional wicketkeeper**
Test debut	**New Zealand v Australia at Perth 2001-02**
ODI debut	**New Zealand v Sri Lanka at Auckland 2000-01**

THE PROFILE Lou Vincent started with a bang – a memorable hundred on Test debut against Australia at Perth in 2001-02, followed by 54 in the second innings – then slipped back as he struggled for consistency, managing only one more century (106 against India on a shirtfront at Mohali) in his next 18 Tests. Part of the problem has been finding a settled spot in the batting order: something of a reluctant opener, he was miffed when this led to his being left out of the Test team. "It was just a preference, I wasn't insisting on anything," he explained early in 2006. Before this setback Vincent, a stylish right-hander with a penchant for sixes, had worked his way back into both national sides, first re-establishing himself at Test level with a measured 224 (from No. 4) against the Murali-less Sri Lankans to set up an innings victory at Wellington in April 2005, then cementing his one-day spot with a national-record 172 – off 120 balls, with nine sixes – against the outclassed Zimbabweans at Bulawayo in August. He remained in the one-day shake-up throughout 2005-06, making 102 against West Indies at Napier in March not long after fracturing a finger, but his Test career seems to have stalled. His Auckland coach Mark O'Donnell thinks he'll be back: "Lou's had to cope with failure, work his way back into favour, and over time figure out a method that would prove successful at Test level."

THE FACTS Vincent was the sixth of seven New Zealanders to score a century on Test debut: the others are Jackie Mills, Bruce Taylor, Rodney Redmond, Mark Greatbatch, Mathew Sinclair and Scott Styris ... He averages 92 against Sri Lanka in Tests, but only 11.50 v Bangladesh: he has not played against South Africa ... Vincent's 172 against Zimbabwe in August 2005 is New Zealand's highest ODI score, beating Glenn Turner's 171 not out against East Africa in the first World Cup in 1975 ... He played a few matches for Worcestershire in 2006 ...

THE FIGURES

Batting and fielding

	M	Inns	NO	Runs	HS	Avge	S/R	100	50	4s	6s	Ct	St
Tests to 11.9.06	22	38	1	1295	224	35.00	46.93	3	9	156	11	19	0
ODIs to 11.9.06	83	80	9	1867	172	26.29	69.02	2	7	169	30	33	0
First-class to 11.9.06	79	126	9	4390	224	37.52	–		10	27	–	–	99	0

Bowling

	M	Balls	Runs	Wkts	BB	Avge	RpO	S/R	5i	10m
Tests to 11.9.06	22	6	2	0	–	–	2.00	–	0	0
ODIs to 11.9.06	83	2	3	0	–	–	9.00	–	0	0
First-class to 11.9.06	79	897	448	6	2–37	74.66	2.99	149.50	0	0

SHANE WARNE

Full name **Shane Keith Warne**
Born **September 13, 1969, Ferntree Gully, Victoria**
Teams **Victoria, Hampshire**
Style **Right-hand bat, legspinner**
Test debut **Australia v India at Sydney 1991-92**
ODI debut **Australia v New Zealand at Wellington 1992-93**

THE PROFILE First there were nerves, and chubbiness. Then wild soaring legbreaks, fame, flippers. Then women, a bookmaker, diet pills, more women ... and headlines, always headlines. Now he has come out the other end, somehow intact. The man who in 2000 was one of *Wisden's* Five Cricketers of the 20th Century is bowling better than ever. Shane Warne has taken a Test hat-trick, won the match award in a World Cup final, and inspired several books. He was the first to 650 Test wickets. He is probably the wiliest captain Australia never had. The ball that gazoodled Gatting in 1993, bouncing outside leg stump and cuffing off, is the most famous in history. Warne revived legspin, which was thought to be extinct. For all that, his greatest feats are arguably more recent. Returning from a 12-month drug ban, he swept aside 26 Sri Lankans in three matches, and in 2005 scalped a world-record 96 victims. Forty of those came in the thrilling Ashes series, in what sometimes seemed to be a lone stand. Nowadays he is helped by a stockpile of straight balls: zooter, slider, toppie and back-spinner, in-drifter, out-sloper, and another that doesn't budge. Yet he seldom gets his wrong'un right, and rarely lands the flipper, relying more on excruciating accuracy and an exquisite legbreak. His bowling has never been simpler, nor more effective, nor lovelier to watch. Maybe we don't fully appreciate his genius: maybe, like Bradman's, it will become ever more apparent with time. One thing's for sure – we'll weep when he's gone.

THE FACTS Warne was the first bowler to reach 600 Test wickets: his 600th, during the 2005 Ashes series, was Marcus Trescothick, who had been Glenn McGrath's 500th victim two matches previously ... Warne has taken 172 wickets against England (129 of them in England), passing Dennis Lillee's previous Ashes record of 167 during 2005 ... His most frequent victim is Alec Stewart (14), ahead of Nasser Hussain and Ashwell Prince (11) ... Warne has scored more Test runs without a century than anyone else: his highest score is 99, against New Zealand at Perth in 2001-02 ... His record includes one ODI for the World XI ...

THE FIGURES

Batting and fielding

	M	Inns	NO	Runs	HS	Avge	S/R	100	50	4s	6s	Ct	St
Tests to 11.9.06	140	194	16	2958	99	16.61	56.93	0	11	330	35	120	0
ODIs to 11.9.06	194	107	29	1018	55	13.05	72.04	0	1	60	13	80	0
First-class to 11.9.06	277	378	46	6312	107*	19.01	–	2	24	–	–	237	0

Bowling

	M	Balls	Runs	Wkts	BB	Avge	RpO	S/R	5i	10m
Tests to 11.9.06	140	39257	17297	685	8-71	25.25	2.64	57.30	36	10
ODIs to 11.9.06	194	10642	7541	293	5-33	25.73	4.25	36.32	1	0
First-class to 11.9.06	277	69634	31700	1235	8-71	25.66	2.73	56.38	62	11

SHANE WATSON

AUSTRALIA

Full name	**Shane Robert Watson**
Born	**June 17, 1981, Ipswich, Queensland**
Teams	**Queensland**
Style	**Right-hand bat, right-arm fast-medium bowler**
Test debut	**Australia v Pakistan at Sydney 2004-05**
ODI debut	**Australia v South Africa at Centurion 2001-02**

THE PROFILE Hulklike, blond and spiky-haired, Shane Watson should be the shiny embodiment of modern-day Australian cricket ... if only that body didn't keep cracking up. He is the quintessential young man in a hurry: Queensland Under-17s at 15, the Academy, nipping off at 19 to Tasmania, where he hit his maiden hundred in his fifth match. He missed the 2003 World Cup with stress fractures of the back: until then his batting lacked nothing in swagger, if a little in gap-finding artifice, while his bowling was willing if docile. He bounced back in 2003-04 with four hundreds for Tasmania. He also smashed 300 in a club game, then grabbed 7 for 29. Watson remains the cleanest of hitters and, several remodelled actions later, decidedly sharp. Back home in Queensland (he hated the cold), he's tipped to become Australia's next champion allrounder – not least by their last one: "A fine physical specimen, good athlete – just give him time," noted Alan Davidson in 2002. Picked for his first Test in 2004-05, Watson fell over first ball before finding his feet with Younis Khan's wicket. He didn't play in the Ashes defeat, but his stock rose afterwards, as Andrew Flintoff highlighted the benefits of a genuine allrounder. A dislocated shoulder in the field against West Indies at Brisbane ruined 2005-06, and he watched his mate Andrew Symonds fill in. Watson returned for the one-dayers in South Africa early in 2006, but missed the Tests – although 201 in the Pura Cup final eased the pain.

THE FACTS Watson hit 201 for Queensland in the 2005-06 Pura Cup final demolition of Victoria before retiring hurt: uniquely, four batsmen passed 150 in Queensland innings of 900 for 6 ...... His highest four innings in ODIs are all not out – 77*, 66*, 44*, 35* ... Watson has played county cricket for Hampshire, alongside Shane Warne: in 2005 he scored 203 not out for them against Warwickshire at the Rose Bowl ...

THE FIGURES

Batting and fielding

	M	Inns	NO	Runs	HS	Avge	S/R	100	50	4s	6s	Ct	St
Tests to 11.9.06	3	4	0	81	31	20.25	38.20	0	0	8	0	0	0
ODIs to 11.9.06	43	28	12	507	77*	31.68	70.61	0	2	28	6	12	0
First-class to 11.9.06	52	89	13	3812	203*	50.15	–		11	18	–	–	35	0

Bowling

	M	Balls	Runs	Wkts	BB	Avge	RpO	S/R	5i	10m
Tests to 11.9.06	3	186	123	2	1–25	61.50	3.96	93.00	0	0
ODIs to 11.9.06	43	1738	1376	37	4–39	37.18	4.75	46.97	0	0
First-class to 11.9.06	52	4962	2979	96	6–32	31.03	3.60	57.68	2	1

MICHAEL YARDY

Full name	**Michael Howard Yardy**
Born	**November 27, 1980, Pembury, Kent**
Teams	**Sussex**
Style	**Left-hand bat, slow left-arm orthodox spinner**
Test debut	**No Tests yet**
ODI debut	**England v Pakistan at Nottingham 2006**

THE PROFILE A compact, organised left-hander with a technique not unlike Andrew Strauss's – although involving a wide-open stance before a shuffle across to a more orthodox position as the ball is delivered – Michael Yardy was a Sussex stand-in until he cemented a place with his maiden first-class century in a defeat against Surrey in the final match of 2004. He began 2005 in identical fashion, with another hundred against Surrey, to trigger a run of form that carried him to the top of the domestic batting charts. His zenith arrived against the Bangladeshis at Hove, where he followed a fine double-century with five wickets with his newly adopted left-arm spin, to double his previous tally of first-class wickets. His good form continued, and he finished 2005 with 1520 runs and a place on the England A tour of West Indies. He did little in the Caribbean, but as England looked for someone to bowl slow left-arm in the one-day team, in the absence of the injured Ashley Giles and Ian Blackwell, and with Monty Panesar considered too one-dimensional, Yardy got a chance at the end of 2006. He did well in the Twenty20 encounter with Pakistan, biffing a few late runs and taking an important wicket, then went better still in the full one-day international team, obtaining surprising turn to grab three wickets in his first match, and collecting the winning runs in the second: all in all it was enough to secure him a place in England's 14-man Champions Trophy squad.

THE FACTS Yardy made 257 against the Bangladeshis at Hove in 2005, the highest score for Sussex against any touring team, beating George Cox's 234 against the 1946 Indians ... He also took 5 for 83 in the same match, which remain his best figures ... Yardy took 3 for 24 in his first ODI, against Pakistan at Nottingham in 2006, and hit the winning runs in his second, at Birmingham, sharing a matchwinning eighth-wicket stand of 37 with Sajid Mahmood ... He made 1520 runs at 56.29 in England in 2005, including five of his eight first-class centuries to date ...

THE FIGURES

Batting and fielding

	M	Inns	NO	Runs	HS	Avge	S/R	100	50	4s	6s	Ct	St
Tests *to 11.9.06*	0	–	–	–	–	–	–	–	–	–	–	–	–
ODIs *to 11.9.06*	2	1	1	12	12*	–	38.70	0	0	0	0	1	0
First-class *to 11.9.06*	69	119	13	4065	257*	38.34	–	8	18	–	–	53	0

Bowling

	M	Balls	Runs	Wkts	BB	Avge	RpO	S/R	5i	10m
Tests *to 11.9.06*	0	–	–	–	–	–	–	–	–	–
ODIs *to 11.9.06*	2	102	46	4	3–24	11.50	2.70	25.50	0	0
First-class *to 11.9.06*	69	1748	1044	15	5–83	69.60	3.58	116.53	1	0

YASIR ARAFAT

Full name	**Yasir Arafat Satti**
Born	**March 12, 1982, Rawalpindi, Punjab**
Teams	**Rawalpindi, National Bank, Sussex**
Style	**Right-hand bat, right-arm fast-medium bowler**
Test debut	**No Tests yet**
ODI debut	**Pakistan v Sri Lanka at Karachi 1999-2000**

PAKISTAN

THE PROFILE Yasir Arafat is a typical Pakistan allrounder: he's ideal for one-day cricket, but also looks capable of making a contribution in Tests, although he is yet to play in one. He is a useful lower-order plunderer – he averages in the mid-twenties at first-class level – but his bowling remains much his stronger suit. His straight, full, skiddy bowling, from a slingy action, accounted for Andrew Flintoff in a one-dayer at Karachi in December 2005. It also helped him winkle out nine England wickets in a warm-up game earlier during the same tour, and it once brought him five wickets in six deliveries (the other one was a no-ball) in a domestic game. How straight he bowls is shown by the fact that four of those five were bowled or lbw. Arafat can generate pace and, when conditions are helpful, swing. He travels well, and has wide experience of cricket in the UK, where he played league cricket, and also represented Scotland, before Sussex signed him up in 2006 to join one Pakistani, Mushtaq Ahmed, and replace another, Naved-ul-Hasan. Arafat took 24 wickets in his first four games for them, and was then called up by Pakistan himself, after injuries to other seamers, and was on standby for the second and third Tests, although he didn't actually play in either. Such is the competition – Abdul Razzaq, Shahid Afridi and Shoaib Malik are still ahead of him in the allrounder pecking order – that Arafat still faces an uphill battle to stay in the frame.

THE FACTS Yasir Arafat took five wickets in six balls for Rawalpindi against reigning champions Faisalabad in the Quaid-e-Azam Trophy in December 2004: only three other bowlers had previously done this – Derbyshire's Bill Copson (1937), William Henderson of Orange Free State (1937-38) and Surrey's Pat Pocock (1972) ... Arafat made 100 for Khan Research Laboratories against Defence Housing Authority at Karachi in January 2004 ... He represented Scotland in 2004 and 2005, and Sussex in 2006 ...

THE FIGURES
Batting and fielding

	M	Inns	NO	Runs	HS	Avge	S/R	100	50	4s	6s	Ct	St
Tests *to 11.9.06*	0	–	–	–	–	–	–	–	–	–	–	–	–
ODIs *to 11.9.06*	6	4	1	21	10	7.00	87.50	0	0	0	0	1	0
First-class *to 11.9.06*	98	152	22	3485	100	26.80	–	1	20	–	–	33	0

Bowling

	M	Balls	Runs	Wkts	BB	Avge	RpO	S/R	5i	10m
Tests *to 11.9.06*	0	–	–	–	–	–	–	–	–	–
ODIs *to 11.9.06*	6	204	200	3	1–28	66.66	5.88	68.00	0	0
First-class *to 11.9.06*	98	16244	9305	412	7–102	26.58	3.43	39.42	23	2

YOUNIS KHAN

Full name	**Mohammad Younis Khan**
Born	**November 29, 1977, Mardan, North-West Frontier Province**
Teams	**Peshawar, Habib Bank**
Style	**Right-hand bat, occasional legspinner**
Test debut	**Pakistan v Sri Lanka at Rawalpindi 1999-2000**
ODI debut	**Pakistan v Sri Lanka at Karachi 1999-2000**

THE PROFILE Younis Khan is a fearless middle-order batsman, as befits his Pathan ancestry. He plays with a flourish, and is especially strong in the arc from backward point to extra cover, and he is prone to getting down on one knee and driving extravagantly. But this flamboyance is coupled with grit. His main weaknesses are playing away from his body and leaving straight balls. He started with 107 on his Test debut, against Sri Lanka early in 2000, and scored well in bursts after that, with 153 against West Indies in a Test in Sharjah the highlight. Younis was one of the few batsmen who retained his place after Pakistan's disastrous 2003 World Cup campaign, but he lost it soon afterwards after a string of low scores at home against Bangladesh and South Africa: he was recalled for the one-dayers against India early the following year. Another century against Sri Lanka finally cemented that Test place, and he has been a heavy run-maker ever since, especially against India: in March 2005 he made 147 and 267 in successive Tests against them, and continued in that vein early in 2006, with 199, 83, 194, 0 and 77, before scoring consistently in England too, making 173 at Leeds. He's also a good fielder, pouching four catches in an innings as a substitute during Pakistan's demolition of Bangladesh at Multan in August 2001, and he displayed further versatility by keeping wicket – and winning the Man of the Match award – in a one-dayer against Zimbabwe at Peshawar in October 2004.

THE FACTS Younis Khan averages 106.10 in Tests against India – and 19.75 against South Africa ... He was the seventh of nine Pakistanis to score a century on Test debut, with 107 against Sri Lanka at Rawalpindi in February 2000 ... Against India at home early in 2006 Younis shared successive stands of 319, 142, 242, 0 and 158 with Mohammad Yousuf ... At Lahore in that series he became the sixth batsman to be out for 199 in a Test, following Mudassar Nazar, Mohammad Azharuddin, Matthew Elliott, Sanath Jayasuriya and Steve Waugh ...

THE FIGURES

Batting and fielding

	M	Inns	NO	Runs	HS	Avge	S/R	100	50	4s	6s	Ct	St
Tests to 11.9.06	47	83	4	3884	267	49.16	53.73	12	15	481	17	49	0
ODIs to 11.9.06	139	134	18	3756	144	32.37	74.55	2	25	286	31	71	0
First-class to 11.9.06	101	163	17	7465	267	51.13	–		24	31	–	–	106	0

Bowling

	M	Balls	Runs	Wkts	BB	Avge	RpO	S/R	5i	10m
Tests to 11.9.06	47	264	169	2	1–24	84.50	3.84	132.00	0	0
ODIs to 11.9.06	139	91	101	1	1–24	101.00	6.65	91.00	0	0
First-class to 11.9.06	101	1064	662	12	3–24	55.16	3.73	88.66	0	0

YUVRAJ SINGH

INDIA

Full name **Yuvraj Singh**
Born **December 12, 1981, Chandigarh**
Teams **Punjab**
Style **Left-hand bat, slow left-arm orthodox spinner**
Test debut **India v New Zealand at Mohali 2003-04**
ODI debut **India v Kenya at Nairobi 2000-01**

THE PROFILE Generously gifted, Yuvraj Singh has long been looked upon as a strong, fearless natural destined for great things. Two months short of his 19th birthday he made a lordly entry into international cricket, toppling Australia in the ICC Knockout of October 2000 in Nairobi with a blistering 84 in his first innings (he hadn't batted in his first game) and some scintillating fielding. In time he was to supplement these skills with clever, loopy left-arm spin. While his ability to hit the ball long and clean was instantly recognised, he was soon found to be troubled by quality spin, and also perceived to lack commitment, traits for which he temporarily lost his one-day place. But he returned for the last two ODIs against Zimbabwe early in 2002, and swung the series India's way with a matchwinning innings in each game, then went to England and played key roles in three run-chases in the NatWest Series, culminating in the final, where his 69, and stand of 121 with Mohammad Kaif, set up India's memorable victory over England. It still took another 15 months, and an injury to Sourav Ganguly, for Yuvraj to get a Test look-in. But in his third match, against Pakistan on a greentop at Lahore, he stroked a stunning first-day century off 110 balls. The 2005-06 season proved to be a watershed for Yuvraj, with 1161 runs at 58 in one-dayers, and another Test century against Pakistan, as he became one of the keystones of India's batting line-up.

THE FACTS Yuvraj played 73 ODIs before winning his first Test cap, in October 2003 ... His highest first-class score is 209, for North Zone against South Zone at Faridabad in March 2002 ... Yuvraj average 44.90 in ODIs against England, but only 17.66 against New Zealand ... His father Yograj Singh, a fast bowler, played one Test for India in 1980-81 ...

THE FIGURES
Batting and fielding

	M	Inns	NO	Runs	HS	Avge	S/R	100	50	4s	6s	Ct	St
Tests to 11.9.06	19	29	4	830	122	33.20	52.93	2	3	118	5	21	0
ODIs to 11.9.06	155	140	20	4232	139	35.26	86.63	7	25	444	48	53	0
First-class to 11.9.06	69	109	12	4228	209	43.79	–		14	19	–	–	76	0

Bowling

	M	Balls	Runs	Wkts	BB	Avge	RpO	S/R	5i	10m
Tests to 11.9.06	19	144	90	1	1–25	90.00	3.75	144.00	0	0
ODIs to 11.9.06	155	1899	1558	41	4–6	38.00	4.92	46.31	0	0
First-class to 11.9.06	69	891	473	10	3–25	47.30	3.18	89.10	0	0

NUWAN ZOYSA

Full name	**Demuni Nuwan Tharanga Zoysa**
Born	**May 13, 1978, Colombo**
Teams	**Sinhalese Sports Club**
Style	**Left-hand bat, left-arm fast-medium bowler**
Test debut	**Sri Lanka v New Zealand at Dunedin 1996-97**
ODI debut	**Sri Lanka v New Zealand at Christchurch 1996-97**

THE PROFILE A left-arm seam bowler with a loping, rhythmical run-up and action, Nuwan Zoysa has shown plenty of promise, but his career has been plagued by injury. He was discarded after a disappointing tour of England in 2002, but trained hard and regained pace, nip and bounce off the pitch. Most importantly, though, he returned with the delivery that moves back into the right-hander, a weapon that makes him a far more potent force. A natural striker of the ball, he has also emerged as a useful lower-order strokeplayer. During the Sri Lanka A tour of Kenya in 2003, he was even employed as a pinch-hitter to good effect and, during his comeback to international cricket in the one-day series at home against Australia early in 2004 after missing the World Cup, further underlined his batting potential with a matchwinning unbeaten 47 in the final match. His bowling continued on its upward curve, culminating in a five-wicket haul against South Africa at the Premadasa Stadium during the one-day series in August 2004. Zoysa was first spotted by the canny Arjuna Ranatunga, who encouraged him to join the Sinhalese Sports Club in Colombo, and made his international debut in New Zealand early in 1997. In only his eighth Test, against Zimbabwe at Harare in November 1999, Zoysa claimed a hat-trick in his first over – the second of the match. He hasn't featured in a Test since the 2004 Australian tour, amid murmurs about his commitment, but remains in the one-day frame.

THE FACTS Zoysa's hat-trick against Zimbabwe at Harare in November 1999 came from his first three balls of the Test – it was the second over – and featured the scalps of Trevor Gripper, Murray Goodwin and Neil Johnson ... His average with the ball in Tests against Zimbabwe is 17.26 – but 51.66 against England ... Zoysa made his first-class debut for Sri Lanka A against West Indies A in 1996-97, and later that season took 7 for 58, still his best figures, for Sinhalese Sports Club against Singha in Colombo ...

THE FIGURES

Batting and fielding

	M	Inns	NO	Runs	HS	Avge	S/R	100	50	4s	6s	Ct	St
Tests to 11.9.06	30	40	6	288	28*	8.47	41.43	0	0	31	5	4	0
ODIs to 11.9.06	94	47	21	343	47*	13.19	95.81	0	0	29	7	13	0
First-class to 11.9.06	96	115	21	1344	69	14.29	–	0	4	–	–	17	0

Bowling

	M	Balls	Runs	Wkts	BB	Avge	RpO	S/R	5i	10m
Tests to 11.9.06	30	4422	2157	64	5–20	33.70	2.92	69.09	1	0
ODIs to 11.9.06	94	4259	3213	108	5–26	29.75	4.52	39.43	1	0
First-class to 11.9.06	96	12813	6056	254	7–58	23.84	2.83	50.44	5	0

OVERALL RECORDS

Most appearances

168	SR Waugh	A
156	AR Border	A
140	SK Warne	A
133	AJ Stewart	E
132	SR Tendulkar	I
132	CA Walsh	WI
131	Kapil Dev	I
128	BC Lara	WI/World
128	ME Waugh	A
125	SM Gavaskar	I

Lara's record includes one Test for the World XI

Most runs

			Avge
11505	BC Lara	WI/World	52.05
11174	AR Border	A	50.56
10927	SR Waugh	A	51.06
10469	SR Tendulkar	I	55.39
10122	SM Gavaskar	I	51.12
9049	R Dravid	I/World	58.75
8900	GA Gooch	E	42.58
8832	Javed Miandad	P	52.57
8792	RT Ponting	A	58.22
8540	IVA Richards	WI	50.23

Lara and Dravid's records include one Test for the World XI

Most wickets

			Avge
685	SK Warne	A	25.25
657	M Muralitharan	SL	21.96
542	GD McGrath	A	21.55
533	A Kumble	I	28.75
519	CA Walsh	WI	24.44
434	Kapil Dev	I	29.64
431	RJ Hadlee	NZ	22.29
414	Wasim Akram	P	23.62
405	CEL Ambrose	WI	20.99
395	SM Pollock	SA	23.42

Muralitharan's record includes one Test for the World XI

Highest scores

400*	BC Lara	WI v Eng at St John's	2003-04
380	ML Hayden	Aust v Zim at Perth	2003-04
375	BC Lara	WI v Eng at St John's	1993-94
374	DPMD Jayawardene	SL v SA at Colombo	2006
365*	GS Sobers	WI v Pak at Kingston	1957-58
364	L Hutton	Eng v Aust at The Oval	1938
340	ST Jayasuriya	SL v India at Colombo	1997-98
337	Hanif Mohammad	Pak v WI at Bridgetown	1957-58
336*	WR Hammond	Eng v NZ at Auckland	1932-33
334*	MA Taylor	Aust v Pak at Peshawar	1998-99
334	DG Bradman	Aust v Eng at Leeds	1930

In all 20 scores of 300 or more have been made in Tests

Best innings bowling

10-53	JC Laker	Eng v Aust at Manchester	1956
10-74	A Kumble	India v Pak at Delhi	1998-99
9-28	GA Lohmann	Eng v SA at Jo'burg	1895-96
9-37	JC Laker	Eng v Aust at Manchester	1956
9-51	M Muralitharan	SL v Zim at Kandy	2001-02
9-52	RJ Hadlee	NZ v A at Brisbane	1985-86
9-56	Abdul Qadir	Pak v Eng at Lahore	1987-88
9-57	DE Malcolm	Eng v SA at The Oval	1994
9-65	M Muralitharan	SL v Eng at The Oval	1998
9-69	JM Patel	India v Aust at Kanpur	1959-60

There have been seven further instances of a bowler taking nine wickets in an innings

Record wicket partnerships

1st	413	MH Mankad (231) and P Roy (173)	India v New Zealand at Madras	1955-56
2nd	576	ST Jayasuriya (340) and RS Mahanama (225)	Sri Lanka v India at Colombo	1997-98
3rd	624	KC Sangakkara (287) and DPMD Jayawardene (374)	Sri Lanka v South Africa at Colombo	2006
4th	411	PBH May (285*) and MC Cowdrey (154)	England v West Indies at Birmingham	1957
5th	405	SG Barnes (234) and DG Bradman (234)	Australia v England at Sydney	1946-47
6th	346	JHW Fingleton (136) and DG Bradman (270)	Australia v England at Melbourne	1936-37
7th	347	DS Atkinson (219) and CC Depeiaza (122)	WI v Australia at Bridgetown	1954-55
8th	313	Wasim Akram (257*) and Saqlain Mushtaq (79)	Pakistan v Zimbabwe at Sheikhupura	1996-97
9th	195	MV Boucher (78) and PL Symcox (108)	South Africa v Pakistan at Johannesburg	1997-98
10th	151	BF Hastings (110) and RO Collinge (68*)	New Zealand v Pakistan at Auckland	1972-73
	151	Azhar Mahmood (128*) and Mushtaq Ahmed (59)	Pakistan v South Africa at Rawalpindi	1997-98

Updated records can be found at **www.cricinfo.com/db/stats/tests**

Test Matches — **OVERALL RECORDS**

Most catches

Fielders

181	ME Waugh	*A*
161	BC Lara	*WI/World*
157	MA Taylor	*A*
156	AR Border	*A*
152	SP Fleming	*NZ*

Most dismissals

Wicketkeepers — *Ct/St*

395	IA Healy *A*	366/29
364	MV Boucher	
	SA/World	350/14
355	AC Gilchrist *A*	320/35
355	RW Marsh *A*	343/12
270	PJL Dujon *WI*	265/5

Highest team totals

952-60	**Sri Lanka** v India at Colombo	1997-98
903-7d	**Eng** v Australia at The Oval	1938
849	**Eng** v WI at Kingston	1929-30
790-3d	**WI** v Pakistan at Kingston	1957-58
758-8d	**Aust** v WI at Kingston	1954-55
756-5d	**Sri Lanka** v SA at Colombo	2006
751-5d	**WI** v England at St John's	2003-04
747	**WI** v SA at St John's	2004-05
735-6d	**Aust** v Zimbabwe at Perth	2003-04
729-6d	**Aust** v England at Lord's	1930

There have been four further totals of more than 700

Lowest team totals

Completed innings

26	**NZ** v Eng at Auckland	1954-55
30	**SA** v Eng at Pt Elizabeth	1895-96
30	**SA** v Eng at Birmingham	1924
35	**SA** v Eng at Cape Town	1898-99
36	**Aust** v Eng at B'ham	1902
36	**SA** v Aust at M'bourne	1931-32
42	**Aust** v Eng at Sydney	1887-88
42	**NZ** v Aust at W'ton	1945-46
42*	**India** v England at Lord's	1974
43	**SA** v Eng at Cape Town	1888-89

* One batsmen absent hurt.
There have been seven further totals of less than 50

Best match bowling

19-90	JC Laker	Eng v Aust at Manchester	1956
17-159	SF Barnes	Eng v SA at Jo'burg	1913-14
16-136	ND Hirwani	India v WI at Madras	1987-88
16-137	RAL Massie	Aust v England at Lord's	1972
16-220	M Muralitharan	SL v England at The Oval	1998
15-28	J Briggs	Eng v SA at Cape Town	1888-89
15-45	GA Lohmann	Eng v SA at Pt Elizabeth	1895-96
15-99	C Blythe	Eng v South Africa at Leeds	1907
15-104	H Verity	England v Australia at Lord's	1934
15-123	RJ Hadlee	NZ v Aust at Brisbane	1985-86

Hirwani and Massie were making their Test debuts. W Rhodes (15-124) and Harbhajan Singh (15-217) also took 15 wickets in a match

Most centuries

35	SR Tendulkar *India*	132
34	SM Gavaskar *India*	125
32	BC Lara *West Indies/World XI*	128
32	SR Waugh *Australia*	168
31	RT Ponting *Australia*	105
29	DG Bradman *Australia*	52
27	AR Border *Australia*	156
26	ML Hayden *Australia*	84
26	GS Sobers *West Indies*	93
25	Inzamam-ul-Haq *Pakistan/World XI*	113

Bradman (12) hit the most double-centuries, ahead of Lara (8) and WR Hammond (7)

Test match results

	Played	Won	Lost	Drawn	Tied	% win
Australia	682	315	178	187	2	46.32
Bangladesh	44	1	39	4	0	2.27
England	852	298	245	309	0	34.97
India	400	88	129	182	1	22.05
New Zealand	330	61	130	139	0	18.48
Pakistan	324	100	85	139	0	30.86
South Africa	314	101	113	100	0	32.16
Sri Lanka	165	46	62	57	0	27.87
West Indies	433	149	136	147	1	34.49
Zimbabwe	83	8	49	26	0	9.63
World XI	1	0	1	0	0	0.00
TOTAL	1814	1167	1167	645	2	

OVERALL RECORDS *One-day Internationals*

Most appearances

367	Inzamam-ul-Haq	*P/Asia*
364	ST Jayasuriya	*SL/Asia*
363	SR Tendulkar	*I*
356	Wasim Akram	*P*
334	M Azharuddin	*I*
325	SR Waugh	*A*
308	PA de Silva	*SL*
293	R Dravid	*I/Asia/World*
283	Salim Malik	*P*
281	WPUJC Vaas	*SL/Asia*

A further 13 men have played in 250 or more ODIs

Most runs

			Avge
14148	SR Tendulkar	*I*	44.21
11549	Inzamam-ul-Haq	*P/Asia*	39.82
11104	ST Jayasuriya	*SL/Asia*	32.75
10123	SC Ganguly	*I/Asia*	40.65
9661	BC Lara	*WI/World*	41.11
9537	R Dravid	*I/Asia/World*	40.24
9378	M Azharuddin	*I*	36.92
9284	PA de Silva	*SL*	34.90
9210	RT Ponting	*A/World*	42.44
8823	Saeed Anwar	*P*	39.21

DL Haynes (8648), ME Waugh (8500), MS Atapattu and AC Gilchrist (both 8233) have also passed 8000 runs

Most wickets

			Avge
502	Wasim Akram	*P*	23.52
416	M Muralitharan	*SL/World*	23.28
416	Waqar Younis	*P*	23.84
354	WPUJC Vaas	*SL/Asia*	27.39
348	SM Pollock	*SA/World*	24.29
331	GD McGrath	*A/World*	22.43
329	A Kumble	*I/Asia*	30.76
315	J Srinath	*I*	28.08
293	SK Warne	*A/World*	25.73
288	Saqlain Mushtaq	*P*	21.78

ST Jayasuriya (278), AA Donald (272), Kapil Dev (253) and AB Agarkar (252) have also taken more than 250 wickets

Highest scores

194	Saeed Anwar	Pakistan v India at Chennai	1996-97	
189*	IVA Richards	W Iv England at Manchester	1984	
189	ST Jayasuriya	Sri Lanka v India at Sharjah	2000-01	
188*	G Kirsten	SA v UAE at Rawalpindi	1995-96	
186*	SR Tendulkar	India v NZ at Hyderabad	1999-2000	
183*	MS Dhoni	India v Sri Lanka at Jaipur	2005-06	
183	SC Ganguly	India v Sri Lanka at Taunton	1999	
181	IVA Richards	WI v Sri Lanka at Karachi	1987-88	
175*	Kapil Dev	India v Zim at Tunbridge Wells	1983	
175	HH Gibbs	SA v Aust at Johannesburg	2005-06	

SR Tendulkar has scored 39 ODI centuries, SC Ganguly and ST Jayasuriya 22, RT Ponting and Saeed Anwar 20

Best innings bowling

8-19	WPUJC Vaas	SL v Zimbabwe at Colombo	2001-02
7-15	GD McGrath	Aust v Namibia at P'stroom	2002-03
7-20	AJ Bichel	Aust v Eng at Port Elizabeth	2002-03
7-30	M Muralitharan	Sri Lanka v India at Sharjah	2000-01
7-36	Waqar Younis	Pakistan v England at Leeds	2001
7-37	Aqib Javed	Pakistan v India at Sharjah	1991-92
7-51	WW Davis	West Indies v Australia at Leeds	1983
6-12	A Kumble	India v West Indies at Calcutta	1993-94
6-14	GJ Gilmour	Australia v England at Leeds	1975
6-14	Imran Khan	Pakistan v India at Sharjah	1984-85

Waqar Younis took five wickets in an innings 13 times, Muralitharan 8, GD McGrath 7, L Klusener, Saqlain Mushtaq and Wasim Akram 6

Record wicket partnerships

1st	286	WU Tharanga (109) and ST Jayasuriya (152)	Sri Lanka v England at Leeds	2006
2nd	331	SR Tendulkar (186*) and R Dravid (153)	India v New Zealand at Hyderabad	1999-2000
3rd	237*	R Dravid (104*) and SR Tendulkar (140*)	India v Kenya at Bristol	1999
4th	275*	M Azharuddin (153*) and A Jadeja (116*)	India v Zimbabwe at Cuttack	1997-98
5th	223	M Azharuddin (111*) and A Jadeja (119)	India v Sri Lanka at Colombo	1997-98
6th	161	MO Odumbe (82) and AV Vadher (73*)	Kenya v Sri Lanka at Southampton	1999
7th	130	A Flower (142*) and HH Streak (56)	Zimbabwe v England at Harare	2001-02
8th	119	PR Reiffel (58) and SK Warne (55)	Australia v South Africa at Port Elizabeth	1993-94
9th	126*	Kapil Dev (175*) and SMH Kirmani (24*)	India v Zimbabwe at Tunbridge Wells	1983
10th	106*	IVA Richards (189*) and MA Holding (12*)	West Indies v England at Manchester	1984

Updated records can be found at **www.cricinfo.com/db/stats/odis**

One-day Internationals **OVERALL RECORDS**

Most catches

Fielders

156	M Azharuddin	*I*
127	AR Border	*A*
120	CL Hooper	*WI*
116	SP Fleming	*NZ/World*

Most dismissals

Wicketkeepers   *Ct/St*

393	AC Gilchrist *A/World*	348/45
320	MV Boucher *SA/Africa*	303/17
287	Moin Khan *P*	214/73
233	IA Healy *A*	194/39
220	Rashid Latif *P*	182/38

Highest team totals

443-9	**SL** v N'lands at Amstelveen	2006
438-9	**SA** v Aust at Johannesburg	2005-06
434-4	**Australia** v SA at Jo'burg	2005-06
398-5	**SL** v Kenya at Kandy	1995-96
397-5	**NZ** v Zim at Bulawayo	2005-06
391-4	**Eng** v B'desh at Nottingham	2005
376-2	**India** v NZ at Hyderabad	1999-2000
373-6	**India** v Sri Lanka at Taunton	1999
371-9	**Pak** v Sri Lanka at Nairobi	1996-97
368-5	**Aust** v Sri Lanka at Sydney	2005-06

NZ's 397-5 was made in 44 overs, all the other totals in 50 except SA's 438-9, when the winning run came off the fifth ball of the 50th over

Lowest team totals

Completed innings

35	**Zim** v SL at Harare	2003-04
36	**Canada** v SL at Paarl	2002-03
38	**Zim** v SL at Colombo	2001-02
43	**Pak** v WI at Cape Town	1992-93
45	**Can** v Eng at Manchester	1979
45	**Nam** v Aust at P'stroom	2002-03
54	**India** v SL at Sharjah	2000-01
54	**WI** v SA at Cape Town	2003-04
55	**SL** v WI at Sharjah	1986-87
63	**India** v Aust at Sydney	1980-81

The lowest total successfully defended in a non-rain-affected ODI is 125, by India v Pakistan (87) at Sharjah in 1984-85

Most sixes

216	Shahid Afridi	*Pak/Asia/World*
209	ST Jayasuriya	*SL/Asia*
168	SC Ganguly	*I/Asia*
153	CL Cairns	*NZ/World*
149	SR Tendulkar	*I*
140	Inzamam-ul-Haq	*P/Asia*
126	IVA Richards	*WI*
123	AC Gilchrist	*A/World*
121	Wasim Akram	*P*
119	RT Ponting	*A/World*

BC Lara has hit 117 sixes in ODIs

Best strike rate

Runs per 100 balls   *Runs*

107.83	**Shahid Afridi** *P/Asia/World*	4860
100.96	**MS Dhoni** *I*	1467
99.43	**IDS Smith** *NZ*	1055
97.47	**MEK Hussey** *A*	1156
96.76	**AC Gilchrist** *A/World*	8233
96.76	**V Sehwag** *I/Asia/World*	4608
96.66	**RL Powell** *WI*	2085
95.64	**KP Pietersen** *E/World*	1382
95.07	**Kapil Dev** *I*	3783
92.21	**A Symonds** *A*	3697

Qualification: 1000 runs

Most economical bowlers

Runs per over   *Wkts*

3.09	J Garner *WI*	146
3.28	RGD Willis *E*	80
3.30	RJ Hadlee *NZ*	158
3.32	MA Holding *WI*	142
3.37	SP Davis *A*	44
3.40	AME Roberts *WI*	87
3.48	CEL Ambrose *WI*	225
3.53	MD Marshall *WI*	157
3.54	ARC Fraser *E*	47
3.55	MR Whitney *A*	46

Qualification: 2000 balls bowled

One-day international results

	Played	Won	Lost	Tied	No result	% win
Australia	625	381	219	8	17	63.50
Bangladesh	133	20	111	0	2	15.26
England	445	215	211	4	15	50.46
India	624	296	300	3	25	49.66
Kenya	79	16	61	0	2	20.77
New Zealand	497	210	260	4	23	44.68
Pakistan	641	344	277	6	14	55.39
South Africa	355	216	124	5	10	63.52
Sri Lanka	502	226	255	3	18	46.98
West Indies	539	300	217	5	17	58.02
Zimbabwe	303	78	212	4	9	26.89
Others (see below)	81	11	66	0	4	14.28
TOTAL	2412	2313	2313	21	78	

Other teams: Africa XI (P3, W1, L1, NR1), Asia XI (P4, W1, L2, NR1), Bermuda (P5, W3, L2), Canada (P15, W1, L14), East Africa (P3, L3), Hong Kong (P2, L2), Ireland (P3, W1, L1, NR1), Namibia (P6, L6), Netherlands (P17, W1, L15, NR1), Scotland (P8, W1, L7), United Arab Emirates (P9, W1, L8), USA (P2, L2), World XI (P4, W1, L3).

213

AUSTRALIA
Test Match Records

Most appearances

168	SR Waugh	
156	AR Border	
140	SK Warne	
128	ME Waugh	
119	IA Healy	
119	GD McGrath	
107	DC Boon	
105	RT Ponting	
104	MA Taylor	
100	JL Langer	

10 of the 41 players with 100 or more Test caps are Australian

Most runs

		Avge
11174	AR Border	50.56
10927	SR Waugh	51.06
8792	RT Ponting	58.22
8029	ME Waugh	41.81
7525	MA Taylor	43.49
7422	DC Boon	43.65
7393	JL Langer	45.35
7226	ML Hayden	53.08
7110	GS Chappell	53.86
6996	DG Bradman	99.94

RN Harvey (6149) also reached 6000 Test runs

Most wickets

		Avge
685	SK Warne	25.25
542	GD McGrath	21.55
355	DK Lillee	23.92
291	CJ McDermott	28.63
259	JN Gillespie	26.13
248	R Benaud	27.03
246	GD McKenzie	29.78
228	RR Lindwall	23.03
216	CV Grimmett	24.21
212	MG Hughes	28.38

B Lee (211) and JR Thomson (200) also reached 200 Test wickets

Highest scores

380	ML Hayden	v Zimbabwe at Perth	2003-04
334*	MA Taylor	v Pakistan at Peshawar	1998-99
334	DG Bradman	v England at Leeds	1930
311	RB Simpson	v England at Manchester	1964
307	RM Cowper	v England at Melbourne	1965-66
304	DG Bradman	v England at Leeds	1934
299*	DG Bradman	v South Africa at Adelaide	1931-32
270	DG Bradman	v England at Melbourne	1936-37
268	GN Yallop	v Pakistan at Melbourne	1983-84
266	WH Ponsford	v England at The Oval	1934

At the time of his retirement in 1948 DG Bradman had made eight of Australia's highest ten Test scores

Best innings bowling

9-121	AA Mailey	v England at Melbourne	1920-21
8-24	GD McGrath	v Pakistan at Perth	2004-05
8-31	FJ Laver	v England at Manchester	1909
8-38	GD McGrath	v England at Lord's	1997
8-43	AE Trott	v England at Adelaide	1894-95
8-53	RAL Massie	v England at Lord's	1972
8-59	AA Mallett	v Pakistan at Adelaide	1972-73
8-65	H Trumble	v England at The Oval	1902
8-71	GD McKenzie	v West Indies at Melbourne	1968-69
8-71	SK Warne	v England at Brisbane	1994-95

Trott and Massie were making their Test debuts. Massie took 8-84 – Australia's 11th-best analysis – in the first innings of the same match

Record wicket partnerships

1st	382	WM Lawry (210) and RB Simpson (205)	v West Indies at Bridgetown	1964-65
2nd	451	WH Ponsford (266) and DG Bradman (244)	v England at The Oval	1934
3rd	315	RT Ponting (206) and DS Lehmann (160)	v West Indies at Port-of-Spain	2002-03
4th	388	WH Ponsford (181) and DG Bradman (304)	v England at Leeds	1934
5th	405	SG Barnes (234) and DG Bradman (234)	v England at Sydney	1946-47
6th	346	JHW Fingleton (136) and DG Bradman (270)	v England at Melbourne	1936-37
7th	217	KD Walters (250) and GJ Gilmour (101)	v New Zealand at Christchurch	1976-77
8th	243	MJ Hartigan (116) and C Hill (160)	v England at Adelaide	1907-08
9th	154	SE Gregory (201) and JM Blackham (74)	v England at Sydney	1894-95
10th	127	JM Taylor (108) and AA Mailey (46*)	v England at Sydney	1924-25

Updated records can be found at **www.cricinfo.com/db/stats/aus**

Test Match Records

AUSTRALIA

Most catches

Fielders

181	ME Waugh	
157	MA Taylor	
156	AR Border	
122	GS Chappell	
120	RT Ponting/SK Warne	

Highest team totals

758-8d	v West Indies at Kingston	1954-55
735-6d	v Zimbabwe at Perth	2003-04
729-6d	v England at Lord's	1930
701	v England at The Oval	1934
695	v England at The Oval	1930
674	v India at Adelaide	1947-48
668	v West Indies at Bridgetown	1954-55
659-8d	v England at Sydney	1946-47
656-8d	v England at Manchester	1964
653-4d	v England at Leeds	1993

Australia have reached 600 on 27 occasions, 14 of them against England

Lowest team totals

Completed innings

36	v England at Birmingham	1902
42	v England at Sydney	1887-88
44	v England at The Oval	1896
53	v England at Lord's	1896
58*	v England at Brisbane	1936-37
60	v England at Lord's	1888
63	v England at The Oval	1882
65	v England at The Oval	1912
66*	v England at Brisbane	1928-29
68	v England at The Oval	1886

*One or more batsmen absent.
Australia's lowest total against anyone other than England is 75, v South Africa at Durban in 1949-50

Most dismissals

Wicketkeepers   *Ct/St*

395	IA Healy	366/29
355	AC Gilchrist	320/35
355	RW Marsh	343/12
187	ATW Grout	163/24
130	WAS Oldfield	78/52

Best match bowling

16-137	RAL Massie	v England at Lord's	1972
14-90	FR Spofforth	v England at The Oval	1882
14-199	CV Grimmett	v South Africa at Adelaide	1931-32
13-77	MA Noble	v England at Melbourne	1901-02
13-110	FR Spofforth	v England at Melbourne	1878-79
13-148	BA Reid	v England at Melbourne	1990-91
13-173	CV Grimmett	v South Africa at Durban	1935-36
13-217	MG Hughes	v West Indies at Perth	1988-89
13-236	AA Mailey	v England at Melbourne	1920-21
12-87	CTB Turner	v England at Sydney	1887-88

Massie was playing in his first Test, Grimmett (1935-36) in his last – he took 10 or more wickets in each of his last three

Hat-tricks

FR Spofforth	v England at Melbourne	1878-79
H Trumble	v England at Melbourne	1901-02
H Trumble	v England at Melbourne	1903-04
TJ Matthews	v South Africa at Manchester	1912
TJ Matthews	v South Africa at Manchester	1912
LF Kline	v South Africa at Cape Town	1957-58
MG Hughes	v West Indies at Perth	1988-89
DW Fleming	v Pakistan at Rawalpindi	1994-95
SK Warne	v England at Melbourne	1994-95
GD McGrath	v West Indies at Perth	2000-01

Fleming was playing in his first Test, Trumble (1903-04) in his last. Matthews uniquely took a hat-trick in both innings of the same Test

Australia's Test match results

	Played	Won	Lost	Drawn	Tied	% win
v Bangladesh	4	4	0	0	0	100.00
v England	311	126	97	88	0	40.51
v India	68	32	15	20	1	47.05
v New Zealand	46	22	7	17	0	47.82
v Pakistan	52	24	11	17	0	46.15
v South Africa	77	44	15	18	0	57.14
v Sri Lanka	18	11	1	6	0	61.11
v West Indies	102	48	32	21	1	47.05
v Zimbabwe	3	3	0	0	0	100.00
v World XI	1	1	0	0	0	100.00
TOTAL	**682**	**315**	**178**	**187**	**2**	**46.18**

Updated records can be found at **www.cricinfo.com/db/stats/aus**

AUSTRALIA *One-day International Records*

Most appearances

325	SR Waugh
273	AR Border
251	RT Ponting
244	ME Waugh
241	AC Gilchrist
232	MG Bevan
220	GD McGrath
200	DR Martyn
193	SK Warne
181	DC Boon

A total of 19 Australians have played in more than 100 ODIs

Most runs

		Avge
9095	RT Ponting	42.10
8500	ME Waugh	39.35
8209	AC Gilchrist	36.48
7569	SR Waugh	32.90
6912	MG Bevan	53.58
6524	AR Border	30.62
6068	DM Jones	44.61
5964	DC Boon	37.04
5030	DR Martyn	40.24
4357	GR Marsh	39.97

ML Hayden (4129) also reached 4000 runs

Most wickets

		Avge
330	GD McGrath	22.38
291	SK Warne	25.82
237	B Lee	22.84
203	CJ McDermott	24.71
195	SR Waugh	34.67
142	JN Gillespie	25.42
134	DW Fleming	25.38
114	A Symonds	36.38
108	SP O'Donnell	28.72
107	GB Hogg	27.73

PR Reiffel (106) and DK Lillee (103) also reached 100 wickets

Highest scores

173	ME Waugh	v West Indies at Melbourne	2000-01
172	AC Gilchrist	v Zimbabwe at Hobart	2003-04
164	RT Ponting	v South Africa at Johannesburg	2005-06
156	A Symonds	v New Zealand at Wellington	2005-06
154	AC Gilchrist	v Sri Lanka at Melbourne	1998-99
151	A Symonds	v Sri Lanka at Sydney	2005-06
146	ML Hayden	v Pakistan at Nairobi	2002-03
145	DM Jones	v England at Brisbane	1990-91
145	RT Ponting	v Zimbabwe at Delhi	1997-98
144*	DR Martyn	v Zimbabwe at Perth	2000-01

RT Ponting also made 140 v India at Johannesburg in 2002-03, the highest score in the World Cup final*

Best innings bowling

7-15	GD McGrath	v Namibia at Potchefstroom	2002-03
7-20	AJ Bichel	v England at Port Elizabeth	2002-03
6-14	GJ Gilmour	v England at Leeds	1975
6-39	KH MacLeay	v India at Nottingham	1983
5-13	SP O'Donnell	v New Zealand at Christchurch	1989-90
5-14	GD McGrath	v West Indies at Manchester	1999
5-15	GS Chappell	v India at Sydney	1980-81
5-16	CG Rackemann	v Pakistan at Adelaide	1983-84
5-17	TM Alderman	v New Zealand at Wellington	1981-82
5-18	GJ Cosier	v England at Birmingham	1977
5-18	A Symonds	v Bangladesh at Manchester	2005

DK Lillee took 5-34 against Pakistan at Leeds in the 1975 World Cup, the first five-wicket haul in ODIs

Record wicket partnerships

1st	382	WM Lawry (210) and RB Simpson (205)	v West Indies at Bridgetown	1964-65
1st	212	GR Marsh (104) and DC Boon (111)	v India at Jaipur	1986-87
2nd	225	AC Gilchrist (124) and RT Ponting (119)	v England at Melbourne	2002-03
3rd	234*	RT Ponting (140*) and DR Martyn (88*)	v India at Johannesburg	2002-03
4th	237	RT Ponting (124) and A Symonds (151)	v Sri Lanka at Sydney	2005-06
5th	220	A Symonds (156) and MJ Clarke (82*)	v New Zealand at Wellington	2005-06
6th	145*	MEK Hussey (75*) and SR Watson (66*)	v World XI at Melbourne	2005-06
7th	123	MEK Hussey (73) and B Lee (57)	v South Africa at Brisbane	2005-06
8th	119	PR Reiffel (58) and SK Warne (55)	v South Africa at Port Elizabeth	1993-94
9th	77	MG Bevan (59*) and SK Warne (29)	v West Indies at Port-of-Spain	1998-99
10th	63	SR Watson (35*) and AJ Bichel (28)	v Sri Lanka at Sydney	2002-03

Updated records can be found at **www.cricinfo.com/db/stats/aus**

One-day International Records **AUSTRALIA**

Most catches

Fielders

127	AR Border	
111	SR Waugh	
108	ME Waugh	
103	RT Ponting	
80	SK Warne	

Most dismissals

Wicketkeepers   Ct/St

391	AC Gilchrist	347/44
233	IA Healy	194/39
124	RW Marsh	120/4
49	WB Phillips	42/7
28	GC Dyer	24/4

Highest team totals

434-4	v South Africa at Johannesburg	2005-06
368-5	v Sri Lanka at Sydney	2005-06
359-2	v India at Johannesburg †	2002-03
359-5	v India at Sydney	2003-04
349-6	v New Zealand at C'church	1999-2000
347-2	v India at Bangalore	2003-04
347-5	v New Zealand at Napier	2004-05
344-7	v Zimbabwe at Hobart	2003-04
344-6	v South Africa at Sydney	2005-06
338-6	v West Indies at Melbourne	2000-01
338-4	v India at Visakhapatnam	2000-01

† In World Cup final. All scores made in 50 overs

Lowest team totals

Completed innings

70	v England at Birmingham	1977
70	v New Zealand at Adelaide	1985-86
91	v West Indies at Perth	1986-87
93	v S Africa at Cape Town	2005-06
101	v England at Melbourne	1978-79
101	v India at Perth	1991-92
107	v West Indies at Melb'ne	1981-82
109	v England at Sydney	1982-83
120	v Pakistan at Hobart	1996-97
124	v New Zealand at Sydney	1982-83

Australia scored 101-9 in a 30-overs match against West Indies at Sydney in 1992-93 – and won

Most sixes

122	AC Gilchrist
116	RT Ponting
74	A Symonds
68	SR Waugh
64	DM Jones
57	ME Waugh
50	ML Hayden
43	AR Border
28	SP O'Donnell
22	B Lee
22	GR Marsh

Best strike rate

Runs per 100 balls   Runs

97.47	MEK Hussey	1156
96.71	AC Gilchrist	8209
92.21	A Symonds	3697
88.16	IJ Harvey	715
85.71	WB Phillips	852
84.34	MJ Clarke	2393
83.84	IA Healy	1764
83.41	B Lee	694
82.26	RW Marsh	1225
81.34	DS Lehmann	3078

Qualification: 500 runs

Most economical bowlers

Runs per over   Wkts

3.37	SP Davis	44
3.55	MR Whitney	46
3.58	DK Lillee	103
3.65	GF Lawson	88
3.65	TM Alderman	88
3.84	GD McGrath	330
3.92	PR Reiffel	106
3.94	CG Rackemann	82
3.94	RM Hogg	85
4.03	CJ McDermott	203

Qualification: 2000 balls bowled

Australia's one-day international results

	Played	Won	Lost	Tied	No Result	% win
v Bangladesh	12	11	1	0	0	91.66
v England	85	47	34	2	2	58.02
v India	80	49	27	0	4	64.47
v New Zealand	100	70	27	0	3	72.16
v Pakistan	74	43	27	1	3	61.42
v South Africa	65	34	28	3	0	54.83
v Sri Lanka	62	41	19	0	2	68.33
v West Indies	108	49	55	2	2	47.11
v Zimbabwe	27	25	1	0	1	96.15
v others (see below)	12	12	0	0	0	100.00
TOTAL	**625**	**381**	**219**	**8**	**17**	**63.50**

Other teams: Canada (P1, W1), Kenya (P4, W4), Namibia (P1, W1), Netherlands (P1, W1), Scotland (P1, W1), USA (P1, W1), World XI (P3, W3).

BANGLADESH *Test Match Records*

Most appearances

42	Habibul Bashar
41	Khaled Mashud
35	Javed Omar
33	Mohammad Ashraful
26	Mohammad Rafique
21	Tapash Baisya
20	Mashrafe Mortaza
17	Alok Kapali
17	Hannan Sarkar
17	Manjural Islam
17	Rajin Saleh

Habibul Bashar has missed only two of Bangladesh's 44 Tests

Most runs

		Avge
2838	Habibul Bashar	34.60
1525	Javed Omar	22.10
1511	Mohammad Ashraful	44.85
1361	Khaled Mashud	19.44
982	Mohammad Rafique	21.82
930	Rajin Saleh	29.06
683	Al Sahariar	22.76
662	Hannan Sarkar	20.06
584	Alok Kapali	17.69
530	Aminul Islam	21.20

Habibul Bashar reached 2000 runs for Bangladesh before anyone else had made 1000

Most wickets

		Avge
87	Mohammad Rafique	36.59
50	Mashrafe Mortaza	37.42
36	Tapash Baisya	59.36
32	Enamul Haque jnr	37.43
28	Manjural Islam	57.32
18	Enamul Haque snr	57.04
16	Shahadat Hossain	49.56
14	Mohammad Sharif	65.07
14	Talha Jubair	55.07
13	Khaled Mahmud	64.00
13	Mushfiqur Rahman	63.00

Naimur Rahman (12) also passed 10 wickets

Highest scores

158*	Moh'd Ashraful	v India at Chittagong	2004-05
145†	Aminul Islam	v India at Dhaka	2000-01
138	Shahriar Nafees	v Australia at Fatullah	2005-06
136†	Moh'd Ashraful	v Sri Lanka at Chittagong	2005-06
121	Nafees Iqbal	v Zimbabwe at Dhaka	2004-05
119	Javed Omar	v Pakistan at Peshawar	2003-04
114	Moh'd Ashraful	v Sri Lanka at Colombo	2001-02
113	Habibul Bashar	v West Indies at Gros Islet	2004
111	Moh'd Rafique	v West Indies at Gros Islet	2004
108	Habibul Bashar	v Zimbabwe at Chittagong	2001-02
108	Habibul Bashar	v Pakistan at Karachi	2003-04

† On debut. The only other century for Bangladesh is Khaled Mashud's 103 v West Indies at Gros Islet in 2004*

Best innings bowling

7-95	Enamul Haque jnr	v Zim at Dhaka	2004-05
6-45	Enamul Haque jnr	v Zim at Chittagong	2004-05
6-77	Moh'd Rafique	v South Africa at Dhaka	2002-03s
6-81	Manjural Islam	v Zim at Bulawayo	2000-01
6-122	Moh'd Rafique	v New Zealand at Dhaka	2004-05
6-132	Naimur Rahman	v India at Dhaka	2000-01
5-36	Moh'd Rafique	v Pakistan at Multan	2003-04
5-62	Moh'd Rafique	v Australia at Fatulla	2005-06
5-65	Moh'd Rafique	v Zim at Chittagong	2004-05
5-86	Shahadat Hossain	v Sri Lanka at Bogra	2005-06

Other five-wicket hauls have been recorded by Mohammad Rafique (2) and Enamul Haque jnr

Record wicket partnerships

1st	133	Javed Omar (43) and Nafees Iqbal (121)	v Zimbabwe at Dhaka	2004-05
2nd	187	Shahriar Nafees (138) and Habibul Bashar (76)	v Australia at Fatullah	2005-06
3rd	130	Javed Omar (119) and Mohammad Ashraful (77)	v Pakistan at Peshawar	2003-04
4th	120	Habibul Bashar (77) and Manjural Islam Rana (35)	v West Indies at Kingston	2004
5th	126	Aminul Islam (56) and Mohammad Ashraful (114)	v Sri Lanka at Colombo	2001-02
6th	97	Mohammad Ashraful (98) and Mushfiqur Rahman (44)	v Zimbabwe at Harare	2003-04
7th	93	Aminul Islam (145) and Khaled Mashud (32)	v India at Dhaka	2001-02
8th	87	Mohammad Ashraful (81) and Mohammad Rafique (111)	v West Indies at Gros Islet	2004
9th	74	Khaled Mashud (103*) and Tapash Baisya (26)	v West Indies at Gros Islet	2004
10th	69	Mohammad Rafique (65) and Shahadat Hossain (3*)	v Australia at Chittagong	2005-06

Updated records can be found at **www.cricinfo.com/db/stats/bdesh**

BANGLADESH

Most catches

	Fielders	
19	Habibul Bashar	
11	Rajin Saleh	
10	Al Sahariar	
10	Mohammad Ashraful	
7	Hannan Sarkar	
7	Javed Omar	

Most dismissals

	Wicketkeepers	Ct/St
83	Khaled Mashud	75/8
4	Mohammad Salim	3/1
2	Mehrab Hossain	2/0

Khaled Mashud has missed only three of Bangladesh's 44 Tests

Highest team totals

488	v Zimbabwe at Chittagong	2004-05
427	v Australia at Fatullah	2005-06
416	v West Indies at Gros Islet	2004
400	v India at Dhaka	2000-01
361	v Pakistan at Peshawar	2003-04
333	v India at Chittagong	2004-05
331	v Zimbabwe at Harare	2003-04
328	v Sri Lanka at Colombo	2001-02
319	v Sri Lanka at Chittagong	2005-06
316	v England at Chester-le-Street	2005

The 400 against India came in Bangladesh's inaugural Test

Lowest team totals

	Completed innings	
86	v SL at Colombo	2005-06
87	v WI at Dhaka	2002-03
90	v SL at Colombo	2001-02
91	v India at Dhaka	2000-01
96	v Pakistan at Peshawar	2003-04
97	v Australia at Darwin	2003
102	v SA at Dhaka	2002-03
104	v Eng at Chester-le-Street	2005
107	v Zimbabwe at Dhaka	2001-02
107	v SA at Potchefstroom	2002-03

The lowest all-out total by the opposition is 154, by Zimbabwe at Chittagong in 2004-05 (Bangladesh's only Test victory)

Best match bowling

12-200	Enamul Haque jr	v Zim at Dhaka	2004-05
9-160	Moh'd Rafique	v Australia at Fatullah	2005-06
7-105	Khaled Mahmud	v Pakistan at Multan	2003-04
7-116	Moh'd Rafique	v Pakistan at Multan	2003-04
6-77	Moh'd Rafique	v SA at Dhaka	2002-03
6-81	Manjural Islam	v Zim at Bulawayo	2000-01
6-100	Enamul Haque jr	v Zim at Chittagong	2004-05
6-117	Tapash Baisya	v WI at Chittagong	2002-03
6-122	Moh'd Rafique	v New Zealand at Dhaka	2004-05
6-154	Naimur Rahman	v India at Dhaka	2000-01

Khaled Mahmud took only six other wickets in 11 more Tests

Hat-tricks

Alok Kapali	v Pakistan at Peshawar	2003-04

Alok Kapali's figures were 2.1-1-3-3; he ended Pakistan's innings by dismissing Shabbir Ahmed, Danish Kaneria and Umar Gul. He has taken only three other Test wickets.

Two bowlers have taken hat-tricks against Bangladesh: AM Blignaut for Zimbabwe at Harare in 2003-04, and JEC Franklin for New Zealand at Dhaka in 2004-05

Bangladesh's Test match results

	Played	Won	Lost	Drawn	Tied	% win
v Australia	4	0	4	0	0	0.00
v England	4	0	4	0	0	0.00
v India	3	0	3	0	0	0.00
v New Zealand	4	0	4	0	0	0.00
v Pakistan	6	0	6	0	0	0.00
v South Africa	4	0	4	0	0	0.00
v Sri Lanka	7	0	7	0	0	0.00
v West Indies	4	0	3	1	0	0.00
v Zimbabwe	8	1	4	3	0	12.50
TOTAL	44	1	39	4	0	2.27

Updated records can be found at **www.cricinfo.com/db/stats/bdesh**

BANGLADESH *One-day International Records*

Most appearances

120	Khaled Mashud
100	Mohammad Rafique
84	Habibul Bashar
77	Khaled Mahmud
74	Mohammad Ashraful
55	Alok Kapali
53	Javed Omar
52	Tapash Baisya
44	Akram Khan
41	Mashrafe Mortaza

Habibul Bashar has captained in 42 ODIs, Khaled Mashud in 30

Most runs

		Avge
1777	Khaled Mashud	21.93
1708	Habibul Bashar	21.62
1391	Moh'd Ashraful	20.45
1166	Javed Omar	23.79
1049	Moh'd Rafique	13.62
999	Rajin Saleh	24.36
991	Khaled Mahmud	14.36
976	Akram Khan	23.23
964	Alok Kapali	19.67
863	Aftab Ahmed	24.65

Aminul Islam (794) and Shahriar Nafees (787) have also passed 600 runs

Most wickets

		Avge
95	Mohammad Rafique	39.86
67	Khaled Mahmud	42.76
56	Tapash Baisya	40.48
54	Mashrafe Mortaza	31.18
30	Abdur Razzak	24.43
29	Hasibul Hossain	46.13
24	Manjural Islam	53.50
23	Manjural Islam Rana	29.95
23	Syed Rasel	22.73
19	Enamul Haque snr	57.00
19	Mushfiqur Rahman	51.73

Mohammad Rafique needs only five wickets to complete the double in ODIs. He is close to it in Test cricket too

Highest scores

118*	Shahriar Nafees	v Zimbabwe at Harare	2006
108*	Rajin Saleh	v Kenya at Fatullah	2005-06
101	Mehrab Hossain	v Zimbabwe at Dhaka	1998-99
100	Moh'd Ashraful	v Australia at Cardiff	2005
95	Shahriar Hossain	v Kenya at Dhaka	1998-99
94	Moh'd Ashraful	v England at Nottingham	2005
91	Shahriar Nafees	v Kenya at Bogra	2005-06
89*	Alok Kapali	v West Indies at Dhaka	2002-03
85*	Javed Omar	v Sri Lanka at Dhaka	1999-2000
82	Athar Ali Khan	v Pakistan at Colombo	1997-98
82	Rajin Saleh	v India at Dhaka	2004-05

Bangladesh's highest score in the World Cup is 68, by Minhajul Abedin against Scotland at Edinburgh in 1999*

Best bowling figures

6-26	Mashrafe Mortaza	v Kenya at Nairobi	2006
5-31	Aftab Ahmed	v NZ at Dhaka	2004-05
5-47	Moh'd Rafique	v Kenya at Fatullah	2005-06
4-16	Tapash Baisya	v WI at Kingstown	2004
4-16	Rajin Saleh	v Zim at Harare	2006
4-19	Khaled Mahmud	v Zim at Harare	2003-04
4-22	Syed Rasel	v Kenya at Nairobi	2006
4-33	Moh'd Rafique	v Zim at Dhaka	2004-05
4-34	M'ral Islam Rana	v Zim at Chittagong	2004-05
4-36	Saiful Islam	v Sri Lanka at Sharjah	1994-95
4-36	M'ral Islam Rana	v Zim at Dhaka	2004-05

Aftab Ahmed has taken only five more wickets in 38 other matches

Record wicket partnerships

1st	170	Shahriar Hossain (68) and Mehrab Hossain (101)	v Zimbabwe at Dhaka	1998-99
2nd	150	Mohammad Rafique (72) and Aftab Ahmed (81*)	v Zimbabwe at Dhaka	2004-05
3rd	128	Rajin Saleh (71) and Alok Kapali (69)	v Pakistan at Karachi	2003-04
4th	175*	Rajin Saleh (108*) and Habibul Bashar (64*)	v Kenya at Fatullah	2005-06
5th	109	Aminul Islam (69*) and Khaled Mahmud (47)	v India at Dhaka	1997-98
6th	123*	Al Sahariar (62*) and Khaled Mashud (53*)	v West Indies at Dhaka	1999-2000
7th	89	Alok Kapali (55) and Khaled Mashud (39)	v Kenya at Fatullah	2005-06
8th	70*	Khaled Mashud (35*) and Mohammad Rafique (41*)	v New Zealand at Kimberley	2002-03
9th	62*	Khaled Mashud (30*) and Mohammad Rafique (32*)	v West Indies at Kingstown	2004
10th1	54*	Khaled Mashud (39*) and Tapash Baisya (22*)	v Sri Lanka at Colombo	2005-06

Updated records can be found at **www.cricinfo.com/db/stats/bdesh**

Most catches

Fielders

22	Mohammad Rafique
21	Alok Kapali
17	Khaled Mahmud
16	Habibul Bashar
13	Aminul Islam

Most dismissals

Wicketkeepers		*Ct/St*
119	Khaled Mashud	87/32
2	Hafizur Rahman	2/0
2	Nasir Ahmed	1/1

Highest team totals

301-7	v Kenya at Bogra	2005-06
272-8	v Zimbabwe at Bulawayo	2000-01
267-9	v Zimbabwe at Dhaka	2001-02
257-5	v Zimbabwe at Dhaka	1998-99
257-9	v India at Dhaka	2004-05
257	v Zimbabwe at Nairobi	1997-98
250-5	v Australia at Cardiff	2005
250-8	v Australia at Canterbury	2005
249-6	v India at Dhaka	1999-2000
247-9	v Zimbabwe at Dhaka	2004-05

Bangladesh passed 300 for the first time in their 119th one-day international

Lowest team totals

Completed innings

76	v Sri Lanka at Colombo	2002
76	v India at Dhaka	2002-03
77	v NZ at Colombo	2002-03
86	v NZ at Chittagong	2004-05
87*	v Pakistan at Dhaka	1999-2000
92	v Zimbabwe at Nairobi	1997-98
93	v SA at Birmingham	2004
94	v Pakistan at Moratuwa	1985-86
100	v Kenya at Nairobi	1997-98
103	v Zimbabwe at Harare	2000-01

* One batsman absent hurt

Most sixes

24	Mohammad Rafique
19	Aftab Ahmed
17	Mohammad Ashraful
11	Mashrafe Mortaza
8	Habibul Bashar
7	Khaled Mahmud
5	Hasibul Hossain
5	Khaled Mashud
5	Naimur Rahman
4	Alok Kapali

Exactly one-sixth of Mashrafe Mortaza's runs have come in sixes

Best strike rate

Runs per 100 balls		*Runs*
81.10	Aftab Ahmed	863
72.44	Mohammad Rafique	1049
72.33	Mohammad Ashraful	1391
67.83	Khaled Mahmud	991
66.52	Shahriar Nafees	787
65.66	Alok Kapali	964
61.52	Tushar Imran	547
60.09	Habibul Bashar	1708
56.71	Akram Khan	976
56.59	Aminul Islam	794

Qualification: 500 runs. Mashrafe Mortaza has scored 396 runs at a strike rate of 97.53

Most economical bowlers

Runs per over		*Wkts*
3.82	Abdur Razzak	30
4.42	Mushfiqur Rahman	19
4.49	Mohammad Rafique	95
4.77	Mashrafe Mortaza	54
4.84	Manjural Islam	24
4.95	Naimur Rahman	10
5.01	Alok Kapali	15
5.07	Khaled Mahmud	67
5.24	Enamul Haque snr	19
5.62	Tapash Baisya	56

Qualification: 1000 balls bowled

Bangladesh's one-day international results

	Played	Won	Lost	Tied	No Result	% win
v Australia	12	1	11	0	0	8.33
v England	7	0	7	0	0	0.00
v India	14	1	13	0	0	7.14
v New Zealand	7	0	7	0	0	0.00
v Pakistan	18	1	17	0	0	5.55
v South Africa	7	0	7	0	0	0.00
v Sri Lanka	17	1	16	0	0	5.88
v West Indies	11	0	9	0	2	0.00
v Zimbabwe	23	6	17	0	0	26.08
v others (see below)	17	10	7	0	0	58.82
TOTAL	**133**	**20**	**111**	**0**	**2**	**15.26**

Other teams: Canada (P1, L1), Hong Kong (P1, W1), Kenya (P14, W8, L6), Scotland (P1, W1)

Updated records can be found at **www.cricinfo.com/db/stats/bdesh**

ENGLAND

Most appearances

133	AJ Stewart
118	GA Gooch
117	DI Gower
115	MA Atherton
114	MC Cowdrey
108	G Boycott
102	IT Botham
100	GP Thorpe
96	N Hussain
95	APE Knott

Cowdrey was the first man to reach 100 Tests, in 1968

Most runs

		Avge
8900	GA Gooch	42.58
8463	AJ Stewart	39.54
8231	DI Gower	44.25
8114	G Boycott	47.72
7728	MA Atherton	37.69
7624	MC Cowdrey	44.06
7249	WR Hammond	58.45
6971	L Hutton	56.67
6806	KF Barrington	58.67
6744	GP Thorpe	44.66

ME Trescothick (5825), DCS Compton (5807) and N Hussain (5764) also passed 5500 runs

Most wickets

		Avge
383	IT Botham	28.40
325	RGD Willis	25.20
307	FS Trueman	21.57
297	DL Underwood	25.83
252	JB Statham	24.84
236	AV Bedser	24.89
234	AR Caddick	29.91
229	D Gough	28.39
222	MJ Hoggard	29.76
202	JA Snow	26.66

Willis is the only bowler to take more than 260 Test wickets without ever managing ten in a match

Highest scores

364	L Hutton	v Australia at The Oval	1938
336*	WR Hammond	v New Zealand at Auckland	1932-33
333	GA Gooch	v India at Lord's	1990
325	A Sandham	v West Indies at Kingston	1929-30
310*	JH Edrich	v New Zealand at Leeds	1965
287	RE Foster	v Australia at Sydney	1903-04
285*	PBH May	v West Indies at Birmingham	1957
278	DCS Compton	v Pakistan at Nottingham	1954
262*	DL Amiss	v West Indies at Kingston	1973-74
258	TW Graveney	v West Indies at Nottingham	1957

Foster was playing in his first Test, Sandham in his last

Best innings bowling

10-53	JC Laker	v Australia at Manchester	1956
9-28	GA Lohmann	v SA at Johannesburg	1895-96
9-37	JC Laker	v Australia at Manchester	1956
9-57	DE Malcolm	v South Africa at The Oval	1994
9-103	SF Barnes	v SA at Johannesburg	1913-14
8-7	GA Lohmann	v SA at Port Elizabeth	1895-96
8-11	J Briggs	v SA at Cape Town	1888-89
8-29	SF Barnes	v South Africa at The Oval	1912
8-31	FS Trueman	v India at Manchester	1952
8-34	IT Botham	v Pakistan at Lord's	1978

Botham also scored 108 in England's innings victory

Record wicket partnerships

1st	359	L Hutton (158) and C Washbrook (195)	v South Africa at Johannesburg	1948-49
2nd	382	L Hutton (364) and M Leyland (187)	v Australia at The Oval	1938
3rd	370	WJ Edrich (189) and DCS Compton (208)	v South Africa at Lord's	1947
4th	411	PBH May (285*) and MC Cowdrey (154)	v West Indies at Birmingham	1957
5th	254	KWR Fletcher (113) and AW Greig (148)	v India at Bombay	1972-73
6th	281	GP Thorpe (200*) and A Flintoff (137)	v New Zealand at Christchurch	2001-02
7th	197	MJK Smith (96) and JM Parks (101*)	v West Indies at Port-of-Spain	1959-60
8th	246	LEG Ames (137) and GOB Allen (122)	v New Zealand at Lord's	1931
9th	163*	MC Cowdrey (128*) and AC Smith (69*)	v New Zealand at Wellington	1962-63
10th	130	RE Foster (287) and W Rhodes (40*)	v Australia at Sydney	1903-04

Updated records can be found at www.cricinfo.com/db/stats/eng

Test Match Records

ENGLAND

Most catches

Fielders
120	IT Botham
120	MC Cowdrey
110	WR Hammond
105	GP Thorpe
103	GA Gooch

Most dismissals

Wicketkeepers		Ct/St
269	APE Knott	250/19
241	AJ Stewart	227/14
219	TG Evans	173/46
174	RW Taylor	167/7
165	RC Russell	153/12

Highest team totals

903-7d	v Australia at The Oval	1938
849	v West Indies at Kingston	1929-30
658-8d	v Australia at Nottingham	1938
654-5	v South Africa at Durban	1938-39
653-4d	v India at Lord's	1990
652-7d	v India at Madras	1984-85
636	v Australia at Sydney	1928-29
633-5d	v India at Birmingham	1979
629	v India at Lord's	1974
627-9d	v Australia at Manchester	1934

England have made five other totals of more
than 600

Lowest team totals

Completed innings		
45	v Australia at Sydney	1886-87
46	v WI at Port-of-Spain	1993-94
52	v Australia at The Oval	1948
53	v Australia at Lord's	1888
61	v Aust at Melbourne	1901-02
61	v Aust at Melbourne	1903-04
62	v Australia at Lord's	1888
64	v NZ at Wellington	1977-78
65*	v Australia at Sydney	1894-95
71	v WI at Manchester	1976

*One batsman absent

Best match bowling

19-90	JC Laker	v Australia at Manchester	1956
17-159	SF Barnes	v SA at Johannesburg	1913-14
15-28	J Briggs	v SA at Cape Town	1888-89
15-45	GA Lohmann	v SA at Port Elizabeth	1895-96
15-99	C Blythe	v South Africa at Leeds	1907
15-104	H Verity	v Australia at Lord's	1934
15-124	W Rhodes	v Australia at Melbourne	1903-04
14-99	AV Bedser	v Australia at Nottingham	1953
14-102	W Bates	v Australia at Melbourne	1882-83
14-144	SF Barnes	v South Africa at Durban	1913-14

Barnes took ten or more wickets in a match a record seven
times for England

Hat-tricks

W Bates	v Australia at Melbourne	1882-83
J Briggs	v Australia at Sydney	1891-92
GA Lohmann	v SA at Port Elizabeth	1895-96
JT Hearne	v Australia at Leeds	1899
MJC Allom	v NZ at Christchurch	1929-30
TWJ Goddard	v SA at Johannesburg	1938-39
PJ Loader	v West Indies at Leeds	1957
DG Cork	v West Indies at Manchester	1995
D Gough	v Australia at Sydney	1998-99
MJ Hoggard	v West Indies at Bridgetown	2003-04

Allom was playing in his first match, and went on to
take four wickets in five balls

England's Test match results

	Played	Won	Lost	Drawn	Tied	% win
v Australia	311	97	126	88	0	31.18
v Bangladesh	4	4	0	0	0	100.00
v India	94	34	17	43	0	36.17
v New Zealand	88	41	7	40	0	46.59
v Pakistan	67	19	12	36	0	28.35
v South Africa	130	54	26	50	0	41.53
v Sri Lanka	18	8	5	5	0	44.44
v West Indies	134	38	52	44	0	28.35
v Zimbabwe	6	3	0	3	0	50.00
TOTAL	852	298	245	309	0	34.97

Updated records can be found at **www.cricinfo.com/db/stats/eng**

ENGLAND
One-day International Records

Most appearances

170	AJ Stewart
158	D Gough
125	GA Gooch
123	ME Trescothick
122	AJ Lamb
120	GA Hick
116	IT Botham
114	DI Gower
103	PAJ DeFreitas
100	PD Collingwood
100	NV Knight

A Flintoff has played 99 ODIs for England and 3 for the World XI

Most runs

		Avge
4677	AJ Stewart	31.60
4335	ME Trescothick	37.37
4290	GA Gooch	36.98
4010	AJ Lamb	39.31
3846	GA Hick	37.33
3637	NV Knight	40.41
3170	DI Gower	30.77
2573	A Flintoff	34.30
2419	RA Smith	39.01
2380	GP Thorpe	37.18

N Hussain (2332), PD Collingwood (2251), IT Botham (2113), MW Gatting (2095) and NH Fairbrother (2092) also reached 2000 runs

Most wickets

		Avge
234	D Gough	26.29
145	IT Botham	28.54
115	PAJ DeFreitas	32.82
109	A Flintoff	24.65
80	RGD Willis	24.60
76	JE Emburey	30.86
75	JM Anderson	26.29
69	AR Caddick	28.47
67	MA Ealham	32.79
66	CC Lewis	29.42

Seven further bowlers have taken 50 wickets

Highest scores

167*	RA Smith	v Australia at Birmingham	1993
158	DI Gower	v New Zealand at Brisbane	1982-83
152	AJ Strauss	v Bangladesh at Nottingham	2005
142*	CWJ Athey	v New Zealand at Manchester	1986
142	GA Gooch	v Pakistan at Karachi	1987-88
137	DL Amiss	v India at Lord's	1975
137	ME Trescothick	v Pakistan at Lord's	2001
136	GA Gooch	v Australia at Lord's	1989
131	KWR Fletcher	v New Zealand at Nottingham	1975
130	DI Gower	v Sri Lanka at Taunton	1983
130	ME Trescothick	v West Indies at Gros Islet	2003-04

Trescothick has scored 12 centuries in ODIs, Gooch 8 and Gower 7

Best innings bowling

6-31	PD Collingwood	v B'desh at Nottingham	2005
5-15	MA Ealham	v Zim at Kimberley	1999-2000
5-20	VJ Marks	v NZ at Wellington	1983-84
5-21	C White	v Zim at Bulawayo	1999-2000
5-26	RC Irani	v India at The Oval	2002
5-31	M Hendrick	v Australia at The Oval	1980
5-32	MA Ealham	v Sri Lanka at Perth	1998-99
5-33	GA Hick	v Zim at Harare	1999-2000
5-33	SJ Harmison	v Australia at Bristol	2005
5-35	PW Jarvis	v India at Bangalore	1992-93

Collingwood also scored 112 in the same match.*
All Ealham's 5 wickets at Kimberley were lbw, an ODI record

Record wicket partnerships

1st	200	ME Trescothick (114*) and VS Solanki (106)	v South Africa at The Oval	2003
2nd	202	GA Gooch (117*) and DI Gower (102)	v Australia at Lord's	1985
3rd	213	GA Hick (86*) and NH Fairbrother (113)	v West Indies at Lord's	1991
4th	226	AJ Strauss (100) and A Flintoff (123)	v West Indies at Lord's	2004
5th	174	A Flintoff (99) and PD Collingwood (79*)	v India at The Oval	2004
6th	150	MP Vaughan (90*) and GO Jones (80)	v Zimbabwe at Bulawayo	2004-05
7th	110	PD Collingwood (100) and C White (48)	v Sri Lanka at Perth	2002-03
8th	67	BC Hollioake (53) and D Gough (40*)	v Pakistan at Leeds	2001
9th	100	LE Plunkett (56) and VS Solanki (39*)	v Pakistan at Lahore	2005-06
10th	50*	D Gough (46*) and SJ Harmison (11*)	v Australia at Chester-le-Street	2005

Updated records can be found at **www.cricinfo.com/db/stats/eng**

Most catches

Fielders

64	GA Hick	
54	PD Collingwood	
49	ME Trescothick	
45	GA Gooch	
44	DI Gower/NV Knight	

Most dismissals

Wicketkeepers		*Ct/St*
163	AJ Stewart	148/15
72	GO Jones	68/4
47	RC Russell	41/6
42	CMW Read	40/2
32	RW Taylor	26/6

Highest team totals

391-4	v Bangladesh at Nottingham	2005
363-7	v Pakistan at Nottingham	1992
334-4	v India at Lord's	1975
333-9	v Sri Lanka at Taunton	1983
327-4	v Pakistan at Lahore	2005-06
325-5	v India at Lord's	2002
322-6	v New Zealand at The Oval	1983
321-7	v Sri Lanka at Leeds	2006
320-8	v Australia at Birmingham	1980
307-5	v India at The Oval	2004

England have reached 300 on six other occasions

Lowest team totals

Completed innings

86	v Australia at Manchester	2001
88	v SL at Dambulla	2003-04
89	v NZ at Wellington	2001-02
93	v Australia at Leeds	1975
94	v Aust at Melbourne	1978-79
101	v NZ at Chester-le-Street	2004
103	v SA at The Oval	1999
107	v Zim at Cape Town	1999-2000
110	v Aust at Melbourne	1998-99
111	v SA at Jo'burg	1999-2000

The lowest totals against England are 45 by Canada at Manchester in 1979, and 70 by Australia at Birmingham in 1977

Most sixes

84	A Flintoff*	
44	IT Botham	
41	GA Hick	
41	ME Trescothick	
33	KP Pietersen*	
30	AJ Lamb	
26	AJ Stewart	
24	PD Collingwood	
22	DI Gower	
22	RA Smith	

*Also hit one six for the World XI

Best strike rate

Runs per 100 balls		*Runs*
96.25	KP Pietersen	1364
89.55	A Flintoff	2573
85.21	ME Trescothick	4335
83.84	PAJ DeFreitas	690
79.11	IT Botham	2113
78.21	GO Jones	815
78.13	AJ Strauss	1847
75.55	AJ Lamb	4010
75.45	JE Emburey	501
75.15	DI Gower	3170

Qualification: 500 runs

Most economical bowlers

Runs per over		*Wkts*
3.28	RGD Willis	80
3.54	ARC Fraser	47
3.79	GR Dilley	48
3.84	AD Mullally	63
3.96	IT Botham	145
3.96	PAJ DeFreitas	115
4.01	AR Caddick	69
4.08	MA Ealham	67
4.10	JE Emburey	76
4.17	GC Small	58

Qualification: 2000 balls bowled

England's one-day international results

	Played	Won	Lost	Tied	No result	% win
v Australia	85	34	47	2	2	41.97
v Bangladesh	7	7	0	0	0	100.00
v India	57	26	29	0	2	47.27
v New Zealand	54	25	25	1	3	50.00
v Pakistan	63	35	26	0	2	57.37
v South Africa	34	11	21	1	1	34.37
v Sri Lanka	37	19	18	0	0	51.35
v West Indies	70	29	37	0	4	43.93
v Zimbabwe	30	21	8	0	1	72.41
v others (see below)	8	8	0	0	0	100.00
TOTAL	**445**	**215**	**211**	**4**	**15**	**50.46**

Other teams: Canada (P1, W1), East Africa (P1, W1), Ireland (P1, W1), Kenya (P1, W1), Namibia (P1, W1), Netherlands (P2, W2), United Arab Emirates (P1, W1).

INDIA
Test Match Records

Most appearances

132	SR Tendulkar
131	Kapil Dev
125	SM Gavaskar
116	DB Vengsarkar
110	A Kumble
103	R Dravid
99	M Azharuddin
91	GR Viswanath
88	SC Ganguly
88	SMH Kirmani

Gavaskar played 106 consecutive matches between 1974-75 and 1986-87

Most runs

		Avge
10469	SR Tendulkar	55.39
10122	SM Gavaskar	51.12
9026	R Dravid	59.38
6868	DB Vengsarkar	42.13
6215	M Azharuddin	45.03
6080	GR Viswanath	41.93
5248	Kapil Dev	31.05
5221	SC Ganguly	40.78
4698	VVS Laxman	42.70
4378	M Amarnath	42.50

Tendulkar has scored 35 centuries, Gavaskar 34, Dravid 23

Most wickets

		Avge
533	A Kumble	28.75
434	Kapil Dev	29.64
266	BS Bedi	29.74
242	BS Chandrasekhar	29.74
238	Harbhajan Singh	29.86
236	J Srinath	30.49
189	EAS Prasanna	30.38
162	MH Mankad	32.32
156	S Venkataraghavan	36.11
151	RJ Shastri	40.96

In all 15 Indians have reached 100 wickets

Highest scores

309	V Sehwag	v Pakistan at Multan	2003-04
281	VVS Laxman	v Australia at Kolkata	2000-01
270	R Dravid	v Pakistan at Rawalpindi	2003-04
254	V Sehwag	v Pakistan at Lahore	2005-06
248*	SR Tendulkar	v Bangladesh at Dhaka	2004-05
241*	SR Tendulkar	v Australia at Sydney	2003-04
236*	SM Gavaskar	v West Indies at Madras	1983-84
233	R Dravid	v Australia at Adelaide	2003-04
231	MH Mankad	v New Zealand at Madras	1955-56
227	VG Kambli	v Zimbabwe at Delhi	1992-93

Dravid has scored five double-centuries, Gavaskar and Tendulkar four

Best innings bowling

10-74	A Kumble	v Pakistan at Delhi	1998-99
9-69	JM Patel	v Australia at Kanpur	1959-60
9-83	Kapil Dev	v WI at Ahmedabad	1983-84
9-102	SP Gupte	v WI at Kanpur	1958-59
8-52	MH Mankad	v Pakistan at Delhi	1952-53
8-55	MH Mankad	v England at Madras	1951-52
8-61	ND Hirwani	v WI at Madras	1987-88
8-72	S Venkataraghavan	v NZ at Delhi	1964-65
8-75	ND Hirwani	v WI at Madras	1987-88
8-76	EAS Prasanna	v NZ at Auckland	1975-76

Hirwani's two performances were in the same match, his Test debut

Record wicket partnerships

1st	413	MH Mankad (231) and P Roy (173)	v New Zealand at Madras	1955-56
2nd	344*	SM Gavaskar (182*) and DB Vengsarkar (157*)	v West Indies at Calcutta	1978-79
3rd	336	V Sehwag (309) and SR Tendulkar (194*)	v Pakistan at Multan	2003-04
4th	353	SR Tendulkar (241*) and VVS Laxman (178)	v Australia at Sydney	2003-04
5th	376	VVS Laxman (281) and R Dravid (180)	v Australia at Calcutta	2000-01
6th	298*	DB Vengsarkar (164*) and RJ Shastri (121*)	v Australia at Bombay	1986-87
7th	235	RJ Shastri (142) and SMH Kirmani (102)	v England at Bombay	1984-85
8th	161	M Azharuddin (109) and A Kumble (88)	v South Africa at Calcutta	1996-97
9th	149	PG Joshi (52*) and RB Desai (85)	v Pakistan at Bombay	1960-61
10th	133	SR Tendulkar (248*) and Z Khan (75)	v Bangladesh at Dhaka	2004-05

Updated records can be found at **www.cricinfo.com/db/stats/ind**

Test Match Records

Most catches

Fielders

145	R Dravid	
108	SM Gavaskar	
105	M Azharuddin	
82	SR Tendulkar	
81	VVS Laxman	

Most dismissals

Wicketkeepers		Ct/St
198	SMH Kirmani	160/38
130	KS More	110/20
107	NR Mongia	99/8
82	FM Engineer	66/16
51	NS Tamhane	35/16

Highest team totals

705-7d	v Australia at Sydney	2003-04
676-7	v Sri Lanka at Kanpur	1986-87
675-5d	v Pakistan at Multan	2003-04
657-7d	v Australia at Kolkata	2000-01
644-7d	v West Indies at Kanpur	1978-79
633-5d	v Australia at Kolkata	1997-98
628-8d	v England at Leeds	2002
609-6d	v Zimbabwe at Nagpur	2000-01
606-9d	v England at The Oval	1990
603	v Pakistan at Faisalabad	2005-06

India reached 600 on two other occasions

Lowest team totals

Completed innings

42*	v England at Lord's	1974
58	v Australia at Brisbane	1947-48
58	v England at Manchester	1952
66	v SA at Durban	1996-97
67	v Aust at Melbourne	1947-48
75	v West Indies at Delhi	1987-88
81*	v NZ at Wellington	1975-76
81	v WI at Bridgetown	1996-97
82	v England at Manchester	1952
83*	v England at Madras	1976-77
83	v NZ at Mohali	1999-2000

*One or more batsmen absent.

Best match bowling

16-136	ND Hirwani	v West Indies at Madras	1987-88
15-217	Harbhajan Singh	v Australia at Chennai	2000-01
14-124	JM Patel	v Australia at Kanpur	1959-60
14-149	A Kumble	v Pakistan at Delhi	1998-99
13-131	MH Mankad	v Pakistan at Delhi	1952-53
13-132	J Srinath	v Pakistan at Calcutta	1998-99
13-181	A Kumble	v Australia at Chennai	2004-05
13-196	Harbhajan Singh	v Australia at Kolkata	2000-01
12-104	BS Chandrasekhar	v Australia at Melbourne	1977-78
12-108	MH Mankad	v England at Madras	1951-52

Hirwani's feat was on his Test debut

Hat-tricks

Harbhajan Singh v Australia at Kolkata 2000-01

The wickets of RT Ponting, AC Gilchrist and SK Warne, as India fought back to win after following on.

IK Pathan v Pakistan at Karachi 2005-06

Salman Butt, Younis Khan and Mohammad Yousuf with the fourth, fifth and sixth balls of the match – Pakistan still won the match by 341 runs.

India have never conceded a hat-trick in a Test match

India's Test match results

	Played	Won	Lost	Drawn	Tied	% win
v Australia	68	15	32	20	1	22.38
v Bangladesh	3	3	0	0	0	100.00
v England	94	17	34	43	0	18.08
v New Zealand	44	14	9	21	0	31.81
v Pakistan	56	8	12	36	0	14.28
v South Africa	16	3	7	6	0	18.75
v Sri Lanka	26	10	3	13	0	38.46
v West Indies	82	11	30	41	0	13.41
v Zimbabwe	11	7	2	2	0	63.63
TOTAL	**400**	**88**	**129**	**182**	**1**	**22.00**

INDIA

Most appearances

363	SR Tendulkar
334	M Azharuddin
289	R Dravid
278	SC Ganguly
262	A Kumble
229	J Srinath
225	Kapil Dev
196	A Jadeja
165	AB Agarkar
161	BKV Prasad

Robin Singh played 136 ODIs for India – but only one Test match

Most runs

		Avge
14148	SR Tendulkar	44.21
10101	SC Ganguly	40.72
9416	R Dravid	40.24
9378	M Azharuddin	36.92
5359	A Jadeja	37.47
4435	V Sehwag	32.85
4413	NS Sidhu	37.08
4232	Yuvraj Singh	35.26
4091	K Srikkanth	29.01
3783	Kapil Dev	23.79

DB Vengsarkar (3508), RJ Shastri (3108) and SM Gavaskar (3092) also reached 3000 runs

Most wickets

		Avge
326	A Kumble	30.70
315	J Srinath	28.08
253	Kapil Dev	27.45
252	AB Agarkar	27.15
196	BKV Prasad	32.30
157	M Prabhakar	28.87
154	Harbhajan Singh	31.19
144	Zaheer Khan	29.08
142	SR Tendulkar	43.61
129	RJ Shastri	36.04

IK Pathan (109) has also reached 100 wickets

Highest scores

186*	SR Tendulkar	v NZ at Hyderabad	1999-2000
183*	MS Dhoni	v Sri Lanka at Jaipur	2005-06
183	SC Ganguly	v Sri Lanka at Taunton	1999
175*	Kapil Dev	v Zimbabwe at Tunbridge Wells	1983
159*	D Mongia	v Zimbabwe at Guwahati	2001-02
153*	M Azharuddin	v Zimbabwe at Cuttack	1997-98
153*	SC Ganguly	v New Zealand at Gwalior	1999-2000
153	R Dravid	v NZ at Hyderabad	1999-2000
152	SR Tendulkar	v Nam at Pietermaritzburg	2002-03
148	MS Dhoni	v Pakistan at Visakhapatnam	2004-05

Tendulkar (39) and Ganguly (22) head the overall list for most centuries in ODIs

Best bowling figures

6-12	A Kumble	v West Indies at Calcutta	1993-94
6-23	A Nehra	v England at Durban	2002-03
6-42	AB Agarkar	v Australia at Melbourne	2003-04
6-55	S Sreesanth	v England at Indore	2005-06
6-59	A Nehra	v Sri Lanka at Colombo	2005
5-6	SB Joshi	v South Africa at Nairobi	1999-2000
5-15	RJ Shastri	v Australia at Perth	1991-92
5-16	SC Ganguly	v Pakistan at Toronto	1997-98
5-21	Arshad Ayub	v Pakistan at Dhaka	1988-89
5-21	N Chopra	v West Indies at Toronto	1999-2000

AB Agarkar has taken four wickets in an ODI innings nine times, A Kumble eight and J Srinath 7

Record wicket partnerships

1st	258	SC Ganguly (111) and SR Tendulkar (146)	v Kenya at Paarl	2001-02
2nd	331	SR Tendulkar (186*) and R Dravid (153)	v New Zealand at Hyderabad	1999-2000
3rd	237*	R Dravid (104*) and SR Tendulkar (140*)	v Kenya at Bristol	1999
4th	275*	M Azharuddin (153*) and A Jadeja (116*)	v Zimbabwe at Cuttack	1997-98
5th	223	M Azharuddin (111*) and A Jadeja (119)	v Sri Lanka at Colombo	1997-98
6th	158	Yuvraj Singh (120) and MS Dhoni (67*)	v Zimbabwe at Harare	2005-06
7th	102	HK Badani (60*) and AB Agarkar (53)	v Australia at Melbourne	2003-04
8th	82*	Kapil Dev (72*) and KS More (42*)	v New Zealand at Bangalore	1987-88
9th	126*	Kapil Dev (175*) and SMH Kirmani (24*)	v Zimbabwe at Tunbridge Wells	1983
10th	64	Harbhajan Singh (41*) and L Balaji (18)	v England at The Oval	2004

Updated records can be found at **www.cricinfo.com/db/stats/ind**

Most catches

Fielders

156	M Azharuddin
107	SR Tendulkar
102	R Dravid
96	SC Ganguly
84	A Kumble

Most dismissals

Wicketkeepers		*Ct/St*
154	NR Mongia	110/44
90	KS More	63/27
86	R Dravid	72/14
53	MS Dhoni	44/9
36	SMH Kirmani	27/9

Highest team totals

376-2	v NZ at Hyderabad	1999-2000
373-6	v Sri Lanka at Taunton	1999
356-9	v Pakistan at Visakhapatnam	2004-05
353-5	v New Zealand at Hyderabad	2003-04
351-3	v Kenya at Paarl	2001-02
350-6	v Sri Lanka at Nagpur	2005-06
349-7	v Pakistan at Karachi	2003-04
348-5	v Bangladesh at Dhaka	2004-05
333-6	v Zimbabwe at Guwahati	2001-02
329-2	v Kenya at Bristol	1999

All scored in 50 overs

Lowest team totals

Completed innings

54	v Sri Lanka at Sharjah	2000-01
63	v Australia at Sydney	1980-81
78	v Sri Lanka at Kanpur	1986-87
79	v Pakistan at Sialkot	1978-79
100	v WI at Ahmedabad	1993-94
100	v Australia at Sydney	1999-2000
108	v NZ at Auckland	2002-03
108	v NZ at Christchurch	2002-03
112	v Pakistan at Lahore	1989-90
113	v New Zealand at Perth	1985-86

The lowest score against India is Zimbabwe's 65 at Harare in 2005-06

Most sixes

168	SC Ganguly
149	SR Tendulkar
85	A Jadeja
77	M Azharuddin
67	Kapil Dev
61	V Sehwag
48	Yuvraj Singh
45	MS Dhoni
44	NS Sidhu
41	K Srikkanth
41	Robin Singh

Best strike rate

Runs per 100 balls		*Runs*
100.96	MS Dhoni	1467
96.92	V Sehwag	4435
95.07	Kapil Dev	3783
89.43	SB Joshi	584
86.63	Yuvraj Singh	4232
85.97	SR Tendulkar	14148
84.25	AB Agarkar	1166
83.89	Harbhajan Singh	604
83.54	SM Patil	1005
80.49	IK Pathan	858

Qualification: 500 runs

Most economical bowlers

Runs per over		*Wkts*
3.71	Kapil Dev	253
3.95	Maninder Singh	66
4.05	Madan Lal	73
4.11	Harbhajan Singh	154
4.21	RJ Shastri	129
4.27	M Prabhakar	157
4.29	A Kumble	326
4.33	M Amarnath	46
4.36	SLV Raju	63
4.44	SB Joshi	69
4.44	J Srinath	315

Qualification: 2000 balls bowled

India's one-day international results

	Played	Won	Lost	Tied	No result	% win
v Australia	80	27	49	0	4	35.52
v Bangladesh	14	13	1	0	0	92.85
v England	57	29	26	0	2	52.72
v New Zealand	75	36	35	0	4	50.70
v Pakistan	108	40	64	0	4	38.46
v South Africa	50	18	30	0	2	37.50
v Sri Lanka	90	47	35	0	8	57.31
v West Indies	83	31	50	1	1	38.27
v Zimbabwe	49	39	8	2	0	82.97
v others (see below)	18	16	2	0	0	88.88
TOTAL	624	296	300	3	25	49.66

Other teams: East Africa (P1, W1), Kenya (P13, W11, L2), Namibia (P1, W1), Netherlands (P1, W1), United Arab Emirates (P2, W2).

NEW ZEALAND *Test Match Records*

Most appearances

102	SP Fleming
86	RJ Hadlee
82	JG Wright
79	NJ Astle
78	AC Parore
77	MD Crowe
70	DL Vettori
63	IDS Smith
62	CL Cairns
61	BE Congdon

Vettori also played one Test for the World XI against Australia in October 2005

Most runs

		Avge
6545	SP Fleming	40.15
5444	MD Crowe	45.36
5334	JG Wright	37.82
4650	NJ Astle	37.80
3448	BE Congdon	32.22
3428	JR Reid	33.28
3320	CL Cairns	33.53
3124	RJ Hadlee	27.16
3116	CD McMillan	38.46
2991	GM Turner	44.64

Fleming has reached 50 on 50 occasions, but has gone on to 100 only nine times: Crowe holds the NZ record with 17 Test centuries

Most wickets

		Avge
431	RJ Hadlee	22.29
218	CL Cairns	29.40
218	DL Vettori	34.61
160	DK Morrison	34.68
130	BL Cairns	32.92
123	EJ Chatfield	32.17
116	RO Collinge	29.25
111	BR Taylor	26.60
102	JG Bracewell	35.81
100	RC Motz	31.48

CS Martin currently has 99 Test wickets – and just 48 runs from 31 matches.
Vettori also took one wicket for the World XI

Highest scores

299	MD Crowe	v Sri Lanka at Wellington	1990-91
274*	SP Fleming	v Sri Lanka at Colombo	2002-03
267*	BA Young	v Sri Lanka at Dunedin	1996-97
262	SP Fleming	v South Africa at Cape Town	2005-06
259	GM Turner	v West Indies at Georgetown	1971-72
239	GT Dowling	v India at Christchurch	1967-68
230*	B Sutcliffe	v India at Delhi	1955-56
224	L Vincent	v Sri Lanka at Wellington	2004-05
223*	GM Turner	v West Indies at Kingston	1971-72
222	NJ Astle	v England at Christchurch	2001-02

There have been four other double-centuries: two by MS Sinclair and one each by MP Donnelly and SP Fleming

Best innings bowling

9-52	RJ Hadlee	v Australia at Brisbane	1985-86
7-23	RJ Hadlee	v India at Wellington	1975-76
7-27	CL Cairns	v West Indies at Hamilton	1999-2000
7-52	C Pringle	v Pakistan at Faisalabad	1990-91
7-53	CL Cairns	v Bangladesh at Hamilton	2001-02
7-65	SB Doull	v India at Wellington	1998-99
7-74	BR Taylor	v West Indies at Bridgetown	1971-72
7-74	BL Cairns	v England at Leeds	1983
7-87	SL Boock	v Pakistan at Hyderabad	1984-85
7-87	DL Vettori	v Australia at Auckland	1999-2000

Hadlee took five or more wickets in an innings on 36 occasions: the next-best for NZ is 13, by CL Cairns

Record wicket partnerships

1st	387	GM Turner (259) and TW Jarvis (182)	v West Indies at Georgetown	1971-72
2nd	241	JG Wright (116) and AH Jones (143)	v England at Wellington	1991-92
3rd	467	AH Jones (186) and MD Crowe (299)	v Sri Lanka at Wellington	1990-91
4th	243	MJ Horne (157) and NJ Astle (114)	v Zimbabwe at Auckland	1997-98
5th	222	NJ Astle (141) and CD McMillan (142)	v Zimbabwe at Wellington	2000-01
6th	246*	JJ Crowe (120*) and RJ Hadlee (151*)	v Sri Lanka at Colombo	1986-87
7th	225	CL Cairns (158) and JDP Oram (90)	v South Africa at Auckland	2003-04
8th	256	SP Fleming (262) and JEC Franklin (122*)	v South Africa at Cape Town	2005-06
9th	136	IDS Smith (173) and MC Snedden (22)	v India at Auckland	1989-90
10th	151	BF Hastings (110) and RO Collinge (68*)	v Pakistan at Auckland	1972-73

Updated records can be found at **www.cricinfo.com/db/stats/nz**

Most catches

Fielders

152	SP Fleming	
71	MD Crowe	
69	NJ Astle	
64	JV Coney	
54	BA Young	

Most dismissals

Wicketkeepers   *Ct/St*

204	AC Parore	197/7
176	IDS Smith	168/8
96	KJ Wadsworth	92/4
61	BB McCullum	56/5
59	WK Lees	52/7

Highest team totals

671-4	v Sri Lanka at Wellington	1990-91
630-6d	v India at Chandigarh	2003-04
595	v South Africa at Auckland	2003-04
593-8d	v South Africa at Cape Town	2005-06
586-7d	v Sri Lanka at Dunedin	1996-97
563	v Pakistan at Hamilton	2003-04
561	v Sri Lanka at Napier	2004-05
553-7d	v Australia at Brisbane	1985-86
551-9d	v England at Lord's	1973
545-6d	v Bangladesh at Chittagong	2004-05

671-4 is the record score in any team's second innings in a Test match

Lowest team totals

Completed innings

26	v England at Auckland	1954-55
42	v Aust at Wellington	1945-46
47	v England at Lord's	1958
54	v Australia at Wellington	1945-46
65	v Eng at Christchurch	1970-71
67	v England at Leeds	1958
67	v England at Lord's	1978
70	v Pakistan at Dacca	1955-56
73	v Pakistan at Lahore	2001-02
74	v WI at Dunedin	1955-56
74	v England at Lord's	1958

26 is the lowest total by any team in a Test match

Best match bowling

15-123	RJ Hadlee	v Australia at Brisbane	1985-86
12-149	DL Vettori	v Australia at Auckland	1999-2000
12-170	DL Vettori	v Bangladesh at Chittagong	2004-05
11-58	RJ Hadlee	v India at Wellington	1975-76
11-102	RJ Hadlee	v West Indies at Dunedin	1979-80
11-152	C Pringle	v Pakistan at Faisalabad	1990-91
11-155	RJ Hadlee	v Australia at Perth	1985-86
11-169	DJ Nash	v England at Lord's	1994
11-180	CS Martin	v South Africa at Auckland	2003-04
10-88	RJ Hadlee	v India at Bombay	1988-89

Hadlee took 33 wickets at 12.15 in the three-Test series in Australia in 1985-86

Hat-tricks

PJ Petherick	v Pakistan at Lahore	1976-77
JEC Franklin	v Bangladesh at Dhaka	2004-05

*Petherick's hat-trick was on Test debut: he dismissed Javed Miandad (who had made 163 on **his** debut), Wasim Raja and Intikhab Alam. Petherick won only five more Test caps.*

Franklin is one of only four men to have scored a century and taken a hat-trick in Tests: the others are J Briggs of England, and Abdul Razzaq and Wasim Akram of Pakistan.

The only man to take a Test hat-trick against New Zealand is MJC Allom of England at Christchurch in 1929-30: it was his Test debut, and he took four wickets in five balls in all

New Zealand's Test match results

	Played	Won	Lost	Drawn	Tied	% win
v Australia	46	7	22	17	0	15.21
v Bangladesh	4	4	0	0	0	100.00
v England	88	7	41	40	0	7.95
v India	44	9	14	21	0	20.45
v Pakistan	45	6	21	18	0	13.33
v South Africa	33	4	18	11	0	12.12
v Sri Lanka	22	8	4	10	0	36.36
v West Indies	35	9	10	16	0	25.71
v Zimbabwe	13	7	0	6	0	53.84
TOTAL	**330**	**61**	**130**	**139**	**0**	**18.48**

NEW ZEALAND *One-day International Records*

Most appearances

252	SP Fleming	
250	CZ Harris	
214	CL Cairns	
212	NJ Astle	
179	AC Parore	
175	CD McMillan	
169	DL Vettori	
149	JG Wright	
143	MD Crowe	
121	GR Larsen	
121	KR Rutherford	

Fleming (1), Cairns (1) and Vettori (4) have also played in official ODIs for the World XI

Most runs

		Avge
7154	SP Fleming	32.08
6890	NJ Astle	35.69
4881	CL Cairns	29.22
4704	MD Crowe	38.55
4379	CZ Harris	29.00
4148	CD McMillan	27.47
3891	JG Wright	26.46
3314	AC Parore	25.68
3143	KR Rutherford	29.65
2784	AH Jones	35.69

Astle has scored 16 centuries: Fleming is next with six. Fleming also scored 30 runs and Cairns 69 for the World XI

Most wickets

		Avge
203	CZ Harris	37.50
200	CL Cairns	32.78
159	DL Vettori	34.14
158	RJ Hadlee	21.56
140	EJ Chatfield	25.84
126	DK Morrison	27.53
114	MC Snedden	28.39
113	GR Larsen	35.39
106	SB Styris	31.74
103	C Pringle	23.87

NJ Astle currently has 99 wickets. Vettori also took eight wickets, and Cairns one, for the World XI

Highest scores

172	L Vincent	v Zimbabwe at Bulawayo	2005-06
171*	GM Turner	v East Africa at Birmingham	1975
145*	NJ Astle	v USA at The Oval	2004
141	SB Styris	v Sri Lanka at Bloemfontein	2002-03
140	GM Turner	v Sri Lanka at Auckland	1982-83
134*	SP Fleming	v SA at Johannesburg	2002-03
130	CZ Harris	v Australia at Madras	1995-96
122*	NJ Astle	v England at Dunedin	2001-02
120	NJ Astle	v Zimbabwe at Auckland	1995-96
120	NJ Astle	v India at Rajkot	1999-2000

Turner's 171 was the highest individual score in the first World Cup*

Best bowling figures

6-19	SE Bond	v India at Bulawayo	2005-06
6-23	SE Bond	v Australia at Port Elizabeth	2002-03
6-25	SB Styris	v West Indies at Port-of-Spain	2001-02
5-22	MN Hart	v West Indies at Margao	1994-95
5-22	AR Adams	v India at Queenstown	2002-03
5-23	RO Collinge	v India at Christchurch	1975-76
5-25	RJ Hadlee	v Sri Lanka at Bristol	1983
5-25	SE Bond	v Australia at Adelaide	2001-02
5-26	RJ Hadlee	v Australia at Sydney	1980-81
5-26	JDP Oram	v India at Auckland	2002-03

In all Hadlee took five wickets in an ODI on five occasions

Record wicket partnerships

1st	204	L Vincent (172) and SP Fleming (93)	v Zimbabwe at Bulawayo	2005-06
2nd	156	L Vincent (102) and NJ Astle (81)	v West Indies at Napier	2005-06
3rd	181	AC Parore (96) and KR Rutherford (108)	v India at Baroda	1994-95
4th	168	LK Germon (89) and CZ Harris (130)	v Australia at Chennai	1995-96
5th	148	RG Twose (80*) and CL Cairns (60)	v Australia at Cardiff	1999
6th	130	KJ Wadsworth (104) and BE Congdon (49*)	v Australia at Christchurch	1973-74
7th	115	AC Parore (78) and LK Germon (52)	v Pakistan at Sharjah	1996-97
8th	79	SB Styris (63) and DL Vettori (47)	v Zimbabwe at Harare	2005-06
9th	74*	BB McCullum (50*) and DL Vettori (23*)	v Australia at Christchurch	2005-06
10th	65	MC Snedden (40) and EJ Chatfield (19*)	v Sri Lanka at Derby	1983

Updated records can be found at **www.cricinfo.com/db/stats/nz**

Most catches

Fielders

115	SP Fleming	
96	CZ Harris	
80	NJ Astle	
66	CL Cairns	
66	MD Crowe	

Most dismissals

Wicketkeepers		*Ct/St*
141	AC Parore	116/25
112	BB McCullum	104/8
86	IDS Smith	81/5
38	TE Blain	37/1
30	LK Germon	21/9
30	WK Lees	28/2

Highest team totals

397-5	v Zimbabwe at Bulawayo	2005-06
349-9	v India at Rajkot	1999-2000
348-8	v India at Nagpur	1995-96
347-4	v USA at The Oval	2004
338-4	v Bangladesh at Sharjah	1989-90
332-8	v Australia at Christchurch	2005-06
324-6	v West Indies at Napier	2005-06
320	v Australia at Wellington	2005-06
309-5	v East Africa at Birmingham	1975
307-8	v Netherlands at Baroda	1995-96
307-8	v Pakistan at Wellington	2003-04

The 397-5 came from 44 overs; all the others were from 50 overs, except 332-8 (49), 320 (49.5) and 309-5 (60)

Lowest team totals

Completed innings

64	v Pakistan at Sharjah	1985-86
74	v Aust at Wellington	1981-82
74	v Pakistan at Sharjah	1989-90
94	v Aust at Christchurch	1989-90
97	v Aust at Faridabad	2003-04
105	v Aust at Auckland	2005-06
108	v Pak at Wellington	1992-93
110	v Pakistan at Auckland	1993-94
112	v Aust at Port Elizabeth	2002-03
116	v SL at Moratuwa	1983-84
116	v WI at Port-of-Spain	1984-85

The lowest score against New Zealand is 70, by Australia at Adelaide in 1985-86

Most sixes

151	CL Cairns	
83	NJ Astle	
65	CD McMillan	
49	SP Fleming	
45	SB Styris	
43	CZ Harris	
41	BL Cairns	
37	MJ Greatbatch	
36	AC Parore	
33	RG Twose	

CL Cairns also hit 2 for the World XL

Best strike rate

Runs per 100 balls		*Runs*
104.89	BL Cairns	987
99.43	IDS Smith	1055
83.77	CL Cairns	4881
78.53	DL Vettori	991
78.12	SB Styris	2503
77.87	CM Spearman	936
77.24	BB McCullum	1120
75.51	RJ Hadlee	1751
75.41	RG Twose	2717
74.93	JDP Oram	1034

Qualification: 500 runs

Most economical bowlers

Runs per over		*Wkts*
3.30	RJ Hadlee	158
3.57	EJ Chatfield	140
3.76	GR Larsen	113
4.06	BL Cairns	89
4.14	W Watson	74
4.17	DN Patel	45
4.17	JV Coney	54
4.20	DL Vettori	159
4.21	SE Bond	87
4.28	CZ Harris	203

Qualification: 2000 balls bowled

New Zealand's one-day international results

	Played	Won	Lost	Tied	No result	% win
v Australia	100	27	70	0	3	27.83
v Bangladesh	7	7	0	0	0	100.00
v England	54	25	25	1	3	50.00
v India	75	35	36	0	4	49.29
v Pakistan	77	28	47	1	1	37.33
v South Africa	45	14	27	0	4	34.14
v Sri Lanka	60	32	25	1	2	56.14
v West Indies	45	17	23	0	5	42.50
v Zimbabwe	28	19	7	1	1	73.07
v others (see below)	6	6	0	0	0	100.00
TOTAL	**497**	**210**	**260**	**4**	**23**	**44.68**

Other teams: Canada (P1, W1), East Africa (P1, W1), Netherlands (P1, W1), Scotland (P1, W1), United Arab Emirates (P1, W1), United States of America (P1, W1).

PAKISTAN
Test Match Records

Most appearances

124	Javed Miandad
112	Inzamam-ul-Haq
104	Wasim Akram
103	Salim Malik
88	Imran Khan
87	Waqar Younis
81	Wasim Bari
78	Zaheer Abbas
76	Mudassar Nazar
70	Mohammad Yousuf

Inzamam-ul-Haq also played one Test for the World XI

Most runs

		Avge
8832	Javed Miandad	52.57
8497	Inzamam-ul-Haq	51.49
5768	Salim Malik	43.69
5737	Mohammad Yousuf	53.12
5062	Zaheer Abbas	44.79
4114	Mudassar Nazar	38.09
4052	Saeed Anwar	45.52
3931	Majid Khan	38.92
3915	Hanif Mohammad	43.98
3884	Younis Khan	49.16

Mohammad Yousuf was known as Yousuf Youhana until September 2005

Most wickets

		Avge
414	Wasim Akram	23.62
373	Waqar Younis	23.56
362	Imran Khan	22.81
236	Abdul Qadir	32.80
208	Saqlain Mushtaq	29.83
185	Mushtaq Ahmed	32.97
177	Sarfraz Nawaz	32.75
171	Iqbal Qasim	28.11
169	Danish Kaneria	32.92
165	Shoaib Akhtar	25.69

Fazal Mahmood (139) and Intikhab Alam (125) also took 100 wickets

Highest scores

337	Hanif Mohammad	v WI at Bridgetown	1957-58
329	Inzamam-ul-Haq	v NZ at Lahore	2001-02
280*	Javed Miandad	v India at Hyderabad	1982-83
274	Zaheer Abbas	v Eng at Birmingham	1971
271	Javed Miandad	v NZ at Auckland	1988-89
267	Younis Khan	v India at Bangalore	2004-05
260	Javed Miandad	v England at The Oval	1987
257*	Wasim Akram	v Zim at Sheikhupura	1996-97
240	Zaheer Abbas	v England at The Oval	1974
237	Salim Malik	v Aust at Rawalpindi	1994-95

Wasim Akram's innings included 12 sixes, a record for a Test innings

Best innings bowling

9-56	Abdul Qadir	v England at Lahore	1987-88
9-86	Sarfraz Nawaz	v Australia at Melbourne	1978-79
8-58	Imran Khan	v Sri Lanka at Lahore	1981-82
8-60	Imran Khan	v India at Karachi	1982-83
8-69	Sikander Bakht	v India at Delhi	1979-80
8-164	Saqlain Mushtaq	v England at Lahore	2000-01
7-40	Imran Khan	v England at Leeds	1987
7-42	Fazal Mahmood	v India at Lucknow	1952-53
7-49	Iqbal Qasim	v Australia at Karachi	1979-80
7-52	Intikhab Alam	v NZ at Dunedin	1972-73
7-52	Imran Khan	v Eng at Birmingham	1982

Wasim Akram took five or more wickets in a Test innings on 25 occasions, Imran Khan 23

Record wicket partnerships

1st	298	Aamer Sohail (160) and Ijaz Ahmed (151)	v West Indies at Karachi	1997-98
2nd	291	Zaheer Abbas (274) and Mushtaq Mohammad (100)	v England at Birmingham	1971
3rd	451	Mudassar Nazar (231) and Javed Miandad (280*)	v India at Hyderabad	1982-83
4th	350	Mushtaq Mohammad (201) and Asif Iqbal (175)	v New Zealand at Dunedin	1972-73
5th	281	Javed Miandad (163) and Asif Iqbal (166)	v New Zealand at Lahore	1976-77
6th	269	Mohammad Yousuf (223) and Kamran Akmal (154)	v England at Lahore	2005-06
7th	308	Waqar Hasan (189) and Imtiaz Ahmed (209)	v New Zealand at Lahore	1955-56
8th	313	Wasim Akram (257*) and Saqlain Mushtaq (79)	v Zimbabwe at Sheikhupura	1996-97
9th	190	Asif Iqbal (146) and Intikhab Alam (51)	v England at The Oval	1967
10th	151	Azhar Mahmood (128*) and Mushtaq Ahmed (59)	v South Africa at Rawalpindi	1997-98

Updated records can be found at **www.cricinfo.com/db/stats/pak**

Test Match Records

PAKISTAN

Most catches

Fielders

93	Javed Miandad	
79	Inzamam-ul-Haq	
70	Majid Khan	
65	Salim Malik	
58	Mohammad Yousuf	

Most dismissals

Wicketkeepers — *Ct/St*

228	Wasim Bari	201/27
148	Moin Khan	128/20
130	Rashid Latif	119/11
106	Kamran Akmal	90/16
104	Salim Yousuf	91/13

Highest team totals

708	v England at The Oval	1987
699-5	v India at Lahore	1989-90
679-7d	v India at Lahore	2005-06
674-6	v India at Faisalabad	1984-85
657-8d	v WI at Bridgetown	1957-58
652	v India at Faisalabad	1982-83
643	v New Zealand at Lahore	2001-02
636-8d	v England at Lahore	2005-06
624	v Australia at Adelaide	1983-84
616-5d	v New Zealand at Auckland	1988-89

Pakistan have made three other scores of 600 or more

Lowest team totals

Completed innings

53*	v Australia at Sharjah	2002-03
59	v Australia at Sharjah	2002-03
62	v Australia at Perth	1981-82
72	v Australia at Perth	2004-05
77*	v West Indies at Lahore	1986-87
87	v England at Lord's	1954
90	v England at Manchester	1954
92	v SA at Faisalabad	1997-98
97*	v Australia at Brisbane	1995-96
100	v England at Lord's	1962

* One batsman retired hurt or absent hurt. The lowest two totals came in the same game

Best match bowling

14-116	Imran Khan	v Sri Lanka at Lahore	1981-82
13-101	Abdul Qadir	v England at Lahore	1987-88
13-114	Fazal Mahmood	v Australia at Karachi	1956-57
13-135	Waqar Younis	v Zimbabwe at Karachi	1993-94
12-94	Fazal Mahmood	v India at Lucknow	1952-53
12-94	Danish Kaneria	v Bangladesh at Multan	2001-02
12-99	Fazal Mahmood	v England at The Oval	1954
12-100	Fazal Mahmood	v West Indies at Dacca	1958-59
12-130	Waqar Younis	v NZ at Faisalabad	1990-91
12-165	Imran Khan	v Australia at Sydney	1976-77

Imran Khan took ten or more wickets in a match six times, Abdul Qadir, Waqar Younis and Wasim Akram five each.

Hat-tricks

Wasim Akram	v Sri Lanka at Lahore	1998-99
Wasim Akram	v Sri Lanka at Dhaka	1998-99
Abdul Razzaq	v Sri Lanka at Galle	1999-2000
Mohammad Sami	v Sri Lanka at Lahore	2001-02

Wasim Akram's hat-tricks came in successive matches: he also took Pakistan's first two hat-tricks in one-day internationals.

RS Kaluwitharana was the first victim in both Wasim Akram's first hat-trick and in Abdul Razzaq's

Pakistan's Test match results

	Played	Won	Lost	Drawn	Tied	% win
v Australia	52	11	24	17	0	21.15
v Bangladesh	6	6	0	0	0	100.00
v England	67	12	19	36	0	17.91
v India	56	12	8	36	0	21.42
v New Zealand	45	21	6	18	0	46.66
v South Africa	11	2	5	4	0	18.18
v Sri Lanka	32	15	7	10	0	46.87
v West Indies	41	13	14	14	0	31.70
v Zimbabwe	14	8	2	4	0	57.14
TOTAL	**324**	**100**	**85**	**139**	**0**	**30.86**

Updated records can be found at **www.cricinfo.com/db/stats/pak**

PAKISTAN
One-day International Records

Most appearances

364	Inzamam-ul-Haq
356	Wasim Akram
283	Salim Malik
262	Waqar Younis
250	Ijaz Ahmed
247	Saeed Anwar
233	Javed Miandad
225	Shahid Afridi
219	Mohammad Yousuf
219	Moin Khan

Abdul Razzaq (213) also played in more than 200 ODIs

Most runs

		Avge
11511	Inzamam-ul-Haq	39.83
8823	Saeed Anwar	39.21
7408	Mohammad Yousuf	41.61
7381	Javed Miandad	41.70
7170	Salim Malik	32.88
6564	Ijaz Ahmed	32.33
5841	Rameez Raja	32.09
4823	Shahid Afridi	23.64
4780	Aamer Sohail	31.86
4248	Abdul Razzaq	31.00

Younis Khan (3756), Wasim Akram (3717), Imran Khan (3709), Moin Khan (3266) and Shoaib Malik (3118) also passed 3000 runs

Most wickets

		Avge
502	Wasim Akram	23.52
416	Waqar Younis	23.84
288	Saqlain Mushtaq	21.78
235	Abdul Razzaq	30.20
202	Shoaib Akhtar	22.96
190	Shahid Afridi	35.95
182	Aqib Javed	31.43
182	Imran Khan	26.61
161	Mushtaq Ahmed	33.29
132	Abdul Qadir	26.16

Azhar Mahmood (122), Mudassar Nazar (111) and Mohammad Sami (109) also reached 100 wickets

Highest scores

194	Saeed Anwar	v India at Chennai	1996-97
144	Younis Khan	v Hong Kong at Colombo	2004
143	Shoaib Malik	v India at Colombo	2004
141*	Mohammad Yousuf	v Zim at Bulawayo	2002-03
140	Saeed Anwar	v India at Dhaka	1997-98
139*	Ijaz Ahmed	v India at Lahore	1997-98
137*	Inzamam-ul-Haq	v NZ at Sharjah	1993-94
137	Ijaz Ahmed	v England at Sharjah	1998-99
135	Salim Elahi	v SA at Port Elizabeth	2002-03
134	Aamer Sohail	v NZ at Sharjah	1993-94

Saeed Anwar scored 20 centuries, Mohammad Yousuf 11, Ijaz Ahmed and Inzamam-ul-Haq 10.

Best innings bowling

7-36	Waqar Younis	v England at Leeds	2001
7-37	Aqib Javed	v India at Sharjah	1991-92
6-14	Imran Khan	v India at Sharjah	1984-85
6-16	Shoaib Akhtar	v NZ at Karachi	2001-02
6-18	Azhar Mahmood	v WI at Sharjah	1999-2000
6-26	Waqar Younis	v SL at Sharjah	1989-90
6-27	Naved-ul-Hasan	v India at Jameshedpur	2004-05
6-30	Waqar Younis	v NZ at Auckland	1993-94
6-35	Abdul Razzaq	v Bangladesh at Dhaka	2001-02
6-44	Waqar Younis	v NZ at Sharjah	1996-97

Waqar Younis took five or more wickets in an innings 13 times, Saqlain Mushtaq and Wasim Akram 6

Record wicket partnerships

1st	204	Saeed Anwar (110) and Rameez Raja (109*)	v Sri Lanka at Sharjah	1992-93
2nd	263	Aamer Sohail (134) and Inzamam-ul-Haq (137*)	v New Zealand at Sharjah	1993-94
3rd	230	Saeed Anwar (140) and Ijaz Ahmed (117)	v India at Dhaka	1997-98
4th	172	Salim Malik (84) and Basit Ali (127*)	v West Indies at Sharjah	1993-94
5th	162	Inzamam-ul-Haq (72) and Mohammad Yousuf (88)	v Australia at Lord's	2004
6th	144	Imran Khan (102*) and Shahid Mahboob (77)	v Sri Lanka at Leeds	1983
7th	124	Mohammad Yousuf (91*) and Rashid Latif (66)	v Australia at Cardiff	2001
8th	92	Mohammad Yousuf (92) and Shoaib Akhtar (36)	v Australia at Karachi	1998-99
9th	70*	Abdul Razzaq (75*) and Naved-ul-Hasan (9*)	v England at Nottingham	2006
10th	72	Abdul Razzaq (46*) and Waqar Younis (33)	v South Africa at Durban	1997-98

Updated records can be found at **www.cricinfo.com/db/stats/pak**

One-day International Records **PAKISTAN**

Most catches

Fielders

106	Inzamam-ul-Haq	
90	Ijaz Ahmed	
88	Wasim Akram	
83	Shahid Afridi	
81	Salim Malik	

Most dismissals

Wicketkeepers   *Ct/St*

287	Moin Khan	214/73
220	Rashid Latif	182/38
103	Salim Yousuf	81/22
62	Wasim Bari	52/10
50	Kamran Akmal	44/6

Highest team totals

371-9	v Sri Lanka at Nairobi	1996-97
353-6	v England at Karachi	2005-06
344-5	v Zimbabwe at Bulawayo	2002-03
344-8	v India at Karachi	2003-04
343-5	v Hong Kong art Colombo	2004
338-5	v Sri Lanka at Swansea	1983
335-6	v South Africa at Port Elizabeth	2002-03
330-6	v Sri Lanka at Nottingham	1975
329-6	v India at Rawalpindi	2003-04
328-2	v New Zealand at Sharjah	1993-94

Pakistan have reached 300 on 28 further occasions

Lowest team totals

Completed innings

43	v WI at Cape Town	1992-93
71	v WI at Brisbane	1992-93
74	v England at Adelaide	1991-92
81	v WI at Sydney	1992-93
85	v England at Manchester	1978
87	v India at Sharjah	1984-85
108	v Australia at Nairobi	2002-03
109	v SA at Johannesburg	1994-95
113	v WI at Multan	1986-87
114	v SA at Cape Town	1997-98

Against India in 1984-85 Pakistan were chasing only 126 to win

Most sixes

214	Shahid Afridi	
139	Inzamam-ul-Haq	
121	Wasim Akram	
100	Abdul Razzaq	
97	Saeed Anwar	
87	Ijaz Ahmed	
77	Mohammad Yousuf	
61	Moin Khan	
45	Imran Khan	
44	Javed Miandad	

Afridi hit 2 other sixes in official ODIs

Best strike rate

Runs per 100 balls   *Runs*

107.68	Shahid Afridi	4823
89.60	Manzoor Elahi	741
88.29	Wasim Akram	3717
86.31	Kamran Akmal	927
84.80	Zaheer Abbas	2572
81.30	Moin Khan	3266
80.97	Abdul Razzaq	4248
80.66	Saeed Anwar	8823
80.30	Ijaz Ahmed	6564
77.98	Shoaib Malik	3118

Qualification: 500 runs

Most economical bowlers

Runs per over   *Wkts*

3.63	Sarfraz Nawaz	63
3.71	Akram Raza	38
3.89	Imran Khan	182
3.89	Wasim Akram	502
4.06	Abdul Qadir	132
4.14	Arshad Khan	56
4.14	Tauseef Ahmed	55
4.24	Mudassar Nazar	111
4.26	Mushtaq Ahmed	161
4.28	Aqib Javed	182

Qualification: 2000 balls bowled

Pakistan's one-day international results

	Played	Won	Lost	Tied	No result	% win
v Australia	74	27	43	1	3	38.57
v Bangladesh	18	17	1	0	0	94.44
v England	63	26	35	0	2	42.62
v India	108	64	40	0	4	61.53
v New Zealand	77	47	28	1	1	62.66
v South Africa	41	13	28	0	0	31.70
v Sri Lanka	106	64	38	1	3	62.74
v West Indies	105	41	62	2	0	39.80
v Zimbabwe	34	30	2	1	1	93.75
v others (see below)	15	15	0	0	0	100.00
TOTAL	**641**	**344**	**277**	**6**	**14**	**55.39**

Other teams: Canada (P1, W1), Hong Kong (P1, W1), Kenya (P5, W5), Namibia (P1, W1), Netherlands (P3, W3), Scotland (P2, W2), United Arab Emirates (P2, W2).

SOUTH AFRICA _Test Match Records_

Most appearances

102	SM Pollock	
101	JH Kallis	
101	G Kirsten	
95	MV Boucher	
79	HH Gibbs	
72	AA Donald	
70	DJ Cullinan	
69	M Ntini	
68	WJ Cronje	
52	JN Rhodes	

Kallis and Boucher also played one Test for the World XI against Australia

Most runs

		Avge
7950	JH Kallis	55.59
7289	G Kirsten	45.27
5728	HH Gibbs	44.40
4554	DJ Cullinan	44.21
3879	GC Smith	50.37
3714	WJ Cronje	36.41
3565	MV Boucher	30.47
3515	SM Pollock	31.95
3471	B Mitchell	48.88
2960	AD Nourse	53.81

Kallis (83 runs), Smith (12) and Boucher (17) also played one Test for the World XI against Australia

Most wickets

		Avge
395	SM Pollock	23.42
330	AA Donald	22.25
274	M Ntini	28.28
199	JH Kallis	31.67
170	HJ Tayfield	25.91
134	PR Adams	32.87
123	TL Goddard	26.22
116	PM Pollock	24.18
104	NAT Adcock	21.10
100	N Boje	42.65

Kallis also took one wicket for the World XI against Australia

Highest scores

277	GC Smith	v England at Birmingham	2003
275*	DJ Cullinan	v New Zealand at Auckland	1998-99
275	G Kirsten	v England at Durban	1999-2000
274	RG Pollock	v Australia at Durban	1969-70
259	GC Smith	v England at Lord's	2003
255*	DJ McGlew	v New Zealand at Wellington	1952-53
236	EAB Rowan	v England at Leeds	1951
231	AD Nourse	v Australia at Johannesburg	1935-36
228	HH Gibbs	v Pakistan at Caoe Town	2002-03
222*	JA Rudolph	v Bangladesh at Chittagong	2002-03

Smith's innings were in consecutive matches. Rudolph's was on Test debut

Best innings bowling

9-113	HJ Tayfield	v England at Johannesburg	1956-57
8-53	GB Lawrence	v NZ at Johannesburg	1961-62
8-64	L Klusener	v India at Calcutta	1996-97
8-69	HJ Tayfield	v England at Durban	1956-57
8-70	SJ Snooke	v England at Johannesburg	1905-06
8-71	AA Donald	v Zimbabwe at Harare	1995-96
7-23	HJ Tayfield	v Australia at Durban	1949-50
7-29	GF Bissett	v England at Durban	1927-28
7-37	M Ntini	v WI at Port-of-Spain	2004-05
7-63	AE Hall	v England at Cape Town	1922-23

Klusener and Hall were making their Test debuts

Record wicket partnerships

1st	368	GC Smith (151) and HH Gibbs (228)	v Pakistan at Cape Town	2002-03
2nd	315*	HH Gibbs (211*) and JH Kallis (148*)	v New Zealand at Christchurch	1998-99
3rd	429*	JA Rudolph (222*) and HH Dippenaar (177*)	v Bangladesh at Chittagong	2002-03
4th	249	JH Kallis (177) and G Kirsten (137)	v West Indies at Durban	2003-04
5th	267	JH Kallis (147) and AG Prince (131)	v West Indies at St John's	2004-05
6th	200	RG Pollock (274) and HR Lance (61)	v Australia at Durban	1969-70
7th	246	DJ McGlew (255*) and ARA Murray (109)	v New Zealand at Wellington	1952-53
8th	150	ND McKenzie (103) and SM Pollock (111)	v Sri Lanka at Centurion	2000-01
	150	G Kirsten (130) and M Zondeki (59)	v England at Leeds	2003
9th	195	MV Boucher (78) and PL Symcox (108)	v Pakistan at Johannesburg	1997-98
10th	103	HG Owen-Smith (129) and AJ Bell (26*)	v England at Leeds	1929

Updated records can be found at **www.cricinfo.com/db/stats/rsa**

Test Match Records SOUTH AFRICA

Most catches

Fielders

94	JH Kallis	
83	G Kirsten	
72	HH Gibbs	
68	SM Pollock	
67	DJ Cullinan	

Most dismissals

Wicketkeepers   *Ct/St*

362	MV Boucher	348/14
152	DJ Richardson	150/2
141	JHB Waite	124/17
59	DT Lindsay	57/2
51	HB Cameron	39/12

Highest team totals

682-6d	v England at Lord's	2003
658-9d	v West Indies at Durban	2003-04
622-9d	v Australia at Durban	1969-70
621-5d	v New Zealand at Auckland	1998-99
620-7d	v Pakistan at Cape Town	2002-03
620	v Australia at Johannesburg	1966-67
604-6d	v West Indies at Centurion	2003-04
600-3d	v Zimbabwe at Harare	2001-02
595	v Australia at Adelaide	1963-64
594-5d	v England at Birmingham	2003

The 620 was scored in the second innings

Lowest team totals

Completed innings

30	v Eng at Port Elizabeth	1895-96
30	v Eng at Birmingham	1924
35	v Eng at Cape Town	1898-99
36	v Aust at Melbourne	1931-32
43	v Eng at Cape Town	1888-89
45	v Aust at Melbourne	1931-32
47	v Eng at Cape Town	1888-89
58	v England at Lord's	1912
72	v Eng at Johannesburg	1956-57
72	v Eng at Cape Town	1956-57

South Africa's lowest total since their return to Test cricket in 1991-92 is 105 against India at Ahmedabad in 1995-96

Best match bowling

13-132	M Ntini	v WI at Port-of-Spain	2004-05
13-165	HJ Tayfield	v Australia at Melbourne	1952-53
13-192	HJ Tayfield	v England at Johannesburg	1956-57
12-127	SJ Snooke	v England at Johannesburg	1905-06
12-139	AA Donald	v India at Port Elizabeth	1992-93
12-181	AEE Vogler	v England at Johannesburg	1909-10
11-112	AE Hall	v England at Cape Town	1922-23
11-113	AA Donald	v Zimbabwe at Harare	1995-96
11-127	AA Donald	v Eng at Johannesburg	1999-2000
11-150	EP Nupen	v England at Johannesburg	1930-31

Hall was making his Test debut. His performance, and Vogler's, were at the old Wanderers ground in Johannesburg

Hat-tricks

GM Griffin	v England at Lord's	1960

Griffin achieved the feat in his second and final Test (he was no-balled for throwing in the same match).

GA Lohmann (for England at Port Elizabeth in 1895-96), TJ Matthews (twice in the same match for Australia at Manchester in 1912) and TWJ Goddard (for England at Johannesburg in 1938-39) have taken Test hat-tricks against South Africa

South Africa's Test match results

	Played	Won	Lost	Drawn	Tied	% win
v Australia	77	15	44	18	0	19.48
v Bangladesh	4	4	0	0	0	100.00
v England	130	26	54	50	0	20.00
v India	16	7	3	6	0	43.75
v New Zealand	33	18	4	11	0	54.54
v Pakistan	11	5	2	4	0	45.45
v Sri Lanka	17	8	4	5	0	47.05
v West Indies	19	12	2	5	0	63.15
v Zimbabwe	7	6	0	1	0	85.71
TOTAL	**314**	**101**	**113**	**100**	**0**	**32.16**

Updated records can be found at **www.cricinfo.com/db/stats/rsa**

SOUTH AFRICA One-day International Records

Most appearances

253	SM Pollock
245	JN Rhodes
226	JH Kallis
215	MV Boucher
188	WJ Cronje
185	HH Gibbs
185	G Kirsten
171	L Klusener
164	AA Donald
138	DJ Cullinan

Pollock (6 matches), Kallis (5) and Boucher (2) also appeared in official ODIs for composite teams

Most runs

		Avge
7966	JH Kallis	45.00
6798	G Kirsten	40.95
6117	HH Gibbs	35.77
5935	JN Rhodes	35.11
5565	WJ Cronje	38.64
3860	DJ Cullinan	32.99
3576	L Klusener	41.10
3389	GC Smith	40.34
3190	HH Dippenaar	44.92
3117	MV Boucher	26.64

Kallis (29 runs), Smith (0), Dippenaar (44) and Boucher (58) also appeared in official ODIs for composite teams

Most wickets

		Avge
342	SM Pollock	24.07
272	AA Donald	21.78
205	M Ntini	22.99
199	JH Kallis	32.42
192	L Klusener	29.95
114	WJ Cronje	34.78
95	N Boje	35.27
95	PS de Villiers	27.74
79	CR Matthews	25.00
72	PL Symcox	38.36

Pollock (6 wickets), Ntini (1), Kallis (4) and Boje (1) also appeared in official ODIs for composite teams

Highest scores

188*	G Kirsten	v UAE at Rawalpindi	1995-96
175	HH Gibbs	v Australia at Johannesburg	2005-06
169*	DJ Callaghan	v NZ at Verwoerdburg	1994-95
161	AC Hudson	v Netherlands at Rawalpindi	1995-96
153	HH Gibbs	v B'desh at Potchefstroom	2002-03
143	HH Gibbs	v NZ at Johannesburg	2002-03
139	JH Kallis	v WI at Johannesburg	2003-04
134*	GC Smith	v India at Kolkata	2005-06
133*	G Kirsten	v India at Johannesburg	2001-02
131*	ND McKenzie	v Kenya at Cape Town	2001-02

Gibbs has scored 16 one-day hundreds, Kallis and Kirsten 13

Best bowling figures

6-22	M Ntini	v Australia at Cape Town	2005-06
6-23	AA Donald	v Kenya at Nairobi	1996-97
6-35	SM Pollock	v WI at East London	1998-99
6-49	L Klusener	v Sri Lanka at Lahore	1997-98
5-20	SM Pollock	v Eng at Johannesburg	1999-2000
5-21	L Klusener	v Kenya at Amstelveen	1999
5-21	N Boje	v Australia at Cape Town	2001-02
5-24	L Klusener	v Australia at Melbourne	1997-98
5-25	L Klusener	v Pakistan at Cape Town	1997-98
5-29	AA Donald	v India at Calcutta	1991-92

Klusener has taken five wickets in an ODI innings six times, Pollock four

Record wicket partnerships

1st	235	G Kirsten (115) and HH Gibbs (111)	v India at Kochi	1999-2000
2nd	209	G Kirsten (124) and ND McKenzie (131*)	v Kenya at Cape Town	2001-02
3rd	172*	HH Gibbs (108*) and JH Kallis (64*)	v Sri Lanka at Kimberley	2002-03
4th	232	DJ Cullinan (124) and JN Rhodes (121)	v Pakistan at Nairobi	1996-97
5th	183*	JH Kallis (109*) and JN Rhodes (94*)	v Pakistan at Durban	1997-98
6th	137	WJ Cronje (70*) and SM Pollock (75)	v Zimbabwe at Johannesburg	1996-97
7th	114	MV Boucher (68) and L Klusener (75*)	v India at Nagpur	1999-2000
8th	91	DM Benkenstein (69) and L Klusener (54*)	v West Indies at Cape Town	1998-99
9th	61	SM Pollock (46) and J Botha (15*)	v Australia at Melbourne	2005-06
10th	67*	JA Morkel (23*) and M Ntini (42*)	v New Zealand at Napier	2003-04

Updated records can be found at www.cricinfo.com/db/stats/rsa

Most catches

Fielders

105	JN Rhodes	
94	SM Pollock	
90	JH Kallis	
77	HH Gibbs	
73	WJ Cronje	

Most dismissals

	Wicketkeepers	*Ct/St*
312	MV Boucher	296/16
165	DJ Richardson	148/17
9	SJ Palframan	9/0
5	N Pothas	4/1
5	ELR Stewart	5/0

Highest team totals

438-9	v Australia at Johannesburg	2005-06
363-3	v Zimbabwe at Bulawayo	2001-02
354-3	v Kenya at Cape Town	2001-02
329-6	v Zimbabwe at Durban	2004-05
328-3	v Netherlands at Rawalpindi	1995-96
326-3	v Australia at Port Elizabeth	2001-02
324-4	v New Zealand at Centurion	2000-01
321-2	v UAE at Rawalpindi	1995-96
321-8	v Pakistan at Nairobi	1996-97
320-7	v India at Nagpur	1999-2000

438-9 was the highest total in all ODIs, and came from 49.5 overs; all the others above were scored in 50 overs

Lowest team totals

Completed innings

69	v Australia at Sydney	1993-94
101*	v Pakistan at Sharjah	1999-2000
106	v Australia at Sydney	2001-02
107	v England at Lord's	2003
117	v India at Nairobi	1999-2000
123	v Aust at Wellington	1994-95
129	v Eng at East London	1995-96
149	v Eng at Jo'burg	1999-2000
152	v WI at Port-of-Spain	1991-92
153	v Pak at Port Elizabeth	2002-03

* One batsman retired hurt. SA also had 50-overs totals of 140-9 (v WI in 1992-93) and 144-9 (v Aust in 1999-2000)

Most sixes

98	JH Kallis
94	WJ Cronje
87	HH Gibbs
76	L Klusener
47	SM Pollock
47	JN Rhodes
42	MV Boucher
35	JM Kemp
33	DJ Cullinan
22	PL Symcox

Kemp also hit a six for the Africa XI

Best strike rate

Runs per 100 balls		*Runs*
92.40	JM Kemp	888
89.92	L Klusener	3576
89.30	N Boje	1410
85.83	SM Pollock	2702
83.61	PL Symcox	694
82.10	HH Gibbs	6117
81.42	AP Kuiper	539
80.91	JN Rhodes	5935
80.36	MV Boucher	3117
79.07	GC Smith	3389

Qualification: 500 runs

Most economical bowlers

Runs per over		*Wkts*
3.57	PS de Villiers	95
3.74	SM Pollock	342
3.94	CR Matthews	79
4.15	AA Donald	272
4.15	PL Symcox	72
4.28	BM McMillan	70
4.40	M Ntini	205
4.44	WJ Cronje	114
4.50	RP Snell	44
4.51	N Boje	95

Qualification: 2000 balls bowled

South Africa's one-day international results

	Played	Won	Lost	Tied	No result	% win
v Australia	65	28	34	3	0	45.16
v Bangladesh	7	7	0	0	0	100.00
v England	34	21	11	1	1	65.62
v India	50	30	18	0	2	62.50
v New Zealand	45	27	14	0	4	65.85
v Pakistan	41	28	13	0	0	68.29
v Sri Lanka	43	20	21	1	1	48.78
v West Indies	38	26	11	0	1	70.27
v Zimbabwe	21	18	2	0	1	90.00
v others (see below)	11	11	0	0	0	100.00
TOTAL	355	216	124	5	10	63.52

Other teams: Canada (P1, W1), Kenya (P8, W8), Netherlands (P1, W1), United Arab Emirates (P1, W1).

SRI LANKA
Test Match Records

Most appearances

107	M Muralitharan
105	ST Jayasuriya
94	WPUJC Vaas
93	PA de Silva
93	A Ranatunga
88	MS Atapattu
83	DPMD Jayawardene
83	HP Tillakaratne
62	KC Sangakkara
52	RS Mahanama

Ranatunga uniquely played in his country's first Test, and their 100th

Most runs

		Avge
6745	ST Jayasuriya	41.12
6361	PA de Silva	42.97
6250	DPMD Jayawardene	49.60
5330	MS Atapattu	38.90
5105	A Ranatunga	35.69
4796	KC Sangakkara	48.93
4545	HP Tillakaratne	42.87
2576	RS Mahanama	29.27
2503	WPUJC Vaas	22.75
2452	AP Gurusinha	38.92

TT Samaraweera (2089) and TM Dilshan (2054) also reached 2000 runs

Most wickets

		Avge
652	M Muralitharan	21.89
307	WPUJC Vaas	29.51
96	ST Jayasuriya	34.07
85	GP Wickremasinghe	41.87
73	RJ Ratnayake	35.10
69	HDPK Dharmasena	42.31
69	CRD Fernando	31.89
64	DNT Zoysa	33.70
62	SL Malinga	32.80
59	ALF de Mel	36.94

KR Paushpakumara (58) and JR Ratnayeke (56) also reached 50 wickets

Highest scores

374	DPMD Jayawardene	v SA at Colombo	2006
340	ST Jayasuriya	v India at Colombo	1997-98
287	KC Sangakkara	v SA at Colombo	2006
270	KC Sangakkara	v Zim at Bulawayo	2003-04
267	PA de Silva	v NZ at Wellington	1990-91
253	ST Jayasuriya	v Paki at Faisalabad	2004-05
249	MS Atapattu	v Zim at Bulawayo	2003-04
242	DPMD Jayawardene	v India at Colombo	1998-99
237	DPMD Jayawardene	v SA at Galle	2004-05
232	KC Sangakkara	v SA at Colombo	2004-05

de Silva scored 20 Test centuries, Atapattu and Jayawardene 16, Jayasuriya 14

Best innings bowling

9-51	M Muralitharan	v Zimbabwe at Kandy	2001-02
9-65	M Muralitharan	v England at The Oval	1998
8-46	M Muralitharan	v West Indies at Kandy	2005
8-70	M Muralitharan	v England at Nottingham	2006
8-83	JR Ratnayeke	v Pakistan at Sialkot	1985-86
8-87	M Muralitharan	v India at Colombo	2001-02
7-46	M Muralitharan	v England at Galle	2003-04
7-71	WPUJC Vaas	v West Indies at Colombo	2001-02
7-84	M Muralitharan	v South Africa at Galle	2000-01
7-94	M Muralitharan	v Zimbabwe at Kandy	1997-98

Muralitharan has taken five or more wickets in an innings a record 56 times

Record wicket partnerships

1st	335	MS Atapattu (207*) and ST Jayasuriya (188)	v Pakistan at Kandy	2000
2nd	576	ST Jayasuriya (340) and RS Mahanama (225)	v India at Colombo	1997-98
3rd	624	KC Sangakkara (287) and DPMD Jayawardene (374)	v South Africa at Colombo	2006
4th	240*	AP Gurusinha (116*) and A Ranatunga (135*)	v Pakistan at Colombo	1985-86
5th	280	TT Samaraweera (138) and TM Dilshan (168)	v Bangladesh at Colombo	2005-06
6th	189*	PA de Silva (143*) and A Ranatunga (87*)	v Zimbabwe at Colombo	1997-98
7th	194*	HP Tillakaratne (136*) and TT Samaraweera (103*)	v India at Colombo	2001-02
8th	170	DPMD Jayawardene (237) and WPUJC Vaas (69)	v South Africa at Galle	2004-05
9th	105	WPUJC Vaas (50*) and KMDN Kulasekera (64)	v England at Lord's	2006
10th	79	WPUJC Vaas (68*) and M Muralitharan (43)	v Australia at Kandy	2003-04

Updated records can be found at **www.cricinfo.com/db/stats/sl**

Test Match Records — **SRI LANKA**

Most catches

Fielders

111	DPMD Jayawardene	
89	HP Tillakaratne	
78	ST Jayasuriya	
57	MS Atapattu	
57	M Muralitharan	

Most dismissals

Wicketkeepers		Ct/St
144	KC Sangakkara	124/20
119	RS Kaluwitharana	93/26
35	HP Tillakaratne	33/2
34	SAR Silva	33/1
24	PB Dassanayake	19/5

Highest team totals

952-6d	v India at Colombo	1997-98
756-5d	v South Africa at Colombo	2006
713-3d	v Zimbabwe at Bulawayo	2003-04
628-8d	v England at Colombo	2003-04
627-9d	v West Indies at Colombo	2001-02
610-6d	v India at Colombo	2001-02
591	v England at The Oval	1998
590-9d	v West Indies at Galle	2001-02
586-6d	v Zimbabwe at Colombo	2001-02
555-5d	v Bangladesh at Colombo	2001-02
555-8d	v England at Lord's	2002

952-6d is the highest total in all Tests

Lowest team totals

Completed innings

71	v Pakistan at Kandy	1994-95
73*	v Pakistan at Kandy	2005-06
81	v England at Colombo	2000-01
82	v India at Chandigarh	1990-91
93	v NZ at Wellington	1982-83
95	v SA at Cape Town	2000-01
97	v NZ at Kandy	1983-84
97	v Australia at Darwin	2004
101	v Pakistan at Kandy	1985-86
109	v Pakistan at Kandy	1985-86

* One batsman absent hurt

Best match bowling

16-220	M Muralitharan	v England at The Oval	1998
14-191	WPUJC Vaas	v West Indies at Colombo	2001-02
13-115	M Muralitharan	v Zimbabwe at Kandy	2001-02
13-171	M Muralitharan	v South Africa at Galle	2000
12-117	M Muralitharan	v Zimbabwe at Kandy	1997-98
12-225	M Muralitharan	v South Africa at Colombo	2006
11-93	M Muralitharan	v England at Galle	2003-04
11-132	M Muralitharan	v England at Nottingham	2006
11-161	M Muralitharan	v South Africa at Durban	2000-01
11-170	M Muralitharan	v West Indies at Galle	2001-02

Muralitharan has taken ten or more wickets in a match a record 18 times; the only others to do it for Sri Lanka are Vaas (twice) and UDU Chandana (once)

Hat-tricks

DNT Zoysa	v Zimbabwe at Harare	1999-2000

He dismissed TR Gripper, MW Goodwin and NC Johnson with the first three balls of his first over, the second of the match.

Four hat-tricks have been taken against Sri Lanka in Tests, all of them for Pakistan: two by Wasim Akram (in successive Tests in the Asian Test Championship at Lahore and Dhaka in 1998-99), Abdul Razzaq (at Galle in 2000-01) and Mohammad Sami (at Lahore in 2001-02)

Sri Lanka's Test match results

	Played	Won	Lost	Drawn	Tied	% win
v Australia	18	1	11	6	0	5.55
v Bangladesh	7	7	0	0	0	100.00
v England	18	5	8	5	0	27.77
v India	26	3	10	13	0	11.53
v New Zealand	22	4	8	10	0	18.18
v Pakistan	32	7	15	10	0	21.87
v South Africa	17	4	8	5	0	23.52
v West Indies	10	5	2	3	0	50.00
v Zimbabwe	15	10	0	5	0	66.66
TOTAL	**165**	**46**	**62**	**57**	**0**	**27.87**

Updated records can be found at **www.cricinfo.com/db/stats/sl**

SRI LANKA
One-day International Records

Most appearances

363	ST Jayasuriya	
308	PA de Silva	
280	WPUJC Vaas	
269	M Muralitharan	
269	A Ranatunga	
253	MS Atapattu	
219	DPMD Jayawardene	
213	RS Mahanama	
200	HP Tillakaratne	
189	RS Kaluwitharana	

In all 16 Sri Lankans have played more than 100 ODIs

Most runs

		Avge
11076	ST Jayasuriya	32.76
9284	PA de Silva	34.90
8233	MS Atapattu	37.76
7456	A Ranatunga	35.84
5865	DPMD Jayawardene	32.22
5162	RS Mahanama	29.49
4715	KC Sangakkara	35.45
3902	AP Gurusinha	28.27
3789	HP Tillakaratne	29.60
3738	RP Arnold	35.26

RS Kaluwitharana (3711) also reached 3000 runs

Most wickets

		Avge
405	M Muralitharan	23.27
353	WPUJC Vaas	27.30
278	ST Jayasuriya	36.79
151	UDU Chandana	31.72
138	HDPK Dharmasena	36.21
116	CRD Fernando	31.00
109	GP Wickremasinghe	39.64
108	DNT Zoysa	29.75
106	PA de Silva	39.40
85	JR Ratnayeke	33.71

During 2005 Muralitharan became the first bowler to take 1000 international wickets (Tests + ODIs)

Highest scores

189	ST Jayasuriya	v India at Sharjah	2000-01
157	ST Jayasuriya	v Netherlands at Amstelveen	2006
152	ST Jayasuriya	v England at Leeds	2006
151*	ST Jayasuriya	v India at Mumbai	1996-97
145	PA de Silva	v Kenya at Kandy	1995-96
140	ST Jayasuriya	v NZ at Bloemfontein	1994-95
138*	KC Sangakkara	v India at Jaipur	2005-06
134*	ST Jayasuriya	v Pakistan at Lahore	1997-98
134	PA de Silva	v Pakistan at Sharjah	1996-97
134	ST Jayasuriya	v Pakistan at Singapore	1995-96

ST Jayasuriya has scored 22 ODI centuries, MS Atapattu and PA de Silva 11

Best bowling figures

8-19	WPUJC Vaas	v Zimbabwe at Colombo	2001-02
7-30	M Muralitharan	v India at Sharjah	2000-01
6-25	WPUJC Vaas	v B'desh at P'maritzburg	2002-03
6-29	ST Jayasuriya	v England at Moratuwa	1992-93
5-9	M Muralitharan	v New Zealand at Sharjah	2001-02
5-14	WPUJC Vaas	v India at Sharjah	2000-01
5-17	ST Jayasuriya	v Pakistan at Lahore	2004-05
5-23	M Muralitharan	v Pakistan at Benoni	1997-98
5-23	M Muralitharan	v Pakistan at Dambulla	2002-03
5-23	M Muralitharan	v Zimbabwe at Harare	2003-04

Vaas's 8-19 are the best bowling figures in all ODIs

Record wicket partnerships

1st	286	WU Tharanga (109) and ST Jayasuriya (152)	v England at Leeds	2006
2nd	170	S Wettimuny (74) and RL Dias (102)	v India at Delhi	1982-83
	170	ST Jayasuriya (120) and HP Tillakaratne (81*)	v NZ at Bloemfontein	2002-03
3rd	226	MS Atapattu (102*) and DPMD Jayawardene (128)	v India at Sharjah	2000-01
4th	171*	RS Mahanama (94*) and A Ranatunga (87*)	v West Indies at Lahore	1997-98
5th	166	ST Jayasuriya (189) and RP Arnold (52*)	v India at Sharjah	2000-01
6th	133	MS Atapattu (59) and RP Arnold (68)	v India at Vadodara	2005-06
7th	126*	DPMD Jayawardene (94*) and UDU Chandana (44*)	v India at Dambulla	2005-06
8th	91	HDPK Dharmasena (51*) and DK Liyanage (43)	v WI at Port-of-Spain	1996-97
9th	76	RS Kalpage (44*) and WPUJC Vaas (33)	v Pakistan at Colombo	1994-95
10th	51	RP Arnold (103) and KSC de Silva (2*)	v Zimbabwe at Bulawayo	1999-2000

*** Note to typesetters Please spell NZ (New Zealand) and WI (West Indies) full out in above table if there's room***

Updated records can be found at **www.cricinfo.com/db/stats/sl**

Most catches

Fielders

109	RS Mahanama	
109	M Muralitharan	
107	ST Jayasuriya	
104	DPMD Jayawardene	
95	PA de Silva	

Most dismissals

Wicketkeepers		*Ct/St*
206	RS Kaluwitharana	131/75
163	KC Sangakkara	121/42
45	HP Tillakaratne	39/6
34	DSBP Kuruppu	26/8
30	RG de Alwis	27/3

Highest team totals

443-9	v Netherlands at Amstelveen	2006
398-5	v Kenya at Kandy	1995-96
349-9	v Pakistan at Singapore	1995-96
343-5	v Australia at Sydney	2002-03
339-4	v Pakistan at Mohali	1996-97
329	v West Indies at Sharjah	1995-96
324-2	v England at Leeds	2006
319-8	v England at The Oval	2006
318-7	v England at Manchester	2006
313-6	v West Indies at Bridgetown	2002-03
313-7	v Zim at New Plymouth	1991-92
313-8	v Netherlands at Amstelveen	2006

The 324-2 was scored in 37.3 overs

Lowest team totals

Completed innings

55	v WI at Sharjah	1986-87
78*	v Pakistan at Sharjah	2001-02
86	v WI at Manchester	1975
91	v Australia at Adelaide	1984-85
96	v India at Sharjah	1983-84
98	v SA at Colombo	1993-94
98	v India at Sharjah	1998-99
99	v England at Perth	1998-99
102	v WI at Brisbane	1995-96
105	v SA at Bloemfontein	1997-98

* One batsman absent hurt

Most sixes

209	ST Jayasuriya	
102	PA de Silva	
64	A Rantaunga	
42	AP Gurusinha	
23	DPMD Jayawardene	
22	UDU Chandana	
21	WPUJC Vaas	
20	RP Arnold	
20	KC Sangakkara	
18	RJ Ratnayake	

Best strike rate

Runs per 100 balls		*Runs*
89.90	ST Jayasuriya	11076
86.81	RJ Ratnayake	612
81.13	PA de Silva	9284
78.52	TM Dilshan	1869
77.91	A Ranatunga	7456
77.70	RS Kaluwitharana	3711
75.71	DPMD Jayawardene	5865
75.07	LRD Mendis	1527
73.79	KC Sangakkara	4715
73.21	WPUJC Vaas	1807

Qualification: 500 runs

Most economical bowlers

Runs per over		*Wkts*
3.84	M Muralitharan	405
4.18	SD Anurasiri	32
4.21	WPUJC Vaas	353
4.27	HDPK Dharmasena	138
4.29	CPH Ramanayake	68
4.29	VB John	34
4.50	DS de Silva	32
4.50	RS Kalpage	73
4.52	DNT Zoysa	108
4.53	GP Wickremasinghe	109

Qualification: 2000 balls bowled

Sri Lanka's one-day international results

	Played	Won	Lost	Tied	No result	% win
v Australia	62	19	41	0	2	31.66
v Bangladesh	17	16	1	0	0	94.11
v England	37	18	19	0	0	48.64
v India	90	35	47	0	8	42.68
v New Zealand	60	25	32	1	2	43.85
v Pakistan	106	38	64	1	3	37.25
v South Africa	43	21	20	1	1	51.21
v West Indies	41	16	24	0	1	40.00
v Zimbabwe	36	29	6	0	1	82.85
v others (see below)	10	9	1	0	0	90.00
TOTAL	502	226	255	3	18	46.98

Other teams: Canada (P1, W1), Kenya (P5, W4, L1), Netherlands (P3, W3), United Arab Emirates (P1, W1).

WEST INDIES
Test Match Records

Most appearances

132	CA Walsh	
127	BC Lara	
121	IVA Richards	
116	DL Haynes	
110	CH Lloyd	
108	CG Greenidge	
102	CL Hooper	
98	CEL Ambrose	
98	S Chanderpaul	
93	GS Sobers	

Sobers played 85 successive Tests between 1954-55 and 1971-72

Most runs

		Avge
11464	BC Lara	52.34
8540	IVA Richards	50.23
8032	GS Sobers	57.78
7558	CG Greenidge	44.72
7515	CH Lloyd	46.67
7487	DL Haynes	42.29
6531	S Chanderpaul	44.73
6227	RB Kanhai	47.53
5949	RB Richardson	44.39
5762	CL Hooper	36.46

Greenidge and Haynes put on 6482 runs together, the Test record by any pair of batsmen

Most wickets

		Avge
519	CA Walsh	24.44
405	CEL Ambrose	20.99
376	MD Marshall	20.94
309	LR Gibbs	29.09
259	J Garner	20.97
249	MA Holding	23.68
235	GS Sobers	34.03
202	AME Roberts	25.61
192	WW Hall	26.38
161	IR Bishop	24.27

In all 17 West Indians reached 100 Test wickets

Highest scores

400*	BC Lara	v England at St John's	2003-04
375	BC Lara	v England at St John's	1993-94
365*	GS Sobers	v Pakistan at Kingston	1957-58
317	CH Gayle	v South Africa at St John's	2004-05
302	LG Rowe	v England at Bridgetown	1973-74
291	IVA Richards	v England at the Oval	1976
277	BC Lara	v Australia at Sydney	1992-93
270*	GA Headley	v England at Kingston	1934-35
261*	RR Sarwan	v Bangladesh at Kingston	2003-04
261	FMM Worrell	v England at Nottingham	1950

Lara has scored 32 Test centuries, Sobers 26, Richards 24

Best innings bowling

9-95	JM Noreiga	v India at Port-of-Spain	1970-71
8-29	CEH Croft	v Pakistan at Port-of-Spain	1976-77
8-38	LR Gibbs	v India at Bridgetown	1961-62
8-45	CEL Ambrose	v England at Bridgetown	1989-90
8-92	MA Holding	v England at The Oval	1976
8-104	AL Valentine	v England at Manchester	1950
7-22	MD Marshall	v England at Manchester	1988
7-25	CEL Ambrose	v Australia at Perth	1992-93
7-37	CA Walsh	v NZ at Wellington	1994-95
7-49	S Ramadhin	v England at Birmingham	1957

Valentine was playing in his first Test, Croft and Noreiga in their second

Record wicket partnerships

1st	298	CG Greenidge (149) and DL Haynes (167)	v England at St John's	1989-90
2nd	446	CC Hunte (260) and GS Sobers (365*)	v Pakistan at Kingston	1957-58
3rd	338	ED Weekes (206) and FMM Worrell (167)	v England at Port-of-Spain	1953-54
4th	399	GS Sobers (226) and FMM Worrell (197*)	v England at Bridgetown	1959-60
5th	322	BC Lara (213) and JC Adams (94)	v Australia at Kingston	1998-99
6th	282*	BC Lara (400*) and RD Jacobs (107*)	v England at St John's	2003-04
7th	347	DS Atkinson (219) and CC Depeiaza (122)	v Australia at Bridgetown	1954-55
8th	148	JC Adams (101*) and FA Rose (69)	v Zimbabwe at Kingston	1999-2000
9th	161	CH Lloyd (161*) and AME Roberts (68)	v India at Calcutta	1983-84
10th	106	CL Hooper (178*) and CA Walsh (30)	v Pakistan at St John's	X1992-93XX

Updated records can be found at **www.cricinfo.com/db/stats/wi**

Test Match Records — WEST INDIES

Most catches

Fielders

161	BC Lara	
122	IVA Richards	
115	CL Hooper	
109	GS Sobers	
96	CG Greenidge	

Most dismissals

	Wicketkeepers	*Ct/St*
270	PJL Dujon	265/5
219	RD Jacobs	207/12
189	DL Murray	181/8
102	JR Murray	99/3
90	FCM Alexander	85/5

Highest team totals

790-3d	v Pakistan at Kingston	1957-58
751-5d	v England at St John's	2003-04
747	v South Africa at St John's	2004-05
692-8d	v England at The Oval	1995
687-8d	v England at The Oval	1976
681-8d	v England at Port-of-Spain	1953-54
660-5d	v NZ at Wellington	1994-95
652-8d	v England at Lord's	1973
644-8d	v India at Delhi	1958-59
631-8d	v India at Kingston	1961-62
631	v India at Delhi	1948-49

West Indies have passed 600 in Tests on seven further occasions

Lowest team totals

Completed innings

47	v England at Kingston	2003-04
51	v Aust at Port-of-Spain	1998-99
53	v Pakistan at Faisalabad	1986-87
54	v England at Lord's	2000
61	v England at Leeds	2000
76	v Pakistan at Dacca	1958-59
77	v NZ at Auckland	1955-56
78	v Australia at Sydney	1951-52
82	v Australia at Brisbane	2000-01
86*	v England at The Oval	1957

*One batsman absent hurt

Best match bowling

14-149	MA Holding	v England at The Oval	1976
13-55	CA Walsh	v NZ at Wellington	1994-95
12-121	AME Roberts	v India at Madras	1974-75
11-84	CEL Ambrose	v England at Port-of-Spain	1993-94
11-89	MD Marshall	v India at Port-of-Spain	1988-89
11-107	MA Holding	v Australia at Melbourne	1981-82
11-120	MD Marshall	v NZ at Bridgetown	1984-85
11-126	WW Hall	v India at Kanpur	1958-59
11-134	CD Collymore	v Pakistan at Kingston	2004-05
11-147	KD Boyce	v England at The Oval	1973

Marshall took ten or more wickets in a Test four times, Ambrose and Walsh three

Hat-tricks

WW Hall   v Pakistan at Lahore   1958-59
The first Test hat-trick not for England or Australia.

LR Gibbs   v Australia at Adelaide   1960-61
Gibbs had taken three wickets in four balls in the previous Test, at Sydney.

CA Walsh   v Australia at Brisbane   1988-89
The first Test hat-trick to be split over two innings.

JJC Lawson   v Australia at Bridgetown   2002-03
Also split over two innings

West Indies' Test match results

	Played	Won	Lost	Drawn	Tied	% win
v Australia	102	32	48	21	1	31.68
v Bangladesh	4	3	0	1	0	75.00
v England	134	52	38	44	0	38.80
v India	82	30	11	41	0	36.58
v New Zealand	35	10	9	16	0	28.57
v Pakistan	41	14	13	14	0	34.14
v South Africa	19	2	12	5	0	10.52
v Sri Lanka	10	2	5	3	0	20.00
v Zimbabwe	6	4	0	2	0	66.66
TOTAL	**433**	**149**	**136**	**147**	**1**	**34.49**

Updated records can be found at **www.cricinfo.com/db/stats/wi**

WEST INDIES *One-day International Records*

Most appearances

266	BC Lara
238	DL Haynes
227	CL Hooper
224	RB Richardson
205	CA Walsh
191	S Chanderpaul
187	IVA Richards
176	CEL Ambrose
169	PJL Dujon
158	AL Logie

In all 23 West Indians have played more than 100 ODIs

Most runs

		Avge
9604	BC Lara	41.57
8648	DL Haynes	41.37
6721	IVA Richards	47.00
6248	RB Richardson	33.41
5761	CL Hooper	35.34
5715	S Chanderpaul	36.40
5134	CG Greenidge	45.03
4864	CH Gayle	38.91
3675	PV Simmons	28.93
3465	RR Sarwan	46.82

Lara scored 19 ODI centuries, Haynes 17, Gayle 12, Greenidge and Richards 11

Most wickets

		Avge
227	CA Walsh	30.47
225	CEL Ambrose	24.12
193	CL Hooper	36.05
157	MD Marshall	26.96
146	J Garner	18.84
142	MA Holding	21.36
130	M Dillon	32.44
118	IR Bishop	26.50
118	IVA Richards	35.83
114	CH Gayle	31.51

WKM Benjamin (100) and RA Harper (100) also reached 100 wickets

Highest scores

189*	IVA Richards	v England at Manchester	1984
181	IVA Richards	v Sri Lanka at Karachi	1987-88
169	BC Lara	v Sri Lanka at Sharjah	1995-96
156	BC Lara	v Pakistan at Adelaide	2004-05
153*	IVA Richards	v Australia at Melbourne	1979-80
153*	CH Gayle	v Zimbabwe at Bulawayo	2003-04
153	BC Lara	v Pakistan at Sharjah	1993-94
152*	DL Haynes	v India at Georgetown	1988-89
152*	CH Gayle	v SA at Johannesburg	2003-04
152	CH Gayle	v Kenya at Nairobi	2001-02

S Chanderpaul scored 150 against South Africa at East London in 1998-99

Best bowling figures

7-51	WW Davis	v Australia at Leeds	1983
6-15	CEH Croft	v England at Kingstown	1980-81
6-22	FH Edwards	v Zimbabwe at Harare	2003-04
6-29	BP Patterson	v India at Nagpur	1987-88
6-41	IVA Richards	v India at Delhi	1989-90
6-50	AH Gray	v Aust at Port-of-Spain	1990-91
5-1	CA Walsh	v Sri Lanka at Sharjah	1986-87
5-17	CEL Ambrose	v Australia at Melbourne	1988-89
5-22	AME Roberts	v England at Adelaide	1979-80
5-22	WKM Benjamin	v Sri Lanka at Bombay	1993-94

Edwards's feat was in his first ODI; he had earlier taken 5-36 on his Test debut

Record wicket partnerships

1st	200*	SC Williams (78*) and S Chanderpaul (109*)	v India at Bridgetown	1996-97
2nd	221	CG Greenidge (115) and IVA Richards (149)	v India at Jamshedpur	1983-84
3rd	195*	CG Greenidge (105*) and HA Gomes (75*)	v Zimbabwe at Worcester	1983
4th	226	S Chanderpaul (150) and CL Hooper (108)	v South Africa at East London	1998-99
5th	154	CL Hooper (112*) and S Chanderpaul (67)	v Pakistan at Sharjah	2001-02
6th	154	RB Richardson (122) and PJL Dujon (53)	v Pakistan at Sharjah	1991-92
7th	115	PJL Dujon (57*) and MD Marshall (66)	v Pakistan at Gujranwala	1986-87
8th	84	RL Powell (76) and CD Collymore (3)	v India at Toronto	1999-2000
9th	77	RR Sarwan (65) and IDR Bradshaw (37)	v New Zealand at Christchurch	2005-06
10th	106*	IVA Richards (189*) and MA Holding (12*)	v England at Manchester	1984

Updated records can be found at **www.cricinfo.com/db/stats/wi**

Most catches

Fielders

120	CL Hooper	
108	BC Lara	
100	IVA Richards	
75	RB Richardson	
62	CH Gayle	

Most dismissals

Wicketkeepers		*Ct/St*
204	PJL Dujon	183/21
189	RD Jacobs	160/29
68	CO Browne	59/9
53	JR Murray	46/7
45	D Williams	35/10

Highest team totals

360-4	v Sri Lanka at Karachi	1987-88
347-6	v Zimbabwe at Bulawayo	2003-04
339-4	v Pakistan at Adelaide	2004-05
333-6	v Zimbabwe at Georgetown	2005-06
333-7	v Sri Lanka at Sharjah	1995-96
333-8	v India at Jamshedpur	1983-84
324-4	v India at Ahmedabad	2002-03
315-4	v Pakistan at Port-of-Spain	1987-88
315-6	v India at Vijayawada	2002-03
314-6	v Bangladesh at Dhaka	1999-2000

All in 50 overs except 333-8 (45) and 315-4 (47)

Lowest team totals

Completed innings		
54	v SA at Cape Town	2003-04
87	v Australia at Sydney	1992-93
91	v Zimbabwe at Sydney	2000-01
93	v Kenya at Pune	1995-96
103	v Pak at Melbourne	1996-97
110	v Australia at Manchester	1999
111	v Pak at Melbourne	1983-84
114	v Pak at Pt-of-Spain	1999-2000
117	v Pakistan at Sharjah	1999-2000
119	v Australia at Sydney	2000-01

The 87 was in a match reduced to 30 overs: Australia made 101-9

Most sixes

126	IVA Richards	
117	BC Lara	
81	CG Greenidge	
75	RL Powell	
66	CH Gayle	
65	CL Hooper	
54	RB Richardson	
53	DL Haynes	
49	WW Hinds	
47	S Chanderpaul	

Greenidge and Powell share the West Indian record with 8 sixes in one innings

Best strike rate

Runs per 100 balls		*Runs*
103.20	DR Smith	611
96.66	RL Powell	2085
90.20	IVA Richards	6721
81.22	CH Lloyd	1977
79.50	BC Lara	9604
78.17	CH Gayle	4864
77.45	RR Sarwan	3465
76.65	MD Marshall	955
76.64	CL Hooper	5761
76.57	DJ Bravo	513

Qualification: 500 runs

Most economical bowlers

Runs per over		*Wkts*
3.09	J Garner	146
3.32	MA Holding	142
3.40	AME Roberts	87
3.48	CEL Ambrose	225
3.53	MD Marshall	157
3.83	CA Walsh	227
3.97	RA Harper	100
4.00	CE Cuffy	41
4.09	EAE Baptiste	36
4.15	WKM Benjamin	100

Qualification: 2000 balls bowled

West Indies' one-day international results

	Played	Won	Lost	Tied	No result	% win
v Australia	108	55	49	2	2	52.88
v Bangladesh	11	9	0	0	2	100.00
v England	70	37	29	0	4	56.06
v India	83	50	31	1	1	61.72
v New Zealand	45	23	17	0	5	57.50
v Pakistan	105	62	41	2	0	60.19
v South Africa	38	11	26	0	1	29.72
v Sri Lanka	41	24	16	0	1	60.00
v Zimbabwe	30	22	7	0	1	75.86
v others (see below)	8	7	1	0	0	87.50
TOTAL	**539**	**300**	**217**	**5**	**17**	**58.02**

Other teams: Canada (P1, W1), Kenya (P6, W5, L1), Scotland (P1, W1).

ZIMBABWE   *Test Match Records*

Most appearances

67	GW Flower	
65	HH Streak	
63	A Flower	
60	ADR Campbell	
46	GJ Whittall	
37	SV Carlisle	
30	HK Olonga	
29	DD Ebrahim	
27	CB Wishart	
26	BC Strang	

Zimbabwe's most recent Test match was against India in September 2005

Most runs

		Avge
4794	A Flower	51.54
3457	GW Flower	29.54
2858	ADR Campbell	27.21
2207	GJ Whittall	29.42
1990	HH Streak	22.35
1615	SV Carlisle	26.91
1464	DL Houghton	43.05
1414	MW Goodwin	42.84
1273	T Taibu	29.60
1225	DD Ebrahim	22.68

CB Wishart (1098) and GJ Rennie (1023) also reached 1000 runs

Most wickets

		Avge
216	HH Streak	28.14
70	PA Strang	36.02
69	RW Price	35.86
68	HK Olonga	38.52
56	BC Strang	39.33
53	AM Blignaut	37.05
51	GJ Whittall	40.94
32	M Mbangwa	31.43
30	DH Brain	30.50
26	EA Brandes	36.57

GW Flower, TJ Friend and AG Huckle all took 25 wickets

Highest scores

266	DL Houghton	v Sri Lanka at Bulawayo	1994-95
232*	A Flower	v India at Nagpur	2000-01
203*	GJ Whittall	v New Zealand at Bulawayo	1997-98
201*	GW Flower	v Pakistan at Harare	1994-95
199*	A Flower	v South Africa at Harare	2001-02
188*	GJ Whittall	v New Zealand at Harare	2000-01
183*	A Flower	v India at Delhi	2000-01
166*	MW Goodwin	v Pakistan at Bulawayo	1997-98
156*	GW Flower	v Pakistan at Bulawayo	1997-98
156	A Flower	v Pakistan at Harare	1994-95

Of Zimbabwe's 42 Test centuries, 18 came from the Flower family – 12 by Andy and six by Grant

Best innings bowling

8-109	PA Strang	v New Zealand at Bulawayo	2000-01
6-59	DT Hondo	v Bangladesh at Dhaka	2004-05
6-73	RW Price	v West Indies at Harare	2003-04
6-73	HH Streak	v India at Harare	2005-06
6-87	HH Streak	v England at Lord's	2000
6-90	HH Streak	v Pakistan at Harare	1994-95
6-109	AG Huckle	v New Zealand at Bulawayo	1997-98
6-121	RW Price	v Australia at Sydney	2003-04
5-27	HH Streak	v WI at Port-of-Spain	1999-2000
5-31	TJ Friend	v Bangladesh at Dhaka	2001-02

AJ Traicos took 5-86 in Zimbabwe's inaugural Test, against India in 1992-93: he was 45, and had played three Tests for South Africa 22 years previously

Record wicket partnerships

1st	164	DD Ebrahim (71) and ADR Campbell (103)	v West Indies at Bulawayo	2001
2nd	135	MH Dekker (68*) and ADR Campbell (75)	v Pakistan at Rawalpindi	1993-94
3rd	194	ADR Campbell (99) and DL Houghton (142)	v Sri Lanka at Harare	1994-95
4th	269	GW Flower (201*) and A Flower (156)	v Pakistan at Harare	1994-95
5th	277*	MW Goodwin (166*) and A Flower (100*)	v Pakistan at Bulawayo	1997-98
6th	165	DL Houghton (121) and A Flower (59)	v India at Harare	1992-93
7th	154	HH Streak (83*) and AM Blignaut (92)	v West Indies at Harare	2001
8th	168	HH Streak (127*) and AM Blignaut (91)	v West Indies at Harare	2003-04
9th	87	PA Strang (106*) and BC Strang (42)	v Pakistan at Sheikhupura	1996-97
10th	97*	A Flower (183*) and HK Olonga (11*)	v India at Delhi	2000-01

Updated records can be found at **www.cricinfo.com/db/stats/zim**

Test Match Records ZIMBABWE

Most catches

Fielders

60	ADR Campbell	
43	GW Flower	
34	SV Carlisle	
19	GJ Whittall	
17	DL Houghton/HH Streak	

Most dismissals

Wicketkeepers		*Ct/St*
151	A Flower	142/9
52	T Taibu	48/4
16	WR James	16/0

Flower also took 9 catches in the field

Highest team totals

563-9d	v West Indies at Harare	2001
544-4d	v Pakistan at Harare	1994-95
542-7d	v Bangladesh at Chittagong	2001-02
507-9d	v West Indies at Harare	2003-04
503-6	v India at Nagpur	2000-01
462-9d	v Sri Lanka at Bulawayo	1994-95
461	v New Zealand at Bulawayo	1997-98
457	v Bangladesh at Bulawayo	2000-01
456	v India at Harare	1992-93
441	v Bangladesh at Harare	2003-04

Zimbabwe's 456 in 1992-93 is the highest by any country in their first Test match

Lowest team totals

Completed innings

54	v SA at Cape Town	2004-05
59	v NZ at Harare	2005-06
63	v WI at Port-of-Spain	1999-2000
79	v Sri Lanka at Galle	2001-02
83	v England at Lord's	2000
94	v Eng at Chester-le-Street	2003
99	v NZ at Harare	2005-06
102	v SA at Harare	1999-2000
102	v WI at Kingston	1999-2000
102	v Sri Lanka at Harare	2003-04

Zimbabwe were bowled out twice in a day by New Zealand at Harare in 2005-06, only the second such instance in Test cricket

Best match bowling

11-255	AG Huckle	v New Zealand at Bulawayo	1997-98
10-158	PA Strang	v New Zealand at Bulawayo	2000-01
10-161	RW Price	v West Indies at Harare	2003-04
9-72	HH Streak	v WI at Port-of-Spain	1999-2000
9-105	HH Streak	v Pakistan at Harare	1994-95
9-235	RW Price	v West Indies at Bulawayo	2003-04
8-104	GW Flower	v Pakistan at Chittagong	2001-02
8-105	HH Streak	v Pakistan at Harare	1994-95
8-110	AM Blignaut	v Bangladesh at Bulawayo	2000-01
8-114	HH Streak	v Pakistan at Rawalpindi	1993-94

Blignaut was playing in his first Test, Huckle in his second

Hat-tricks

AM Blignaut v Bangladesh at Harare 2003-04

Blignaut dismissed Hannan Sarkar, Mohammad Ashraful and Mushfiqur Rahman to reduce Bangladesh to 14-5.

The only Test hat-trick against Zimbabwe was taken by DNT Zoysa for Sri Lanka at Harare in 1999-2000, when he removed TR Gripper, MW Goodwin and NC Johnson with the first three balls he bowled, in the second over of the match

Zimbabwe's Test match results

	Played	Won	Lost	Drawn	Tied	% win
v Australia	3	0	3	0	0	0.00
v Bangladesh	8	4	1	3	0	50.00
v England	6	0	3	3	0	0.00
v India	11	2	7	2	0	18.18
v New Zealand	13	0	7	6	0	0.00
v Pakistan	14	2	8	4	0	14.28
v South Africa	7	0	6	1	0	0.00
v Sri Lanka	15	0	10	5	0	0.00
v West Indies	6	0	4	2	0	0.00
TOTAL	**83**	**8**	**49**	**26**	**0**	**9.63**

ZIMBABWE
One-day International Records

Most appearances

219	GW Flower	
213	A Flower	
188	ADR Campbell	
187	HH Streak	
147	GJ Whittall	
111	SV Carlisle	
95	PA Strang	
90	CB Wishart	
83	T Taibu	
82	DD Ebrahim	

A Flower missed only 5 matches between his debut in 1991-92 and his enforced retirement after the 2002-03 World Cup

Most runs

		Avge
6786	A Flower	35.34
6536	GW Flower	33.69
5185	ADR Campbell	30.50
2901	HH Streak	28.44
2740	SV Carlisle	27.67
2705	GJ Whittall	22.54
1818	MW Goodwin	27.13
1719	CB Wishart	23.32
1679	NC Johnson	36.50
1530	DL Houghton	26.37

DD Ebrahim (1443), T Taibu (1400), BRM Taylor (1325) and PA Strang (1090) also reached 1000 runs

Most wickets

		Avge
237	HH Streak	29.81
104	GW Flower	40.25
96	PA Strang	33.05
88	GJ Whittall	39.55
70	EA Brandes	32.37
61	DT Hondo	35.59
58	HK Olonga	34.08
50	GB Brent	38.28
49	AM Blignaut	41.24
46	BC Strang	37.34

Brandes took Zimbabwe's only ODI hat-trick, against England at Harare in 1996-97

Highest scores

172*	CB Wishart	v Namibia at Harare	2002-03
145	A Flower	v India at Colombo	2002-03
142*	GW Flower	v Bangladesh at Bulawayo	2000-01
142*	A Flower	v England at Harare	2001-02
142	DL Houghton	v New Zealand at Hyderabad	1987-88
140	GW Flower	v Kenya at Dhaka	1998-99
132*	NC Johnson	v Australia at Lord's	1999
131*	ADR Campbell	v Sri Lanka at Harare	1994-95
124	ADR Campbell	v Australia at Hobart	2000-01
121*	SV Carlisle	v Sri Lanka at Harare	1999-2000
121	DD Ebrahim	v Bangladesh at Dhaka	2001-02

Campbell made a record seven ODI centuries for Zimbabwe

Best bowling figures

6-19	HK Olonga	v England at Cape Town	1999-2000
6-20	BC Strang	v Bangladesh at Nairobi	1997-98
6-28	HK Olonga	v Kenya at Bulawayo	2002-03
5-21	PA Strang	v Kenya at Patna	1995-96
5-22	PA Strang	v Kenya at Dhaka	1998-99
5-28	EA Brandes	v England at Harare	1996-97
5-32	HH Streak	v India at Bulawayo	1996-97
5-41	EA Brandes	v India at Paarl	1996-97
5-44	ACI Lock	v New Zealand at Napier	1995-96
4-8	HH Streak	v West Indies at Sydney	2000-01

Lock's feat came in the second of his eight ODIs, six of which were in the World Cup

Record wicket partnerships

1st	161	GW Flower (79) and A Flower (81)	v Bangladesh at Nairobi	1997-98
2nd	150	GW Flower (78) and GJ Rennie (76)	v Kenya at Nairobi	1997-98
3rd	166*	CB Wishart (172*) and GW Flower (78*)	v Namibia at Harare	2002-03
4th	202	SV Carlisle (109) and SM Ervine (100)	v India at Adelaide	2003-04
5th	186*	MW Goodwin (112*) and GW Flower (96*)	v West Indies at Chester-le-Street	2000
6th	114	S Matsikenyeri (89) and E Chigumbura (70*)	v Bangladesh at Harare	2006
7th	130	A Flower (142*) and HH Streak (56)	v England at Harare	2001-02
8th	117	DL Houghton (142) and IP Butchart (54)	v New Zealand at Hyderabad	1987-88
9th	55	KM Curran (62) and PWE Rawson (19)	v West Indies at Birmingham	1983
10th	47	HK Olonga (31) and DT Hondo (15*)	v Pakistan at Harare	2002-03

Updated records can be found at **www.cricinfo.com/db/stats/zim**

Most catches

Fielders

86	GW Flower
76	ADR Campbell
45	HH Streak
39	SV Carlisle
36	GJ Whittall

Most dismissals

Wicketkeepers   *Ct/St*

165	A Flower	133/32
80	T Taibu	72/8
25	BRM Taylor	19/6
12	DL Houghton	10/2

Highest team totals

340-2	v Namibia at Harare	2002-03
338-7	v Bermuda at Port-of-Spain	2005-06
325-6	v Kenya at Dhaka	1998-99
312-4	v Sri Lanka at New Plymouth	1991-92
310-6	v Bangladesh at Dhaka	1998-99
309-6	v Bangladesh at Dhaka	2001-02
308-4	v Bangladesh at Bulawayo	2000-01
305-4	v Bangladesh at Nairobi	1997-98
301-6	v Australia at Perth	2000-01
301-8	v Netherlands at Bulawayo	2002-03

Zimbabwe also scored 300-7 against New Zealand at Taupo in 2000-01

Lowest team totals

Completed innings

35	v Sri Lanka at Harare	2003-04
38	v Sri Lanka at Colombo	2001-02
65	v India at Harare	2005-06
69	v Kenya at Harare	2005-06
92	v England at Bristol	2003
94	v Pakistan at Sharjah	1996-97
99*	v WI at Hyderabad	1993-94
102	v England at Harare	2004-05
104	v SL at Rawalpindi	2004-05
105*	v Sri Lanka at Harare	1994-95

* One batsman absent or retired hurt

Most sixes

48	HH Streak
44	ADR Campbell
37	GW Flower
28	SV Carlisle
26	A Flower
26	GJ Whittall
21	DL Houghton
21	CB Wishart
19	BRM Taylor
17	E Chigumbura

Best strike rate

Runs per 100 balls   *Runs*

106.65	AM Blignaut	625
85.54	SM Ervine	698
83.47	E Chigumbura	677
75.94	CN Evans	764
75.69	TJ Friend	548
74.60	A Flower	6786
73.61	HH Streak	2901
71.00	DL Houghton	1530
70.81	DA Marillier	672
70.57	CB Wishart	1719

Qualification: 500 runs

Most economical bowlers

Runs per over   *Wkts*

3.79	P Utseya	31
3.88	AJ Traicos	19
4.13	BC Strang	46
4.14	RW Price	15
4.37	PA Strang	96
4.37	AR Whittall	45
4.50	HH Streak	237
4.52	AH Shah	18
4.63	GW Flower	104
4.66	DH Brain	21

Qualification: 1000 balls bowled

Zimbabwe's one-day international results

	Played	Won	Lost	Tied	No result	% win
v Australia	27	1	25	0	1	3.84
v Bangladesh	23	17	6	0	0	73.91
v England	30	8	21	0	1	27.58
v India	49	8	39	2	0	17.02
v New Zealand	28	7	19	1	1	26.92
v Pakistan	34	2	30	1	1	6.25
v South Africa	21	2	18	0	1	10.00
v Sri Lanka	36	6	29	0	1	17.14
v West Indies	30	7	22	0	1	24.13
v others (see below)	25	20	3	0	2	86.95
TOTAL	303	78	212	4	9	26.89

Other teams: Bermuda (P2, W2), Canada (P1, W1), Kenya (P20, W15, L3, NR 2), Namibia (P1, W1), Netherlands (P1, W1).

Updated records can be found at **www.cricinfo.com/db/stats/zim**

WORLD CUP
Records 1975-2003

Most appearances

38	Wasim Akram	P
35	PA de Silva	SL
34	J Srinath	I
33	Javed Miandad	P
33	SR Tendulkar	I
33	SR Waugh	A
32	Inzamam-ul-Haq	P
30	M Azharuddin	I
30	A Flower	Z
30	A Ranatunga	SL

Javed Miandad uniquely appeared in each of the first six World Cups

Most runs

			Avge
1732	SR Tendulkar	I	59.72
1083	Javed Miandad	P	43.32
1064	PA de Silva	SL	36.68
1013	IVA Richards	WI	63.31
1004	ME Waugh	A	52.84
998	RT Ponting	A	41.58
978	SR Waugh	A	48.90
969	A Ranatunga	SL	46.14
956	BC Lara	WI	43.45
915	Saeed Anwar	P	53.82

The most runs in one tournament is 673 by SR Tendulkar in 2002-03

Most wickets

			Avge
55	Wasim Akram	P	23.83
45	GD McGrath	A	20.77
44	J Srinath	I	27.81
38	AA Donald	SA	24.02
36	WPUJC Vaas	SL	20.94
34	Imran Khan	P	19.26
32	CZ Harris	NZ	26.90
32	SK Warne	A	19.50
30	IT Botham	E	25.40
30	M Muralitharan	SL	23.10

The most wickets in one tournament is 23 by WPUJC Vaas in 2002-03

Highest scores

188*	G Kirsten	SA v UAE at Rawalpindi	1995-96
183	SC Ganguly	India v Sri Lanka at Taunton	1999
181	IVA Richards	WI v Sri Lanka at Karachi	1987-88
175*	Kapil Dev	India v Zim at Tunbridge Wells	1983
172*	CB Wishart	Zim v Namibia at Harare	2002-03
171*	GM Turner	NZ v E Africa at Birmingham	1975
161	AC Hudson	SA v Netherlands at Rawalpindi	1995-96
152	SR Tendulkar	India v Nam at P'maritzburg	2002-03
145	PA de Silva	Sri Lanka v Kenya at Kandy	1995-96
145	R Dravid	India v Sri Lanka at Taunton	1999

SC Ganguly, SR Tendulkar and ME Waugh have all scored four centuries in the World Cup

Best bowling figures

7-15	GD McGrath	Aust v Namibia at P'stroom	2002-03
7-20	AJ Bichel	Aust v Eng at Port Elizabeth	2002-03
7-51	WW Davis	WI v Australia at Leeds	1983
6-14	GJ Gilmour	Australia v England at Leeds	1975
6-23	SE Bond	NZ v Aust at Pt Elizabeth	2002-03
6-23	A Nehra	India v England at Durban	2002-03
6-25	WPUJC Vaas	SL v B'desh at P'maritzburg	2002-03
6-39	KH MacLeay	Aust v India at Nottingham	1983
5-14	GD McGrath	Aust v WI at Manchester	1999
5-21	AG Hurst	Aust v Canada at Birmingham	1979
5-21	L Klusener	SA v Kenya at Amstelveen	1999
5-21	PA Strang	Zimbabwe v Kenya at Patna	1995-96

Record wicket partnerships

1st	194	Saeed Anwar (113*) and Wajahatullah Wasti (84)	Pakistan v New Zealand at Manchester	1999
2nd	318	SC Ganguly (183) and R Dravid (145)	India v Sri Lanka at Taunton	1999
3rd	237*	R Dravid (104) and SR Tendulkar (140*)	India v Kenya at Bristol	1999
4th	168	LK Germon (89) and CZ Harris (130)	New Zealand v Australia at Madras	1995-96
5th	148	RG Twose (80*) and CL Cairns (60)	New Zealand v Australia at Cardiff	1999
6th	161	MO Odumbe (82) and AV Vadher (73*)	Kenya v Sri Lanka at Southampton	1999
7th	98	RR Sarwan (75) and RD Jacobs (50)	West Indies v New Zealand at Port Elizabeth	2002-03
8th	117	DL Houghton (142) and IP Butchart (54)	Zimbabwe v New Zealand at Hyderabad	1987-88
9th	126*	Kapil Dev (175*) and SMH Kirmani (24*)	India v Zimbabwe at Tunbridge Wells	1983
10th	71	AME Roberts (37*) and J Garner (37)	West Indies v India at Manchester	1983

Updated records can be found at www.cricinfo.com/db/stats/wc

Most catches

Fielders

18	RT Ponting	A
16	CL Cairns	NZ
15	ST Jayasuriya	SL
14	PA de Silva	SL
14	A Kumble / SR Waugh	A

Most dismissals

Wicketkeepers		*Ct/St*
35	AC Gilchrist A	33/2
30	Moin Khan P	23/7
23	AJ Stewart E	21/2
22	MV Boucher SA	22/0
22	RD Jacobs WI	21/1
22	Wasim Bari P	18/4

Highest team totals

398-5	Sri Lanka v Kenya at Kandy	1995-96
373-6	India v Sri Lanka at Taunton	1999
360-4	WI v Sri Lanka at Karachi	1987-88
359-2	Aust v India at Jo'burg	2002-03
340-2	Zim v Namibia at Harare	2002-03
338-5	Pakistan v SL at Swansea	1983
334-4	England v India at Lord's	1975
333-9	England v SL at Taunton	1983
330-6	Pakistan v SL at Nottingham	1975
329-2	India v Kenya at Bristol	1999

Australia's 359-2 was scored in the final.
In 1975, 1979 and 1983 the innings were of 60 overs; since then the maximum has been 50

Lowest team totals

Completed innings

36	Canada v SL at Paarl	2002-03
45	Canada v Eng at Manchester	1979
45	Nam v Aust at P'stroom	2002-03
68	Scotland v WI at Leicester	1999
74	Pak v Eng at Adelaide	1991-92
84	Nam v Pak at Kimberley	2002-03
86	SL v WI at Manchester	1975
93	England v Aust at Leeds	1975
93	WI v Kenya at Pune	1995-96
94	E Africa v Eng at Birmingham	1975

There have been no other all-out scores of less than 100

Best strike rate

Runs per 100 balls		*Runs*
115.14	Kapil Dev I	669
100.70	Wasim Akram P	426
94.18	AC Gilchrist A	632
88.05	JN Rhodes SA	354
87.70	BC Lara WI	956
87.56	SR Tendulkar I	1732
86.57	PA de Silva SL	1064
86.17	ST Jayasuriya SL	698
85.05	IVA Richards WI	1013
83.49	MD Crowe NZ	880

Qualification: 20 innings

Hat-tricks

Chetan Sharma
India v New Zealand
at Nagpur 1987-88

Saqlain Mushtaq
Pakistan v Zimbabwe
at The Oval 1999

WPUJC Vaas
Sri Lanka v Bangladesh
at P'maritzburg 2002-03

B Lee
Australia v Kenya
at Durban 2002-03

Most expensive bowling

12-1-105-2	MC Snedden	NZ v Eng at The Oval	1983
10-0-97-1	ALF de Mel	SL v WI at Karachi	1987-88
10-0-92-0	RJ van Vuuren	Nam v Aust at P'stroom	2002-03
10-0-87-0	J Srinath	India v Aust at Jo'burg	2002-03
9-0-85-1	MA Suji	Kenya v SL at Kandy	1995-96
10-0-84-1	WPUJC Vaas	SL v India at Taunton	1983
10-0-83-0	DR Pringle	Eng v WI at Gujranwala	1987-88
11-1-83-0	KD Ghavri	India v Eng at Lord's	1975
12-1-82-1	PJW Allott	Eng v SL at Taunton	1983
10-0-80-0	KEA Upashantha	SL v India at Taunton	1999

The most economical full spell is BS Bedi's 12-8-6-1 for India v East Africa at Leeds in 1975

World Cup finals

		Man of the Match
1975	West Indies (291-8) beat Australia (274) by 17 runs at Lord's	CH Lloyd
1979	West Indies (286-9) beat England (194) by 92 runs at Lord's	IVA Richards
1983	India (183) beat West Indies (140) by 43 runs at Lord's	M Amarnath
1987-88	Australia (253-5) beat England (246-8) by 7 runs at Calcutta	DC Boon
1991-92	Pakistan (249-6) beat England (227) by 22 runs at Melbourne	Wasim Akram
1995-96	Sri Lanka (245-3) beat Australia (241-7) by 7 wickets at Lahore	PA de Silva
1999	Australia (133-2) beat Pakistan (132) by 8 wickets at Lord's	SK Warne
2002-03	Australia (359-2) beat India (234) by 125 runs at Johannesburg	RT Ponting

Updated records can be found at www.cricinfo.com/db/stats/wc

THE WORLD CUP 2007

GROUP A
All matches in St Kitts

March 14	Australia	v Scotland
March 16	Holland	v South Africa
March 18	Australia	v Holland
March 20	Scotland	v South Africa
March 22	Holland	v Scotland
March 24	Australia	v South Africa

GROUP B
All matches in Trinidad

March 15	Bermuda	v Sri Lanka
March 17	Bangladesh	v India
March 19	Bermuda	v India
March 21	Bangladesh	v Sri Lanka
March 23	India	v Sri Lanka
March 25	Bangladesh	v Bermuda

GROUP C
All matches in St Lucia

March 14	Canada	v Kenya
March 16	England	v New Zealand
March 18	Canada	v England
March 20	Kenya	v New Zealand
March 22	Canada	v New Zealand
March 24	England	v Kenya

GROUP D
All matches in Jamaica

March 13	West Indies v Pakistan
March 15	Ireland v Zimbabwe
March 17	Ireland v Pakistan
March 19	West Indies v Zimbabwe
March 21	Pakistan v Zimbabwe
March 23	West Indies v Ireland

SUPER EIGHT

March 27	A1 v D2	Antigua
March 28	A2 v B1	Guyana
March 29	C1 v D2	Antigua
March 30	C2 v D1	Guyana
March 31	A1 v B2	Antigua
April 1	B1 v D2	Guyana
April 2	B2 v C1	Antigua
April 3	A2 v D1	Guyana
April 4	B1 v C2	Antigua
April 7	A2 v B2	Guyana
April 8	A1 v C2	Antigua
April 9	C1 v D1	Guyana
April 10	A2 v D2	Grenada
April 11	B2 v C2	Barbados
April 12	B1 v C1	Grenada
April 13	A1 v D1	Barbados
April 14	A2 v C1	Grenada
April 15	B2 v D1	Barbados
April 16	A1 v B1	Grenada
April 17	A2 v C2	Barbados
April 18	B1 v D1	Grenada
April 19	B2 v D2	Barbados
April 20	A1 v C1	Grenada
April 21	C2 v D2	Barbados

SEMI-FINALS

April 24	Second v Third of Super Eight	Jamaica
April 25	First v Fourth of Super Eight	St Lucia

The World Cup Final will be played on Saturday, April 28, at Bridgetown, Barbados.

All matches have been assigned one reserve day.

VENUES

St Kitts	Warner Park, Basseterre
Trinidad	Queen's Park Oval, Port-of-Spain
St Lucia	Beausejour Stadium, Gros Islet
Jamaica	Sabina Park, Kingston
Antigua	Sir Vivian Richards Stadium, St John's *(new ground)*
Guyana	Providence Stadium, Georgetown *(new ground)*
Grenada	Queen's Park, St George's
Barbados	Kensington Oval, Bridgetown